Simply My Window

by

P.K.HODEL

CONTENTS

Dedication vii
Introduction xi
Preface xiii

PART 1: PRE-AFRICA YEARS 15
Chapter 1: Wapello, Iowa: *A Place to Grow* 17
Chapter 2: Iowa City, Iowa: *On My Own* 44
           Quito, Ecuador
           Lakeland, Florida
Chapter 3: Roanoke, Illinois: *A New Life Together* 58
           Port Au Prince, Haiti
Chapter 4: Schroon Lake, New York: *Wonderful Words of Life* 66
           Danforth, Maine
Chapter 5: Return to Roanoke, Illinois: *Transplanting*
           My Roots 71
Chapter 6: Cicero, Illinois: *A Windy City Window* 76
Chapter 7: Hampton, Tennessee: *Beauty Resurfaces* 86

PART 2: EAST AFRICAN YEARS 101
Chapter 8: Dodoma, Tanzania: *Becoming Acquainted*
           with Missions 103
Chapter 9: Rolling Prairie, Indiana: *Becoming Acquainted*
           with Home Assignments 131
Chapter 10: Morogoro, Tanzania: *Another Language*
           to Love 137

Chapter 11: Return to Dodoma: *Becoming Acquainted
    with Disillusionment* 142
Chapter 12: Goodfield, Illinois: *The Next Step Outlined* 160
    Pearl River, New York
Chapter 13: Kijabe, Kenya: *Spurring One Another on
    Towards Love and Good Works*.............................167
Chapter 14: Bloomington, Illinois: *Ugly Strikes the
    Land of the Free* 182
Chapter 15: Return to Kijabe: *Pressing On*...........................190

PART 3: THE EFFECTS 209
Chapter 16: Normal, Illinois: *Out of Africa, Into Normal*..........211
    Orr Street
    Ballyford
    Tompkins
    Kemise, Ethiopia
Chapter 17: Vientiane, Laos: *A People of the Heart in the
    World's Most Bombed Country* 230
    Colorado
    Hanoi, Viet Nam
    Guiyang, China
    Seoul, South Korea
    Chiang Mai, Thailand
Chapter 18: Bloomington, Illinois/Wheaton, Illinois:
    Forever Transitioning, Continual Liminality.......250
    Barnes' Basement
    Salt Lake City, Utah
Chapter 19: Lhasa, Tibet: *The Enemy's Trophy Showcase* 255
    Beijing, China
Chapter 20: Fresno, California: *A Safe Place to Breathe Easy* 278
    Tenting across America
Chapter 21: Washington, D.C.: *Justitia Omnibus* 296
Chapter 22: Glen Ellyn, Illinois: *A Divine Spanking* 313
Chapter 23: Monrovia, Liberia: *The Enemy's Playground*.........338
Chapter 24: From Pillar to Post: *Homeless in the U.S.A.*...........372

Acknowledgements 387

DEDICATION

To my perfectly awesome husband,
who from his own window,
becomes more of a soulmate
and less of a prisoner with me every day.

NOTE

I have given different names to those characters in this book from
whom it was necessary to distance myself in order to see them
more objectively as I wrote.

INTRODUCTION

Two men, both seriously ill, occupied the same hospital room. One man was allowed to sit up in his bed for an hour each afternoon to help drain the fluid from his lungs. His bed was next to the room's only window. The other man had to spend all his time flat on his back.

The men talked for hours on end. They spoke of their wives and families, their homes, their jobs, their involvement in the military service, where they had been on vacation.

Every afternoon, when the man in the bed by the window could sit up, he would pass the time by describing to his roommate all the things he could see outside the window.

The man in the other bed began to live for those one hour periods where his world would be broadened and enlivened by all the activity and color of the world outside.

The window overlooked a park with a lovely lake. Ducks and swans played on the water while children sailed their model boats. Young lovers walked arm in arm amidst flowers of every color, and a fine view of the city skyline could be seen in the distance.

As the man by the window described all this in exquisite details, the man on the other side of the room would close his eyes and imagine this picturesque scene.

One warm afternoon, the man by the window described a parade passing by. Although the other man could not hear the band — he could see it in his mind's eye as the gentleman by the window portrayed it with descriptive words.

Days, weeks and months passed.

One morning, the day nurse arrived to bring water for their baths, only to find the lifeless body of the man by the window, who had died peacefully in his sleep. She was saddened and called the hospital attendants to take the body away.

As soon as it seemed appropriate, the other man asked if he could be moved next to the window. The nurse was happy to make the switch, and after making sure he was comfortable, she left him alone.

Slowly, painfully, he propped himself up on one elbow to take his first look at the real world outside. He strained to slowly turn to look out the window besides the bed.

It faced a blank wall.

The man asked the nurse what could have compelled his deceased roommate who had described such wonderful things outside this window.

The nurse responded that the man was blind and could not even see the wall.

She said, "Perhaps he just wanted to encourage you."

~ By unknown author

PREFACE

We see the world, not as it is, but as we are -
or, as we are conditioned to see it. ~ Stephen Covey

While writing this book, it became increasingly clear to me that the way I see things is uniquely my own. Someone could be standing right beside me, even all my life, looking out the same physical window, at the same natural scene, and yet interpret it completely differently than I do. Their interpretation would be every bit as valid as mine.

For that reason, I want to stress upfront that this book is simply my interpretation of what I have seen from the windows of my life. I do not ask or expect you to take it as your own view. I only ask from you the privilege and honor of allowing me to share with you what and how I've seen from my windows. I have learned the hard way that my interpretation of reality can have little or nothing to do with God's. Nevertheless, what I've seen out my window is the real world to me and I have a passion to share with you the Beauty that simply overflows my little cup.

Some, such as the window of the hospital I was born in, I was obviously too young to remember, but fortunately or unfortunately, had the opportunity of returning to at more mature stages of my journey. I will tell you what it looked like from that particular window at that later time. And as you know, when you return to a window that you spent time looking out of as a youth, you are surprised how different everything looks from how you remembered it. This, too,

I have tried to capture in hopes of, like the anonymous blind man above, encouraging you by what I saw.

I've tried hard to learn as much as I possibly could from each and every character seen through my window – with the result that, in a very real sense, ***nothing*** I have written is original with me. It's simply what I've observed and experienced as a result. On my own, I realize I can do nothing, not even produce the air I breathe, the blood my heart pumps, or the words my hands type. I had a professor at Illinois State University who told me that I thought in metaphors. Indeed, I do – and I've come to recognize that most of those metaphors are directly connected to the ancient text of the Bible.

Life's windows come in different sizes and shapes and we sit at them for different lengths of time. Therefore, I may have more or less to describe, depending on the amount of time I spent at that specific window of my life – although I feel I did my level best, looking as intensely as I possibly could with the time I had at each window. For glory and for beauty. Please come along with me and see.

PART I

Pre-Africa

A Psalm of David (139)

O LORD, Thou hast searched me and known me. Thou dost know when I sit down and when I rise up; Thou dost understand my thought from afar. Thou dost scrutinize my journeying and my laying down, and art intimately acquainted with all my ways. Even before there is a word on my tongue, Behold, O LORD, Thou dost know it all. Thou hast enclosed me behind and before, and laid Thy hand upon me. Such knowledge is too wonderful for me; it is too high, I cannot attain to it.

Where can I go from Thy Spirit? Or where can I flee from Thy presence? If I ascend to heaven, Thou art there; if I make my bed in Sheol, behold, Thou art there. If I take the wings of the dawn, if I dwell in the remotest part of the sea, even there Thy hand will lead me, and Thy right hand will lay hold of me. If I say, "Surely the darkness will overwhelm me, and the light around me will be night, even the darkness is not dark to Thee, and the night is as bright as the day. Darkness and light are alike to Thee.

For Thou didst form my inward parts; Thou didst weave me in my mother's womb. I will give thanks for Thee, for

I am fearfully and wonderfully made; wonderful are Thy works, and my soul knows it very well. My frame was not hidden from Thee, when I was made in secret, and skillfully wrought in the depths of the earth. Thine eyes have seen my unformed substance; and in Thy book they were all written, the days that were ordained for me, when as yet there was not one of them.

How precious also are Thy thoughts to me, O God! How vast is the sum of them! If I should count them, they would outnumber the sand. When I awake, I am still with Thee.

. . . .

Search me, O God, and know my heart; try me and know my anxious thoughts: and see if there be any hurtful way in me, and lead me in the everlasting way.

1

Wapello, Iowa

A Place to Grow
1956 - 1977

Apparently, after being knit together in Mary Elizabeth's womb, I was born happy. They tell me that I was a joyful little girl. They tell me that my happiness bubbled over, like vinegar poured on baking soda, akin to salt in their wounds. Little could they or I know, this was to be a primary window of my life—joy in sorrow, alone in my happiness.

I was three years old when Teddy, my seven-year-old brother died of leukemia. From down on that busy street in Burlington, Iowa, holding my father's hand, I waved up to Teddy in his hospital window, clearly having no idea that I was waving goodbye. *Goodbye* to our entertainment, *goodbye* to the one who sent me into gales of giggles by jumping out at me from around the corners in our happy little home. *Goodbye, Teddy.*

I was waving goodbye to him in the same hospital where I had been born, my father lovingly proclaiming that my infant eyes were so black that they looked like two holes burnt in a blanket. Unbeknownst to us, this hospital in Burlington, Iowa, would come to hold even more windows for us, both for good and for ill. In the meantime after Teddy's death, my parents were torn as to whether my continual bubbling joy lessened or worsened their deep sadness.

My next memory was of sitting there alone on the back steps of our humble little brown-shingled farmhouse, seven miles from our small rural town, soaking in the July sun, quietly and joyfully anticipating the arrival of my parents. They were coming home from the same hospital, but this time with the bundle from which my happy childhood would emerge and flower. When Baby Jacob got there, my parents were very strict in telling me that I could not touch him now or ever if I didn't first wash my happy little hands. Oh, I would, I would. I'd be happy to wash my hands, just as they commanded me. As I looked at his tiny, perfect face, how could he or I know that I had just met my best lifelong friend? Thus began our idyllic childhood, shadowed only by sorrow, both past and future that we could not comprehend, even if we tried.

There came a day that, for whatever reason, I brought a stick in from the yard and with my unwashed hands hit Baby Jacob with it as he lay contentedly asleep! I don't remember the emotion, though it must have been a valid one — according to the psychologists. Though I know not what possessed me to commit the action, when my mother told me to go outside and tell my father what I had just done to my baby brother, my conscience instinctively knew judgment was about to be pronounced upon me. Putting one little obedient foot in front of the other, I approached him and told him my sin and waited for the sentence. When none came, I returned to the house, where Mom asked me, "And what did your father say?" I answered her honestly, "He said, 'Uh-huh.'" That was the truth; that was what he said!

I can't say for sure the effect this had on me, but I'm pretty certain that from my little window, I had to be all the more convinced that the love of my father was unconditional, in spite of the fact that my dirty little hands had hit his perfectly innocent son. From later windows it was, of course, clear that my father had his mind so intently on earthly matters that he, more than likely, wasn't even aware I was beside him, confessing something. If he was aware of me at all, he probably figured I was asking the endless questions little girls ask. No matter—what impacted me for glory and for beauty, was that I was loved with an inseparable love.

Another of my earliest memories is my mother quietly crying in church. It perplexed me and made me sad. I loved her oh so much, and it hurt me inside to see her always crying. Other mothers were not crying. Why was my mom the only mother crying every Sunday? Mom never did get over losing Teddy. Well, she still had the three of us - my older brother, Adam, me, and Jacob - and she held to us tenaciously; *nothing* was going to let us get away from her. I remember often wishing my mom would be more like other moms and just not care so much about me.

In spite of that, when I became a parent I naturally adopted this enmeshed style of parenting as the norm, just as it had been so beautifully modeled for me. And thus, there were ways I became the bane of my children's existence, something my mother never lived long enough to be to me.

Like Mom, our family dog could not get over Teddy's absence either. Dad repeatedly had to go down our quarter-mile lane and retrieve our dog from where he waited for the school bus to arrive and for Teddy to get off. Dad would bring him home again, only to have that faithful friend return to wait for the bus and Teddy. When I think back to this window, I have to wonder if our dog's commitment to Teddy made my brother, Adam, seven years older than me, feel somehow unworthy of being alive. After all, although he loved Teddy, they had fought, as brothers do, and then Teddy had died. I think that might be true because I remember Dad telling about the time he found Adam quietly crying, alone behind the barn.

On Sundays, we faithfully drove the twenty-seven miles to our church in Oakville, Iowa. I would sometimes sit with Daddy on the men's side. He would sit me beside him, smoothing the ruffled skirt of my dress around me, real proud of his little flower, his darling daughter. On my part, I simply knew for sure he could do anything and would always love and protect me. With him, I was completely safe. Nothing could harm me. I was safe, extremely loved and provided for, and had no need or want of anything.

Much, much later, I discovered his pride in me was because I made him look good. It wasn't about me at all. Rather than being disappointed by this discovery, I found it a relief. Maybe that's because there have been so many times in my life that I'd rather die than be noticed – I've never wanted it to be about me. And perhaps that's because experience has increasingly taught me that getting noticed for doing what I believe to be right leads to negative consequences, like being mocked and booed, which can be fascinating or extremely painful, depending on how you look at it. Either way, I've never been big enough to welcome anyone's hate, nor small enough to truly fear it. As a child, I didn't conform to the old adage that many grew up with at the time, that children should be seen and not heard. I've always wanted so badly to be heard and not seen! If I found myself mocked or booed, well, at least I had been heard.

It eventually became clear from another window, later in life, that it wasn't about me, even as my dad's only daughter. This happened when my brothers married. To my father, anyone in the family was "In." Period. While he recognized the physical reality of in-laws, to him, there was no difference: family was family. So it followed naturally that he considered each of my sisters-in-law as his darling daughters-in-law, and called them that accordingly. Now this was really something, because one wasn't at all fond of my father. Even more amazing to me, it didn't faze my father in the least. He went right on being as proud of her as he was of me, until the day he died! In his pride and jealousy that she was "his," it mattered not whether or not she cared for him. That man had monumental influence on my concept of what or who Beauty really is.

We must have brought our parents so much joy, my younger brother, Jacob and I together. We were constant companions, year round, in season and out of season, with summer being our favorite. Oh, the games we invented in our imaginations, making mush for the 100 young chickens we received every spring. We pretended they were all our children, and we would ask each other why we had so many children. We weren't bothered at all by the reality that the very heads we were feeding today would be chopped off on that post beside the shed, either tomorrow or later that summer.

Our older brother, Adam, was usually somewhere else, working on a project or figuring out another way to make money. We didn't know where he was, but our father almost always did. I guess that was how he found him that time, there behind the barn, crying. Jacob and I played on, oblivious in our happiness until Mom called us in for dinner. Then we always bowed our heads and prayed, thanking

God for all His abundant provision towards us there in that poor little brown-shingled farmhouse.

As we grew, the little house became too small for us. So my father set out to build me a bedroom of my own. He went out into the yard with his tools and measured off where and how big my room would be, then took a shovel and dug the foundation. Seeing this, I was horrified at the prospect and just had to tell him so. I timidly approached him at work and stood watching. After a time, he took notice of me.

"What do you think, Pigeon?" (His nickname for me – I have no idea why. Maybe because of my black, shiny eyes. Anyway, I liked being his pigeon.) I cried, "But I don't want to sleep out here all by myself, Dad." I thought I saw him smile, or was it a wink, at my childish ignorance!

When my room was complete, although I could see it was connected to the rest of the house, I still did not want to sleep there alone. I begged Adam to sleep there with me. Being older and wise enough to enjoy the privileges of his own room, he lined up all my stuffed animals on either side of me in my bed and told me to go to sleep, that I'd be just fine. And I was. Mostly. Except for the occasional scary dream of snakes entwining themselves all around my legs as I slept, or the fear of the shadow at my door being mass murderer Richard Speck on the loose. Fortunately for me, those bad dreams were gradually replaced with a recurring one of flying higher and higher and higher in a Tibetan blue sky – a recurring, sporadic dream that climaxed in a final one in a far future window on another continent.

Growing up on a Midwestern farm was so healthy. There was all that fresh garden produce, watermelon eaten on the tailgate of the pickup with neighboring farmers, plates of steaming hot sweet corn, delicious beyond description, radish sandwiches, eggs fixed in all manners – fried, deviled, creamed, with macaroni and cheese, sandwiched, and more besides that! Besides food, there was all the healthy growth of 4-H Club, county fairs, and learning a work ethic from the daily gathering of eggs from our 900 adult chickens, followed by washing and casing those eggs. We watched the cycle of life through animals mating, giving birth and dying, and repainting the white fence every year or so. We fished in the river, mowed the yard while getting a tan, learned to ride a Shetland pony, and enjoyed the faithfulness of Brownie, our beloved dog. What more could children want? We had no need.

Yet we had more than we needed – more weeds, that is! As Jacob and I did our duty, weeding the garden, we discussed why there were weeds in the first place. Finally pinning the cause of this curse on Adam and Eve, we thoroughly blamed them, saying how we wished they would have just been happy with the rest of that beautiful garden and left that apple alone. Then we wouldn't have the nuisance of these pesky weeds – damned weeds, ruining our mother's perfectly beautiful garden.

I loved to hang around my dad when he worked in his shop or on a tractor under the shade of our big hickory nut tree. I would ask him so many questions, and usually his answer would only lead me to more questions. His final answer to my persistent *But why?* was simply, "To make little girls ask questions." That's pretty much how I've come to see it as I continue to change windows in life – somehow, questions usually get closer to the heart of the matter than answers ever can. Perhaps that led me to my current study of searching out every single question recorded in The Ancient Words, whether asked by humans, an animal, or God Himself – which of course, *He's* not asking to gain information! Not even when He appears to be asking questions concerning what He's doing with His chosen![1]

My father's word was always the final authoritative word to me, and when he told me the reason was to make little girls ask questions, then that was that. I accepted it and have never stopped asking questions. But Father knew then what I know now: a lot of questions cannot be answered. Nevertheless, from future windows, that desire to know *why* would come to be my passion and sorrow in life.

Yes, growing up in our home, what Father said was the law. Period. He said exactly what he meant and meant what he said. Instinctively knowing that he was my father and I his creation, I received his word as truth that I could know, even if I could not yet understand it. As his little daughter, I never doubted it. I knew better than to doubt it; it was clear to me where that got me. About that,

I had no other choice. I had to believe it because it served my best interests.

Fortunately for us, he loved us all more than life itself. And though he was sometimes extreme, he wasn't unreasonable, because what he said, he intended for our good. For example, the church culture we grew up in did not, at that time, allow women to wear pants. However, one cold December evening as I was preparing to leave the house to go Christmas caroling, in a skirt, with 'the young group' (our denomination's terminology for anyone unmarried), Dad told me in no uncertain terms, "You're not leaving the house until you put pants on, Missy. I don't care what they say." Yes, my father was a father of nearly perfect love, in my view, but he would not be mocked. I had no doubts on that. In obedience, I went into my bedroom, put my pants on (*trousers* to you, my dear British friends; yes, I already had my *pants* on) and left the house – as yet undecided if I cared what they said about me or not.

Dad, a tall, strong, lean man, said that some ate to live, but that he lived to eat. However, he was so preoccupied during the height of planting or harvest season that my mother was sure if she asked him, after he ate his last bite, what he had eaten, he would be hard-pressed to answer. Having lived through the Depression, quitting school after eighth grade to help his father feed his younger siblings, the hard work of farming was second nature to him, like breathing out and breathing in.

I remember my mother occasionally saying, "I don't know why we say we don't believe in gambling. Farming is the biggest gamble there is." This would usually be said in a season of flood or drought. It's true, I can remember Dad watching the sky, longing for rain clouds. I remember one particular early summer day during one of those dry times. Thankfully, it began to rain as Mom was driving Jacob and me the seven miles home from Wapello. When we rattled across the second cattle crossing and pulled up to the house, my father was standing there in the rain, waiting for us. No sooner had Mom gotten out of the car than Dad picked up her tiny self and spun her around and around, both of them laughing in the rain. They had risked the cost of planting, and apparently the rain assured them of a big win. I guess that was what Mom meant about farming being a big gamble.

Yet it wasn't that simple, I knew, because Dad, who normally encouraged plenty of talk and banter at the table as we ate, would suddenly shush us quiet and turn up the radio that had been playing softly in the background to hear the markets. That information was what he'd been waiting for – why the radio was on in the first place. The problem with a good crop, it seemed, was that the prices went down. It's hard to win at gambling. Seems like the best that you can hope for is to break even and die in your sleep – or so sings Kenny Rogers in *The Gambler*.

Later on, when I heard Dad discussing Christian doctrines such as 'once saved, always saved' with fellow believers, he would wax eloquent. He always won the argument with his analogy of pointing to my brother Adam and saying, "See him? He's my son. He'll always be my son. There's nothing he nor I can do to change that fact. But if his sin against me is grievous enough, I can disinherit him. And that's how it is with God and us. We'll always be His children, but if we sin badly enough against Him, He can disinherit us from heaven."

I felt proud that my father carried such authority and outsmarted the others, but his cleverness didn't fool me. I knew there was never anything that I could do to make him disinherit me. No, though I feared him when I knew I had done wrong, knowing for a surety he would not spare the rod when it was in our best interest (the only thing I hated worse than getting a spanking myself was watching my little brother, Jacob, get one!), in my little heart, I felt it was impossible that he would disinherit me or either of my brothers. I was just that safe in his love for us. Besides, I had no intention of ever doing anything that would make him even consider disinheriting me.

Many years later, looking through the window at my aging father, I did fear him enough to not vote a Democratic ballot, whether or not I wanted to, lest he disinherit me. This seemed especially odd since that was the party he had staunchly upheld for years, much to my mother's distress. Though she cared nothing for or about politics, Mom could hardly bear the discord he provoked in family circles, his own and hers, by his extremely uncommon views. By the time I saw my father through this latter window, I had reached a maturity where I knew this fear of his displeasure had no connection to any theological doctrine at all. He was, after all, just my earthly father, a far cry from my Heavenly Father. Oddly enough, as my father aged, he became increasingly proud of his darling daughter being a missionary, even while I became increasingly ashamed and embarrassed by its connotations. But I digress from this present window. Please forgive me.

Though my father could easily provoke others with his strong opinions (as he did to me, one particular time I remember as a teenager), when I was younger he was always amazingly patient with me. For example, one fall season in my youth, he allowed me to drive the tractor to disc the fields after the harvest was finished. Having received instructions how to shift the tractor to a lower gear when necessary, I kept doing just that when the going got rough, until I had completely buried the disc under dirt and the remaining cornstalks! When Dad saw the situation and came to my rescue, I knew I deserved a hearty bawling out, but it never came. Not a bit of it. In fact, I think I saw him smile at my efforts, or maybe he winked at my ignorance again, I'm not sure. Once again, I didn't get at all what I thought my mistake deserved.

However, one April 1st, my mom got more than she deserved. Dad was working on the far side of the field west of the house. He intentionally slipped the rear tire of the tractor a couple of times, so to Mom's inexperienced eye, especially from a distance, it appeared that he was stuck. He walked all the way across that big field just so she would have farther to drive the tractor he said he needed to pull him out. Knowing how badly she hated to work with anything mechanical, he made her drive the tractor across the field while he stood behind her on the drawbar. It's easy to picture him grinning from ear to ear as she fretted and focused on trying to drive that big green John Deere tractor. While hating being on the tractor, she no doubt dreaded the worse that was yet to come when she would actually have to pull him out. As they pulled up to the "stuck" tractor, he hopped off, said, "April Fool's Day and thanks for the ride!" jumped on his tractor, and was on his way. It's pretty easy to imagine my dad going across the field laughing as she sat there fuming.

Sometimes in the summer, Mom would go to visit her mother in the itsy bitsy town of Pulaski, Iowa, where she had grown up. She never really knew her father, who had died of an ear infection in those pre-antibiotic days. He left this world while her mother was pregnant with their lastborn, who, of course, never met his father. So raising her five children alone and nearly penniless, Grandma took in boarders, including the tramps who hopped off any passing box car of the railroad that ran alongside their huge white house with its upper level porch.

That porch always fascinated me, maybe because by the time Jacob and I arrived on the scene, it was unsafe to play on it. That was okay, because there were plenty of other wonderful things to do – such as comb Grandma's long, long hair which, in accordance with her denominational beliefs, had never been cut. Grandma also obeyed her church's tradition of always wearing her long hair wrapped up on her head, with an additional head covering over that. So, when she took off that little doily-like head covering and let her hair down for me, I felt so special. I would comb it for as long as she would let me. A simple pleasure of life. Fortunately for me, it continued into the next generation with the joy of combing and arranging not one, but two, daughters' beautiful heads of hair.

One fine summer day when we were at Grandma Miller's, playing under the weeping willow tree, she came out the kitchen side door and asked if Jacob and I would like to go pick up her mail from the post office. *Oh yes, we would.* Since we lived seven miles out of the nearest town, even walking to the post office in Pulaski, Iowa was a fun adventure for Jacob and me. Grandma told us her box number was 123 and we should just ask the man behind the counter for her mail. Well, it doesn't get any simpler than that, but nevertheless, I repeated it over to Jacob the few blocks to the post office: One, two, three. One, two, three. Arriving at the tall counter, I looked up to the kind white-haired man behind it and said, "We want to get our grandma's mail from box three, two, one." Jacob looked at me in disbelief; what an unbelievable idiot he had for a sister! Unbelievable, but true. I am a lover of words, whether by word of mouth or by letter.Numbers, however, remain a mystery to me – though I do love a good mystery!

Our church, with its Anabaptist roots, was a separatist Christian culture, concerned with keeping themselves pure and unstained from the worldly corruption surrounding them. However, my parents bravely went against the flow of their religious culture by allowing me to attend a child evangelism event with a friend 'from the world' – the term the members of our church used to describe outsiders, and a term my mother always laughed at, asking us where that left us, as extra-terrestrials?!

Whether or not it was explicitly taught, I had already caught from our denomination that salvation is not just a simple matter of 'accepting Jesus.' I knew there was a whole lot more to it than that. For one thing, did Jesus accept us? I now know the insidious nature of that concept, but from the young window of my Sunday School, it made perfect sense.

So when it came to the invitation time at this Good News Club meeting I attended with my friend 'from the world,' I felt really uncomfortable about the situation. On the one hand, from seven years of age, I had known I loved Jesus, He loved me, and I wanted to be His forever. On the other hand, from our church's teaching, I knew I hadn't yet reached the age of accountability and thus was too young to come to repentance and salvation. So, being called to make a commitment to Jesus at this meeting, and wanting to do so publicly, but not knowing if it was the right way for it to happen, gave me reason to resonate with Langston Hughes' memoirs, *The Big Sea*, in which he wrote an essay entitled *Salvation*.

I was saved from sin when I was going on thirteen. But not really saved. It happened like this. There was a big revival at my Auntie Reed's church. Every night for weeks there had been much preaching, singing, praying, and shouting, and some very hardened sinners had been brought to Christ, and the membership of the church had grown by leaps and bounds. Then just before the revival ended, they held a special meeting for children, "to bring the young lambs to the fold." My aunt spoke of it for days ahead. That night I was escorted to the front row and placed on the mourners' bench with all the other young sinners, who had not yet been brought to Jesus.

My aunt told me that when you were saved you saw a light, and something happened to you inside! And Jesus came into your life! And God was with you from then on! She said you could see and hear and feel Jesus in your soul. I believed her. I had heard a great many old people say the same thing and it seemed to me they ought to know. So I sat there calmly in the hot, crowded church, waiting for Jesus to come to me.

The preacher preached a wonderful rhythmical sermon, all moans and shouts and lonely cries and dire pictures of hell, and then he sang a song about the ninety and nine safe in the fold, but one little lamb was left out in the cold. Then he said: "Won't you come? Won't you come to Jesus? Young lambs, won't you come?" And he held out his arms to all us young sinners there on the mourners' bench. And the little girls cried. And some of them jumped up and went to Jesus right away. But most of us just sat there.

A great many old people came and knelt around us and prayed, old women with jet-black faces and braided hair, old men with work-gnarled hands. And the church sang a song about the lower lights are burning, some poor sinners to be saved. And the whole building rocked with prayer and song.

Still I kept waiting to see Jesus.

Finally all the young people had gone to the altar and were saved, but one boy and me. He was a rounder's son named Westley. Westley and I were surrounded by sisters and deacons praying. It was very hot in the church, and getting late now. Finally Westley said to me in a whisper: "God damn! I'm tired o' sitting here. Let's get up and be saved." So he got up and was saved.

Then I was left all alone on the mourners' bench. My aunt came and knelt at my knees and cried, while prayers and song swirled all around me in the little church. The whole congregation prayed for me alone, in a mighty wail of moans and voices. And I kept waiting serenely for Jesus, waiting, waiting – but he didn't come. I wanted to see him, but nothing happened to me. Nothing! I wanted something to happen to me, but nothing happened.

I heard the songs and the minister saying: "Why don't you come? My dear child, why don't you come to Jesus? Jesus is waiting for you. He wants you. Why don't you come? Sister Reed, what is this child's name?"

"Langston," my aunt sobbed.

"Langston, why don't you come? Why don't you come and be saved? Oh, Lamb of God! Why don't you come?"

Now it was really getting late. I began to be ashamed of myself, holding everything up so long. I began to wonder what God thought about Westley, who certainly hadn't seen Jesus either, but who was now sitting proudly on the platform, swinging his knickerbockered legs and grinning down at me, surrounded by deacons and old women on their knees praying. God had not struck Westley dead for taking his name in vain or for lying in the temple. So I decided that maybe to save further trouble, I'd better lie, too, and say that Jesus had come, and get up and be saved.

So I got up.

Suddenly the whole room broke into a sea of shouting, as they saw me rise. Waves of rejoicing swept the place. Women leaped in the air. My aunt threw her arms around me. The minister took me by the hand and led me to the platform.

When things quieted down, in a hushed silence, punctuated by a few ecstatic "Amens," all the new young lambs were blessed in the name of God. Then joyous singing filled the room.

That night, for the first time in my life but one for I was a big boy twelve years old – I cried. I cried, in bed alone, and couldn't stop. I buried my head under the quilts, but my aunt heard me. She woke up and told my uncle I was crying because the Holy Ghost had come into my life, and because I had seen Jesus. But I was really crying because I couldn't bear to tell her that I had lied, that I had deceived everybody in the church, that I hadn't seen Jesus, and that now I didn't believe there was a Jesus anymore, since he didn't come to help me.

* *

Fortunately for me, my Sunday School teacher had explained salvation in simpler and more tangible terms for his students than Langston's aunt did for him. My Sunday School teacher told us God was kind of like our father and Jesus was like our mother. Both of them love us, but God, like our father, is the Boss and says what's right and wrong, while Jesus, like our mother, is always there to help us. That worked real fine for me, but one girl sitting near me, blurted out, "But my dad is waaaay nicer than my mom!" I knew her parents and I could easily see she was right about that. I guess I've always just been a lucky girl, inexplicably lucky. As for the other girl, our teacher didn't have an answer for her, or at least not one that I can remember.

There were others besides my parents who were willing to see beyond our self-contained church culture. One sister among those of our local Oakville congregation, who lived close to Wapello, had noticed the value of Vacation Bible School in other churches, something our own local congregation did not participate in. She quietly stepped out of the norm and invited church kids from around the Wapello area to her home and provided us with a wonderful little Vacation Bible School all our own for a week, complete with a small program at the end.

With the gap of Teddy in our family circle, the years between Adam and me seemed to place him in some outer circle in my childhood memories. But I do remember him when we were amongst our cousins. He was like a rock star; they all laughed and talked and had great times together. One time as our family was traveling back to Iowa from Illinois, where most of our cousins lived, Adam commented to me, "How's come you don't ever say anything? Why do you just sit there with your mouth shut like you can't talk?" It stung and I didn't know how to answer. Had I known then what I know now, I could have given him the late John Nash's answer in *A Beautiful Mind,* [I am] "terrified . . . mortified . . . petrified

. . . stupefied . . . by you." But I didn't, and now, looking back at that window, I think it was also because they were all older than me, and so charming and confident in who they were. Anyway, if I had said something loud enough for them to hear me, they would have probably all stopped and looked at me, and then what would I have done? I wouldn't have minded being heard, but I didn't want to be seen.

For most of my life, I've feared public speaking more than death. I've since learned that according to studies, that is common to our population. By public speaking, I mean something as simple as giving an oral report in school. I would dread it increasingly from the time the assignment was given until it was over. I would practice and practice at home. Giving a report in front of my small seventh grade geography class, my hands trembled so badly the paper I held was visibly, more like violently, shaking, and I spoke so fast in a quivering voice that my fellow students couldn't help but laugh out loud! What was there to possibly be afraid of? We were friends, I was an excellent student, teachers all loved me, what could I possibly be nervous about?

I honestly don't know, but I do know that even if I raised my hand to answer a question in class, I would feel my heart beating in my chest. It had always been like this ever since I started school and continued on into my higher education. The main thing I was interested in when learning the requirements of any course was, *Am I, at any point in this semester, going to have to stand in front of this class?* I was happy to do research, write very long papers, anything, just not be up front.

Even though I was shy as a child, I nevertheless loved going to school from kindergarten onwards. I enjoyed the ride to and from school on the big yellow school bus. I loved all my teachers. I loved learning and got good grades. I had plenty of friends. But one thing always made me know I was different. In keeping with our denomination's culture, I grew up without a TV. No one knows how often TV comes up in conversation, both in and out of class, except for those of us who dreaded those conversations and always tried to be invisible when they happened. Funny thing is, I now consider my

31

parents NOT providing a TV to rank high on the list of life-giving skills they unknowingly gifted to me.

Parent-teacher conferences were always positive experiences, except for maybe the first one. Apparently, one day in kindergarten, something set me off and I threw paint everywhere! The teacher told my mother had no idea what caused her otherwise sweet, timid, model student to suddenly act like this and could hardly believe her eyes. Though I don't remember it, I can picture it true, even if my teacher couldn't believe her eyes. I still have no idea why my parents only smiled at each other as my mother relayed the story to my father. It sure wasn't the reaction I expected for such behavior.

Without knowing he was doing it, my father continued to lay the foundation of my life as he picked up his shovel one day, and went to the north side of our little house. By then it was covered in white siding and had a concrete walk running from the front door we rarely used, to the back door everyone came to. Starting directly beneath their bedroom window, my father dug, the shovel scraping against the concrete as it broke the dirt. Looking back to this window, I find it more unbelievable than I did when seeing it happen. How does one dig a basement underneath an existing house? By taking a shovel and digging a hole under it. I just watched in innocence then. Now I shake my head in wonder and amazement.

The area where Dad started with his shovel became the steps down to the hole, which eventually became a plainly carpeted and paneled basement, complete with kitchen, large chest freezer, ping pong table, and furnace room with a shower, wringer washing machine, and a sump pump, also dug by Dad's hand. As the hole became big enough, posts were, of course, required to hold up the house.

For me, however, the experience of this basement that left the most indelible impression on me (other than my father digging it!) was the snake I met on the second to bottom step. Though the basement was not yet finished, we were already keeping some things down there. Mom asked me to run down and get whatever she needed at the time. Happily scampering down the stairs, I stopped abruptly, mid-step, with a sudden sharp intake of breath. There he was, the startlingly crafty creature, wriggling like lightening across the step – the step where my heel was about to land! This creature, in the realest sense of the term, scared the hell out of me – for good. Quickly releasing the startled breath I had been holding in fear, I bolted back up the stairs yelling, "SNAAAAKE!!!!"

The amazing effect of that snake was that I continued to visualize the terrifying beauty of the creature every single time I went down those stairs, for a very long time. In fact, over the next ten or fifteen years, it became an unconscious habit of mine to skip the second to bottom step.

A better memory of that basement came with a terrible storm brewing outside, as occasionally happens in the Midwest. The winds howled at the windows and the sky was darkening fast, as we watched for the tornado tails we had seen other times. My mother, brothers and I wanted to go down to the basement to be safe from the storm, but my father was never afraid of anything. He told us it wasn't necessary to go to the basement – the storm wasn't going to blow the house over. He stayed in his recliner (which he called his 'roost' and would affectionately call out, "Who's sitting in my roost?" whenever he entered the living room and caught me there) reading as usual, occasionally checking the sky. As Mom and I got more worried, I finally went to him, pleading, and took his big hand in my little one and said, "Please, please, Dad, let's go to the basement."

He looked at me with a tenderly amused smile and said, "Okay, Pigeon, if you really want to," and let me lead him by the hand to the basement, with my mother and brothers following close behind. We waited out the storm and sure enough, he was right. There was nothing to worry about. The house didn't blow over.

The Christmas break of Adam's senior year in high school, we took a big vacation in our pickup truck topped with a camper. Jacob and I were ecstatic for weeks ahead of time – we were going to California! We'd swim in the ocean, go to Disneyland, and more! Finally, in the cold wee hours of a December morning, we got in the prepared vehicle, rattled across the cattle crossings and were off to the West Coast for the time of our lives! In Oregon, we visited Mom's Miller relatives. What I still remember about them was the word "beautiful," as in *beee-oooo-ti-ful!* It was a word that we didn't seem to use in our family, so to me it sounded kind of like a foreign word, whose meaning I instinctively understood and resonated with its full abundance. Indeed, Oregon was beautiful, and the eyes these strangers-to-me beheld it with, gave me a new window toward who Beauty really is and how Mother Nature proclaims Him.

I think it was the following summer that Mom woke me up in the middle of the night. Having spent the previous day at Lake Odessa, Jacob and I were, no doubt, sleeping the sleep of healthy children who had a fun day playing outdoors. It was hard to adjust to the reality of Mom gently shaking me awake, telling me to get in the car. In a daze, I learned that Adam had been in a serious car accident and he was in the hospital in Burlington. Burlington Hospital again? *No, please God, No.* But I obediently did as I was told, pulling on some clothes over my pajamas in the dark and getting in the car, confused.

It happened that Adam and his friends had been stopped by a cop. As the policeman approached the '67 Plymouth Hemi Roadrunner to ask for the driver's license, the friend sitting behind the driver, who had two charges against him for driving while drinking and could hear the prison door clicking behind him, whispered, "Go, Speed, go!" (*Speed* was the driver's nickname.) Speed obeyed his friend. The last thing Adam remembered was seeing Speed's hand reaching for the gearshift. Next thing he knew, he woke up in a white room between clean white sheets and he hurt. Bad. What he didn't remember was the speed, sliding through the bridge sideways at 130 miles per hour. Nor did he remember seeing the oncoming car. Thankfully Adam, Speed, and the other friend lived to tell about it. The friend who issued the command did not.

I distinctly remember the effect this incident had on me. I promised myself I would never ever hurt Dad, and especially Mom, as I saw Adam doing, seemingly unbeknownst to himself. Dad was tough, but Mom was tender, almost fragile, I just hated watching either of them suffering pain. What I couldn't know from this window was that my precious mother would have to die because she wouldn't be able to handle the pain that would be hers if I fulfilled the call on my life. To her, it would truly be the *Heart of Darkness.* So, in spite of my well-intentioned promise to myself, I see my future windows as having been more likely to kill her than anything that I had watched transpire with my older brother.

In her nurturing of us, our mother was a worrier by nature. She worried about everything. Not only the weather's effect on our farm, but our health, our safety, our comfort, our cleanliness, our present, our future. My father always said he never had to worry at all because my mother did enough for the two of them. For all of us, really. She even worried that Adam had 'asked for' his wife for all the wrong reasons. (In our denomination, to get married, a young man was required to go to his local elder and 'ask for' the desired lady's hand in marriage. This elder got the message to the lady, later received her affirmative or negative answer, and then relayed her answer to the young man's local elder, who would inform the young man of her decision.) Anyway, Mom worried that beautiful blue eyes and wealth weren't a good basis for marriage. In this situation, as in others, it turned out that Mom wasn't only a worrier; she was a visionary. Knowing what we all know now, we thank God that He didn't allow Mom to live long enough to see the grief that Adam's wife's deep unhappiness brought to our family.

Seeing her propensity towards worry, it was strange that when my perfectly tiny, humble Mom told me that something was wrong with her stomach, she was completely peaceful, without any anxiety at all. Her abdomen, she said, was swelling and she didn't know why. She showed me and it was true. She looked a few months pregnant. She felt fine, she said. She was just very tired. She wished for harvest to be over before she went to the doctor. When she did go to the doctor, he was puzzled and immediately put her in the hospital for testing. After three days, all the tests were inconclusive and the medical team decided an exploratory laparotomy was necessary. They came draped in green and rolled Mom away on a stretcher to the operating room. We waited for the word.

The wait felt long, but wasn't. Our doctor, a short man who was normally as feisty as his red hair, came out and was very kind. He simply told us that he was sorry. Mom's body was full of cancer. They opened her up, saw it everywhere, and closed her back up.

I don't know why, or what I said, but I do remember going to the sanctuary of the hospital ladies' restroom to pray. Little did I know, kneeling beside that cold white toilet bowl, there on the cold gray-speckled tiled floor in that stall, how very often I would find myself kneeling in the bathroom prayer closets at so many other windows of the world. It would become my custom, giving me cause to resonate with the late John Updike who viewed "a cathedral and a toilet bowl with the same peeled-eyeball intensity."

I left the restroom and took my turn sitting by Mom's bed, waiting for her to wake up. I was there when she opened her eyes. She looked at me, her eyes full of love and hope, and said, "Pam. . .it was bad, wasn't it?" I nodded and said nothing. Mom closed her eyes and looked so at peace. I ached.

Grandma Miller came from Pulaski within the next day or so, as they were trying to drain the liquid out of Mom's abdomen. They had already put in an agonizing feeding tube. I wasn't in the room when Grandma was, but met her in the hallway as she came out. She, the quiet, tough, tiny old lady she had had no choice in becoming, was weeping, and repeating over and over, "Why couldn't it be me? Why her and not me? She's so young. I'm so old." I pitied her so and was helpless to answer. Dear Grandma, who had thought it was somehow her fault that my brother Teddy had gotten leukemia – because there had been thirteen of us, in total, sitting around the table the last meal we had eaten together as a family before Mom took him to the doctor to see why he bruised so easily when he was such a tough little boy.

But Grandma's '*why*' was a question Mom never once asked. In fact, she said lots of people get cancer every day, why *shouldn't* she be one of them? "God," she said, "is no respecter of persons." Totally unlike the merchant's servant in Bagdad or Elisabeth Kubler-Ross' five stages of grief, Mom skipped right over denial, anger, bargaining, and depression, and immediately went to acceptance. In fact, hers was *more than* acceptance, she was excited! I recall her saying, "Oh, if only I could take you all with me, this would be *just perfect!*" Well, she couldn't take us with her and to us, it wasn't perfect at all. Not from any of our windows but hers.

Once she was back home, she talked to each of us individually and privately, telling us what it would be like for us when she was gone. The thing that most clearly stuck in my memory was that she would consider it a compliment to their marriage if Dad wanted to be married again. Whoever he chose to marry, she wanted me to welcome the woman with open arms, but, she said, "Don't call her *Mom*, because I'm your Mom."

Beauty allowed her to stay with us for a little over a year. That was the year she taught me to live one day at a time, living each day to the fullest, simply because we have it to live. I was a senior in high school and had enough credits to graduate after the first semester. Though I still attended graduation with my class in the spring, I took the second semester off to do whatever came to Mom and me to do on any given day.

Mom was extremely practical and frugal. One day as we were shopping, I remember her trying on something new that she liked and saying, "This is so silly of me to buy this when I'm just going to die. Here – you try it on, and if it fits you, I'll get it and then you can wear it after I die!" I did. It did. She did. I did.

We filled our days with a lot of fun things and tried to enjoy even what wasn't fun. We refinished furniture, went on a family vacation to see Niagara Falls, went to doctor and lab appointments, and had a Christmas trying hard to be happy, all with Mom taking only oral chemotherapy and that without side effects.

But too soon for us, Mom's get-up-and-go left her. Though I had started registered nurse training in Burlington, it was Dad who learned to give her the necessary morphine shots at home. Then came the time when the tumors inside her blocked off her elimination, both urine and bowel. Watching her struggle through this – watching as a dear friend of Mom's, also a nurse, came to our home and pushed a catheter into her body, around the tumors – left a surprisingly profound and long-term impression on me. It never ceases to amaze me that food and drink, so essential to our well-being, in a short time becomes toxic to the same body it nurtured, if not eliminated. To this day, so many windows later, I remain mindful and thankful my body is healthy enough to so effortlessly rid itself of what was earlier essential to its existence.

Then came the day when Dad carried Mom to the car and we crossed those cattle crossings of our quarter-mile lane one last time with her. Dad drove us to that same Burlington Hospital. There, our red-headed family doctor told Mom, as he stood beside her bed, that she had taught us how to live and that now, at forty-nine years of age, she was teaching us how to die.

And she taught us so well, making us realize that how we die reveals who we really are. During those days of waiting, Mom remained lucid, although she herself questioned whether she was hallucinating from the morphine or having visions. Once she opened her eyes and murmured, "Must have been dreaming. . . .just saw Teddy. . . .so happy. . . . .jumping from cloud to cloud yelling, *'Mom's coming home! Mom's coming home!'*"

Mom's visitors and flowers continued in a constant stream: a single yellow rose, from one of Dad's sisters, with a tag signed, "to the best friend I ever had," and renewed as soon as it faded; a blood relative of Dad's – husband of our little vacation Bible school teacher years before – entering Mom's hospital room in his usual loud joking manner, saying, *"You were sick and in prison and I visited you,"* lightening the somberness of the room and making us all laugh; the mother of Jacob's future wife returning to the car and telling her preteen daughter who was waiting there, of poor Mary's concern over leaving young Jacob at such a critical age. All this love and care lifted and sustained us. But none of us were remotely able to touch the hem of what would happen.

It was February. My older brother, Adam, who was married and had a son, had been driving every weekend from Indiana to Burlington, to spend as much time as possible with Mom while she was with us on earth. A gentle snow was falling outside Mom's hospital window, there in room 333 on the third floor. If felt as if God were whispering that all was well. Adam said softly, "I just never imagined death like this, as peaceful as snow falling." Every first snowfall of each year since, as I watch the flakes fall so gracefully, I think back to this window of my youth and experience afresh that same ache, that melancholy ache of Beauty.

But she didn't die that night. So Adam and I drove back to Wapello to spend the night.

I got up very early the next morning, while it was still completely dark. I was daily commuting the thirty miles between Wapello and my nursing program in Burlington. Stepping out of the house, I saw it had snowed a great deal during the night. If Dad had been home, he would go ahead of me with the snow plough on a tractor, but he wasn't home. He had stayed the night with Mom in the hospital. Not knowing what else to do, I headed down the quarter-mile lane alone in my Camaro. Sure enough, about half way down the lane, I was absolutely and utterly hopelessly stuck in the deep snow. With difficulty, due to the amazing amount of snow, I pushed my car door open and stepped out into the fresh fallen snow.

As I did so, I was awestruck by the absolute stillness and inconceivable vastness of the Presence of Beauty surrounding me. It took my breath away. Overcome, I stood all alone under the huge black sky sprinkled with twinkling stars. The white snow lay glistening across the fields, and I took a deep breath of the cold crisp winter air. Standing quietly alone in the Great Silence, I felt small, insignificant, and helpless, yet surrounded by a Presence larger than life itself, its Silence more meaningful than I could comprehend. Enraptured in the Creator God's Presence, I envisioned Him as Beauty Personified. Unable to take it in, I stood spellbound.

How long I stood there, I don't know, but when I came to, I saw the reality of how hopelessly I was stuck, and again felt my helpless aloneness. Lifting one foot at a time, high, up over and back into the drifts of snow, I slowly made my way across the distance, back to the house where Adam was still sleeping. I woke him to ask his help in getting me unstuck. He did so and I continued on my way to my nursing training in Burlington hospital – just as though I had not been forever changed by the deep impression left on my soul, those few moments there, all alone with Beauty Himself, in the middle of that lonely lane.

When Mom's death angel actually arrived to take her home, I was asleep on a couch in the nurses' conference room. Adam woke me up, saying, "Pam, you'd better get in there if you want to be there when Mom dies." I did. She did.

I drove home alone in the lightly falling snow. When I reached the lane, it had been plowed clear. I parked, went in, got ready for bed, wrote on the February 28th square of the calendar hanging on my closet door, *My best friend went Home to Jesus,* fell in bed and slept.

When I awoke, the cold winter sun was streaming in my bedroom window. I reached for the white Bible lying in the gray sliding headboard of my bed and opened it. My gaze fell on the words, *Precious in the sight of the LORD is the death of His saints*.! (Psalm 116:15) It was not a verse I was familiar with and it gave me mixed emotions – how different God and I were! But somewhere deep inside, I was glad we were different. I knew He was always right and it gave me a sense that all was truly well.

In the kitchen, I could already hear my Moser aunts preparing food. I got up and went to my piano, which Mom and Dad had surprised me with when I entered the house one day after piano lessons years before. Mom would always tell me I could go practice on it while she did the dishes because she loved to hear me play, especially hymns. And it was hymns I wanted to play now, for her, for God, who was apparently happy she was with Him. I did. I played happy hymns and sang along.

Later, Dad told me that his sisters looked a little surprised by my behavior when Mom had just died. But he just said, "She's okay, let her go." When I think of that now, it makes me smile. Dad's words remind me of Jesus saying, "Let her alone" of the woman who was, some felt inappropriately, anointing His feet with expensive perfume.

A staggering number of people came to the visitation at the Wapello funeral home, and even more to the funeral at our church in Oakville. Three things stand out to me as I look back at this window. One is the single tear running down the cheek of the young lady who was to marry my cousin in our church. Mom was so worried that her death and funeral would coincide with the wedding date and ruin their plans. Her last needless worry.

The second is my cousin, daughter of the sender of single yellow roses, crying and telling me so sincerely that she would share her mom with me.

And the last one is the memory of my Grandpa Moser, sitting over against a wall, away from the crowd, looking beyond the crowd and smiling peacefully. Jacob saw him first and pointed him out to me, saying, "Grandpa is looking at the bright side of things." Yes, that was how Grandpa always seemed to look at things, as though, in spite of the mess, all was well.

Sitting on the front bench at the Apostolic Christian Church in Oakville, Iowa, Mom's casket in front of us, I had the distinct impression that it was simply my turn to be there. The reality is, we take turns here on the front bench of funeral services. We have a few turns here on the front bench, several to many in the succeeding benches, and then one in the casket. It's just how it works.

Though I had sat beside Mom's bed, longing to just bear her pain for her for an hour, if only I could, nothing about watching my mother die came close to the agony of watching my father try to go on living without her. Coupled with that and my own sorrow was the helplessness I felt in helping Jacob cope with his. Hearing him crying in his room one night, I went in only to have him ask me, "Why did God take my mom, when other boys don't even like their moms?" It was true, the love between Jacob and our mom was unusually beautiful, as was her love for each of us. Each of us were loved deeply and uniquely by her. For Jacob, I had no answer. The ache inside settled deeper.

Many years and windows later, Jacob would write a poem from a beautiful sunny space on Marco Island, Florida, that I want to share with you here, dear reader, to encourage you before I continue on to the next window of my youth.

> *What would she think if she saw us today*
> *so much has transpired since she went away.*
> *Sometimes it seems but a few days have gone,*
> *sometimes a lifetime past,*
> *since our dear mother told us good-bye*
> *and we watched her breathe her last.*
>
> *On that lonely old hill down by the*
> *church is where we laid her to rest.*
> *Twenty-six years is not very long,*
> *but in them she gave us her best.*
> *People were kind on that day with prayers*
> *and words they hoped would ease our sorrow*

but none-the-less we walked away
with a fear and dread of tomorrow.

Adam was first to get back on the track,
his life was already a blur;
with kids to raise and a business to run, his love was no less
he just had less time to miss her.

Pam was next to jump back into life
without her mother and friend;
with the grit of her dad and the compassion of mom,
she had the perfect blend.

Only Dad knows the roads he went down and
the spiritual battles he fought,
while deep in despair he could not yet
see the future God had wrought;
but in answer to our mom's prayers finally a new love he sought.
Now the course of life takes crazy turns and
sometimes the road gets rough
and God had so much to teach our dad
that even two wives weren't enough.
Not only would our mom be pleased, it'll be added to her glory,
that Dad counted married life so sweet that
there are three wives in his story.

For a momma's boy who's lost his mom
the world's a confusing place,
especially when that foolish boy will not apply God's grace.
But God said unto His own dear Son, "Bring Jacob here to me,
for I still can hear his mother's prayers and
I'll honor them, you'll see."
Salvation is a wondrous thing and this one was even more sweet,
for when Jacob gave his life to God,
Dad's family circle was complete.
With four of us now running hard and two across the line,
no matter what else life deals out, our souls will be just fine.

What would she think and what would she say
if she saw us today?
I think she'd bow her head and give thanks for all the ways
that God equipped each one of us His mighty Name to praise.
We loved her so and to let her go none of us were ready,
but God knew then and we know now,
it was best she go wait with Teddy.

The Good Book says glories await
that by us cannot even be guessed,
but if I dare to be so bold I do have one request.
Sometime in eternity I'd like to see our dad
experience just once a wondrous joy that I have often had.
If he could sit down at a table with all his children there,
to think he'd not get to do this once is more than I can bear;
For Teddy left before I came and even with all God's grace
our dad has never ever seen all his family in one place.
Then we could sit and share a meal and laugh and cry and talk
about the rich and bounteous ways God blessed our earthly walk.

It is a fact we've taken some hits and
many times been on the ropes,
but bigger far than all our fears is the Source of all our hopes.
We're no strangers to discouragement and we've many times
been tried
but He's dealt us all innumerable joys
for each single tear we've cried.
Our dad's family has a message that we'll tell as well we should,
for God's let us be a living proof that He is very good.[2]

* *

Lessons learned:
Sometimes The Beauty is enough. He just has To Be.
Heaven is Real and it's our Home.

2

Iowa City, Iowa

On My Own
1977 - 1980

Having graduated from nursing school, taken and passed my state boards, worked for a year in the Cardiac Care Unit in Muscatine, Iowa, while driving back and forth to help Dad and Jacob at home, I felt ready to move on. Starting out my career in Intensive Care as a new nurse had presented a tremendous learning curve, causing my habit of praying in the restroom to increase! I recall earnestly praying that the vitamin K that I had just given intravenously instead of subcutaneously would not do as the warning said and cause a severe reaction or fatality! It didn't. Whew.

Some of our most critical patients related near-death experiences to us as they were recovering. Some reminded me of Mom, who had described seeing a bright door opening for her. However, one particular case was quite the opposite – he claimed that he had seen hell and Satan waiting and he was now completely terrified of death. The doctor didn't seem to take too much stock in any of the stories. As a good doctor, he was mainly invested in making sure none of them died on his watch, no matter where they were headed. Part of his strategy in accomplishing that goal was to send them on to the University of Iowa Hospitals and Clinics in Iowa City if their condition warranted more than our small unit could provide.

After a year working in Muscatine Hospital, I wanted to go see what happened to those patients we sent to Iowa City.

Thus began my career in the 4th floor Surgical Intensive Care Unit at the University of Iowa Hospital. Here were twelve beds in the main unit, two of those set up as isolation units, plus an additional four beds in the annex for post-operative open heart surgery patients. The annex became my favorite place to work. I loved it.

Learning to draw arterial blood gases was a scary but heady experience. The success of the bright red blood surging into the syringe reminded me of the feeling of successfully springing out of the lake water a few summers earlier. Dad had taken me out one afternoon to try until I mastered getting up on skis. The many monitors, respirators, beepers, and yards of tubing of all different manners on the patients, who lay silently breathing in and out at the will of their respirators, gave the place an eerie, futuristic aura. Here I learned, especially when I became charge nurse, to earnestly pray as I pushed open the door to enter the unit for my shift. Generally, there was no time for bathroom prayers here. Though the patients lay still as corpses, their monitors indicated more than enough going on inside them to keep us hopping most all the time!

Concerning ethics and morality, my life had been pretty much black and white up until this time. Right was right and wrong was wrong. Here, I began to learn that a lot depends upon context and interpretation, even when it comes to life and death. With living wills, people can decide ahead of time when and if they want to die in certain situations. Fortunately for me, in this ICU, I was not forced to inject what amounted to lethal injections, but could draw it up and hand it to another nurse who was willing. One day as I was gowned up and suctioning a patient in one of the isolation rooms, the doctor came in, turned down all the machines, told me he hoped it didn't bother me morally, and left. I stood with suction catheter mid-air, unsure what to do, not absolutely certain about any of it. After all, who was I to say that the patient waiting in the Emergency Room wasn't more viable than the one I was caring for?

It was always a relief to make it successfully through the stressful eight-plus hours and get back to the safety of the apartment I shared with roommates from my home church culture. In our sunny kitchen apartment, a large poster greeted me with a glorious golden sunrise, and the words, *"If God is for us, who can be against us?"* (Romans 8:31 ESV) It was a question that I loved, especially in light of the question the author had penned right before it: *What then shall we say to these things?* I was growing to exceedingly love the fundamental truths that showed themselves so clearly in questions.

When I wasn't at work or at our apartment, I was most often on my bike, riding alone, leaving my beautiful roommates to plan their love lives. Though it made riding more difficult, there was something that I especially loved about biking on windy days. I knew not whence it came or where it went, but the rushing mighty wind always seemed to blow away my troubles and sweep my mind clean.

As part of planning our futures, my roommates and I bought a set of Lifetime Pots and Pans for a premium from a salesperson promoting them house to house. Little did I know that, in spite of their proclaimed quality and endurance capacity, my pots and pans were destined to spend nearly a lifetime of being packed away and stored in some out-of-the-way space a continent or two away from whatever kitchen window I found myself looking out.

In the meantime, my father had found a reason to go on living, in the form of a widow with six children. Her name, Naomi Elizabeth, was not so different than my mother's – their middle names being exactly the same and both of their respective names being biblically rich. As I got to know this beautiful woman, seasoned by sorrow, I was more convinced than ever that Beauty really loved me. How else could I be so inexplicably lucky to have the best mother in the world, followed by the best step-mother in the world?? Our own mother's request for us to welcome Dad's new wife with open arms was an impossibly simple one to fulfill.

With my father happily taken care of, I felt freedom to fully enjoy my single life in Iowa City with my friends from work and church. Normally, in our church, at that time, those two worlds didn't mix. But because my parents had been so instrumental in making me clearly aware that religion consisted of so much more than rules, I was lucky enough to have the best of life, security and amusement.

A less fortunate church friend of mine, very close to my heart, once asked me about this apparent duplicity of mine. "Pam, don't you ever feel guilty when you wear your hair down to work?" (Meaning that I didn't have it wrapped up onto my head, in the tradition of my grandmother and all those who followed the church traditions.)

I considered her question for a brief second before replying with a laugh, "Only for five minutes." My precious conservative friend laughed and laughed in delight at such an incredulously irreligious answer. We had such a wonderful relationship, benefitting us both, except for the time that I accidentally locked the keys in the car on a dark night in Paducah, Kentucky. That benefitted neither of us, nor the other friends along with us on that vacation. But fortunately for us all, the memory is now a precious one.

Yes, I was gifted with awesome church friends and roommates. The father of one of my roommates was known for his contagious joy in life, in spite of having suffered hard times. This exuberant joy was not always considered appropriate in our culture, and was even questioned by a concerned brother in the church. My roommate's father replied, "Well, I'm just so happy. I can't help it. It's just my nature." The reply he received: "Scripture teaches us we are to go up against our nature." Sometimes there's just nothing you can say.

While it was a great carefree time of life for me, there was still the occasional flicker of wondering if what they taught might be true. Say for instance, what if it was wrong to go to a movie theater? Would I really want to be found there watching a movie if Jesus suddenly came back? Was it true that I would be ashamed of my behavior in that circumstance? I couldn't be certain. And it kind of ruined a good movie.

Somehow, even in my seeming duplicity of enjoying the church and 'the world' at the same time, I was never accused of losing my religion, as happened to another conservative church friend. She had been working in her yard, and somehow, maybe by a low-hanging branch or the wind, I don't know, her doily-like head covering had, unbeknownst to her, fallen off. The young neighbor girl in the next yard saw this, and pointing to it, sincerely called out to her, "Oh! Miss Shirley, you lost your religion!!"

* *

As I mentioned before, our church practiced what could be classified as marriage by mediation. Though it's not so unusual throughout the world, people outside of our church culture seem to find it a nearly unbelievable story here in America. The first time I told a friend of mine how engagements and weddings came to happen in our church culture, she listened so intently that I felt hot and embarrassed relating how I had experienced my own proposals, engagement and marriage.

To my surprise, when I finished she asked in amazement, "Do you mean to tell me that you and Harrison got engaged without ever even kissing?? That is the most romantic story I have ever heard!!" Yes, that was what I meant, but no, I had never once thought of it as 'the most romantic' story ever. Here is how it happened:

The stress of that ICU unit took its toll on us nurses. The turnover was very high. One day, another nurse and I got to discussing things and decided it would do us good to get back to the basics of nursing, somewhere that the patients could at least talk to us. "Yes!" said my colleague. "Maybe somewhere like a mission field!"

"A mission field?" I repeated. I was not at all familiar with 'mission fields.' Our separatist denomination, at the time, in its effort to keep itself unpolluted by the world, did not encourage evangelism. But I had heard of one man in our denomination who personally knew some missionaries from other churches. "*Yes,*" I told Dawn, "I'll go ask him if he knows of anywhere we could get back to nursing at its basics."

One of the following weekends, I drove to Illinois, visited the Roanoke congregation and talked to this man, Tobin Hodel. He told me he had a cousin named Bob working as a missionary in Quito, Ecuador, and would get me in touch with this cousin in hopes of finding a way for Dawn and me to go to Quito.

When he got home from church, Tobin spoke to his son, Harrison, who was the ninth child out of seven sons and four daughters, saying, "I talked to Pam Moser at church today. She and her friend want to go to Quito this coming winter. Maybe you could fly down together." As it happened, Harrison and one of his older brothers were planning a trip to travel South America during the winter months when they were not busy farming.

Harrison answered his father with, "Pam Moser?? I barely know her. What would I talk to her about for four hours on an airplane?!"

Because it was his father's suggestion, he did call me in spite of not knowing what to talk about. But as it turned out, Harrison and his brother were ready to leave for their South American adventure before Dawn and I had completed our paper work with the mission of Heralding Christ Jesus' Blessings (HCJB), so they left without us.

As Harrison tells it, one of the adventures that he and his brother experienced included leaving Quito by bus (not a Greyhound, mind you), careening through treacherous narrow mountain roads towards the coast, and stopping frequently alongside the road (no guard rails to be seen) to replenish the brake fluid. Though these stops provided a scenic overview of the deep gorge outside the bus windows, they also caused the bus to arrive late to the town. In fact, it didn't even get to its designated destination, and they ended up in a different town than where they were supposed to go. Getting off the bus, the two tourist white boys, who didn't know anyone, didn't speak Spanish, and didn't have any contacts, realized they were basically stranded. By this time it was early evening. Suddenly, someone they didn't know came along, grabbed them, and said, "Get in the boat!"

So they got in a small rowboat with an outboard motor, and were propelled in a northerly direction along the coast. When they stopped, they were taken out of the rowboat and hustled into a dugout canoe, powered by an outboard motor. By this time it was 10:00 pm and a pitch black, starless night. For the next two hours they travelled upriver, not knowing where they were going, but thankfully the moon came out, lending them some weak comfort as they dodged fallen trees and floating logs.

To their amazement, about midnight they arrived at the welcoming home of Lester and Sharon, a missionary couple who lived along the river! Exhausted, they fell into bed and slept.

Harrison and his brother stayed there ten days. During this time, these missionaries and their dedication to the work of planting a church, even in the face of extreme adversity, such as burying some of their own children, made such an impression on Harrison's life that he believed this was what he wanted to do with his life – leave the confines of the farm and live out what had also been his father's dream.

He was only too aware the problem with this was that, being a member of the church, he could only marry someone inside the denomination. Who would be interested in being a missionary with him when the church didn't support missions? Then the obvious dawned on him – Pam Moser! She was currently working as a nurse in Hospital Voz Andes in Quito! Of course.

Passing a local shop, Harrison went in, purchased a postcard pictured with a busy city scene entitled *La Paz*. On it he penned in blue ink:

Pam,

Welcome to Quito from Bolivia. I was glad to hear that you were able to make it down here. Bruce and I spent 3 weeks there with Bob and had a wonderful time. I know you will enjoy your 3 months. Plan to spend another month traveling, it's starting to look all the same so maybe it's time to get home. Will look forward to hear of your experience abroad back in the good old U.S.A.

Harrison

We landed Quito in the early morning, the sun reflecting off the city and the surrounding Andes Mountains, giving us the impression that we were landing in a new Jerusalem, Dawn and I were ecstatic with the adventure lying in front of us. True to promise, the three months were filled with experiences not only meeting, but even exceeding, our expectations. We not only got back to the basics of nursing, but found ourselves playing medical roles we hadn't anticipated while on a medical safari through remote villages in the jungles. Bumping over the roads between villages, in our little dental clinic on wheels, taking in the lush green beauty, I recall singing the little song that still takes me back to this window every time I've heard it since: *Thank You, Lord, for saving my soul. Thank You, Lord, for making me whole. Thank You, Lord, for giving to me,*

Thy great salvation, so rich, so free.[1] If this was missionary life, I wanted it.

Ruth Riggs, the precious elderly lady who was assigned to host us in her little apartment, had given her whole life to serve those less fortunate than her in a foreign land. Being the first missionary I had ever known, the impact and gift of her life on mine was lasting and can be summed up in the message of her favorite Bible verse: *I want to know Christ—yes, to know the power of his resurrection and participation in his sufferings, becoming like him in his death.* (Phil. 3:10 NIV)

In fact, the astonishing thing to me, as I look back at the view out this window, is how precisely clear it remains in my mind's eye. I not only remember Ruth's favorite Bible verse and how she lived it out, but I can also still hear the words of the sermons that were preached in the international church that I attended.

Sitting in that international church, my mind's eye went far back to when I was a small girl, sitting on the dining room floor, there by the big picture window, with the light shining in from the west, playing with my paper doll set – children from many lands with their different dress. I had been fascinated by the different skin tones, different hair types, and spent hours playing alone with them and wondering about their different lives. Now, as I sat in the international church in Quito, Ecuador, it seemed I had arrived at a dream come true. Simply put, I loved the nations. My heart was captured.

Oddly enough, as the preacher expounded on his series on the very letter from which our gracious hostess, Ruth, had lived her life, it appeared clear to me, that, in spite of the differences that I reveled in, in reality, our international hearts were all the same! For better or for worse – well, mostly for the worse, I realized. In my mind's eye, I saw back to the window of Jacob and me, as we toiled by the sweat of our brow, weeding Mom's big beautiful garden. Loitering in the memory, I smiled ruefully at Jacob's and my well-intentioned proclamations as we accused and condemned Adam and Eve for making a choice that we would never have made.

Our experience in Ecuador extended beyond the missionary community. Dawn and I were fortunate to be able to spend some days with a Peace Corp volunteer living in a village near Cotopaxi, a volcano that we spent some time climbing one bright sunny day.

That night, I was awakened in the Peace Corp volunteer's room by pain. My eyes were burning with such an intensity that I knew I had to do something. But what? A wet cloth, I thought, that's what I need. Remembering that there was a pail of water outside, I groped about with difficulty in the dark and found a rag. I could barely see anything and didn't know if it was because of the burning, the darkness or a combination of the two. As the wet rag soothed the burning, I fell back to sleep.

When I awoke in the morning, I could hardly see a thing! Stumbling outside the little adobe room into the light, I was horrified to discover I could only distinguish a hazy outline of the huge snow-covered volcano we had climbed on the day before! Only being guided by someone's hand was I able to make it to the bus to ride back to the city where I could seek help. Once there, I found out that I had sun blindness, a common malady, especially for people with dark eyes, who climb snow-covered mountains in the sun's harsh light, without sunglasses. It felt worse than receiving the light of a five-mile flashlight in a dark tent in the middle of the night. So, there I was, like Saul of Tarsus – blinded by the light.

* *

Before leaving Ecuador, Dawn and I had made arrangements with a traveling nurses company to work in a hospital in Lakeland, Florida, en route back to the Midwest. There we worked nights, spent most of our days by a pool, and the few hours that we did sleep were interrupted by the hallway loudspeakers, especially disturbing when they were proclaiming Code Blue! Yes, the room we were given to live in was in an unused section of the hospital, though the P.A. system was still connected. We slept in hospital beds – providing us with an unusual, sometimes disorienting, and always eerie, window from which to view our current short-term career!

* *

I got back to the States in time to be in the June wedding of a close friend. Because the bride was a mutual friend, Harrison was also at the wedding. Here he received the fulfillment to his comment on the postcard he had sent to me in Quito from La Paz, '*Will look forward to hear of your experience abroad back in the good old U.S.A.*' When he asked about my trip to Ecuador, of course I was aglow with excitement as I related it all to him. Later, he told me that my happy reply was the answer to his prayer for a sign. He had decided that if I complained of cold showers and big bugs, that would be a sign I was not the one for him. If I had enjoyed the experience, he would take it as a sign that I was, indeed, the bride for him.

I had more than enjoyed this time on a short-term mission to Ecuador – I was filled to overflowing with it. Harrison wasted no time in getting to his local church's elder to ask for my hand in marriage.

My local elder, perhaps weary of taking the time to personally convey proposals, called my father's home phone in Wapello, where I happened to be at the time. We were having a party to celebrate Jacob's twentieth birthday. My father answered the phone and I took the call on the basement phone, directly at the bottom of the stairs. The elder told me of a brother in Roanoke who wished to ask me to marry him. Then he hung up, leaving me with the challenge of praying about whether I was to answer *yes* or *no* to this proposal.

After the party, my father asked about the call. I began to cry. He smiled. Naomi looked concerned.

Back at my apartment in Iowa City, life resumed its normal happy course. Sometimes the infamous topic of proposals would inevitably come up. One of my darling roommates had had so many proposals that she sometimes would get mixed up if a certain brother had 'asked for' me or her. We laughed. But I didn't really think it was funny. No, I knew for sure that this 'for better or worse' thing was serious business.

About a month later, I knew I must give an answer to this proposal. The elder had contacted me by phone. I would remove it one more step. I would write him a letter, saying, as I had with other proposals, that I had received no answer from God at all – no *yes* or *no*, leaving me with no choice, that I could see, except to say *no*.

I sat down and began to write the letter. Shortly after the greeting, I found it difficult to continue. There was a nagging sensation in my mind and spirit. I thought of the book I was currently reading on prayer. It explained the absurdity of going to a medical doctor, reciting all your aches, pains, and complaints, and then getting up and walking out of the office without waiting to hear what the doctor had to say! Likening it to prayer, the author said that when we pray, we should wait to see what the Healer has to say. Just listen. Okay, I'd try it. Grabbing my Bible, I got on my bike and left.

Sitting in the breeze of a gentle wind under a beautiful tree in a nearby park, I prayed. I opened the Bible to read. I didn't know how else to 'hear' God speak. I happened to read a letter that Saul of Tarsus, turned Paul, had written to some people in the Grecian city of Corinth, a very long time ago. It was interesting and had a lot of provoking thoughts, and better yet, numerous questions, along with advice about when not to ask questions! But suddenly as I neared the end of the chapter, some words seemed like they were in bold letters, or jumped off the page, or something that I can't quite describe otherwise! *Whether, then, you eat or drink or whatever you do, do it all for the glory of God.* (1 Cor. 10:31)

A gentle breeze rippled the pages of my beloved Book. I waited. I listened to see. And I had a very clear thought that was not in the first person of me. *You and Harrison together would be a glory to Me.*

Whether it was reality or not, I cannot tell you. I can only tell from the experience of my window. That's what happened to me.

The announcement of our engagement, given by the elder following the morning service, came, as was common, as a big surprise to many. The suppressed stir of excitement was fun for me, as I sat there on the women's side in the congregation. I also enjoyed the many congratulations and well wishes over the usual lunch of donuts and coffee. Following his afternoon service, Harrison drove from Roanoke, Illinois, to our home in Wapello, Iowa where we officially met as an engaged couple and had dinner together with my family. It wasn't, however, until weeks later that Harrison told me that when he received my answer from his elder, he totally panicked, thinking, "Oh no! What have I done??"

The wedding took place in the old Oakville church, which today no longer exists, except in the hearts of those who, like me, preserve memories of being nurtured, baptized by immersion, and burying our loved ones there. I wore a replica of my mother's wedding dress, sewn with love by dear Naomi. It was egg-shell in color. White, being the color 'the world' weds in, was contrary to the traditions of our church at that time. An off-white color, 'egg-shell', was as close as my mother could get by with. Whether or not she had an easier time than me in this, I can't say; but I know that God saw my tears over the condemnation placed upon me by my plan of also wearing an off-white wedding dress - a color so near the white of the 'world's' wedding dresses.

My maid of honor was my sole remaining roommate. She is also my dear cousin, daughter of the sender of single yellow roses to my dying mother, and constant friend through thick and thin to this day. It was she who blessed my decision of saying *yes* to Harrison with her comment of, "You and Harrison have matching spirits." I received her blessing, little knowing that the ensuing years of journeying life together would reveal that the Beauty that matched our spirits and made us one flesh certainly endowed us with different ways of looking out our mutual windows!

We should have known when the wedding started that our union was going to be atypical, if compared to the countless couples who had married here before us. Something happened that had never happened before or since. Just as the wedding march began, which in our church is Psalm 23 sung acapella by the entire congregation, the lights in the church dimmed until nearly extinguished! I can't say for sure, but I imagine that all 600 guests gathered in our small church remember that to this day, because it was such a highly irregular happening! There was no way we had of knowing that highly irregular events were destined to happen to us on a regular basis in the adventures of our future life together.

Even the seating of the guests at our wedding turned into an irregularity. Tradition held that men and women sat on opposite sides of the church for all services. In our local church, weddings were included in that tradition. However, one of my father's sisters, not being of this conservative mindset, saw it as ridiculous not to sit as husbands and wives for a wedding. (To be fair to the church's traditions, I must add that weddings were held in lieu of the regular Sunday afternoon service – which was always held after the lunch of donuts and coffee following the morning service. Weddings were, in that respect, treated like any normal Sunday afternoon service, it was just that some people happened to be getting married. On this particular Sunday afternoon, us!)

The way I remember hearing about this irregularity in seating is that when the church usher attempted to separate my aunt from her husband, she wouldn't have it. But this aunt of mine remembers it much differently. The way she remembers it is that, without thinking, she and my uncle innocently went in and sat on the women's side. It wasn't until they were sitting that my uncle noticed he was surrounded by all women, and whispered to her, "I don't think I'm supposed to be here!"

Either way, the result was the same – there sat my uncle, the sole man in the middle of a sea of veiled sisters! (Yes, we women all wore veils to church, not heavy veils like in Islam, but light lacy black pieces about four inches wide and two feet long.) There they were, my aunt and uncle, a rare gem, as the only couple sitting next to each other in the entire church at our wedding. It was beautiful to see them sitting there together, smiling as I walked down the aisle as a newly married woman (without having been kissed by the groom, of course).

Getting back to the actual wedding service: just before we said our vows, promising to be true to each other so long as we both shall live, for better or for worse, I suddenly had a moment of dizziness. I felt it was connected with the totally unexpected, but distinct, feeling that Mom was watching our wedding from somewhere above, looking down at it with pleasure. Though I was happy to sense her pleasure, I was relieved the moment passed quickly. I felt it was important that I not be dizzy just then.

The wedding service itself was centered around another letter from Saul of Tarsus, turned Paul – this one addressed to some people in Colossae, modern-day Turkey. Though reading and expounding on the whole chapter, this lay preacher, who was also my father's cousin, focused on the verse that says, in the exclusively used King James Bible, *And let the peace of God rule in your hearts, to the which also ye are called in one body; and **be ye thankful**.* (Col. 3:15 KJV)

Be ye thankful. And I still am. For everything. In fact, that preacher so emphasized those few words that it became like a mantra of ours. Sometimes one or the other of us would say it, especially in our early years together, and we would both just laugh. A happy, heart-felt laugh.

Our wedding reception was held at the Holiday Inn in Burlington. Though it was a large, happy event, it was unlike the weddings in Jesus' day because there was no wine or dancing, of course. When it was finally over, we escaped, driving away in the dreariness of that drizzly November night.

Lessons Learned:

For better or for worse, we all share in the plight of being human. Happy thankfulness can cover over a multitude of darknesses.

3

Roanoke, Illinois

A New Life Together
November 1980 - August 1983

Harrison's father picked us up at the airport when we arrived back in Peoria from our beautiful honeymoon in Hawaii. On the way back to their farmhouse in Roanoke, he asked us if we had heard that my parents were going on a short-term mission trip to Ecuador to help Les and Sharon – the very missionaries whom Harrison and his brother had spent time with when they were in Ecuador! I was completely dumbfounded by this news – the reason being that my parents had been so concerned about me going earlier that same year! In fact, they had been wary of it to such an extent that I had wondered, at the time, if I was sinning by going against my father's wishes.

I was aware that their concerns had something to do with my father-in-law's cousin having been a member of our church culture before he had become a missionary. Naturally, my parents were concerned about where my going overseas on a mission trip would lead. Would I end up leaving the flock, going out from them as though I didn't really belong to them? I understood that, but it now served to increase my surprise at this turn of events! In a matter of minutes, my incredulousness turned to joy at the prospect of my parents and others from our church experiencing Ecuador as I had!

Being a missionary-lover, my father-in-law, was, of course, really pleased with this turn of events, especially so because his third-born daughter, Harrison's closest sister, and her husband were also planning to go on this same trip with my parents. (My dad's wife, Naomi, was the mother of Harrison's sister's husband – complicated, but true.)

Harrison's father had a quiet way of entering into or facilitating any type of mission work he could, coordinating with the Mennonite Mission Committee to send heifers to Haiti, entertaining missionaries in their home, anything that was helpful to others. He made his children aware of the world beyond the immediate one surrounding them. Through their teen years, he took his children, one or two at a time to various different countries, simply for the experience it afforded.

I so loved and respected my father-in-law and looked forward to my husband being just like him. There are two things about him that I have continued to think of at all the windows I have looked through. One is something that Jesus, during the time that He was walking on earth as a man, is recorded as saying to Peter immediately after he declared that Jesus was the Messiah: *And I tell you that you are Peter, and on this rock I will build my church, and the gates of Hades will not overcome it.* (Mt. 16:18) My father-in-law did not focus on any controversy surrounding this verse, but rather on the fact that Jesus' church would happen and there was nothing that hell could do to prevent it. An awesome comfort, the way I saw, and continue to see, it.

The other thing that I remember this father-in-law of mine (and of quite a few others, too!) often saying was, "Every day is a gift." *Yes,* each one is, even the hard ones.

My mother-in-law, too, quickly connected and became a real friend to me. Our relationship was not one of meaningful talks, but we shared so many good times laughing together. One day, however, as we were lightly discussing something or other, she made the remark that she hated ugly. Though I didn't know if she and I meant the same thing by ugly, I resonated soundly with her statement. I hated ugly, too. To me, he looks like the ultimate terrorist, the twister of Beauty.

Our first home was in a new set of apartments in Roanoke, a set of two buildings, looking for all the world like two Pizza Huts sitting side by side – which was what they were known as, the Pizza Hut apartments. I was delighted to discover that I could climb up into the parapet – my own private place to sunbathe and read! While doing so one sunny day, I read some ancient words that said Beauty had the ability to keep me from tripping up in life, that He could even make me stand in the presence of His glory blameless, plus with great joy on top of it! (Jude 1:24) I could hardly believe my eyes! I sat in my lawn chair, simply amazed, hardly aware of the sun's welcome rays soaking into my skin. If those words had any chance of being true, I realized that I knew precious little about the power of Beauty.

Meanwhile, we had happily set up house. The little embroidered plaque that I had received from a good friend at one of my many bridal showers said it all for me: *A Little Home to Keep, There's No Joy So Deep.*

And yet, it wasn't all joy. My new husband accidentally discovered that he could make me furious, simply by loudly singing, *"I am a rock, I am an island."* I suppose my anger was a result of hurt and fear – fear of living life alone, isolated on a rocky island, like I was married to someone with attachment disorder or something, instead of to the perfect man I just knew I had married.

It was a lot of fun being a part of his big family. Though his three older sisters had married and now lived in other states, Harrison and his four older brothers farmed together with their father, giving us wives a camaraderie as well. Even the pain of one of their farms being eight hours away in Hayti, Missouri, turned out some grand times of family travel and get-togethers.

I was happy that my family approved of my husband, too. Harrison and my brother, Jacob, went together on trips to both Haiti and Ecuador to help out with local mission projects. When they completed their work on the Haitian project, my parents, one of my step-brothers, and I flew to Port au Prince, met Harrison, and spent a week or so experiencing Haiti. And my older brother, Adam, invited Harrison to participate in a business venture in Chesterton, Indiana, that would require us relocating there to manage it. Unsure about what to do, we didn't. And perhaps it was that inadvertent choice not to that has made all the difference.

All things considered, we started out conventionally enough, living our new life together in the apartment for a year or so before finding a partially built new home on Carol Street. Having looked at several other options, both in town and in the surrounding countryside, we bought this one, finished it out, with the help of family, and moved in.

* *

Meanwhile, the company that Dawn and I had worked for in Lakeland, Florida, called to ask if I would consider taking another nursing contract with them. It was at the Pontiac Penitentiary, a male maximum security prison in a town about forty-five minutes away. I accepted and thus gained an entirely new window, a view so entirely different from my own experience that I had almost nothing, apart from my human condition, to hang it on.

While my father had formed the basis of my reality, the vast majority of these men did not know their fathers' whereabouts, and many of them did not even know who their fathers were! Interestingly, as I got to know them, many of them had mothers praying for them, and even more of them spoke of grandmothers praying for them. I found this fascinating. Along with that, even men who were in their thirties would sometimes mention a grandchild of their own.

But what surprised me more than any of that was the spectrum of the ways they treated me! I mostly worked the 3-11pm shift. The first evening that I ventured out of the prison hospital to pass out medication cell to cell, I got the shock of my life. More than the unsavory whistles, language and comments ("Well, well, look what they sent us to play with now!"), was the surprise that I received when I checked what they had told me against their medical records. Never had I ever been so utterly lied to in all my life. Granted, it was possible that I had almost never been lied to thus far in my happy innocent life, but this was too much! All of them, as far as I could tell, were liars! Not only liars, but what kind of human would throw urine on someone who was there to help them?

On the other end of the spectrum, I honestly came to consider a few among them to be good friends who, if a riot were to break out, I felt I could trust more than I would some of the state employed security guards. However, all in all, my experience at the window of this maximum security male penitentiary caused a tectonic shift in my view of our human species, specifically males. And in hearing their stories, I came to understand why, when once released from this awful place, I could expect to see them back within months. I came to understand that those of us who make good choices oftentimes have the cream of the crop of choices to choose from when making them. It makes me wonder if the praise for making good choices should go to the chooser, or to the ones who provided the choices.

But the view wasn't totally dark. There were bright spots, like when the Mennonite Gospel Heirs got permission to enter the walls to sing. I was struck by what vastly different windows the singers and the audience were viewing life from, and yet many of the prisoners seemed able to really appreciate the change of view.

We also laughed a lot, sometimes at things that weren't really funny, like the gloomy young guard who always greeted my cheery greeting of, "Good morning! How are you?" with the same response, "Like a sharp stick in the eye."

A positive change happened for me when a classmate of Harrison's, one who had befriended me in my new life in Roanoke, also began to work at the prison, followed by another church member, a lady our parents' age. Both of these coworkers were extremely cheerful people, the one my age being perhaps the happiest friend I have ever had. If I ever even got close to having a pity party for myself, well, she laughed me right out of it! It was her father who liked to say, "Every day is a good day; some are just better than others." Something I have never forgotten.

I worked at this job until I was overdue with our firstborn child. The prisoners were marvelous about my pregnancy, often joking with me as my tummy grew that that baby would be born in the prison, wouldn't be able to leave, and they would have to raise it. One precious man saved his cigarette cartons and made booties out of them for our newborn, an unusual item kept with the baby book until this day.

* *

During my pregnancy, we heard the news that Les and Sharon, the missionaries who had made such an impression on Harrison's life, were going to be speaking at a church in Washington, Illinois. I don't remember the name or denomination of this church, but the important part was that it was not our church. Visiting other churches was questioned, even frowned upon by our church culture. I remember hearing it referred to as 'spiritual adultery.' But because they had been instrumental in changing the trajectory of Harrison's life, we decided to sneak away and go to the service at this church and listen to Les preach.

Arriving a little late, we entered the unknown territory of this church's sanctuary and found a place to sit. The congregation was singing. We noticed Les lean over and whisper something into the pastor's ear. Later, Les told Harrison and me that he had seen us walk in, recognized Harrison, remembered that he had gotten married, but just didn't think we would actually be in another church, other than our own. For that reason, he had whispered to the pastor, "Who is that couple that just walked in?" The pastor replied to him, "I've never seen them before." Les smiled and replied, "Then I know who they are."

During the service, as Les told the congregation about his mission work, he included Harrison in the sermon by mentioning, "Sometimes we even end up going upriver by canoe in the dark of night, don't we?" looking directly at Harrison. After the service, the pastor of the church gave an invitation for any to come forward who might be feeling the call to give their lives to be a missionary. During his prayer, I felt, I'm not sure what to call it – 'stirred' might be a good word. But it was so unlikely, us here in a strange church, at an altar call, which was completely foreign to us. This just wasn't how we did or experienced things. Plus, I thought, what if Harrison isn't feeling any of this? I opened my eyes and looked up at him in time to see a single tear escape his closed eyes and run down his cheek. I shut my eyes again but didn't hear any of the rest of the prayer.

Three days after the due date for our baby's delivery, traveling home from work, the tabletop-flat fields of central Illinois beginning to sprout with green life, I experienced some pangs in my abdomen. *Odd,* I thought, *it feels like I need to have diarrhea but I don't feel sick.* By the time I reached Roanoke and laid down on the couch, I realized that this must be the beginning of birth pangs. *Apparently this is what it feels like.*

Harrison had left me a list of the different farms that he might be working on. It was 1983 and cell phones were unheard of. The list included the telephone numbers of the neighbors nearest to each of the farms. I went down the list. Cornell – the lady who answered went to her window and looked and said she couldn't see anyone working anywhere. I waited while the lady who answered in Wenona went outside to see. She came back with good news. Yes, she could see tractors working in a field in the distance. She would send somebody out to see if it was Harrison and tell him to come.

In the meantime, my water broke, giving me cause for alarm, because it was green. Maternity had not been my favorite rotation in nurse's training, but the words *fetal distress* came at me full force. I dialed my sister-in-law, wife of Harrison's oldest brother, who also lived in our small town. She said she was on her way. Though my water had already broken at home, it continued to seep, making a mess in their car. We raced to Peoria without a policeman stopping us. The hospital personnel in the emergency driveway helped me into a wheelchair and whisked me into the hospital.

When Harrison received the news, he dashed home to Roanoke, took a shower, grabbed a camera, and headed to the hospital at high speed. Passing through Metamora, a policeman stopped him, lights flashing, to ask why on earth he was going so fast.

"My wife's having a baby!"

Glancing at his wet hair and anxious face, the policeman saw it was true and responded with, "Well, slow down a bit, be safe. . . And congratulations!"

I was in too much pain to fully appreciate his appearance when he arrived. Clutching at his arm as another pain overtook me in spite of our Lamaze classes, I unintentionally drew blood on his upper arm. Wincing, he said, "That hurt. You scratched me." I retorted, "Try having a baby!" I only vaguely remember this. Harrison remembers it clearly.

The doctor came in and informed us the baby was breach and that a C-section would be necessary. Off I went to the OR. Things happened fast, and the doctor said, "I'll have this baby out in three minutes." I was able to watch in a big round mirror above us. Harrison was there, taking pictures. Later, he said the worst of all for him was watching the scalpel make that initial incision. But all was forgotten in the joy of the cry of our firstborn child, a pure gift from heaven above.

As I lay in the recovery room with our precious daughter in my arms, I was filled with a joy I had never before known. The best that I can compare it to is the excitement the most excited child might have over the best Christmas present ever – only it was bigger and realer than that. At the same time, sorrow appeared. How my mom would want to be here, to see her, to hold her. But again, like at our wedding, I felt her presence for a few brief seconds, just like she was there, or at least nearby, seeing us.

Choosing the name of Cherith may have been prophetic. The kings of old recorded that the Lord sent Elijah, a settler of Gilead, modern day Jordan, to the brook Cherith, a hiding place of beauty and comfort. I'm sure there are other means that Beauty could use to bring me joy and comfort at life's various windows, but I can't think of any more wonderful way than providing me with my own Cherith.

When she was three months old, we went to my extended family's annual campout in Iowa and spent several nights in a tent. Soon after that, we sold our newly finished home to Harrison's father, packed up all our belongings in a four-by-eight U-Haul trailer and pulling it behind our black 1976 Monte Carlo, headed off to the new adventure of being full-time students at Word of Life Bible Institute in Schroon Lake, New York.

Lessons learned:

Life is beautiful. (Ugly is simply twisted beauty.)
Our significance is found in the whole - not as separate puzzle pieces, or as a rock or an island.

4

Schroon Lake, New York

Wonderful Words of Life
1983 - 1984

Since it was a two-day car trip from Roanoke, Illinois, to our destination of Schroon Lake, New York, we made plans to spend the weekend with the friends whose wedding we had attended on our return from Ecuador as singles, when Harrison was wondering if he should ask me to be his wife. These friends were now living in Cleveland, Ohio, a good half-way point on our trip. In the U-Haul that we were pulling we had a twelve-cubic-foot chest freezer that my parents had given us as a wedding gift. It was filled with the applesauce we had recently made from fresh apples, along with all the home-frozen meat and produce that Midwesterners kept in their freezers in those days. Our friends figured out a way that we could plug the freezer in for the weekend, running a fifty-foot extension cord from the U-Haul in the parking lot up to their second floor apartment. We had a great weekend with them, going to see a production of Steinbeck's *Of Mice and Men,* and taking in a polo game, something neither Harrison nor I had seen before.

Monday morning, we hit the road again. It was a long trip with a three-month-old. The closer we got to our destination, the narrower the roads became as they wound around the Adirondack Mountains. Darkness was just beginning to settle in the mountains and I felt as though we must be somewhere near the end of the world. But to Harrison, it was familiar territory because his sister, Susie, her husband and their daughters lived in Pottersville, which is just eight miles or so from the Word of Life Bible Institute, the school where Susie's husband still teaches, and where we were just about to become students!

Winding these narrow roads with dusk falling, my mind returned to the familiarity of our home on Carol Street in Roanoke. I recalled the neighbor on the next street behind our house asking another neighbor, who was a member of our church, "Now what's bad about going to Bible college?"

You see, reader, not only Beauty, but everything is in the eye of the beholder. Apparently this neighbor had heard the talk of Harrison and Pam, and how they were leaving with their newborn daughter and heading to upstate New York to go to Bible college. Going to Bible college simply was not done in our church culture, and thus was spoken of in terms that made this 'outsider' neighbor understand that we were doing something wrong. But for the life of her, she couldn't understand what was wrong about going to Bible college, so was asking for some clarity on it from her neighbor on the inside. The insider was unsure exactly how to answer this question. Some questions cannot be answered.

When I awoke the first morning in the boathouse that would be our home for nine months, I could hear the water lapping rhythmically between the boats and the walls beneath our bedroom. Getting up and walking to the big window, I breathed, *"Ohhh, it's beautiful!"* The abundant trees lining Schroon Lake were just tinged with the faintest of autumn glory that they would become. I knew it was going to be a good year. And it was.

To me, sitting in those classes at Word of Life Bible Institute was not unlike sitting at the feet of Jesus. I soaked in every word of the teaching, though on occasion wondering what those believers on the other side of any given issue would present if given a chance. Not that it mattered very much to me as I absorbed it for all it was worth, eager to receive these words of life that it seemed my heart was starving for.

At Word of Life, they were big on Jesus being Lord and on evangelism. As I look back on this window, I clearly see and hear white-haired Jack Wyrtzen standing strong on the stage and leading us all in the song *He is Lord*. I also see his daughter-in-law, Christine, standing in front of Mountainside Bible Chapel (where we found ourselves every Sunday morning and Wednesday evening) in tears, but still singing:

But just think of stepping on shore – And finding it Heaven!
Of touching a hand – And finding it God's!
Of breathing new air – And finding it celestial!
Of waking up in glory – And finding it Home![1]

Both songs became an integral part of who I am and always will be.

So unlike the separatist culture we had been raised in, the emphasis on the urgency of evangelizing the whole world nearly overwhelmed us. We so wanted to be among the wise who win souls, but felt unsure as to how to go about it. With the foundation laid, they went ahead and taught us methods, like doing a rope trick in the subways to get people's attention as they waited for their train, and then cleverly turning it into a presentation of the Gospel. Later, as I watched Harrison perform the magic, I hoped and prayed that somebody, anybody would respond.

At Christmas break, we made the trip back to Illinois to be with family there. We met some single students from Chicagoland who also wanted to return for the holidays. We joined together, left after the last class in the afternoon, and drove straight through the night with seven-month-old Cherith sleeping at my feet in Harrison's black Monte Carlo.

* *

The spring semester passed too quickly. Almost immediately after we celebrated Cherith's first birthday, we packed up and left for our required summer ministry at Living Waters Camp in Danforth, Maine.

For 45 summers, Living Waters Camp has been providing the ideal place to "come apart and rest". It is a fantastic place to ditch the distractions and focus on family, friends, and your relationship with God. The demands of work, school, and the daily pressures that come with life in general can be extremely draining. Physical refreshment, spiritual renewal and a relaxing atmosphere can be the break you and your family are looking for. Plan to join us this summer for your vacation with a purpose.

This, along with *Be still and know that I am God. . . Psalm 46:10*, is how Roger and Karen Black, hosts of the camp, began their summer 2015 brochure. The camp has, no doubt, grown since Harrison and I were on staff there thirty-one years ago. From May through October, different camps and retreats are held. Each week the camp is a specific group – such as pastors and Christian workers, ladies, children (age specific), teens, families, Christian law enforcement, and Living Waters staff alumni.

Harrison's role was to oversee the grounds, though he spent a good deal of time helping to bake the huge amount of bread consumed by the campers each week. My job was to be the camp nurse. Cherith's role, at one year of age, seemed to be to wish she could have more of our attention, something we had not experienced while in Bible classes, when she was being well taken care of and entertained by Harrison's sister and her adorable daughters.

Dr. Wendell Calder, who still speaks at the camp, and his wife, were in charge when we were there in the summer of 1984. Wendell left an impact on my life that is still present today and every day. He provided me with what could be termed my mantra; every day before I read God's Word, I ask, as Wendell suggested, for Beauty to show me 1) myself and my sin, 2) my Savior and His salvation, 3) souls and my service. And He does.

On the other hand, both Harrison and I also remember receiving an emphatic teaching during this summer: "If you don't know the exact day and time you were born again, then you aren't saved!" I believed it at the time and can still resonate with the black and white truth that was being proclaimed, but since this window, I've gotten to know some real people, and heard of others, such as Billy Graham's wife, Ruth, who didn't know the date or time of their rebirth, but simply found it was a path they were on. Even I myself am unable to decidedly say if I entered the Kingdom of God at age seven when I knew I loved Jesus with all of my heart and wanted to be His forever, or if it was at age sixteen when, convicted by my upbringing and the sudden death of my best friend's mother, I knelt by my bed and asked Beauty to take over my life *kabisa*. Or if I'd always been 'saved,' since I have never been aware of a day of being apart from Him, as stated in the Anglican tradition of desire for their children.

Lesson learned:

Extract the precious from the worthless.[2]

5

Return to Roanoke

Transplanting My Roots
Fall 1984 - Summer 1986

It was with pleasure that we settled back into rural life in our small town in central Illinois. We rented a three-bedroom house on Joseph Street and took up where we left off. Almost.

There were some differences now that we had officially completed the thirty hours of Bible training typically required by many mission boards. There were sisters in our church culture who were eager to study the Bible in a group setting. One of them in particular was keen to organize it, having me be the leader. Putting aside my natural inhibitions, I agreed.

A wonderful group of like-minded sisters of various ages from our local congregation on the prairie began to meet together. We initially met at our home on Joseph Street, but then took turns hosting and leading. We began with prayer and spent the rest of our time together sharing our thoughts on sections of Scripture as it related to our lives and the particular study we were doing. Having no desire to cause trouble, we didn't make a big deal out of our weekly gatherings because we knew it would be frowned upon by our church authorities.

But inevitably, the word got out. Our local elder brother (there is one at, or assigned to, each congregation) approached me to tell me he had heard we were meeting. He very seriously, politely, and kindly asked if he could attend one to see what we do while together. Of course, we welcomed him to the very next one. We were aware of the things he would probably be looking for – if we wore our head coverings, if we prayed out loud (traditionally in our culture, women did not pray aloud, at church or in homes), what it was that we were studying along with the Bible (our pastors were elected from the local congregation, did not have any seminary training, and relying upon the Holy Spirit, did not prepare sermons in advance – instead simply opened the Bible, read it and then preached on the text that had fallen open) and perhaps most importantly, what we had to say about it. If I remember correctly, we passed on everything except our thinking. I recall some grave concerns later that there were some amongst us who believed that once gained, salvation could not be lost.

Our first and only son was born to us at this window. Because he also, like Cherith before him, preferred sitting upright in my womb, the doctor let us pick his birth date. Although it was not so common in the 1980s for parents to know, or even want to know, the sex of their unborn child, we knew because of the sonograms monitoring to see if he would move from his breach position into the normal in utero position. The first time the technician was confident of our baby's sex, she asked me if I wanted to know. I was sure that I did, but not at the moment. I was alone at the appointment, Harrison being busy on one of their family farms. I asked her to write it down and put it in a sealed envelope so that Harrison and I could open it together later. She did. We did. And the note said, *"It's a boy!!!!!!!"* We were thrilled and so thankful! So thrilled, in fact, that when at our first family get-together after Tobin's birth, Harrison's brothers nodded, in serious agreement with each other, that our infant son looked just like E.T., it had not the slightest negative affect on me. On the contrary, it made me love the little guy all the more!

I have many precious memories of time spent at this window of my life. I'm glad that I didn't miss enjoying the little things – like two-year-old Cherith who, reveling in her bowl of popcorn, suddenly held up her tiny hands with their long thin fingers and began crying, "My hands are all salty!" Dirty hands bothered her. She liked them clean. May she always.

Harrison, being like his father, loved to entertain any missionaries he could get his hands on. So one evening, he invited a newly married couple, who were raising support to go overseas as Wycliffe Bible translators, to have dinner with us. We didn't know them well and were just beginning to hear their story when Tobin, sitting in his high chair, had gotten what he could off of his chicken and tossed the bone on the floor. Still hungry, he repeated the process. The polite missionaries-to-be ignored each toss with an effort, perhaps thinking their training had already begun.

Because the hair that God gave me is naturally very wavy in the back and naturally very straight in the front, I decided to get a perm to make it all the same – curly. When I got home, Harrison was already there. He took one look at me and simply said, "Now THAT is ugly." We both found ourselves holding our breath, he out of fearful disbelief that he had let those words cross his lips – and I out of disbelief of him stepping so far outside of his character, and in doubt as to how to respond. Then I burst out laughing and he joined in. We laughed and laughed, laughing our silly simple heads off. *The Cat in the Hat* is right – *It's fun to have fun, but you have to know how.*

Harrison came home one day after dropping an envelope in the local post office box and was a changed man. It was obvious that a huge burden had been lifted from his shoulders. He had stopped putting it off and just did it, even though it was too late for the upcoming year of '86. Just like that, he had filled out the application to Moody Bible Institute in Chicago and mailed it. He had no idea what kind of a missionary he could be – he knew he wasn't a preacher or church planter or anything like that. He was the practical type who liked to fix things, mechanical and otherwise. His mother had told me that even when he was very young, she would get so frustrated with him because he would do things like take the sweeper apart to see how it worked.

He wondered about aviation. He thought he might like that. Calling his father's favorite mission board, he was told that there was 'more to life than flying.' I saw the hurt on his sensitive face as he shrugged it off, saying, "I wasn't asking to be a pilot; I don't even want to be a pilot. I was just wondering if they could use an airplane mechanic."

Moody surprised Harrison by not only accepting him, but accepting him for the semester that would begin in a few weeks. We made a quick trip to Chicago to talk with an advisor, since Harrison still didn't know how he could fit into missions. It was an ordained meeting. As the advisor listened to Harrison's dilemma, feeling called but inadequate for missions, we were startled to see tears in his eyes! When Harrison finished, this dear advisor told us his story and the similarities between the two were uncanny.

On the road back to Roanoke, Harrison and I rejoiced, having the assurance that he would be a Moody student in a few short weeks, finishing what prerequisites were not already met by our time at Word of Life Bible Institute, and then, Beauty willing, we would transfer to Moody's aviation program in Tennessee.

We made a second trip to Chicago to look for housing and ended up securing an apartment in Cicero in a building where some other Moody students also lived. Then we began packing boxes in anticipation of the move. One day, Harrison's oldest brother stopped by for a few minutes. As he stepped into the kitchen, he looked around at the disarray and half-packed boxes and innocently asked, "Going somewhere?" This was all the proof that I needed to support my theory that this family I married into had an unspoken rule: The more important something is, the less it should be talked about. That was sure a completely new window for me. Never had I ever even considered such a view.

Nevertheless, word did get out that we were going before we were gone. Again, Dad and Naomi were concerned about where this was leading. Harrison's father was excited about it, but his mother was not at all enthused because it involved them moving from the old homestead in the country where they had lived their entire married life and into town, into our new house.

In our church on the prairie, there was also concern over us going. One of Harrison's uncles told him that if he would just stick around and be patient, he would undoubtedly be voted in as a preacher, just like his grandfather had been.

In the ensuing years, when I would return to Roanoke to visit family and friends, I would be amazed how everything there was always the same, exactly as we had left it, except that people grew older. The sameness amazed me – same houses, same people living in them, sitting on the same front steps, going the same places at the same times. It always filled me with a sense of appreciation for the joy of our uncertain journey. From the adventurous window of my life, the American Dream looked to me as boring as sin, the "same ole thing" over and over again, without any new and different thing happening. I loved new and different. Little did I know at that window, there would come a time when I would long for normalcy, even seek it carefully with tears, but would not be able to find it.

But as for now, we were young and adventurous and ready to face the future with open arms.

Lesson applied:

The time had come. The time was now.
So Harrison and Pam went.

6

Cicero, Illinois

A Windy City Window
1986 - 1988

E ver since reading *Secret Power,* by D.L. Moody, I've been convinced that sometimes books just fall into hands exactly when
they're supposed to; that they are just one of the endless good gifts
provided us by our Father, as Moody himself is quoted as saying:
*Every good gift that we have had from the cradle up has come from
God. If a man just stops to think what he has to praise God for, he
will find there is enough to keep him singing praises for a week.*

It was good to be at Moody, founded by this man of secret
power, even if it did mean living in Cicero, a western suburb twelve
miles from downtown Chicago, where Moody Bible Institute was
located. The drive to school for Harrison could take twenty minutes,
or an hour and twenty minutes, depending on traffic. The view from
our Cicero window was not beautiful. Looking out from the living
room there were just rows of old brick buildings, all looking tired
and disinterested, similar enough to be nearly indistinguishable one
from the other. For this reason, I created a little tune for our address
and sang it over and over to Cherith and Tobin in hopes that should
it ever happen, God forbid, that they got lost alone, they could sing
it to a kind stranger or neighbor.

Looking out the back from our minuscule, dark kitchen, the
view consisted of a narrow, cluttered alley with many sets of

peeling wooden ghetto steps leading down to it. Our five-by-ten-foot landing on the second floor was just big enough for a child's little round plastic swimming pool. I remember being really glad for the cool water in that little pool, as I sat in it, our second summer there, feeling like a beached whale, large with our third-born child inside me.

Initially, the unceasing noise of the night traffic with its persistent sirens, directly outside our bedroom window, caused us to wonder how a person could ever even fall asleep here, much less stay asleep. Yet in an amazingly short time we learned how to do both without any problem at all. Part of it may have been exhaustion from the schedule we had no choice but to maintain.

Maintain was even the word that Harrison used when I would ask him what he had accomplished during the evening hours while I was working the evening shift wherever the nursing company I worked for placed me - Children's Memorial ICU, Shriner's Children's Hospital, or at the home health case of a very active preschool boy on a ventilator. Harrison went to school by day while I was at home with our kids. Then we would literally meet on the stairs, he would hand me the car keys, and I would go to work while he took his turn at childcare. Thus, his answer when I would return home around midnight and inquire, "What did you do this evening, honey?" *Maintain*, he replied, *I maintained.*

I knew what he meant. He had entertained, fed, and put to bed a one-year-old and a three-year-old. That is so much simpler to write than to do; there are infinitely more steps in the doing. And unfortunately for me, I also learned that some evenings he had done more than maintain. I knew, because those were the nights that he had finished writing some paper or the other and it needed to be typed. That night.

Before leaving Roanoke, Harrison had bought an electric type-writer with a cartridge that allowed backspace correction. It was simple; you just had to hit backspace, then type the letter again to erase it, and finally type the correct letter that had been intended in the first place. It was so much easier than holding correction tape over the mistyped letter and retyping it. Or worse yet, using a type-writer eraser and tearing a hole in the paper – which was what I had been accustomed to doing as I typed my papers in nursing school a few years earlier. Harrison always tried his very best to simplify my life when he could, and I appreciated that. It only made sense that I type while he slept because I could type so much faster. His one semester typing class on manual typewriters as a sophomore in high school hadn't served him well.

Sometimes Harrison was already asleep when I got home from work. Cicero wasn't known for being a safe place. (Drive-by shootings at our small nearby park, blood remaining on our neighbor's steps of a morning, and other news let me know that I couldn't possibly let the kids out of my sight for a moment. On the rare times that they convinced me to let them play in our negligible front lawn, I stayed at the window, watching from above, which defeated any purpose of not being down there with them!) Therefore, Harrison and I had a plan to help me travel unharmed from whatever parking space I could find on the dark, narrow one-way streets to the safety of our apartment. He would leave a light on in the living room of our apartment, and as I neared our apartment, I would wave happily to the window to let anyone on the street clearly see that someone was watching over me, probably even expecting my arrival imminently. Hopefully they wouldn't notice I was simply waving to a lighted, empty room.

Harrison even told me that he was thinking of spending the money for a car phone in case I had car or other trouble traveling to or from work. When he told me this, I was incredulous!

"A *car* phone! Whatever is that??"

He told me that he had heard about phones that could be installed in a car. There was an accompanying antenna to attach to the car window somehow. I could hardly believe such a thing! What would they think of next?

Well, it didn't take long at all before that question of mine was answered. Our neighbors downstairs were fellow Moody-ites; Randy, the husband, worked part-time at *The Chicago Tribune* and was on the cutting edge of innovation. One day he and Harrison were commiserating together about all the work and papers they had to get done for their classes. This led Randy to ask Harrison if he knew about this thing called a computer that hooked to other computers. He said it was amazing and was inviting Harrison into his apartment to show him one when I happened to come up the stairs, holding the mail I had just collected from our box in the apartment entryway. Pointing to our mail, Randy asked me if I believed a time would come when my mail would come electronically over wires. *No, I didn't think so. What a preposterous idea.* I went on into our apartment as Harrison followed Randy into their apartment to see this thing.

When Harrison returned to our apartment, I asked him about the thing Randy had just shown him. What was it like? What did it do? Harrison shrugged and said, "Well, Randy says it's really great because through it you can have access to other college libraries, like Harvard and Yale – so you can read research documentation from their libraries. He says it's called *Internet*. Randy's really excited about it, but I don't know. I'm not that interested in academic research and don't really care about Harvard, Yale, or Cambridge's libraries. But it's good for Randy, I suppose."

These interesting neighbors of ours were both on the cutting edge of technology and on the current trend of returning to the natural. The wife, Annette, when pregnant with their second child, decided to have the baby at home there in the apartment. When the time came, everything went quicker than expected and she ended up having the baby on the toilet seat, which she found most comfortable. If I remember correctly, the midwife was there, catching the newborn, while Harrison and I were upstairs sleeping.

Because all four apartments in our little section of the building were Moody students and because the outside entrance consisted of two doors, the outer one being locked at all times, we sometimes used the situation to enjoy spending time together as couples while our children were sleeping in their beds upstairs or down, depending on whose apartment we were gathering in. When we did this, one or the other of each couple would frequently check the sleeping children to make sure they were still fast asleep. By this time, Cherith was sleeping in a big girl bed, but Tobin was still in the crib. So imagine our surprise when during one of these parties – this one downstairs – in walked Tobin, in his blue, fuzzy footed pajamas, his sleepy cherub face happy as could be. He had let himself *fall* over

the edge of his crib (it had to be a fall, he simply was not big enough
to manage crawling out of it!) and made it safely down a flight of
stairs to enter the party as though he were invited and didn't want to
disappoint!

A few months after arriving to Cicero, we discovered Beauty
had blessed us with a third child. Again, we were so very glad and
thankful! As time went on, I realized that it was easier to be pregnant
on the wide prairies of central Illinois than it was in a upstairs apartment in a less-than-desirable Chicago suburb. Carrying groceries
upstairs, living in the confines of a hot apartment, two other children who could not be turned loose like they could in the country,
working as a nurse, all while preparing, in the back of our minds, to
move overseas for life.

The good thing about this was that I was not alone. There were
many of us at Moody. If we hadn't already met some other way, we
met at Women's Guild, a Moody group for the female spouses of
students. There we could glean from the wisdom and maturity of
teachers and other speakers. Not only that, we found huge support
in each other – both the many gathered and the few with whom we
formed deep friendships. When the late Elizabeth Elliot came and
spoke to us, reminding us not to overburden our already burdened
student husbands, she told us that even if all three of her husbands
were alive at the same time, they could not meet her deepest needs.
Only God could do that for a woman. I was glad for her reassurance
that God was able, because from what I could see, Harrison and
I, along with all these other couples, seemed unlikely subjects to
become missionaries to take the answer to life's problems around
the world. To me, it was evident that we all had plenty of problems
ourselves, that we'd likely take with us wherever we went. Maybe
Beauty was just looking for anybody willing to be completely His,
and then He'd take care of us as we fumbled along in our willingness.

Moody events were not the only way to connect. Via church, I
became a part of Mothers of Preschoolers (MOPS), forming supportive relationships there while also giving Cherith and Tobin time
to interact with others their ages. The friendships made extended
to doing so many other things together – taking the kids to the zoo,
aquarium, and museums, especially on the free days.

The Moody wife with whom I most often did these things was also pregnant at the same time I was. On her recommendation, I decided to go to an office of midwives. At my first appointment, I was thrilled to discover that the midwife to whom I was assigned was a member of our home denomination! What were the chances? She became not only my midwife, but a lifelong friend and supporter of us. Beauty is so good!

Because of already having one year of Bible classes at Word of Life Bible Institute in New York, by the end of our first year at Moody, Harrison had fulfilled all the requirements necessary to be invited to Moody's 'flight camp.' At that time, Moody's missionary aviation program was based in Hampton, Tennessee. Flight Camp consisted of a week of being watched by Moody instructors to determine whether or not a student had the aptitude to be a mission aviator. They were observing not only skills necessary for aviation, but also observing interpersonal reactions in and out of the hangar setting. Not only were the actual applicants being observed, but also the spouses of the married students.

Leaving Cherith and Tobin with my parents, Harrison and I headed to Tennessee, taking along another applicant, Paul, who was also from the Roanoke church. Harrison had thought he would like to be a missionary aircraft mechanic, but when we arrived at Moody Tennessee and he walked into the hangar, all tentativeness was gone and he was absolutely sure – this, without the shadow of a doubt, was exactly what he wanted to do! The pressure was on. Aware that we were being observed during our waking hours, we both tried to be our natural selves.

In spite of the blunt truth (proved within a few years) presented by one of the Moody aviation leaders in talking to us wives, telling us that some among us would lose our husbands as a result of this service, I wanted so badly for Harrison to be accepted. I was concerned when we heard the success rate of flight camp was fifty percent. One day I took my Bible and found a quiet place under a tree. As I read the words of a psalmist, I was encouraged to be like those who have no fear of bad news, whose hearts are steadfast, trusting in the Lord. I took it as an encouragement that I need not fear, that Harrison would be accepted into this program that he so desired to be a part of. And he was.

Rejoicing, we began the road trip back to Illinois. We were in a hurry to retrieve our kids from Dad and Naomi, not only because we missed them like crazy, but also because Naomi's youngest son was about to have a bone marrow transplant for his leukemia and Naomi wanted to be there with him and his wife. Pregnancy tiredness overcame me and I laid my head in Harrison's lap as he was driving and fell asleep. Our traveling companion, Paul, was in the back seat. I was awakened by a huge thud as our car came to an abrupt halt. Bolting upright, I asked, "What happened??"

Near midnight, a deer had suddenly leaped out in front of our car as we were traveling along interstate 75, approaching Corbin, Kentucky. Getting out of the car, we encountered the awful sight of a *pregnant* deer, split open and breathing her last. Our car was damaged beyond driving. Thus began days of a grueling ordeal trying to get ourselves and our car back to Illinois. Remember, dear reader, as you read the next paragraph, that cell phones as we know them were not yet invented.

After much ado, Harrison located the only U-Haul car carrier within a hundred-mile radius. Unfortunately, U-Haul was unable to confirm that we could have it if another customer arrived before we did, even though Harrison gave them his credit card number in an attempt to hold it, explaining our situation of physically not being able to get there. Then Harrison contacted his good friend, Gary, back in Roanoke, who left after work in a pickup truck to come collect us and our car. Harrison called U-Haul back to say our help was on the way. U-Haul said they were sorry, someone else had come in and taken the only available car carrier. Harrison slammed down the hotel phone in the fury of utter frustration. I had never seen this side of him before and had no idea how to respond.

As we had no way to contact Gary and tell him not to come, he arrived to help us, only to have Harrison tell him that it was impossible. The only help he could give was to return Paul and me safely to Illinois. Paul could get on with his life, having not been accepted into the Moody aviation program, and I could free Dad and Naomi to go be with her son undergoing bone marrow transplant.

In the end, Harrison's brother, Herbert, brought his pickup along with a borrowed trailer from a neighboring farmer, and collected Harrison and our ruined car.

Those who pass flight camp and are welcomed into Moody's aviation program typically return to Moody Chicago for their second year of school. Because Harrison had already completed the requirements, he had the next year free from school. He got a job with a small crew who did remodeling of houses. I was especially glad for him not to have the stress of school as we neared the time of our third child's birth.

Elizabeth, named so after my mother and step-mother's middle names, was born on August 7, 1987. The midwives and I were determined that I could and would do exercises until this baby flipped to the head-down position in which other babies entered the world. Lizzie was more determined to sit in my womb, just as her sister and brother had before her, head-up, as in an adult thinking position. Lizzie's birth, however, turned out to be an emergency C-section because my blood pressure was suddenly unexplainably high.

Harrison's parents came and took Cherith and Tobin to stay in Indiana with Harrison's oldest sister, her husband, and their four teenaged kids. Later, these teenage cousins told us stories about their time together. One of them was about Tobin spilling his milk at the dinner table. One of these strapping big cousins looked to the other and said, "Tobin needs a spanking for spilling his milk." The other agreed, saying, "Yeah. Give him a spanking, Dad." Tobin looked at them in concern and quickly offered an alternative. "Just wipe it up! Just wipe it up!"

Although my pregnancy with Lizzie had been more difficult than the previous two, the adjustment to her as a newborn was, in some ways, easier than the other two – partly for that reason: there were two of them to entertain each other, which they did marvelously, freeing me to care for the newest member of our little fivesome.

When Cherith turned four, she was eager to go to school. We came into contact with a kindergarten for four-year-olds (K-4) through a local church. It turned out to be a real good thing in every way. Miss Rivera will probably never know the powerful impact for good she had on our little Cherith's life. Besides her genuine personal touch, Miss Rivera was also effective at planting God's Word in these kids' little hearts and minds. They had to memorize portions of verses from the King James Bible, starting with each letter of the alphabet. A - *All have sinned, and fall short of the glory of God* (Rom. 3:23), B - *Believe on the Lord Jesus Christ and thou shalt be saved* (Acts 16:31), C - *Children, obey your parents in the Lord, for this is right* (Eph. 6:1), and so forth. It was the Q verse that became a family joke: Q - *Quit you like men.* (1 Cor.16:13) "That's right," Harrison said to Cherith while grinning at me, "Be a man, be a man, be a man!" We laughed and laughed. Cherith, confused, laughed, too.

One cold morning as I was driving Cherith to school, with Tobin in his toddler car seat, and Lizzie in her infant one, I was quizzing Cherith on her verses. Normally she answered them immediately, but as she hesitated on this particular verse, Tobin, from his car seat in the back, completed the verse perfectly! I was struck by the absorbing power of a child's mind and felt confident that they would be able to sing our Cicero address if needed – and probably long into the future as well!

During this time, Cherith remarked to me one day out of the blue, "Mommy, I know what people are made for."

"What's that, honey?" I responded.

Her simple answer was, "Telling other people about Jesus."

It may have been this same sensitivity at work when she came to Harrison one evening and told him that she felt Jesus was whispering in her heart. Though this was uncharted territory, Harrison was only too glad to pray with Cherith to fortify this whispering. And I was affirmed in a clear statement I thought I heard, sitting in the auditorium of Word of Life Bible Institute at the Schroon Lake window: *Don't worry about Cherith. She will be okay.* This thought contained an imperative and a promise, and was also not spoken in the first person of me.

Our home denomination, left behind on the prairie, had a church that was half an hour's drive away from Cicero, but during our time at Moody we chose to attend a Bible church in the neighborhood. We did make the drive to the other church now and then, and were reminded that with all its foibles, there's nowhere like home.

The one sermon that I remember, looking back at this window, is one in which the pastor compared a personal story from his youth with the spiritual reality of having God as our Father. He told the details of how scared he had been on a certain walk at night in the woods with his dad. But when his father picked him up and put him on his shoulders, it just seemed like everything changed immediately and the fear left him. Same situation. Different perspectives.

We were ready to leave this old apartment by the time the end of our second year there rolled around. It was in this apartment that Tobin first developed asthma. And it was here that Lizzie had one ear infection after another. Our last visit to the pediatrician, he gave me a prescription for antibiotics for Lizzie, telling me that way the first person I could see in Tennessee would be a pharmacist. As it turned out, I never had to fill that prescription.

When it was time for the actual move to Tennessee, that happy-natured father of my Iowa City roommate offered to bring one of his semi-trailer trucks to move us and two other Moody aviation families. It was a generous offer none of us could refuse; indeed, we were deeply grateful.

Lesson learned:

The eyes of the LORD move to and fro throughout the earth finding those that need the most work done in their hearts, but who consider themselves to be completely His – a foolish thought that is sure to lead to all kinds of wars, through which He will strongly support them.[1]

7

Hampton, Tennessee

Beauty Resurfaces
1988 - 1990

Good as it had been to be at Moody Chicago, even better was to be at Moody Tennessee – in fact, *so* much better. At least for me. Harrison was stressed with the high learning curve, though immensely enjoying the material and his new longed-for surroundings. But as for me, sitting there on our porch swing, holding sleeping Lizzie in my arms, hearing the childish chatter and glee of Cherith and Tobin playing beside the babbling creek that ran along two sides of the Little Doe Freewill Baptist Church parsonage in which we were living, I felt sure that life simply couldn't get any better than this. It was absolutely idyllic.

It hadn't begun so perfectly. The Moody family who was living in the parsonage before us decided to stay through the summer, so we had to find somewhere else to live for the time being. Fortunately, we found out about a second year Moody Aviation couple who were away for the summer. Their place was in Elizabethton, the city where Moody's school was located. It was convenient in that it was all set up for living. All we had to do was move in and use their household items – dishes, towels, sheets and all.

We were just settling in when Cherith broke out in chicken pox. Only then did she inform us that the little girl she sat next to at school had these spots, too. Naturally, it wasn't long before Tobin and Lizzie also broke out in the same. Lizzie's were especially bad, not only awful on her face and trunk, but even inside her mouth and throat! As it happened, this was one way I was introduced to the difference between living in Chicagoland and in Tennessee.

Moving my grocery cart along the aisles of Winn Dixie with Lizzie sitting in it and five-year-old Cherith and three-year-old Tobin in tow behind me, I was surprised to hear a lady I didn't know saying, "Oh, honey, look at your poor baby! Why she must feel miserable, poor little thing!" I looked up from the freezer section to see that, sure enough, she was talking to me! We chatted a bit, and she moved on.

If I had been more culturally aware and less focused on getting my groceries and getting home, that encounter would have prepared me for the friendliness of the checkout clerk. As I began to place our groceries on the belt, keeping an eye on the three kids, the checkout lady finished with the previous customer, whom she seemed to know personally and turned to me, "Well, hello! How are you doing today?" Not only the fact that she said it, but also the tone in which she said it, made me think that she had mistaken me for someone she knew. But then the contrast between this grocery-getting experience and all of those of the past two years clicked in, and I began to understand. When I had gotten groceries at the small grocery store in Cicero, it was not uncommon for me to never hear a single word of English. When I had gone to large supermarkets in the area to get groceries, I realized that I had gathered and purchased them without anyone ever speaking to me, or if they spoke it was by rote and certainly without ever making eye contact. As I continued to think about this, I wondered if there was more than simply the airspace and surrounding physical environment that caused Moody to move their aviation program to Tennessee, reasoning it was easier to recreate a typical mission flying in the hills of Tennessee than at Midway Airport in Chicago.

Once the chicken pox were over, I remember this window of my life as being one of thoroughly and absolutely enjoying the three most precious of gifts that Beauty had bestowed on Harrison's and my union. Because of Lizzie's constant ear infections, her crying had become a normal background sound in our impossibly overheated

Cicero apartment. (In the dead of winter, we simply had to open the windows above the old, but unstoppable cast iron hot water radiator!) That was the reason her kind pediatrician had given me a prescription to fill upon arrival in Tennessee. But once her chicken pox left, Lizzie turned the happiest of toddlers, a real joy, just like that! Tennessee was so good to us.

Even so, we were aware of being outsiders, both in the neighborhood and then in church. For one thing, there was the language barrier, which presented itself in fun ways. One early example of this involved the little neighbor boy in Hampton, who was glad to have our kids next door. He began to come daily, always greeting me with, "Can the young'uns come out to play?" They were happy to go and I was happy to let them do so. Then one day, Tobin asked me, "Mom, when he comes to the door, why does he always call us 'onions'?" At first I didn't understand the question, but when I did I thoroughly enjoyed it.

Where to go to church was an easy decision for us in Tennessee. When we had made our survey trip to find a place to live, we had learned that Little Doe Church rented out their parsonage because their pastor had his own home. Because it was a dreary rainy day when we first saw it, we didn't get the full picture of what a perfectly lovely place it was, with the Simmerly creek running by and the church's fellowship building and large field nearby. But we did get the finances – $300 if we did not attend church there, $100 if we did. As I type those figures, I feel sure that my memory cannot be serving me correctly. Anyway, no matter the numbers, we were going to go to church somewhere, why not there?

The first Sunday there, we walked over our little bridge, crossed the highway and entered the church, were greeted warmly, and sat down, the five of us taking up most of one bench. We became aware of every eye in the church on us. We instinctively wondered if we were taking someone's spot. If so, they were very gracious about it, allowing it to become our spot for the following two years.

After church, everyone was eager to meet us. I recall not being sure how to answer the question regarding Lizzie, "Is this your least'un?" I didn't want to agree to her being 'less' than the other two, but instinctively knew I was being asked if she was our youngest and knew the correct answer was *Yes*.

In spite of our cultural differences, we soon came to feel an integral part of this little church. Harrison and another neighboring Moody student taking turns speaking every Wednesday evening service. Participating in their monthly Sunday evening practice of foot washing. Teaching Sunday School. Harrison singing in the choir. Loving the southern food at the potlucks held in the fellowship hall, being invited into their homes, and welcoming them into ours. In short, they became our life-long friends and supporters. We felt success when the pastor's adult son finally announced to us, "You guys are really all right, even if you are Yankees!"

Aware that our view was narrow, we welcomed this new window to the church experience. After one of the rousing services of their week-long evening revival meetings, Tobin pulled on Harrison's pant leg as he was talking to one of the members mingling outside the church in the afterglow of the meeting. Looking down to see what Tobin wanted, Harrison saw his son's young face was in earnest as he said, "Dad! That preacher said that if you're not saved, you need to get saved tonight! I wanna be saved!" Harrison smiled, uncertain. This was just not the way we personally did things. But not having any desire to discourage a good thing, he quietly told Tobin they would talk about it when we walked home (a stone's throw away, just across the highway and over the little stream's bridge into our drive).

True to his word, when we arrived home, Harrison prayed with Tobin to 'be saved.' Tobin was gleeful, wanting to telephone everyone he knew, starting with Mildred, the very special neighbor who lived half a stone's throw behind us, directly the other side of our hedge. We let him joyfully call with his good news. Brother Bill, the pastor, also announced the good news the next Sunday morning in church.

It was sweet to see the love for, and comfort from, Jesus continue in little Tobin's life. I don't remember where it came from, but we had a ten-inch cardboard bust figure of Jesus. One evening as I was putting Tobin to bed, he asked if I would put that little cardboard Jesus right near his bed, in case he woke up at night (which he often did, sometimes getting up to play because he was 'bored' with sleeping). He wanted to be able to see Jesus right next to him.

"Hodel!! I didn't know you were married!! And you have ALL THOSE KIDS???"

Harrison looked up from what he was doing, saw that I was coming across the hangar, and checked that there were still only three kids. Looking back at his fellow Moody student, he shrugged and said, "Yep. They're mine." It ran in the Hodel family to look younger than they were, and most of the Moody students were single guys, with the exception of one single female, so it was not surprising that the single guys assumed he was one of them.

One of these single guys was a tall Sudanese named Tartisio. He was blacker than black, a color he termed "purple." We had no earthly idea how entwined our lives would become with this young man, who grew up in a remote village in southern Sudan. From future windows, Harrison and Tartisio would come to discover that they were so alike in spirit that they joked they must be twins. But at this current window, we were just getting to know one another.

One day when the kids and I were at the school, Tartisio greeted Tobin cheerily by name. Tobin, forgetting that he was wearing a cap with his name on it, asked, "How do you know my name?" Laughing, Tartisio answered him, "Don't you know? It's written on your forehead!" Having not heard the conversation, I didn't know what was happening when Tobin came up to me, rubbing his forehead and asking, "Mom, does it say 'Tobin' here?"

Here, perhaps even more than at Moody Chicago, there was a great camaraderie between the students, and in the case of married students, between the wives. One of the wives was riding her bike to the school. As she was riding across some railroad tracks, one of her bike tires slipped into the crevice between the track and the road, causing her to fall. An oncoming truck driver either did not see her or could not stop in time. Either way, this young, vivacious wife was immediately called home. My mind returned to the warning that we wives had received from the Moody teacher – that some of our husbands would lose their lives in missionary service. This accident was not part of that deal, clearly reminding us all that there are no guarantees in this earthly life.

The nursing job that I had in Tennessee was teaching part-time in the licensed practical nurse program at the vocational school in Elizabethton. It involved some classroom teaching, but more often I was a clinical instructor, assisting the student nurses as they applied practically in the hospital setting what they had learned theoretically in the classroom. It lent itself to some tense moments, such as very quickly applying force on top of the timid student's hand on the syringe when giving her first shot to a black patient. As we had walked down the hall together toward the patient's room, I had reminded this student that black skin was typically tougher than white and that she would need to remember this as she injected the needle into the buttocks. It wasn't that she didn't believe me. It's just that experience speaks louder than words – whether coming from a book or a teacher.

Though Cherith had gone to K-4 in Cicero, I decided that I would do as other Moody wives were doing and homeschool her during her fifth year of life. At the same time, I did what I considered preschool with Tobin. It had become increasingly clear to me that our three children were very different from one another. From the beginning it was obvious that Cherith and Tobin were as different as night and day. Then Lizzie joined us and was completely different than either sibling, causing me to change my comparison from 'night and day' to 'three corners of a triangle.' To me, there's nothing so fascinating as people, big or small.

While Cherith had been content to sit and soak up the letters of the alphabet and their corresponding sounds, I quickly learned that Tobin needed to be handed the magnetic letter, allowed to jump over furniture and snap it on the fridge before connecting it with a sound. Much later, I would learn, as with most of my experiences, there's an official name for what I've already experienced – in this case, it's called differences in learning styles.

Lizzie, like the other two, had learned to walk early. Though I did not yet know her learning style, I discovered the hard way that she was very adept at quietly getting wherever there was to be gotten to! One day, as I was hanging up freshly washed clothes on the line between our house and the fellowship hall, Gilbert, a dear man from the church, called from behind me. I turned to see him approaching from the bend in the highway that passed between us and the church. Though this highway curved around the mountains, cars seemed to really speed on it, perhaps because it was so smooth. As I turned towards his voice, I was astonished to see that he was carrying Lizzie! He had been mowing at the church and had looked up to see tiny Lizzie toddling in the middle of the highway!! As he safely delivered Lizzie into my arms, I knew I could no longer think of him as Gilbert, but rather as the angel Gabriel.

Just as Lizzie surprised me early on with her agility in getting away, her early vocabulary was also amazing. I had purchased some small juice boxes from a discount place that we Moody students frequented because of its cheap prices on nearly expired items. Putting her in the car seat to return home with these groceries, I opened a box and handed it to her to drink on the way home. She had only taken one sip when she began to announce – and then paused to find the right word, "This juice is so. . . LOUD!" I tasted it, and indeed, it had loudly expired. This adjective continues to have the ability to describe taste for our family to this day.

After some months of homeschooling, one of the moms organized a recital so that each child could present something they had been working on. Each of the presenters were completely precious, but now it's only our own that I recall clearly. Cherith did an excellent, even theatrical, presentation of Emily Dickinson's poem, *I'm Nobody! Who Are You?* and three-year-old Tobin, in his little red suspenders, performed a perfect recitation of the pledge of allegiance to our flag.

An advantage that I can see of homeschool life is that the students get to know not only the other homeschoolers, but also get to know the parents of those kids. Cherith's experience with this may have eliminated her fear of dogs. When one of the mothers saw this fear of Cherith's in action, she asked if she could pray for Cherith. Neither Cherith nor I objected. As this mother began to pray for Cherith, she started in English and then broke out in tongues. Other than reading and hearing about it, this was a first for us.

This same mother became a dear friend to me. I was honored when she once described our friendship as wine compared to water. It was through her that I first recognized that the difference between reading the Bible and actually experiencing it could be considered much like the difference between eating delicious food ordered from the menu at a fancy restaurant and eating the menu itself! Reading the Bible to see what I could experience, without experiencing what it had to offer, was tasteless at best. She seemed to always have a different spin on things than I did.

I have only had two intricately detailed, vividly colored dreams in my life. In both of them, not only the color, but the texture of cloth was clearly visible, almost tangible. One of these dreams occurred at this window of my life. It came to me seemingly unprompted, out of nowhere, in the middle of an ordinary night. When I casually happened to mention it the following evening at a Moody gathering in the church's fellowship hall beside our house, this same friend listened carefully and said, "Pam, this dream is holy ground." I said nothing, because I didn't have anything to say.

Though Harrison only intended to do the Moody course to become an airframe and powerplant (A&P) mechanic, he decided it would be valuable experience for him, as a mechanic, to have taken at least enough flight lessons to solo. So when his flight instructor called me on the phone, one beautiful day the second summer we were there, and asked me if I knew where my husband was, I knew enough to answer, "If you are down here on the phone talking to me right now, that must mean that Harrison is up in the sky in an airplane by himself for the first time." *Yes, he was!*

Though I had thoroughly enjoyed doing home school for our first year in Tennessee, when Cherith turned six, our pastor's wife suggested that perhaps Cherith would enjoy going to school at Hampton public school, where she was a teacher. Cherith would technically only be ready for first grade, but our pastor's wife believed that she would be able to slip into second grade – the class that she taught. We discussed it and decided together to give it a try. After the initial adjustment of skipping a class, it seemed to be a positive experience for Cherith. Not only did she have new experiences academically and riding the school bus, but the Valentine's Day gift wrapped and lying on her desk when she arrived at school on February 14th was the beginning of her romantic admirers. The close friend she made, whose father would chase the two of them around the kitchen table in their home, pretending he was going to burn them with his cigarette, was the beginning of her having friends other than what her parents considered customary.

Looking back at this window of life, with Harrison more than consumed with his aviation training, it seems the majority of my experiences centered around our three children. And the three of them seemed intent on giving us a variety of experiences, just like others experience raising children. Like the time we were all together shopping in a large Walmart-type store, and suddenly Tobin was nowhere to be found. Harrison and I split, one going through the store vertically, the other horizontally, checking every aisle. We checked the changing rooms. Our panic was mounting. Finally there was nowhere else to look, so I headed outside into the cold to look. There, lo and behold, was Tobin, standing beside the smiling Salvation Army man, ringing the bell himself, happy as could be, oblivious to the distress he caused us! Overjoyed as I was to see him, I didn't know whether to scold or hug first. Adorable as he was, standing there ringing that Salvation Army bell, the decision was simple. I hugged and hugged him.

That same season of Christmas, while at the mall, Harrison and I decided to let our children experience the American Santa Claus before taking them away to a foreign land. We had always told them there was no Santa, but they didn't have to tell their friends so. We told them the truth because we wanted to gain credibility with them for later years and didn't see how lying about Santa would build that. Now here they were, in line waiting to see Santa, whom they knew was a man in a red suit – always reminding me of another impostor in a red suit with the same name, only the last three letters are mixed around. When it was Tobin's turn, he climbed into Santa's lap and waited. Satan asked him what he wanted for Christmas. Tobin shrugged. Santa tried again. "Would you like some toys?" Unfazed, Tobin answered with a slight shrug of his little shoulders. "Got a lot of 'em."

Later that same winter, as I was crossing the yard between Mildred's house and ours, I stopped awestruck. The morning sun was shining brightly on the crisp, untouched snow, causing a million glittering diamonds to dance on the cold whiteness. The dazzling beauty was breathtaking and a clear impression settled over me, "The beauty of holiness!" That moment has uncannily continued to return to me throughout the years, as a reminder, I think, that Beauty is determined to have His children be as Oswald Chambers describes, *pure, clean, and white as driven snow*.[1]

During the two years in Tennessee, Harrison continually considered where we would go to serve. Through a fellow student, he had become acquainted with the aviation division of Regions Beyond Missionary Union (RBMU). He was very interested in the possibility of putting his newly acquired skills to work in Irian Jaya, but when he applied, he found out that the area where he would be working was extremely remote. It was a small aviation program and he would be the lone mechanic, with no one to turn to if he had questions. Though the mission welcomed him, they suggested that he first get some aircraft mechanic experience under his belt and then come.

Another fellow student, this one from England, told Harrison that he knew of a place where he could get bountiful experience and be on the mission field at the same time. We learned that this perfect place was Dodoma, Tanzania, an aviation base for Mission Aviation Fellowship U.K. And thus we started down the path leading to our next window. Harrison graduated from Moody Aviation the first of June and our expected departure from the States was set for August.

One week in late June, Cherith and Tobin attended Camp Ta Pa Win Go, a Christian-based camp in Watauga, Tennessee. Because they were attending day camp, they came home each evening, filled with stories of a fun day. When I picked them up on Friday, Tobin looked decidedly unhappy. In questioning him, he told me that he had hurt his leg. Cherith didn't seem to know much more, so I couldn't be sure but that he was very tired from a full week of fun. When we got home, he limped to the recliner and sat looking miserable. To cheer him up, I asked if he would like a Coke, a rare treat in our home. Exclaiming, "Yeah!!" he jumped out of the chair in excitement, and a step later fell to the floor, crying. Then I knew there was really a problem and it was not tiredness. I took him directly to the emergency room of the hospital where I had been a clinical instructor. The x-rays revealed his leg was indeed broken. The technician told me that he would call the doctor on call to come put a cast on it, but that it could be some time before the doctor would get there. I asked who the doctor on call was. The technician told me the doctor's name and asked if that was all right. I had seen this doctor's unpleasant bedside manner and questioned his competency. Even so, I could hardly believe it when I heard my voice saying, "No, I'm sorry. That is not okay. Is it possible to get someone else?" When I caught myself and started to apologize, the technician said, "No, that's okay. You are not the first to say this." As it turned out, another doctor was present who I was happy to trust with my son's broken leg. Before long we left the hospital, with Tobin gleeful over the bright purple cast he had chosen. The cast was to remain on six weeks – exactly the number of weeks we had left in the U.S.A. before heading to Africa. The wildest part of this story is that I would one day come face to face with the doctor whose care I had refused – but in a similar yet much different setting: a hospital in Africa.

After graduation, Harrison built a 4 x 4 box that we filled with everything we thought we would need during the next three years in Tanzania. Max Gove, the head of Mission Aviation Fellowship U.K., had come from England to spend time with us, getting to know us, and we him, and helping us know what to expect from life in Dodoma, Tanzania. We packed our big box according to what he informed us was and was not available locally in Dodoma, our next window of life. It wasn't easy deciding how many bandages our family would need for three years. It was even harder to estimate how much our kids and their feet would grow in three years. Max explained as much to Harrison as he could about life as an aircraft engineer in East Africa. He simply told me that life would be much the same for me as it was now, except that I'd feel like I had one arm tied behind my back while doing it. It was a little hard for me to be as excited as Harrison was about the venture, but I tried and think I succeeded.

After getting the box shipped off, we were ready to return to the Midwest to spend time with family and friends before leaving the continent. Harrison's oldest brother, Steve, and his wife and daughters came to help us move what was left of our earthly belongings to put them in storage in Harrison's sister's basement in Missouri.

We longed for a church to send us out with their blessing, but there was no chance that the church we had been in since birth was going to do that. In fact, the elder of our church on the prairie had heard we were in town and wanted to get together at the local coffee shop. We did. He patiently explained to us that, for the sake of unity and keeping the body pure, he would have to remove us from the church. He further explained that we were likely to be taking communion with, well, he didn't know what kind of believers, and that was the main reason we could no longer belong to our church. He was kind and asked if we understood. *Yes, we understood.* We were born and raised in that thinking; of course, we understood.

Harrison's oldest sister and her husband, who had been a preacher in our church culture, had recently made a decision to leave the denomination and were starting their own independent church. As it happened, their first Sunday meeting as a new church was during this time we were in transition between Tennessee and leaving for Africa. They were more than willing, even considered it an honor and privilege to commission missionaries in their very first service! It was what they wanted to be about and what a beautiful beginning it was – for them and us! There were about 150 of us gathered together there in the gymnasium of a local school to birth Faith Evangelical Bible Church. Looking back, the thing that stands out most to me is the following song, sung so beautifully by a couple at that service.

> *Pierce my ear, O Lord, my God.*
> *Take me to Your door this day.*
> *I will serve no other god.*
> *Lord, I'm here to stay.*

> *For You have paid the price for me.*
> *With Your blood You ransomed me.*
> *I will serve You eternally.*
> *A free man I'll never be.*[2]

The other song that stayed strong in my memory from that service was *Faithful Men.*

> *Come and join the reapers*
> *All the kingdom seekers*
> *Laying down your life to*
> *Find it in the end.*
>
> *Come and share the harvest*
> *Help to light the darkness*
> *For the Lord is calling faithful men.*[3]

I can never hear either of those songs without picturing our little family right there at Faith's first church service, being blessed and commissioned to go out into the harvest of souls for the Kingdom.

We had spent the time between leaving Tennessee and departing for Africa wandering from pillar to post. Every now and then, Lizzie, tired and confused, would say, "I wanna go home." Tobin, who seemed to be enjoying all the variety, explained to her very factually, "Lizzy, we don't *have* a home." Through a later window, and too late, I would learn there is a term for what was beginning here; it's *liminality.* And it was only going to get a whole lot worse.

One night shortly before we were scheduled to leave, I woke up in the darkness violently sick. We were staying in the basement of friends in Roanoke. I had a raging headache, vomiting and diarrhea. The following day, a rash broke out across my abdomen and my joints were hot and circled with red. The doctor in Eureka told me he believed I had lupus. I told him I couldn't have lupus because I was leaving for Africa in a few days. He told me that I wasn't going to Africa or anywhere else, but he would try to get me in to a specialist as soon as possible, but even that might not be for a week or two at the earliest.

I spent a sleepless night worrying. I didn't think Harrison would approve of me putting our mission on hold. I just couldn't be sick with something as serious as lupus.

In the morning, I received a call from the specialist's office. They could fit me in right away! I went. The specialist examined me thoroughly and asked me lots of questions. Then he told me that I didn't have lupus or anything else. I could leave for Africa. I spontaneously began to praise Beauty, saying aloud, "I don't? I can? I'm fine? Oh, praise the Lord! This is such wonderful news! I'm so thankful!" I was oblivious at the time, but looking back, I wonder what that doctor thought. As far as I can remember, he just sat there and smiled at me.

I walked outside of that doctors' complex. The summer sun was shining so gloriously. The sky was so beautifully blue and clear. I had to restrain myself to keep from hugging the people who walked by me on the sidewalk. I wanted to tell them I was fine!! That life was so good. And so beautiful!

The day before leaving, Harrison purchased a used Toshiba laptop from the missionaries who we had gotten to know much better since the time they had watched Tobin throw his chicken bones on the floor some years earlier. The problem was that Harrison wasn't sure that he knew how to turn the computer on if he should be asked to do so in the customs and immigration line.

Lessons learned:

The act of seeing is itself glorious,
and of hearing, and feeling, and tasting![4]
To taste and see just how beautiful holiness is!

PART II

East African Years

Psalm 23 / *Zaburi 23*

The LORD is my shepherd, I shall not want.
BWANA ndiye mchungaji wangu, Sitapungukiwa na kitu.

He makes me lie down in green pastures;
Katika malisho ya majani mabichi hunilaza,

He leads me beside still waters.
Kando ya maji ya utulivu huniongoza.

He restores my soul;
Hunihuisha nafsi yangu;

He guides me in the paths of righteousness for His name's sake.
Na kuniongoza katika njia za haki kwa ajili ya Jina lake.

Even though I walk through the valley of the shadow of death,
Naam, nijapopita kati ya bonde la uvuli wa mauti,

I fear no evil; for Thou art with me;
Sitaogopa mabaya; kwa maana wewe Upo pamoja nami,

Thy rod and Thy staff, they comfort me.
Gongo Lako na fimbo Yako, vyanifariji.

Thou dost prepare a table before
me in the presence of my enemies;
Waandaa meza mbele yangu, machoni pa watesi wangu;

Thou dost anoint my head with oil;
Umenipaka mafuta kichwani pangu;

My cup overflows.
Na kikombe changu kinafurika.

Surely goodness and lovingkindness
will follow me all the days of my life,
Hakika wema na fadhili zitanifuata siku zote za maisha yangu;

And I will dwell in the house of the LORD forever.
Nami nitakaa nyumbani mwa BWANA milele.

8

Dodoma, Tanzania

Becoming Acquainted With Missions
1990 - 1993

Lizzie was twirling, dancing and singing at the airport as we waited to board the plane for London, "I'm a missionary kid! I'm a missionary kid! I'm a missionary kid!!" She had apparently picked up the term somewhere along the line, and in her excitement over it had forgotten her homelessness. Harrison had told Lizzie that she would turn three years old when we were in England. So as we landed in London and he announced, "Kids, we're in England!" Lizzie, quick as a wink, unbuckled her seat belt, and believing that she had just turned three, flew down the aisle shouting, "I'm freeeeeee!!!!" The flight attendant, misinterpreting Lizzie's excitement, quickly returned her to her seat.

Mission Aviation Fellowship's headquarters were in Folkestone, England. We were met, welcomed, and driven to our hosts' home, where we stayed for a three-day orientation along with two other newbies. We were unaware at the time that a three-day orientation entering a new foreign mission for the first time was negligible. The only thing I remember taking from it was a verse someone shared in one of the morning devotionals (Rom. 8:37) – that is, we are not only conquerors, but we are ***more than*** conquerors through Beauty who loves us! In our attempt to fit in, we watched what others around us were doing and tried to do the same – which included eating

Kentucky Fried Chicken with a fork and knife, while balancing the plates on our laps during a staff picnic that we were invited to our second evening there. Everything around us looked so different – glass milk bottles being delivered to each little door, small houses, small yards that they called gardens, small cars; in fact, everything seemed in miniature, except for the gigantic red mail boxes.

When orientation was over, we took some time to visit Clive and Liz, the British friends who were with us at Moody in Tennessee and had pointed Harrison towards this mission. Along with Clive helping Harrison to put a British-style plug on his new computer, they also showed us a great time of experiencing England. We saw the changing of the guards at the Buckingham Palace, fed pigeons in the park, saw Big Ben, went to a petting zoo, went to Stonehenge, and to Westminster Abbey, and saw Churchill's memorial stone near the grave of the Unknown Warrior, and they even got us connections to get into Parliament.

Then it was time to fly to Africa for our very first time! First we flew from London Heathrow to Jomo Kenyatta Airport in Nairobi, Kenya. We were to stay there for the weekend before our MAF flight on Monday morning to our new home in Dodoma, Tanzania.

Computers were still uncommon in Kenya and officials collected exorbitant duty on each computer brought into the country. They confiscated ours and wrote in Harrison's passport that he had brought a computer into the country. Their concern was that it left the country with us and that we didn't sell it in the meantime without them collecting duty from us. We did as we were told, but felt bad that it necessitated making somebody go to the airport on Sunday afternoon to get the computer out of customs, take it to Wilson, the small airport that we would be flying out of on Monday morning, and lodge it in customs there. But this was what we had to do. After spending Saturday night and Sunday in the MAF guest house in Nairobi, early Monday morning, we flew to Tanzania on a Beech 99 MAF flight, with our computer safely in hand. The plane held about fifteen people, and every seat must have been full because we have a picture of Cherith sitting on my lap and Lizzie on Harrison's.

Looking out the plane window as we circled to land in Dodoma for the first time, I swallowed hard. The whole place looked so dry and unbelievably barren. The description *God-forsaken* came to my mind. The beauty was so stark that it was difficult for me to recognize it as such. But I needn't have worried, Beauty is everywhere. It wouldn't be long before giraffes, zebras, elephants, and an occasional lion or rhino against an African sunset, or a campfire under a humongous jet black sky with a myriad of diamond pinpoints sparkling against it, would assure me that Beauty abounds in Africa, too, Awesomely and too big to grasp.

We landed, descended the steps and onto the tarmac, the little airport in front of us looking more like an abandoned house than an international airport. Well, it was really only this flight from Nairobi on Monday mornings that made it an international airport. As we were being warmly received by missionaries, I happened to look over to see Tobin and another MK his age, each wearing one strap of Tobin's travel bag around their respective necks. I hoped that Beauty had given us the right kids for this adventure.

Max Gove had prepared me well. Our three-bedroom home was basic, plainly furnished and lovely. Being American, I did wonder how a college dorm-size refrigerator was going to do for the five of us. Our Swedish neighbors next door had us come over for something to drink and a snack. Then showing us around the compound, we saw there were eight houses similar to ours and one duplex, plus a guest house and a swimming pool. We learned that the compound had been built by and for a German construction company for its workers who were building roads in Tanzania. When they left, MAF purchased it and built a modern spacious hangar with offices included.

Max had also forewarned me well. Initially, just not knowing what to fix my family to eat brought me to tears. The outdoor market had so few things – onions, potatoes, lots of cabbage and sometimes carrots. Though it was a challenge, especially traipsing through the mud in the rainy season, this market became an enjoyable experience, once I got on friendly terms with the sellers. The outdoor meat market, however, was another story. It happened on Saturdays and it seemed to me that the cattle and pigs entered on one side and we the other. Bone chips and blood droplets flew through the air as the vendors chopped at their wares, asking which part you wanted.

When we got the meat home and laid it on the counter, it was still quivering!

Even when I was introduced to the food container that we had on the compound, the British names and items were unfamiliar to me. It takes a while for an American to get used to Marmite, and Weetabix we never did develop a taste for.

About the time I was getting really comfortable with, even enjoying, the outdoor market experience, something happened that made me think again. I was getting my usual things, had placed a large can of Blue Band (margarine) in my basket, and was buying more produce, when suddenly I became aware of a commotion a short distance away in the market. The shouting and yelling was increasing, as was the surrounding mob. Just then I happened to see our neighbor, the new Canadian avionics technician at MAF. I asked him what was happening. He told me he heard that a man had stolen some Blue Band from someone and the crowd was giving him 'justice.' The thief was clearly being beaten by anyone who could swing at him in the mob.

I glanced down at my basket. My Blue Band was gone! "Lindell!" I said, "My Blue Band is gone!" Though it was surely wrong thinking, it nevertheless immediately felt to me that this man's beating was somehow my fault, initiated by my presence here. I watched in horror as someone lifted a metal chair and moved forward towards the thief at the same time that Lindell managed to squeeze in and come between the thief and his accusers. A white man in the mix immediately changed things. Everyone became uncertain and the shouting and commotion lessened. Just then an old blue police pickup truck pulled up to the curb and several policemen pushed their way through the crowd, grabbed the thief, dragged him to the back of the trunk, hoisted him in and drove away. I was temporarily relieved until I heard, "The police will probably just beat him to death." I was visibly shaking and wished this were just a bad dream I was having. Knowing it was real made me aware that I was at a truly new window – one very foreign when compared to the freedom, justice, and security to which I was accustomed. Being convinced that this black thief was created glorious at his core, equal to me in the eyes of our Maker, I felt something vital slipping from my grip.

We had learned to sleep through traffic horns and sirens outside our bedroom window in Cicero, and here we eventually learned to sleep through the thick eerie wail of the Moslems' early morning call to prayer coming over the loud speaker of a nearby mosque. The other four calls to prayer also became just a part of the backdrop of our daily lives, heard but not necessarily noticed. And every evening, year round, between 6 and 6:30 p.m., the sun would go down, just like someone pulling a shade, and another day drew to an end.

Because we had broken our trip from America to Africa by a stay in England, we were not able to bring all our luggage with us. Luggage allowance was less leaving England than leaving the States. MAF had planned to send us our remaining luggage as air freight, but it had somehow been delayed. Had we known we would have packed differently. As it turned out, Harrison only had one pair of blue jeans to last for over a month! Some months later, the box Harrison had built in Tennessee arrived and we had great fun unpacking and enjoying pieces of American life.

One piece that was very special to me was the keyboard that Little Doe Freewill Baptist church had given us as a gift at the farewell party they had for us. Before leaving Tennessee, we had moved my old upright piano, one that I had bought second hand in Iowa City, to the Sunday School area in the church's basement. Using this new keyboard, I gave lessons to our three kids as well as other missionary kids who lived in the compound. Later on, we again purchased an old upright piano from another missionary who was leaving the country, and our keyboard went to some missionaries who lived out in one of the remoter areas of Tanzania.

Another small but important piece to me, in that box we shipped from America, was our tape player. I had really missed music. As I worked in my little kitchen with the barred windows and slatted window panes, through which I could see the sweet little bananas growing on their trees, I was especially comforted by the refrain,

Leaning, leaning, safe and secure from all alarms;
Leaning, leaning, leaning on the everlasting arms.[1]

Listening to the song, in my mind's eye, I was a little girl again, sitting on that church bench so long ago, there beside my father in the Oakville church, feeling safe and secure, knowing that I was protected from all harm. Then the Blue Band thief came to my mind again, reminding me of my presence here and making me wonder how my being here was helping.

In those days, it was a big deal for a telephone call to get through from the States. One of the early ones that I remember was from a good friend still at our church on the prairie in Illinois. Amongst other news, she told me about the closed meeting for members only, which was held specifically to announce our excommunication. She said she really felt sorry for the elder conducting it. According to what she told me, he began by saying, "We all love Harrison and Pam and they love all of us. But for the sake of unity we need to remove them from us." Then he continued with more explanation, which was when she felt sorry for him because he was waffling so with the difficulty of coming up with clear reasoning. The really unusual thing about our excommunication was that it also took place in the Oakville church where I had grown up. Normally it is only announced in one church, so I guess we were a special case. The heart-warming part of this story came when we received, first one, and then another, warm letter from the elder on the prairie, the second letter containing a generous check of financial support for us. Beauty is so good.

There were actually two MAF compounds in Dodoma. The one we lived on was the older of the two, called Compound A; the other one consisted of four new houses in a row and was called Compound B. One day as I was walking the half-mile dirt path between the two, a knowledge settled over me that this had always been me – ever since playing with my paper dolls from other lands, I somehow always knew that I was not just my daddy's pigeon; I was also 'other' – the poor girl walking a dusty path with poverty all around (well, except for the missionary and other expatriate homes). Though I hadn't known what 'other' entailed, I now knew this was at least part of it.

Looking back at it now, I think perhaps I can sum it up by saying that I've always failed to share the hole that Richard Stearns writes about in his book, *The Hole in Our Gospel*. I had always somehow been aware that life doesn't consist of the abundance of one's possessions - or at least I had never been under the illusion that it does. For whatever reasons, I'd never been blind to poverty, to others' or my own. Nor had I been blind to wealth, including my own. I don't see this as making me any better than anyone else, in fact, maybe worse, because it seems like once that 'hole' gets filled and people can see the need, they are empowered to fill what's lacking in others' lives. I don't see me as having the resources or ability to ever fix what's wrong. I can only see me as, at least partly, *being* the other. How it happens that the poverty I encountered struck me more as natural than unnatural, I don't know, but I do know that I can relate to the words penned by Rainer Maria Rilke in 1903 in Paris,". . .for the creator [of poetry] there is not poverty and no poor, indifferent place."[2] And of course, Jesus Himself said, "The poor you will always have with you. . ."[3] so I guess it shouldn't really come as any surprise. And in many ways, life felt richer here – in real ways, in relationships, in the primal beauty of nature. It made me unsure of the real definitions of poverty and riches.

Soon after arriving, we learned that we were expected to have a house helper and a gardener, just like rich folks in America do! Apparently I initially showed some hesitation at the idea, because it was quickly explained to me that the Tanzanians would think poorly of us should we not employ them to do this work for us; it would be selfish of us. I certainly didn't want to be selfish and I'm sure I looked very foolish the first time our house helper, Monika, scrubbed our red concrete kitchen floor, and I felt the necessity to get on my knees to show her that I could do this work, too. I still can't be completely sure of my motivation, whether it was to show her that the work was not beneath me or to show her that I didn't actually need her, that I was just being 'unselfish' in allowing her to do it. What a mixed bag I was!

Whatever Monika's reaction to a white woman scrubbing her own floor, I'm still sure that she surprised me more when, a few days later, I came back from the market and found her sitting in the middle of our little kitchen floor, mixing bowl between her legs, as she mightily stirred the batter in the bowl! Seeing the shock on my face, she put her finger in her nose. Fortunately for me, I did not have to choose my words, because a veteran missionary had followed me into the house and immediately handled the situation by kindly explaining to Monika in Swahili that this was not acceptable practice in a *mzungu's* (*white person's*) home. Then this dear missionary explained to me that it is common for Tanzanians to do what we would consider to be picking their noses when they feel ill at ease, embarrassed or ashamed. I was, and am, so thankful for those who understand things I don't.

As Beauty would have it, Monika's family and ours became very close friends, even sharing our sorrows and joys. Monika's husband was a pastor and lived in the village, Mpwapwa, a couple hours outside of Dodoma. They had a son, and three daughters, all of whom we also got to know well as we spent time in each other's homes and sometimes travelled to Mpwapwa together. Monika understood that I didn't know much and was a wonderful resource to me. I came to understand that a woman's value was in having children and that women were known as 'Mama _____', the blank being filled with the name of one of their children. When I noticed that I was generally known as Mama Tobin, but occasionally Mama Cherith and sometimes Mama Lizzie, I asked why that was. She explained to me that the usual name was that of a son, but sometimes people simply used the name of the child that they were most familiar with. As far as my real name, if I offered 'Pam' as my name, no one ever seemed to understand. So I learned to use my full name of 'Pamela,' and without exception, they would respond, "Oh, Pa-may-la! Yes, a beautiful name!" And as I learned to speak Swahili, it was simple to see that Swahili used vowels in the straightforward method of many languages, unlike English. As I quickly took to the simplicity of Swahili, any remaining Spanish I had left vanished.

It was encouraging to me that Tanzanian Christians greeted each other and us, not only in church, but on the street, at the market, at work, anywhere they were, with *Bwana Asifiwe!* (*The Lord He should be praised!*) And the greeting was typically followed by many questions beginning with *habari* (*news*). So the questions would consist of *What's your news? What's the news of your family? What's the news of your work? What's the news of the many days since I have seen you?* etc. The answer, no matter how untruthfully, was always *Nzuri (good)*. An extreme example of this was the morning that a missionary in Compound B went through all of the usual *habari* questions with her security guard when he arrived to work in the morning. She received the expected *Nzuri* from each question, so at the end was not expecting what was coming after the *Nzuri, lakini*. . . (Good, but. . .). The guard had dutifully answered all the questions with *Good,* but at the last had to reveal the news that his wife had died during the night.

Not long after we arrived and began living and working in Dodoma, Tartisio, the Sudanese friend from Moody Aviation, arrived to work alongside Harrison and the other mechanics. Tartisio had the advantage of being black, but the disadvantage of not being able to speak Swahili. This caused the Tanzanians who didn't know him to think he was putting on superior airs. Fortunately, Tartisio already had experience learning languages and caught on to Swahili more quickly than most of us. Tartisio had grown up in a village outside of Juba, South Sudan. MAF had an aviation base there and Tartisio became the house boy for one of the MAF engineers. Tartisio's outstanding work ethic was noticed, and with MAF's help, he progressed from house boy, to hangar help, to language school in England, followed by All Nations Bible College, on to Moody Aviation in Tennessee, and finally to MAF's program in Dodoma, Tanzania.

Tartisio became as a member of our family. We ate many meals together, celebrated birthdays together, he took our kids on motorcycle rides, and in short, we did life together. I remember when Lizzie in a moment of youthful exuberance exclaimed, "T, I love you!" Shortly after that statement, she added another when she saw what was for dinner, "I LOVE green beans!" to which Tartisio inquired, "Lizzie, am I like a green bean?!"

When Harrison returned to the States for his parents' fiftieth wedding anniversary, Tartisio made the trip with him. While there, they also visited my parents at the home of my youth. While there, Tartisio, the boy who grew up in rural Southern Sudan, asked Harrison if I hadn't been very lonely, living down a quarter-mile lane seven miles outside of the nearest small town of Wapello, Iowa.

In those days of no email and limited international telephone service, I spent a considerable amount of time writing letters to family, friends, and supporters of our work. The first time that I went to the Dodoma post office to buy stamps and aerograms, I didn't realize that I was in for another new window of experience. Though I went soon after the post office opened, people were already mingling inside. Or at least I thought they were mingling, because though they were near the windows open for service, they didn't necessarily seem to be *behind* any of them. Uncertain, I got behind the closest thing that could possibly resemble a line. More people were coming in all the time. And as one customer got served and moved from the window, I tried to take a step forward only to have one or more people intentionally move in front of me! As the place got more crowded and this continued to happen, I wondered if it was really possible that my dream of becoming invisible had been realized. I could see that without using some force, it was going to be impossible for me to ever get my turn at any of these windows.

If *this* was what it was like to be invisible, I guessed I didn't like it after all. I wanted to be seen and serviced – just the same as they did! I now recognized just what an extremely efficient and beautiful method the postal service at my home window was, but I had to accept the fact that I was no longer there; I was here. And it didn't take long before I learned that I, too, could get a turn at this window. I quickly assimilated, realizing that if I were to accomplish my goal of getting stamps, my shoulders and elbows, too, had to develop their voice.

~ ~ ~

In her sweet speech, little Lizzie often told us how she loved the 'flack' babies at church. She thought they were *so* cute. Harrison was relaying this story to the guys at the hangar one Monday morning when one of the Tanzanian mechanics asked in all seriousness, "Say, you wouldn't be interested in taking care of one of those black babies, would you?" Harrison quickly asserted that he would not. However, as he was telling the story to us at dinner that evening, when he got to the part about wanting one, the four of us listening to his story all got very excited – to Harrison's consternation. I guess, being the practical guy that he is, he, like Eliza Dolittle in *My Fair Lady,* was looking ahead and wondering what was to become of the little 'flack' baby, should we actually accept the deal.

This baby boy had been born to a mother in distress in a village outside of Dodoma. It was decided that a Caesarean section was necessary for the birth to happen. The mother had quickly died as a result of blood loss. The baby was now three months old and had been passed from nursing mother to nursing mother to stay alive. How could we possibly say *No*?

And thus John entered our family. We heard later, true or not, that when Tanzanians don't think the baby is going to live long enough to give them a name, they just call him *John*. This John became a part of us; he didn't know that he hadn't always been or wouldn't always be ours. Unforeseen by us, John was our ticket into the hearts and lives of Tanzanians. We had accepted one of them like our own. We were in. And it didn't only work in one direction. John was often the center of missionary attention, by both adults and kids.

After, or more likely because of, his slow start, John became an avid eater, crying when the spoon we were feeding him with scraped the side of the jar or bowl, indicating to him the food was nearing an end. The local British missionary doctor told us that a mechanism triggers in newborn brains when their stomach is full, but in John's case it was likely that this mechanism did not develop because his stomach didn't get full. The result was that John became a short, chubby bubble of absolute joy with whom everyone immediately fell in love. He was so much fun to be with and was loved by all.

Staying in touch with John's father, Emmanuel, and his *shangazi* (paternal aunt), we discussed adoption. In time Emmanuel agreed. The Tanzanian lawyer, having had no experience with such a case, struggled to draw up the papers, and we met together to sign. As he sat at the table, pen in hand, John's father began to sweat and his hand quivered. He laid down the pen, saying (in Swahili), "I can't do it. I can't sign. He is my firstborn, my only son. I just can't."

Our hearts went out to him. No, we would not be able to do it either if we were him. "But what now?" we asked. How would we go about returning him to the culture he was born into – a vastly different one than he had become accustomed to, living with us? Well, his father wanted us to continue taking care of his son, just not adopt him as our own. We found out shortly thereafter that there were those among his friends and family who didn't know why Emmanuel's son should get to go to America while theirs would not, so they warned him that a curse from his forefathers would surely befall him if he gave up his own son to white people.

After further discussion with John's father and the lawyer, we came to what might have been the most harmful conclusion of all – or perhaps not, who's to say? We decided that it would be best to have John adapt to both of our worlds. We would keep him during the week, he could attend the expatriate nursery school where Lizzie had attended when we first arrived, and then on the weekends, we would take him to his father's village where his aunt would care for him.

It was pretty awful. I got so that I would have our gardener bicycle John out to his aunt's on the weekend because I couldn't bear to see his long face and sometimes his tears as I drove away, leaving him standing forlornly by the mud house that was his home for another weekend. I am not proud of this, but what was I to do? I'm sure that Beauty sovereignly places people in families, but I was not at all sure how this mess was a part of that plan.

Long story short: at the time of this writing, John's loving care and affection for us continues as he shares with us, via Facebook from Tanzania, his troubles and successes. Many mornings I awake to a message that may simply say, "Good morning, Mum." I'm so thankful for the technology that I didn't believe would happen.

~ ~ ~

During this first term of working in Tanzania, we felt abundantly loved and supported by our families. Considering the distance and the cost involved, both we and the missionaries we worked with were impressed by the love of the family visitors we received from home. Naturally, Harrison's father was the first to visit. As Beauty would have it, his visit coincided with us receiving baby John into our home. Having had eleven babies of his own, taking in this new baby was a much bigger deal to us than to him. It was comforting to have his steady presence there with us. But he also got to experience the Tanzania outside our home in a big way. Via a Cessna 206 single engine plane, he and Harrison had the privilege of accompanying MAF's Malambo safari, an outreach to the colorful Maasai tribe. As they were flying there, little did they know that when they landed, they would enter a boma (traditional neighborhood enclosed by thorny bushes and consisting of a variety of small huts made of mud and cow dung), to find numerous fifteen-to-eighteen-year-old males lying on their stick beds, dealing with the pain of having been freshly circumcised that morning! Harrison and his father were introduced to the old shriveled up warrior who had performed the rites. The warriors in between the ages of the newly initiated and the circumcision performer were still celebrating the occasion, dancing wildly and jumping up and down in the style that they are famous for. Harrison, not wanting to miss an opportunity, joined in with them, as his father and the old warrior sat watching.

Though we had learned a lot, we were still fairly new to Tanzanian culture, and this was our first family member to visit us. I appreciated the manner in which one of the Tanzanian engineers informed me of what was acceptable and unacceptable behavior. I felt close to my father-in-law and was so happy to have him with us. One day during his visit, in the course of the morning we happened to meet each other in the hangar and greeted warmly with a hug. Soon afterwards, this engineer, who had also become a good friend, pulled me aside to let me know that he understood himself, but it was sure to be misinterpreted by others. I was completely confused as to what he was talking about, so he had to spell it out to me. A Tanzanian father-in-law and daughter-in-law would never greet each other such as we had. If they do, and anyone sees it, everyone will think the worst. There was so much to learn in a new culture. Things that are, of course, completely foreign to one's thinking.

Our next visitors came in our second December on the field; Harrison's sister, Jan, her husband, Kent (Naomi's son, thus my step-brother), and their three children, whose ages were similar to our children's, came to spend the Christmas holidays with us. They brought many items that we now considered luxuries, such as Velveeta cheese, Ranch dressing, Ramen noodles, Dream Whip packages and Pampers! We had actually seen Pampers for sale in the capital city of Dar Es Salaam, but at $60 for a large box, decided we could easily do without! One day when one of the nieces was changing John's diaper, she called for her sister to bring her a fresh diaper. Her sister, knowing that we had been using them, responded with, "Do you want a cloth diaper?" The answer was quick and certain, "No, not cloth! I want a real diaper!"

We delighted in showing them our daily life in Tanzania. Kent, being the owner of his own construction business, had the great idea of building a tree house for our kids. Not long into the day, Kent gained a new respect for Harrison's calm patience and ability to take into stride all the endless frustrations encountered in simply trying to obtain the necessary wood and nails to begin the project. The normal place to buy wood was closed for inventory, leaving them to buy it two or three boards at a time, as they could find it, from street peddlers. Fortunately, Harrison had brought a hammer from the States and a fellow missionary loaned them his electric handsaw. In the end, Kent and Harrison, together with their sons, produced a splendid tree house, which, with local help, moved with us when we later moved to another house on the compound.

Kent, Jan and their family got to be with us for the big hangar party that the missionaries planned as a Christmas get-together for all MAF staff, expatriate and national. The children put on a darling program, singing, *Who is the King of glory? Who is the Prince of Peace?* This was followed by welcoming the Tanzanians to a table laden with cakes and sweets of every kind imaginable. This being our first experience, we were unprepared for the mad dash to the table, and were thankful no one got hurt. Afterwards, we had invited a couple of the families we knew best to our home for dinner, wanting to share our Tanzanian friendships with our family from home. It was a beautiful time of togetherness.

Jan had gone to her local library and had researched all she could find about Tanzania, so she knew many more facts than we did. She was a great tour guide for us all as we traveled from Dodoma to a local guest house in Babati, to a tented camp in the famous Ngorogoro Crater, and on to Tarangeri National Park, where we spent Christmas Eve and Christmas morning by a decidedly feeble makeshift Christmas tree. We made many special memories that will last a lifetime.

The rest of the crew also went by a small MAF plane on the Malambo safari to see the life of the colorful Maasai tribe (no circumcision rites this time), but Lizzie had a slight fever, so I stayed home with her and John. When the time came for their departure, we drove them the six hours to the airport in Dar Es Salaam in a van without air conditioning. After battling the many mosquitoes while eating at a typical tourist restaurant by the ocean, we delivered them to the airport drenched in sweat, thanking them profusely for their visit, and returned to life in Dodoma.

Our next visitors, my parents, came in February of 1992. It was also a very special time as we celebrated my father's and John's birthdays. They were born a few days apart, but with seventy years between. Later, as we traveled from Arusha towards Mt. Meru, it was music to my ears to hear Naomi express her awe at seeing giraffes running across the savanna, "Oooh, *now I know* I'm in Africa!" She especially loved the giraffes, so we were extra pleased when we woke up the next morning and stepped out to see perhaps a dozen or more giraffes eating just outside our rustic cabin at the foot of the mountain. A glorious sight under the African sun of a fresh new day.

Harrison tirelessly showed the *Jesus Film* in many villages. He welcomed Dad's help in setting up the reel to reel film projector, run by gasoline generator, and hanging the white sheet which improvised well as a screen. Many times the film was shown under the night sky, but this particular showing was in a building. As was usual, a crowd gradually emerged, many barefooted, out of the darkness. Because it was being held indoors, the crowd was too big for the indoor space, also not unusual. When everything was nearly ready to roll, suddenly Lizzie became aware that she was quite separated from any of her family members. Though she sometimes tired of being in the villages because her long blond hair was tantalizing to the African children and they just had to touch it, to feel its smoothness, this night was different. As she cried out in her separation, she didn't mind the strong black hands that lifted her above the crowd passed her to other black hands and so on, until she had traversed the width of the building on top of the crowd and was safely at my side!

Weddings, too, were something that we were often included in to one degree or another. Dad and Naomi happened to be with us as one of Harrison's Tanzanian coworkers was getting married, and Cherith and Tobin were participants as flower girl and ring bearer. I was happy to have my parents get to experience not only the wedding, which was quite western, apart from the bride not being allowed to smile (that would show she was happy to be leaving her parents and home and/or she was not a respectable girl!). I found it painful to watch the bride repress positive emotion, and rejoiced to sometimes see a forbidden smile play at her lips!, They also experienced the traditional meal of pilau afterwards, along with the hand washing ritual that always precedes formal eating, a tradition with an essential, if not always effective, purpose in this setting!

As we spent time with Dad and Naomi, both at home and traveling, Dad commented more than once that watching our little family interact, he was continually reminded of his own family growing up – that we didn't need anybody but ourselves to have fun. *Yes, I* too loved watching our kids enjoy each other, and was thankful that a three-fold cord is not easily broken. And John was quite content to be in the center of it!

Dad's brother, Uncle Arnie, was our next visitor from the States. He was big into the Gideons International Bible Society, and had come to Nairobi, Kenya for that purpose. We were really glad when he made plans to come spend some time with us, meeting at Arusha. We weren't clear in our communication and he ended up flying to Kilimanjaro airport while a MAF plane was waiting for him at Arusha airport. Or was it the other way around? I'm not sure – the point being that the MAF pilot, who had asked me if I'd like to fly along to pick up my uncle, and I waited for hours for Uncle Arnie to arrive. When we finally discovered and corrected the mistake, it was too late for us to return to Dodoma via air. The MAF pilot, Uncle Arnie, and I stood alone on the tarmac, not knowing what to do next. A private pilot, walking away from the plane that he had just parked some distance away, took note of us standing, uncertainly, by the MAF plane. He came over, introduced himself, and asked if we needed something. The MAF pilot explained our conundrum. The pilot listened, thought a moment and said, "Well, you're welcome to come stay at my home tonight." So, a few minutes later, there we were, sitting on the porch, cool drinks in hand, looking out over the scenic view, feeling exactly like we were in *Out of Africa*. I overheard our host's wife tell their worker, Mohammed, that there would be five for dinner tonight. And what a lovely dinner it was. The next morning after breakfast, we flew back to Dodoma to show Uncle Arnie our life there. Because of the difficulty of communication, it had been some time before Harrison had gotten word via radio for the reason for our delay. When I asked him if he had been worried, he said, "No, I knew wherever you were, you were probably having a good time." True, that.

It was hard to say if Uncle Arnie enjoyed our kids more or if they enjoyed him more! Since they hadn't had opportunity to get to know each other before this, they made good use of the present time. I remember Uncle Arnie being concerned about the busyness of our lives, and wondering about its sustainability. I remember appreciating him noticing and caring. Uncle Arnie also stayed busy; whenever we didn't know where he was, we could find him witnessing to any Tanzanian he came across about Jesus' love for everyone and how it had changed his life. Then he would leave a small Gideons' New Testament in their hands. When it was time for him to leave, we drove him the fourteen hours to Nairobi, stopping overnight and to see sights along the way. He simply could not get over how bad the roads were, saying that he wasn't even going to try to tell anybody back home about them, because they wouldn't be able to believe it anyway.

By the time the last guests of our first term came, we had moved to a house off of the MAF compound and were living in a regular neighborhood in Dodoma. Though we had initially gloried in the easy transition from our home in America to our German-built house on a fenced and guarded compound with a lovely in-ground swimming pool, complete with a small (unstocked) bar, barbecue pit, and sauna, it didn't take long before we noticed some discrepancy in our ideology. We had not come this distance in search of comfort, pleasure, and security. We wanted to think that we had come not only for Harrison to do aircraft mechanics and me to carry on normally, though with one arm figuratively tied behind my back, but that there was something more. We wanted to think that the 'more' was building relationships with the people surrounding us. And we were. The missionaries surrounding us had become very dear friends. The Tanzanians we worked with in the hangar and at home had also become very close friends. So what exactly made us want to live in a less desirable house, with Tanzanian neighbors six feet away on either side, one of whom was experiencing significant morning sickness with her pregnancy, meaning that we woke up daily to the sound of her retching?

Looking back now to that window, I ask myself this question in all seriousness, and I see that, for one thing, it had become trendy thinking. As the mission in Dodoma grew, we had run out of compound houses, and a family or two had no choice but to live off compound. Then others of us began to see advantages in this. Perhaps it made us feel better about ourselves and the image we were portraying to those who were financially making our lives possible. Perhaps we honestly wanted to experience a life more representative of the people we were there to serve. Perhaps we then felt that we were a bit better than missionaries who lived in a huddle of their own privileged society. It's hard to say definitively. Maybe the old joke is true: Missionaries are like manure. Heaped up in one place they really stink, but spread them out and they can do a lot of good. Anyway, for whatever reason, we chose to live off compound when the opportunity presented itself, and that was where Rod and his son, Brett, found us.

Rod is the husband of Harrison's oldest sister, Mary, and he is the one who started the church that commissioned us as we left the States to come to Tanzania. Brett is their second son, one of those teens who had 'threatened' two-year-old Tobin with a spanking for spilling his milk at the dinner table. Now when the electricity was off, we were no longer covered by MAF's generator, and so I ended up cooking our meals outside on a kerosene camp stove. I imagine that this, along with other similar things, gave Rod and Brett a different picture of our life than our other visitors had received. One reason that we were especially glad to have them was that, as the time of our first term of service was coming to an end, we needed to decide whether this experience was what Harrison was looking for, to go on to work with Regions Beyond Missionary Union in Irian Jaya, or whether Dodoma, Tanzania was where we wanted to stay indefinitely, or at least for the foreseeable future. As both family and pastor of our main supporting church, we valued Rod's thoughts, guidance, and prayers. Our time with him was valuable, helping us to see that Dodoma had become our home. Harrison had quickly gained experience, moving from his role as a mechanic on the floor, to hangar foreman, and then to chief engineer within the three years. Each of our kids and I were all happy campers. We decided to stay.

I had become part of a puppet team that did shows with Swahili-speaking puppets and African animals. Our puppets often performed prior to showing the *Jesus Film* in the late afternoon while it was still light out. The intent was for the puppets to present a Christian message with the Swahili children as the targeted audience, but we were often tickled to see that the adults crowding in behind the kids were every bit as taken in as the children were. I recall doing a puppet show, while Rod and Brett were there, that didn't go as smoothly as we would have liked.

Another afternoon we spent climbing Lion Rock (aka Simba Rock) together. Lion Rock is simply a rocky hill jutting up out of the flat dry land of Dodoma. It takes maybe a half hour or so to climb to the top. As we were climbing, Rod was impressed that Tobin, when in doubt of risking his safety, would always first check with Harrison, "Is it okay, Dad? Should I try it?" Pastor Rod told us later that he likened Tobin's questions to how we should all be towards our Father God, trusting that He knows all, wants us to fully experience life, and at the same time stay safe and secure, out of harm's way. As he watched our family, he said he imagined that our kids would never live 'goofy lifestyles.' We were encouraged and knew time would tell.

When we took them to Dar Es Salaam for their departing flight, Rod wanted to treat us to a night in a nice hotel. We chose Bahari Beach Hotel, the best thing going, which we saw as offering all the amenities, including live entertainment featuring African dancers. Rod, however, was a little shocked. To him, it didn't offer much and the cost of $100/night for each of our bungalow huts came as quite a shock!

All in all, our family visits left us with wonderful lifetime memories, and along with all the bountiful love offerings that came to us in many other forms – packages, prayers, words, and deeds (one precious older lady from Tennessee sent us a card with a package of Kool-Aid every single holiday!) – we felt we must be the most well-loved missionaries alive.

~ ~ ~

The Christian fellowship that we experienced from day one in Africa was a beautiful thing. Both the weekly MAF prayer meetings and the international ladies' Bible study that I attended represented a rainbow of nationalities, languages, and denominations, but we were one in heart, mind, and spirit. This new window of Christianity that Harrison and I marveled at, our kids accepted as the norm along with all the rest of their experiences.

When it came time to choose a church to attend on Sundays, we naturally enough looked to see where those we were already praying with went to church. With few exceptions, they were divided between two denominations – Anglican and Assemblies of God. Neither of those were familiar from our church experience so far, so we visited them both. Though the formality of the cathedral with its beautiful stained glass windows and the liturgical nature of the service were strange to us, it was comfortable, there were many white faces we had already met, and it was in English.

The next Sunday we rode to the AoG church with a British family in a Land Rover shared by the MAF families. The church was on the campus of an AoG Bible college about five miles outside of Dodoma. After bouncing along a dusty, extremely bumpy dirt road, we turned left and saw what they called the church. It was a very large pole building. When we entered, the singing was already under way. Approximately 300 black voices were raised in what was apparently heartfelt praise. Not understanding the Swahili, I whispered, no, just asked, she could not have heard me whisper, my British friend what the words meant. She told me, "They're singing, *In my heart, I'm living in Jerusalem.*"

Wow. I looked around and remembered landing in Quito in the early morning, the sun reflecting off the city and the surrounding mountains, giving me the impression that I was landing in a new Jerusalem. And I knew for sure the Jerusalem these people of God saw was in their hearts, because it sure wasn't here. It was stifling hot. The place was packed. We chose seats near the back where there were a few other white faces, none American. We were sweating. Now and then a hot breeze would come in through the open windows. I welcomed it.

When the singing was over, the people's voices rose in prayer, all of them speaking at once – in Swahili or tongues? How would I know? That done, we all sat down and it was time for greetings or prayer requests or something that involved one person at a time, from anywhere in the congregation, standing up and talking. At one point a nursing mother, with her breast still very exposed, stood and said something. Many murmured assent. Finally it was time for the sermon to begin. My friend occasionally gave me the gist of the message. I don't remember at all what is was, but I do remember seeing a woman, down the row of folding chairs from us, lifting her baby out away from her lap. The baby peed. The mother was wearing red plastic flip flops. She used her foot to wipe the urine, spreading it on the dusty concrete floor, and resumed listening to the sermon.

After the sermon there was more loud praying, and then everyone filed out singing. Outside, they formed a large circle where, still singing, everyone entering the circle shook hands with those who had already formed the circle and when they got to the end, they either joined the circle or went home.

In an effort to integrate, we chose this church.

Though our children never complained about sitting through the services (Come to think of it, those three never complained about anything – how is that possible???), the British mother started an English Sunday School and the few of us with English-speaking children took turns teaching. When it came time for the Christmas program, Cherith, Tobin, and Lizzie agreed to sing a short song in Swahili. I don't know if they actually knew the meanings of the words or if it was just a simple song to catch on to. Either way, there they were, in no way expecting what would happen next. Our three little white kids, standing in front of that big church full of

Tanzanians. They opened their mouths to sing, only got out three words, *Siku gani leo?* and the entire church went electric with ululation! Undaunted, they kept singing - *Duniani po pote; Kristo kazaliwa. . .* but the entirety of the rest of their song was drowned out by a multitude of tongues moving rapidly, back and forth in mouths, producing the high-pitched trill of emotional celebration. The kids, not knowing what else to do, finished the song, though no one could hear, got off the stage and sat down, making absolutely nothing out of it.

Later on, an American team of two families, both with children near the ages of ours, came to Dodoma to start a Bible Baptist church. There weren't many Americans around, and living and working with mostly Europeans, we were happy to welcome someone from home. Our families connected immediately, and for some time we assembled with their little church plant. The Christmas program there was quite different from the one we had experienced the year before, and much closer to what we were accustomed to. It was accompanied by a sermon on the beautiful simplicity of the first Christmas, a very fitting message here where there were little to no Christmas trimmings and trappings.

As we increasingly caught that the goal of this team was to build a church for Tanzanians, and perhaps we were a distraction, we began attending another new church in town, the Pentecostal Assemblies of God (PAOC) where I played the piano for the English service. The pastor and his wife there were Canadian and also had children the ages of Cherith and Lizzie. For some reason, my mind, or maybe it's my ear, still returns to a sermon this pastor preached on something the prophet Isaiah once said: "Whether you turn to the right or to the left, your ears will hear a voice behind you, saying, 'This is the way; walk in it.'"(Isaiah 30:21) So, after all our years of growing up in a separatist church, we had become church hoppers. The elder on the prairie had been right; who knew what kind of Christians we would be associating with?

So when Tobin led Lizzie to the Lord while they were playing one day, it apparently seemed very natural to them that she was giving her life to Jesus, and they never even thought to connect it to a church experience. For a few years, we celebrated the anniversary of each child's 'spiritual birthday' with a birthday cake, in hopes of supporting the spiritual with a concrete physical reality.

Actually, we had a whole slew of family traditions, particularly on Sundays. For starters, I made the same coffee cake every Sunday morning for years – throughout this window and many future ones to come. Plus, as we ate the coffee cake, we always had the same tape playing in the recorder we shipped in our 4x4 box. It was the 2nd Chapter of Acts, a sibling trio popular during the 1970s and 80s. Tobin later remarked that whenever he heard that music, or even thought of it, he could smell coffee cake! After church we would grill some meat, usually chickens that had been delivered to my door, headless and plucked. In the afternoon, we always took a family bike ride, becoming familiar with most every little trail possible, although sometimes they led us to simply nowhere, which we affectionately labeled an *uh-oh*. Then in the evening, in place of dinner, we would fire up the air popcorn popper, also from our 4x4 box, and enjoy popcorn and board games. Because of our close quarters, even on the MAF compound, one of our British neighbors finally asked us, "What is that noise I hear every Sunday about dinnertime coming from your house?" We said, "Come and see!" He was fascinated to watch the popcorn fly out of the air popper and wondered what Americans would think of next.

These traditions seemed important to maintain some boundaries in identifying the six of us as a family unit. Apart from those boundaries, compound living was one big happy family for the most part. It was not so unusual for me to come home from the market to find maybe six or seven children playing in my home, and none of them being mine! And this was okay, because if mine weren't outside somewhere, then they were undoubtedly playing in someone else's home. It was a good life.

Of course, amongst all the carefree play, some discipline had to be taught. Insisting on them practicing the piano became one means towards that goal. Again, it was fascinating to watch how different three kids in one family could be in their learning styles. Lizzie, in particular, did not need me to correct her. I would often overhear her interrupt her practicing with, "NO, Lizzie, that's NOT RIGHT! Now do it right!!"

It seemed odd to me, too, to have my own child speak with a British accent, but that's what happened. If I would give Lizzie several commands at one time, such as "Pick up your toys, brush your teeth and get ready for bed," she would respond with, "I CAUNT do everything at once, Mum!" Though the accent was what I noticed at the time, the simple purity of the message is still what often comes to my mind when I'm expecting too much of myself.

Lizzie loved to talk. Sometimes she would stand by me in the kitchen while I was working and talk, endlessly. Thinking about what I was doing, or letting my mind go elsewhere, I would continue to interject *uh-huh,* every now and then as though I were listening to her. Finally she had had it and burst out, "Mum, stop saying *uh-huh* and answer me!!" Caught, I recalled my own father's *uh-huh* response to my early childhood confession and realized, *Like father, like daughter.* It dawned on me, too, that Lizzie had a lot more awareness of what was actually happening than I did at her age – or maybe it was just that she wanted an answer and I, in my situation, did not! Either way, I watched this awareness of hers develop through the windows of life to the point of it becoming a family joke in later years – Lizzie and her *so-called's*. She seemed to have a knack for seeing right through what others only nodded at with an *uh-huh,* and even now often makes us laugh with her descriptions of things *so-called*, such as *so-called Christians*.

As I watched, I came to discover that not only were each of our children created unique in themselves and in their learning styles, but also in their love for me. It may have happened the day Lizzie professed her sincere love for me with, "I love you, Mom, even if you are old!" Her love for me was undoubtedly pure, Tobin's was so wide, and Cherith's so deep – reminding me of the *Deep and Wide* song that they sang so cutely at school, and also of Beauty's unique love for each of us.

Lizzie's British accent wasn't the only linguistic entertainment we had going on. John, in his unique situation of living in both the English and the Swahili worlds, learned not only to speak both languages, but could also choose to speak Swahili like a Tanzanian or like a *mzungu*. To listen to him imitate a white person speaking Swahili was absolutely hilarious – and he loved entertaining. But his standard answer when I directed him to do something that wasn't so entertaining was, "*Kesho, Mom.*" Tomorrow, he would do it tomorrow.

John was priceless to watch the first time we told him the story of Jesus' birth. He sat absolutely still at the dinner table, where we had just finished eating. When I got to the part about an angel suddenly appearing and scaring the shepherds, followed by more angels appearing in the sky, without moving his head, John's big brown eyes moved to the nearby window and checked the darkness, as if expecting something to happen. I guess the story is not so far-fetched to a Tanzanian boy who daily sees flocks and herds being shepherded, often by boys not so much older than himself.

Because there was only one radio station and no TV station in Tanzania, it was always an exciting week for the kids when it was our turn to have the MAF video box. The thirteen-inch TV, accompanied with a VCR and a box of twenty or so movies that never changed the whole three years, rotated house to house in turn. It was amazing how many times kids could enjoy watching films like *Willie Wonka and the Chocolate Factory* and not tire. Truth be told, I think they enjoyed their adventurous outdoor life more; it was just that they had to get the most use possible out of their video week.

School life at Canon Andrea Mwaka Primary School (CAMPS) was simple, rich, and full. We moms took turns collecting the school-age kids at Compound A and B in first a Land Rover, and then later on, as the number grew, in a new white minibus. We drove them the four miles through the sleepy, dusty center of town to the school on the other side and then picked them up in the heat of the afternoon when school was over.

Each of our kids loved this school from the beginning and on to the end. When we arrived, Lizzie, at three years of age, began at the nursery school, which was on the grounds next to CAMPS's so-called soccer field. I picture her yet, marching into her first day of nursery school, pigtails a'bobbin', hand in hand with Jonathan, her Swedish buddy with whom she would play for hours, each speaking their own languages. I volunteered at the nursery school, and as usual, received more than I gave. The Tanzanian teacher and I became friends and she gave me great insight into the window of a Tanzanian female. Listening to the stories of a friend who had undergone the terrors of female circumcision, aka female mutilation, is as close as I ever want to come to knowing about it – or understanding why successive generations of mothers allow, even promote, the same to their daughters.

Cultures have their horrors and religion has its limits. When I had reached my limits with my sympathy for it, I told the boys at Tobin's birthday party that the hotdogs were made of whatever meat they wished them to be. Maybe I should explain. Tobin invited the boys from his class to a wiener roast at a stone fort on a hill half an hour outside of Dodoma. Some of the boys' religions did not allow them to eat beef, others were not allowed pork. Since hotdogs were not available, one of the MAF pilots had brought them to us from a Nairobi flight. The first time through the line, the hotdogs were clearly divided into beef and pork, but as they came back for seconds and thirds, I was no longer sure which hotdogs were where. The boys, wanting to do what was right, would check with me if they were getting the right one for them. No longer certain which was beef and which was pork, I agreed that whichever one they pointed to was whatever they wanted it to be. They ate it and no one seemed the wiser, or harmed either, and no gods appeared to get angry.

It was really nice to have our kids at a school where the principal was willing to ride his motorbike to the house midday to tell me, "Today is swimming day and Tobin forgot his swimming togs (Kiwi for trunks). He told me that his mom forgot to pack them, but I told him his mom didn't forget, HE forgot. Anyway, just thought I'd run over and pick them up for him before it's time for swimming." We mothers also took turns helping the teachers to transport the various classes of students the two or so miles to The Climax Club when it was their day for swimming. The Climax Club, consisting mostly of a swimming pool, racquet ball court, and a place where sodas and fresh chips (french fries) were sometimes served, could have been an oasis in the middle of dry, dusty Dodoma, but instead was run down and unkempt. Nevertheless, the kids usually loved to go there, unless the pool water got too bad. Even then, some of the boys thought it was fun to dive in and go under the thick green scum where they couldn't be seen!

In comparison, the pool in the MAF compound was pristine. The MAF maintenance man worked hard to keep it so. It was a lovely spot for the children to have fun swimming together weekday afternoons while we mothers sat beside the pool, chatting and keeping an eye on the kids. On Sunday afternoons, the pool would often get crowded as more families were free. One Sunday afternoon, Cherith swam to the edge of the pool and told Harrison that she couldn't get out because her leg hurt so much. When he helped her out, it was obvious that her leg really did hurt. She had told me a time or two before that she had had to stop running at recess at school because her leg hurt, and once she had come in from riding her bike saying it hurt. But now, she was almost unable to walk. After calling the British missionary doctor on the other side of town, we carried her to the car and drove her to his home to see what he thought.

Long story short, it turned out to be synovitis of her hip joint and she lay for weeks on the couch in our living room in traction, made by Harrison from bits and pieces from the hangar, using beans as weights. We carried her to the bathroom, to bed at night, and back to the couch in the morning. Her school teacher brought or sent her work to our home. Some weeks into this, she one day announced that she was sure Jesus had healed her hip and she could get up now. We were glad for her faith and didn't want to discourage it. We shared the news with the kind, understanding British missionary doctor. He came over, examined Cherith, told her he was sure Jesus had healed her, but that she still needed to lay here and rest for the time being. Disappointed with our unbelief, Cherith nevertheless submitted, with only a little grumpiness.

What more shall I say then – of endless safaris, riding humongous turtles on the island of Zanzibar, snorkeling in coral reefs, asthma attacks when there was no doctor, bouts of malaria, prayer partners who truly understood, daily bike rides, unbelievable chance meetings, and endless funny and not-so-funny cultural misunderstandings? Time and space do not permit me to tell the depth of the highs and lows of this, our first term of service in Africa.

Throughout the experiences, I gradually came to the realization that I was somehow different than other overseas workers. I didn't share their intense longing for home, where everything seemed better. I was content to be where I was. Where all five or six pairs of our flip flops were lined up neatly by the screen door. That was where home was to me.

The second leg of our airline trip to return to the States for our first furlough happened to fall on Tobin's eighth birthday. We had chosen the cheapest tickets we could find, which this time happened to be on Sabena, a Belgian airline. One of the MAF pilots suggested we let the airline know in advance that it would be our son's birthday when we flew with them. We did.

Somewhere in the skies between Brussels, Belgium and Chicago O'Hare airport, several airline hosts gathered in the aisle near our seats and sang a cute little bee-bop version of 'Happy Birthday' to Tobin, presented him with a small cake to share, and gave Harrison and me champagne. Later on, a steward returned to ask Tobin if he would like to go see the cockpit and talk to the pilot. Oh, he would! "Okay," the steward said, "and you might as well bring your family along."

The pilot was a character. The landing in Chicago was quite rough. As we were taxiing to a stop, his voice came over the speaker announcing, "Sorry, but I just want to tell you. That was not my fault. That was not the plane's fault. That was asphalt."

The following afternoon, we arrived to O'Hare airport in Chicago. The immigration officer stamped our passports, and handing them back, said, "Welcome home!" Pushing our burdensome luggage trolley out into the crowd, we scanned the faces, each waiting expectantly for their own, and were so happy to quickly spot the beautiful head of white hair belonging to Harrison's father. Yes, we were home. But once in the car, traveling first through Chicago traffic and then out into the wide open spaces of central Illinois, everything looked more than familiar; it looked super strange and too sparkling clean.

Lessons Learned:

Life's not fair and I'm inexplicably lucky.
Life in Africa is so rich and so raw.

9

Rolling Prairie, Indiana

Becoming Acquainted With Home Assignments
July 1993 - January 1994

A family of farmers was a big part of the new church that had begun on the Sunday we were commissioned. They had a small, unoccupied house on one of their tomato farms and offered it to us as a home for our first furlough. Another member of the same church loaned us a Ford Taurus as our second car. Before leaving for Africa, Harrison had put moth balls in the motor and trunk of our 1985 Chevy Celebrity before parking it in the shed at the Hodel farm in Roanoke. The moth balls had served their purpose of keeping the mice out, but the smell had so permeated the inside of the car, people we visited with would admit they thought we smelled funny! We took to leaving all four doors wide open when we weren't using it, causing our new country neighbors to also wonder about us. So it's easy to see how grateful we were to the lenders of the Ford Taurus! Not only did the Ford not reek of moth balls, it talked! First, it *listened* to where we wanted to go, and then it *told* us how to get there! It's no wonder that, in contrast with *our* car, the kids dubbed this one '*God's Car.*'

One fine summer day, an older member of the church invited us to go blueberry picking with him. Harrison was busy, but the kids and I went along. Once there, buckets in hand, ready to pick, this precious man put us on pause by saying, "I always like to pray first."

And there, right beside the blueberry bushes, he thanked Beauty for the day, the sunshine, the good air, our health, and this holy ground of the blueberry farm! I don't know if it happened with the kids, but for me that perspective put a whole new spin on my day of blueberry picking – like I really was on holy ground.

And eating those fresh blueberries was a real treat. We were surprised at how much being in Africa had changed our taste buds. Our kids were especially sensitive to it, pointing out that American bananas tasted like cardboard in comparison with the sweetness of the bananas they had become accustomed to. It was the same with pineapples. It wasn't only fruit that they found disturbing. Tobin, having taken one gulp from his McDonald's milk carton, exclaimed, "What is wrong with this milk?!" Recalling Lizzie's *loud* juice, we checked, but no – the only problem with Tobin's milk was that it was two percent. Later when he rode along to the store with Grandpa to get milk for Grandma, Grandpa asked Tobin what kind of milk he liked and he responded with, "100 percent!". Indeed, our milk in Tanzania had come to our door straight from the cow's udder. When we were first there, we boiled this milk – thick cream forming a layer on top. Later, we got a pasteurizer, which caused the cream to homogenize throughout the milk.

~ ~ ~

Because of having been excommunicated from our home church, our situation was a little different than typical missionaries. We weren't sure exactly how to handle sharing our experiences of the last three years living in Tanzania. We were not allowed to use the fellowship hall connected with the church. Harrison's father came up with an idea. He arranged for us to use the activity room in a nursing home in Eureka, Illinois. We prepared a slide show, our children agreed to sing in Swahili, and Harrison's father set up a dozen or so folding chairs in hopes that somebody would come listen to us. What happened next was simply astonishing.

Well over a hundred people came! And they kept coming even after there was standing room only!! We were completely overcome with this outpouring of love. Whether it was curiosity, or the natural human draw towards crossing the line of what is allowed, or something else, we didn't mind. We just received it as another abundant gift from Beauty. He is *so* good. And here we were simply doing what we wanted to do because we thought it was the right thing to do – or vice versa; it's always hard to be sure. Either way, we had no way of knowing we were on the edge of what was already happening in that church culture.[1] It wasn't about us at all!

By this time, my older brother, Adam, was a preacher in the Valparaiso, Indiana congregation of our home church and my younger brother, Jacob, and his wife had left our home church in Oakville, Iowa to help some friends start a Baptist church plant in Wapello. Both brothers welcomed our family to their churches, Adam stepping out of protocol by welcoming us from the pulpit, and Jacob and his wife, arranging for us to share our mission work with their group.

The Baptist church that Jacob helped to start met in the Wapello movie theater, a place I had fond memories of, from being allowed to go once at Christmastime to watch *The Three Stooges*. Jacob had laughed and laughed out loud the whole movie, and it had made me happy to hear him laugh. And now he was beginning a church here in the same spot. Oddly enough, the same effect took place as our family attended the service now as had happened at the movie: we got the giggles, inappropriate as it was! It happened when an elderly lady sang a solo in a priceless, croaky voice, "*It is written, Vengeance is mine; I will repay, saith the Lord.*"[1] Though it added to the effect, it was not the lady's voice that struck us as funny; what was funny was such fierce words being repeatedly sung so sweetly. The contrast struck us as hilarious, and though we stifled our amusement at the time, afterwards we laughed and laughed, and still smile about it to this day. However, the truth of it is dead serious business. I thought of the atrocities of the genocide we had just seen on TV, taking place in Rwanda, the country neighboring Tanzania, where 800,000 people had just been killed in ninety days and wondered, but didn't see how or if it related.

~ ~ ~

The kids were excited about going to first, third, and fifth grades in America. They went ahead of time to check out the building (from the outside) and the playground. So Tobin was totally unprepared for what would happen when, on the first day, his teacher in this tiny Midwestern school was introducing him to the other third graders and asked him what school he went to last year. He quickly replied, "Canon Andrea Mwaka Primary School." After asking him to repeat it several times, which he did, she asked, "And where is that school?"

"In Africa."

"Africa? I want you to go to the principal's office and tell him that."

After finding out where the office was, he obediently went and told them his teacher had sent him. That was how Tobin and Mrs. Wells' relationship started, but not how it ended. Once aware of the situation, Mrs. Wells was thrilled to have someone from the outside in her class and made total use of it every chance she got, especially at the school's open house. She made Tobin feel extraordinarily special and we were glad for that.

We settled into a routine and once again had our shoes (no longer flip flops) lined up at the door. The kids got on the school bus in the morning, Harrison got a chance to help farm again – this time harvesting something he had never harvested before, tomatoes! – and I had the joy of a little home to keep. One evening I had made a casserole for dinner. As I was taking it out of the oven, I accidentally bumped into Tobin and the casserole slipped from my hands and crashed to the floor. I struggled to maintain my composure. So I could hardly believe my ears when, later that evening on the phone with his Grandpa, Tobin relayed what had happened with the casserole, saying that I had yelled at him! When he got off the phone, I said, "Tobin, I cannot believe you told Grandpa that I yelled at you! I purposely did not say a single word – much less yell at you!!" His answer stayed with me for a long time, "Oh, I know you didn't, Mom, but I heard you loud and clear."

Having been three seasons without the sights of Christmas lights glowing in the cold, we decided to take advantage of being near Chicago this year. Arriving in the early dark in heavy traffic, we were eager to park God's car so we could walk the sidewalks looking in the windows of Marshall Field and other stores. The problem was that finding a parking place seemed nigh on impossible. Then Lizzie's voice came from the back seat, "I'll pray for one!" Lizzie, our little 'prayer' – who prayed for lost things and they were found, who prayed for parking spaces in impossibly packed cities and there they were.

Dad and Naomi came for one last visit together before they headed to Marco Island for the winter. After a wonderful weekend together, they packed up on Monday morning and were standing at the door with their coats on when Harrison thought to suggest we pray together before they go. I'm so thankful we did. It's a beautiful way to part.

Wanting to make the most of our time, we took the kids out of school to make a road trip to Disney World in Florida. We had a good trip down and tons of perfect fun there. Perhaps foolishly, we decided that to save another night's lodging, Harrison and I would drive through the night, taking turns driving and sleeping, while the kids slept in the back seat. It was the one time in my life that I can remember being so tired that I would see mirages of strange things standing on the road. But nothing so strange as the dream that Cherith, suddenly sitting upright in the back seat announced. "I just had a really scary dream! We were waiting in line to see Mickey Mouse and he scared us by turning into the Antichrist!"

Once again, and too soon, it was time to pack up and change to our life on the other side of the world. I again began to see myself as different than other missionaries. I had heard those missionaries say how they missed their overseas field so much when they were in the States. That they thought of that as home now. To me, I would have been content just to stay here – where all of our boots were lined up neatly by the door. That was where home was to me.

But I was looking forward to our upcoming opportunity to go to language school. I loved language and I loved Swahili speakers. To be able to combine the two was incentive enough to be excited about the adventure ahead.

Lessons learned:
There's so much happening that's not about me.
Beauty knows what He's up to.

10

Morogoro, Tanzania

Another Language to Love
Spring 1994

In the spring of the year, when other missionaries go out to do battle on the front lines, we felt lucky that our mission was giving us the gift of time off to officially learn the language of the people we were living amongst. The Evangelical Lutheran Church in Tanzania (ELCT) had established an excellent Swahili language school near the foothills of the lush Uluguru Mountains in Morogoro, Tanzania, a three-hour drive from Dodoma. During our first three years in Tanzania we had learned what Swahili we could from daily life among the Tanzanians. Jean, a Canadian MAF wife, and I had also been tutored weekly by a Tanzanian friend who was the mother of Baraka (meaning *blessing* in Swahili), one of Tobin's best friends. Our tutor's name was Frida, and being married to a man from Holland, she was proficient in several languages, including English. Jean and I struggled to understand the grammar, but thought we were doing well when the two of us carried on a complete conversation in Swahili at one of our lessons. We were crushed, but at the same time thought it was hilarious that, though we had perfectly understood each other, Frida couldn't make heads or tails of our conversation!

Our first morning in language school we received a big red binder that said *Mtu ni Watu* on the cover. *A Person is People.* Wow, I knew there was a reason I loved this language which, like all languages, reflects the culture of its speakers, or vice versa, depending on whether thought or language come first. Either way, I liked the idea of this culture of connectedness, that we are all a part of each other and of the whole, none of us alone as a rock or an island.

But the surprise came when we opened those big red three-ring binders to find them empty! What kind of a language book was this?? The answer to that question was that it was the kind of language book whose makers believed that spoken language comes before written. So every day, we would *listen* to the new lesson several times, in the form of a live conversation between two or more Tanzanian teachers, feeling, I suppose, just as a baby or toddler does, trying to get a gist of the conversation. Only then would we receive the printed text of the conversation along with notes on the sentence structure and grammar, which was then clearly expounded on by our European teacher. It was here that everything that Frida had taught me clicked into place. I loved it. But then Harrison remarked that I liked talking in any language more than he did.

During our orientation, the director of the campus had stressed to us the importance of *expecting the unexpected,* as we were guests in a foreign country and learning a new language. We had no idea of the relevance of that saying in our personal lives until one morning when we received an unexpected visit from Peter and Heather Candy, the MAF Dodoma program manager and his wife. Harrison had just returned from dropping the kids off at the international school, when we saw the MAF Land Rover pull in to the language school campus. When we saw Peter and Heather get out, we couldn't imagine why they were there on a weekday morning.

Their news was even more unexpected than their appearance. They had received a tragic message from America. Having no other means to send it to us, they drove the three hours from Dodoma to Morogoro to tell us. We were glad they did. It was good to receive the comfort of their presence and prayers.

My snowbird parents, Dad and Naomi, had been in a terrible car accident in Florida. It happened the night before they were to return to their home in Missouri. After Wednesday evening church in Ft. Meyers, a group of them went out to get a bite to eat as usual. On the way back home to Marco Island, the driver of an empty car-carrier semi-truck had lost his way and was making a U-turn on the highway when his engine stalled and died. Without headlights and empty of cars, his truck was not visible as the car carrying my parents and aunt and uncle sped along the four-lane highway. My father and uncle were seated in the front and Naomi and my aunt (Dad's sister, Ruth, giver of the single yellow roses to my mom) were riding in the back. All but my dad were wearing their seat belts. My aunt only uttered a few words before dying. Though Naomi made it to the operating room, the rupture in her aorta bled faster than the blood could be replaced. Dad and Uncle Art were banged up bad, but were alive and admitted to the hospital.

Peter and Heather could not relay any of this to us, because they had only received news via Uncle Arnie of a terrible accident without any details. Blessedly, they had already booked airline tickets for the five of us to return to the States. In an attempt to find out more news than just that there had been a bad accident, we went to the Morogoro Hotel to see if they could place a phone call to the States for us. Yes, they could, but it would be 400 USD. Cost prohibitive. Fortunately for us, the Smiths, friends of the same mission as our Baptist friends in Dodoma, had recently installed a way to make international calls without going through an operator. It was at their place in Morogoro that we were able to make contact with family in the States to find out the grim details. And still there were all the physical details in front of us to deal with before getting in the car to go to the airport in Dar Es Salaam – like our wet laundry hanging on the line, consisting of most of the clothes we had brought to language school with us. Harrison returned to the international school to pick up the kids. Everything became a blur.

Somehow we made it to Dar Es Salaam and onto the flight that night. Landing at O'Hare the following evening, we were met by Adam's wife. Adam, along with Jacob, several of Naomi's children, and some of Art and Ruth's seven children were already in Florida with Dad and Uncle Art. Though I hadn't been there to hear it, the recounting of it left just as big an imprint on me as if I were there – my uncle's statement the morning after the accident in which he lost his truly beloved wife, "I loved Jesus yesterday and I love Him more today than I did yesterday." Wow, Uncle Art kind of reminded me of what Job of old is recorded as saying when he tragically lost all his grown kids and all his earthly property: "The Lord gave and the Lord has taken away. Blessed be the Name of the Lord." (Job 1:21)

Leaving Harrison and the kids in the Midwest, where Naomi and Aunt Ruth's funerals were to be held, I flew to Florida to be with my dad in the hospital there. Uncle Art was well enough to make it to the funerals but Dad was not. When he was able to go, Adam and I traveled with him on a special medical flight from Fort Meyers hospital in Florida to Blessing Hospital in Quincy, Missouri. Not long after the funerals, Harrison and the kids flew back to Tanzania. I stayed with Dad for a few more weeks, tending to his needs in what had been his and Naomi's home in Missouri.

Before leaving to return to Tanzania, I helped move Dad from Missouri to the house outside of Wapello, where I had grown up and where Jacob, his wife and their sons were now living. I felt so torn and burdened leaving Dad there in his pain, but then a strange thing happened – driving down the lane, I felt comforted, like angels were present. I hoped they'd watch over Dad for me, too. Then I thought of the precious letter that I had received from Lizzie just days before, while I was caring for Dad in Missouri. She had begun the letter with *Do you not know, have you not heard?* (Isa.40:28) It had struck me funny because, being in her sweet first grade handwriting, I hadn't immediately recognized the author as Isaiah, and for a skinny second I thought she was about to tell me some important news from her little life in Morogoro! Thinking of it now as I was leaving Dad and heading back to Africa, I did know, and I had heard, and was comforted by the fact that Beauty's understanding is unfathomable and that he never gets tired or weary like I do.

~ ~ ~

Greeted by the familiar heavy blanket of hot humid air as I stepped off the plane in Dar Es Salaam, I thought back to eight-year-old Tobin's question one day as we came out of Blessing Hospital in Quincy, the hospital to which Dad's medical flight from Fort Meyers had delivered him. It was early April and spring was definitely in the air. Tobin, skipping a few steps, had asked me, "Mom, what is it about the air here that makes me feel like bouncing?!" As I collected my bag and headed out of customs and immigration to meet the most precious people in all the world to me, I felt like bouncing, too, in spite of the oppressive heat.

Together again as a family in Morogoro, I tried hard to make up for lost time in learning the language. And while Harrison and I labored away at the language, Cherith, Tobin, and Lizzie were swimming lengths of the beautifully clean pool at the International School in the other part of town. Not only did this school have an excellent academic program, it was here that our kids' swimming skills went from excellent to awesome, considering their ages. In fact, one morning while Harrison and I were in class for hours, we kept reminding each other, "They're *still* swimming!" Indeed, they were trying to see just how many meters they could swim, with the reward being a badge I would sew onto their beach towels. In an effort to keep up their energy, the staff would give them snacks at the end of the pool – snacks that they could receive and eat without stopping, such as a peeled banana. They had also been awarded swimming badges from their school in Dodoma for their incremental progress as they were learning to swim, but we were super proud of them here in Morogoro – 4,000 meters!!

We all considered our time in Morogoro as very worthwhile, in spite of the occasional bad food and the cold showers, which tiny little Lizzie had to work up a great deal of courage to step into. The friendships made, both in and outside the language school, were genuine at the time, even if we were only a'passing through. We were well-prepared and set to return to our normal Swahili life in Dodoma, one of our homes.

Lessons learned:

Expect the unexpected; uncertainty is certain.
There are no guarantees in this life.

11

Return to Dodoma

Becoming Acquainted with Disillusionment
1994 - 1997

Having experienced off-compound living, we were happy to return to the ease of living on the MAF compound. We were assigned to a different house than the one we had previously lived in, and this too, suited us fine. It was only a hundred feet to the hangar and on the opposite side of the compound from the swimming pool, which could become quite noisy at certain times, albeit the noise had never bothered us because it was always happy noise. Because we didn't break our trip from the States with an extended stay in England this time, we were able to bring our allowance of two fifty-pound suitcases per person with us. Harrison is gifted with excellent packing skills and we made the best use of our allotted space by packing such things as living room curtains.

For the other two houses that we had lived in here, I had bought material locally in Dodoma and stitched together curtains with the Viking sewing machine we had packed in our initial 4x4 box. It had been a trying experience, especially because while in-between shops, I had foolishly placed my purse on the front seat of the car. Leaving the door open, I went around the car and was busy strapping John in his car seat when someone grabbed my purse and ran, taking all the shillings that I had hoped to use to buy material for our curtains. But at least no crowd had seen the act, so the thief got away free. I was glad for that.

Actually being back in Dodoma seemed exactly as the saying painted on several of the local buses said – *Kama jana*. 'Like yesterday'. Indeed, it did seem like nothing changed here, that every day was just like the day before. But I guess that Africa is known for moving slowly, making change seem negligible. The contrast between the African culture and our Western culture shows up vividly in the word that Swahili uses to describe white people – *mzungu*. The *m* beginning the word indicates a living being, but the root of the word – *zungu* means *dizzy*. Apparently the Swahili world sees white people as going around in busy circles until they're dizzy! Standing back and looking at myself, it's clear they've got a point!

But I did feel that I had made the necessary adjustments when it came to taking time in relationships. I was able to warmly greet the surprise visits from Tanzanian friends at my door with the many questions beginning with *habari. The Lord He should be praised,* followed with inquiring as to how she is, how her children are, how her parents are, her home, her work, her everything and everyone I can think of. She would then reciprocate with the same questions to me. This could take a full five minutes. Only after having invited her in and served her chai with some more small talk were we able to move on to why she came. There was usually a reason. It rarely happened that there was not a request for something coming. Those rare times were really beautiful and worth being around for.

On the other hand, the truth is that too many times I failed. A seemingly endless stream of Tanzanians would *hodi* (a word called out to replace knocking at the door; the door is often simply a curtain, in our case a screen door) and tell me the *shida* (problem) of a sick wife, baby, parent, or other relative, the hospital or school wanting fees, their house falling in due to last night's heavy rain, or some other problem. Knowing the need was legit (except for the odd con artist now and then), I did not feel I could turn them away empty handed when I had it within my power to help, so I would find myself stomping, yes stomping, back to the bedroom where we kept our shillings, grab an adequate amount of them, and give them, less than graciously, into the patiently waiting hands. Though angry at I don't know what, I'd still feel bad, knowing that with the cheerless attitude in which I had just given, I had really missed Beauty's blessing. Love was not having its way.

Harrison had it much worse than I did. For whatever reason, everybody seemed to turn to him for everything. Not just the Tanzanians, but even the missionaries. I recall the time he got a request from a missionary nurse about a Tanzanian woman who was having difficulty getting pregnant and wanted to know if he could help. Harrison laughingly asked me exactly what kind of help did I think she was asking for!

Language school had definitely improved my Swahili. I was rewarded by Tanzanians telling me I was now *mswahili* (a Swahili person). I didn't miss the fact that the Tanzanians that knew Harrison best had always called him 'one of us.' Tanzanians and Harrison seemed to share a recognized mutuality that I felt was rare. That mutuality, it seemed, was even deeper than a shared language. I smile now as I remember Harrison crossing the hangar hand in hand with a Tanzanian mechanic, a common occurrence between same sexes, but not one that Harrison had been used to before arriving in Tanzania.

We were all six thrilled to have a puppy join us this term. She came from a litter born to the dog of our Baptist missionary friends in Morogoro. Chichi was an excellent dog, whose barking woke us one night to find a huge snake in our yard, and another night just as a burglar was breaking into our neighbor's house. Though our little yard was fenced to keep Chichi in, if anyone unsuspecting opened the gate, Chichi would rush out to chase anything in sight. More than once Harrison found himself burying stray (we hoped) cats after dark. Then there was the time that she killed a rooster. Now this rooster wasn't just any rooster. It had been given as a gift to the British single female engineer named Annie, who lived in a duplex just on the other side of our fence. She was a vegan who had become upset when Harrison and the Tanzanians were trying to kill a rat they found in the hangar. At her insistence, they let it go free. Annie's rooster being visible through the fence had driven Chichi nearly mad, so when she found her chance to fly through the gate, the rooster quickly met his demise. We were nearly worried sick about what Annie would say when she found out. But to our surprise, Annie laughed her always pleasant laugh and simply commented, "That's how God made dogs. Chichi was just doing what she was made to do." *Even Chichi doing what Beauty intended.* Whew, Annie's words were a blessed relief. Chichi was just doing what came natural to dogs to do.

Apparently Chichi was also made to take little girls for walks, because that's what she did with Lizzie. Though Lizzie was now six years old and could sure give Chichi a tongue lashing, she remained helpless at her end of the leash when she was trying to be nice and take Chichi on a walk outside of the compound. The rabbits that we had had for pets first term were more cooperative towards receiving Lizzie's love for them than was Chichi. But Chichi was more entertaining than the rabbits, especially at our Sunday lunches when we usually grilled chicken and ate outside. The kids liked to place a chicken bone on Chichi's nose and command her with, "Chichi, stay, stay, stay. . ." which she would actually do until someone would release her with, "Good girl!" – Chichi's permission to toss the bone off of her nose, catch it in the air and gobble it up. That was more of a challenge for her than simply catching in her mouth the bones they tossed up in the air.

Along with continuing to take my shifts of following the MAF pilots via radio communication, doing puppet shows, hospitality meals, school runs and the other usual routines of last term, I now taught an English class in the chai room of the hangar. Several of the Tanzanians had been asking me to do this, and now that I had more Swahili with which to do it, it seemed more feasible. I found this to be very rewarding and something that I truly loved doing. Not only was the teaching of language enjoyable, but the friendships formed with the Tanzanians made it really fulfilling.

Though we found many ways in which to serve Tanzanians, one particular moment stands out in my mind. MAF employed one gardener to take care of the grounds around the guest house and the other areas that weren't a part of our individual yards. This gardener's name was Simon and what a faithful worker he was! This particular day, I stepped out onto our veranda and heard a voice call my name, "Mama Tobin!" I didn't see anyone at first, and as he called again, I saw a glimpse of Simon through the tall fence of reeds that separated our place from the empty lot outside of the compound. He was working out there under the hot African sun to clear some brush away. He asked if he could have a drink of water. Eager to please him, I hurried into the house to get him a glass of ice water. As my hand forced the crunchy dry brown reeds apart to place the glass of water into his waiting hand, I was reminded of Jesus' words, *"And if anyone gives even a cup of cold water to one of these little ones who is my disciple, truly I tell you, that person will certainly not lose their reward."* (Mt. 10:42 NIV) In that moment, I felt that in the midst of all my busy serving, this act was perhaps the most significant thing I had done, and the one for which I would be most richly rewarded. So I was a little disheartened when I saw that my own culture had gotten in the way again! When I asked Simon if he would like another glass, he said (in Swahili), "Oh yes, but please don't put any ice in it. It's too cold!"

It wasn't for lack of trying that we continued to lack a full understanding of the culture we were living in. We had become good friends with a team of three missionary families who lived in a small rural village some distance outside of Dodoma. This team consisted of what we (and they) jokingly said was a Bible translator, a pastor, and another man who did all the work. The man who 'did all the work' did so in an effort to facilitate the other families being able to live there and effectively fulfill their roles. The village they worked in had an open well, and every year or so a child would fall in and tragically drown. With every death the village people, even in their mourning, would show their acceptance of this death by attributing it to the *kazi ya Mungu*. The work of God. None of the three, the pastor, the Bible translator, or the 'man who did all the work,' were able to change the thinking of the people – to give them an understanding of their responsibility to keep the well covered so that it would not be possible for a child to accidentally fall in. And thus, in our cultural thinking, Beauty was sorely misinterpreted.

Sometimes I just didn't know what else to do other than to scream. Like the late evening that we heard the screams of a woman being beaten in a house just outside of the compound, not far from where thirsty Simon had been clearing the brush. At first, though horrified, we recognized it as an accepted happening here, a part of life. But as the screams continued in spite of our prayers against the evil, I felt I had little control over myself as I went outside and, in my fury at that horrible man, yelled at the top of my lungs, "STOP that!!! Stop it NOW!!!" Mercifully, for whatever reason, it stopped. I do not claim to be the reason.

I've never really felt qualified to see myself as a real missionary. Real missionaries do not act like that. Someone who I do see as a real missionary told me a story recently that happened to her on the other side of the continent, in Ansongo, a rural village in the desert of Mali, West Africa. Here is her story as she relayed it to me, given to you here, with her permission:

Late one night I was awoken by loud, hysterical screaming. Over and over, I would hear a woman screaming behind my compound and then a desperate plea for Allah to be merciful. Since people seemed to be tortured most heavily at night by spirits, it was not completely unusual for this to occur. However, with it being RIGHT behind me, I couldn't escape the desperate hopelessness of this woman's cry. So, after what seemed like hours of listening to her screams, I prayed to the Lord, asking for the Holy Spirit to give me the gift of healing, just for this occasion, so that this woman could be delivered from her oppression. I quoted the scripture that Jesus himself quoted when teaching others why he had come, "He has sent Me to proclaim release to the captives, and recovery of sight to the blind, to set free those who are oppressed. . ." And, by faith, I claimed that anything I asked in the name of Jesus would be given to me, that anything I bind in heaven will be bound in heaven and anything I bind on earth will be bound on earth. In a sense, I was preparing myself for the battle I was all too familiar with. And, also, I was pushing back the doubt that came from multiple failed attempts to deliver those who are oppressed by demons. This time would be different. I would muster the faith to set this woman free! I would be strong in the face of my enemy by the power of the Holy Spirit and under the banner of the name of Jesus Christ. I put on my armor, so to speak, with my shield of faith and the sword of the Word, and marched in the direction of sounds that peeled through the desert night air, confident that the Lord would make Himself known as the One True God, and glorify Himself in this village. There was even a surge of excitement deep in my spirit.

As I approached the lady, I whispered the name of Jesus over and over, "Jesus, sweet Jesus, Mighty God, Jesus Christ." If my faith failed, then surely just the mention of His Name would make the demons shudder and flee. I knelt down beside her as she held her knees, rocking back and forth, whispering prayers to Allah. I asked her if she wanted to be set free. She looked at me with desperation and said, "Yes, Oh Allah, help me." I explained to her that Allah has a Son, who came to set her free and that if she cries out to Him, He will hear her prayer. She just kept rocking and repeating, "Allah, help me." I began praying over her and declaring the name of Jesus. . .Nothing. I prayed for healing and deliverance. . .Nothing. I spoke to the demons with authority. . .Nothing. I spoke in tongues, so that the Spirit could pray for me, knowing things I could never know. . .Nothing. I continued like this for over an hour, trying to persevere in prayer. . .Nothing. The sun began to come up, and I walked away, feeling defeated and confused.

Why? Why did He not heal her? Why did He not listen to our cries? Did He not love this woman more than I? Did He not desire to set those in bondage free? Why had He, well, failed?

The next night, the screams began again, but instead of going over there, afraid of making Jesus look like a fool (and myself, if I am honest), I silently lifted up a short prayer, "Heal her God, please!"

The next night, I listened for her screams, but nothing. I thought to myself, "Maybe He heard us. Maybe He set her free." With excitement, the next day I went to her house. Her niece informed me, "Oh, we finally raised enough money for the black goat as an offering. Then, the spirit left her. She is okay now and in her right mind. She left this morning to go back home." My heart sank. Satan had won! Whether God had healed her or not, by all human perception, it was the sacrifice of the black goat that healed this woman.

The questions became flying through my mind again. How could this be? Why would God not reveal Himself? Why would He not take the glory due His Name? Why would He make us all look like fools and leave the village to believe the Spirits have more power than Jesus?

There are a lot of reasons I can come up with- I didn't have enough faith, I don't have the gift of healing, I didn't persevere in my prayers, she didn't believe in Jesus, it wasn't His will, etc. The list goes on. But when it comes right down to it, is this whole worldly experience not just a training ground for His elect to learn and know about Him? And what have I learned? He does what He wants, when He wants, and how He wants. It does not depend on my prayers (although I am sure He is pleased with me asking) but on His good pleasure.

That is my friend Faith's story. My own story is simply that Beauty abounds everywhere, awesomely and too big to grasp, too big to even put our little minds around. Along with knowing, as the elderly lady sang in church, that vengeance is His, He will repay, I also know for sure that He won't be mocked (Gal. 6:7), nor will He share His Glory with another.[1] And, as Faith says, we are here for His pleasure. Pleasure – that's what my life verse is all about: *You will make known to me the path of life; In Your presence is fullness of joy; In Your right hand there are pleasures forever.* (Psalm 16:11) A pleasures forever seeker. That's the real me.

On the lighter side, it was during this term, too, that we found a way to get the braces on Cherith's teeth that the dentist in La Porte, Indiana had told us she needed. There was an orthodontist from Nairobi, Kenya, who flew to an office in Dar Es Salaam once a month to see any patients in Tanzania who were willing and able to come there. It worked out well because there were a few other MKs who also needed orthodontic work, so we would take our turns in driving the 'patients' down to Dar Es Salaam and sometimes stay at the beach, making a mini-vacation out of it. Trips to the capital city were always fun because there was often something new to see. One time we were so excited to find a fast food place modeled after KFC, but were disappointed to find, upon attempting to order, that they were out of chicken.

In 1996, Tanzania decided to change the capital from Dar Es Salaam on the coast to centrally located Dodoma. What this mostly meant was that when it was time for parliament meetings to be held, all the diplomats flew from Dar Es Salaam to Dodoma, pretty much guaranteeing that our small dusty city would have water and electricity available for those several days. But as for us on the MAF compound, we had a generator that would kick in with a welcome roar whenever the power went out.

Besides traveling to Dar Es Salaam for orthodontic appointments, and traveling to do the puppet shows and to show the *Jesus Film*, we also traveled simply for pleasure. Road trips were always long, bumpy, and often hazardous, but as a family we have good memories of spending the traveling hours listening to *Adventures in Odyssey* on cassette tape or else listening to me reading aloud children's classics such as *I Am David*, or *The Cay*.

On one of these trips, we came upon a tour bus that was stopped along the highway with engine problems. The tourists were standing in small groups along the ditch. We stopped to see if there was anything we could do to help. They said that they had a minibus on the way, but that not everyone would fit on it, so if we could take a few to the Tanzania/Kenya border it would be helpful. We had already picked up someone who had been in Morogoro language school with us and had walked to the main road looking for a ride just when we had come along! So we squeezed together and fit three of the tourists in along with us in MAF's Nissan Patrol, and headed to the border. As we began to chat together, we discovered that the couple we had picked up lived in Chesterton, Indiana and were customers of my brother Adam in Kouts, Indiana! When they returned home from their vacation, they went to Adam's tire store to tell him they had met his sister in Africa. My father happened to be in Indiana visiting Adam at the time, so they had a good time swapping stories of their trips to Africa. It's a small world after all.

On another road trip we drove to Nairobi, Kenya. Once in the city, I foolishly rolled my window down. We were stopped at a red light in thick traffic when, quick as a wink, a Kenyan boy reached in my window, and with a hard yank, grabbed the two gold chains from around my neck and ran. Just as quick, Harrison, after putting the Patrol into park, ran after him!! Everyone stopped to watch. Kenyan businessmen on the sidewalks began to encourage Harrison, "Get 'im!" As the young thief ran between the lanes of stopped cars, people began to open their car doors, forcing the boy to slow his running to avoid them. It didn't take Harrison long to catch the young man. He took my gold chains out of the boy's hand as a Kenyan man shouted his advice, "Hit him!" Harrison acknowledged the man's advice with, "No, I just wanted to get her gold chains back," and returned to the vehicle, put it in first gear and we moved on. The light was green now.

Having gold chains stolen off my neck in Nairobi didn't mess with my mind anything like having Cherith's colorful new bike stolen out of the locked shed next to our front door. Before leaving Rolling Prairie, Harrison had built another 4x4 box to ship to Dodoma. In it had been a very new, very colorful girl's bicycle that Cherith had received for Christmas. Now, every day as I returned from my afternoon bicycle ride, I would count the bikes in the shed before locking it. Bikes were a common thing to have stolen, so I just made a habit of counting them to make sure they were all there. 1,2,3,4,. . . .! There were only four! How could there be only four??Which one was missing? Cherith's – the prettiest one of them all! But how could it be? We kept the shed locked! The lock hadn't been tampered with at all.

Thus began a long saga of questioning, in which the village chief of Niko, our new gardener, became involved and Niko ended up in prison! We were dumbfounded. Though we had not known him long, our whole family was very affectionate of Niko. We had certainly never intended for him to be in prison – and it was our fault! Lizzie, in particular, struggled with this, often crying over the injustice done to Niko. We told the authorities that we wanted the charges dropped – that they should release Niko. They said that we couldn't do that; we must prosecute. During this time we visited

Niko often in prison, taking him soap, which was all that we were allowed to bring. Finally one of the Tanzanian aircraft mechanics that Harrison worked with went as a liaison for us and was able to get Niko released. The thing that we found really amazing about all of this was Niko himself. Though wrongly accused, he never showed even a trace of resentment towards us throughout the whole affair. And he came back to work, with his same unusual cheerful energy as before, as though nothing at all had gone wrong. Inexplicable, thanks be to Beauty!

What did happen to the bike is a really disturbing story of mind-blowing proportions, causing one to doubt their own sanity. A story best forgiven and forgotten.

It might have been about this time that Cherith caught me, at the pool, reading *Disappointment with God*, by Philip Yancey. It was a book I had found lying on Naomi's kitchen table in Missouri when I had been there, caring for Dad after the car accident. Naomi and I had shared a love of good books. I never think of *I Heard the Owl Call My Name* without thinking of her, perhaps the most godly seasoned woman I have ever known. But still, I have to admit that I was very surprised to see a book with this title lying on her table, apparently new and unread. And now, here I was, reading it and finding it very helpful – and timely, as all my illusions of missionary life seemed to be falling away. But when Cherith saw it and read the title aloud, I felt a little trapped when she looked at me in honest surprise and asked, "Mom, how can anyone be disappointed with God??" *How indeed?*

In spite of my disillusionment, or maybe because of it, I'm not sure, there were times that, as I walked wearily along the two hundred feet of dusty, loosely graveled MAF compound drive, leading from our gate to the main MAF gate where the guard shack stood, in my mind I pictured myself as whirling and twirling the entire length, ballerina style, exuberant with great joy. There was no rhyme or reason for when this would happen and I never had an explanation for why it happened when it did. It might just be, as Adam tells me occasionally even today, that I'm just not right in the head. Perhaps.

Adam's description of me might also help explain why the tiny colorful bird that I found lying, apparently injured, at the sink on the far end of the second floor balcony overlooking the hangar, mattered so deeply to me. I honestly have no idea why it affected me as it did, but I think it secretly had something to do with me, wondering if Beauty really saw this little bird, if He cared about its helpless plight, and if He really did see me here so far away from home and to what purpose? Unable to see how anything I could do would help this beautiful little creature, I walked away, desperately hoping that when morning came, it would see the light and be able to fly away on its own.

When I found time the next day to check, the bird was gone. But still I didn't know, did it fly away, or had someone disposed of its dead body without a thought? In my not knowing, I wasn't very comforted.

My friend and prayer partner, the same Heather who came to Morogoro to tell us about my parents' car accident, put a spin on my experiences that was quite different from my brother Adam's perspective of me. It happened at one of our prayer times, sitting in the shade of our front veranda. I was telling her about our recent family vacation to Mombasa on the Kenyan coast. I told her that when we finally arrived, it was near evening. The kids put on their swimsuits and headed for the beach, as Harrison laid down to rest after the exhausting drive, and I began to unpack our clothes to settle in for the week. When I reached a stopping point, I decided to check on the kids just outside the sliding glass door of our hotel room. As I slid the door open, stepped out into the salty wet breeze and headed across the sand, I looked up and stopped in my tracks. There before me lay the most precious beauty I had ever seen. A humongous full moon was rising, hanging low over the waves of the Indian Ocean. At the near edge of those waves were the very most precious children in all the world, my joys in life – busily working together in harmony to build a sand castle. It was absolutely perfect. So why did, at that very moment, a huge sadness well up within me? A sadness too overwhelming for words, too great for tears.

"Oh, don't you know?" replied Heather. "Haven't you heard? That is our deep human ache – our primordial longing to return to the Paradise we were made for!" *Ah, yes. That's exactly what it was. And I far preferred this explanation. Thank you, Heather, my prayerful friend.*

Our many camping trips, though very fun and good for memory-making, were decidedly less idyllic than the beach scene. There was always the possibility that the lions, elephants or other awesome beasts that we could hear in the night would decide they didn't have regard for us or our tent. Then there were the African killer bees who attacked Harrison as we were packing up to leave our camp site in Buigiri, on the fortress up the hill in the same place where Tobin had had his birthday party wiener roast. The kids and I had already taken most of the camping equipment down the hill and put it in the Land Rover, where we were waiting on Harrison to come with the last load. Suddenly Tobin yelled, "WOW! Look at Dad running down the hill!" It was true; he was running pell-mell down the rugged path, not carrying anything with him. As he got closer, we gasped. There appeared to be a million bees surrounding him as he ran to the Land Rover and jumped in! We quickly rolled up our windows and used our flip flops to kill whatever bees we could as they landed. But there were too many and we couldn't roll our windows down even as we drove away, no longer caring about the remainder of our camping gear. A large swarm of bees continued to circle the Land Rover as we headed out the red dirt road of Buigiri towards the main road!

Harrison was not one to go to the doctor. He had only had shorts on when he had thrown out some water over the fort's edge, thus inadvertently disturbing the few, who had then quickly called the many to their defense. At home we counted at least twenty-five angry welts on his torso alone, not to mention his face, neck and extremities. He believed he would be okay and got up the next morning and went to the hangar to work as usual, in spite of his severe headache, fever and nausea. The wonderful kind British missionary doctor who had looked after Cherith and her synovitis got wind of Harrison's harrowing weekend experience. He came to the hangar to firmly tell him that these African bees are known to kill cattle and commanded him to go home right now, go to bed, and let us care for him. He did.

Missionaries are wonderful people. We surely could not have made it without them. Without their knowledge, without their strength, without their healing touch. I could only hope that I would have their same effect as I sat across from one of my dearest and best missionary sisters, and listened to her heart. Since becoming a missionary she wasn't sure she any longer believed in God, at least God as she had thought Him to be. I was stunned and really didn't know what to say, so I just kept listening and didn't say anything. It wasn't like I couldn't relate at all. My own disillusionment had brought me, much to Cherith's chagrin, a certain disappointment with Him. Still, though my view of Christianity itself had weakened considerably, I had never, even for a skinny second, doubted the existence of Beauty Himself. Little could I know that, many windows from now in the years to come, that skinny second *would* appear, and as in my dear friend's case, be missionary-induced. But sitting here now, in silence, continuing to listen to her heart, I was so relieved to hear that she still believed in Beauty. The real God. The God Who *is* Love. I felt weak with relief and thanked Beauty with all of my heart.

Then there was the missionary pilot who had a vision or a dream, I forget which he told me it was. He saw me in a very dark place. But he didn't actually see me. He only saw a house in the darkness and in the window of the house was a light, and without actually seeing me, he knew that I was there, inside that window. A light house in a dark place. An apt description of the very place where my skinny second of disbelief would occur. Though here, at this Dodoma window, neither the pilot nor I had even the faintest idea what it could be about.

~ ~ ~

Because my father phoned occasionally, we weren't necessarily expecting the special news that this certain call contained. When I told the kids at dinnertime that Grandpa was going to get married again, Lizzie immediately exclaimed, "Oh, no! More cousins!!" Lizzie, not being able to remember life before Africa at all, had been totally confused when we had returned to the States for our first

155

furlough. She could not begin to understand who were real cousins, who were step-cousins, who were both (Uncle Kent and Aunt Jan's kids!), and who were simply the children of our good friends. To her, it was an overwhelming perplexity, and now it was to become more complicated yet! That was how it looked to her, but to us – we were just thankful that Beauty had so restored Dad's body and soul that he could add a third wife to his story. Dad's journey had been richly blessed by Mary Elizabeth, Naomi Elizabeth, and now it was time for Ruth Marie to take his hand.

As was common in our home church culture, Dad and Ruth had known each other for many years. In fact, Naomi and Ruth were first cousins. (We didn't bother telling Lizzie this.) William, Ruth's first husband, had had Parkinson's disease for many years, and Ruth, being a nurse, had cared for him up to the end. Sometimes on a Sunday afternoon, Dad and Naomi would stay with William, freeing Ruth to go to the afternoon church service. William had passed away shortly before the car accident that had taken Dad's wife, Naomi, and his sister, Ruth, home. Dad's new wife-to-be, had, and has, four children, all married with children of their own. They and we were very happy for this union of our aging parents.

Soon after their marriage, Dad and Ruth came to visit us in Tanzania. It was a joy to have them, and we considered it an honor to be included as a part of their honeymoon. Because Dad had been to Tanzania earlier, he loved showing Ruth what he knew and delighted in picking fresh bananas from one of our trees every morning after getting dressed.

We went on several safaris together with them, one being to visit our houseworker Monica's husband's church in Mpwapwa, where they gave Harrison the dubious privilege of preaching extemporaneously. Shortly after arriving to Mpwapwa, Ruth expressed a need to go to the bathroom. Watching her head down the footpath in the direction of the makeshift outhouse, whose thin boards didn't always meet, Lizzie giggled and said, "Oh boy. Grandma's going to experience an African toilet!" Later, after her experience, Grandma and we all laughed together as she relayed her confusion as to how to go about the process with what was provided, a hole in the ground and an empty tin can. We laughed and laughed, Grandma laughing most of all. We were thankful to have her here with us and Grandpa.

Another day, we were having lunch at a game park restaurant. I should say we were *trying* to have lunch. We had ordered it at least an hour before and were still waiting for it to be served when the waitress reappeared to our table and announced to Ruth in English, "The chicken is finished." Ruth looked confused, as though she wondered why the waitress didn't just bring it to her if it was finished. Before she had time to articulate her confusion, we quietly explained to her that in this situation '*finished*' meant '*out of*' – there was no chicken available to prepare the meal she had ordered, and thus she was being asked to make another choice. Laughing, Ruth asked if she could see the menu again. We were glad we were enjoying each other's company and weren't in a hurry to eat. Maybe if we sat long enough, the Colobus monkeys that we were hoping to see would grace us with their appearance.

The other visitors we had this second term in Dodoma were Twila and Christina. Twila was a very dear lifelong friend of mine, having grown up with me in Oakville Sunday School. Our real connection had taken place when we were both working in the University of Iowa Hospital and Clinics – she as a respiratory therapist, I as a nurse, both of us as members of our home church culture. In other words, both of us a part of the world *and* of our separatist church. Coming to visit us in Tanzania, she brought along a close Korean friend of hers I had never met. This Korean friend turned out to not only bless us but our whole compound with her absolutely amazing ability on the piano. Not only did she bless us with her playing, but she labored hours at tuning the old upright piano we had gotten from some missionaries who were returning to Canada.

Like Harrison had done some years before with his father and then with his sister, Jan and her family, Twila, Christina and I flew on a MAF plane out to visit the Maasai tribe on the Malambo safari. Afterwards, instead of returning to Dodoma, the MAF pilot flew us to the Ngorogoro Crater and left us there. And from then on, all the details of the adventures we had before returning to good, safe Dodoma could fill a small book of their own!

Nor do time and space permit me to tell of all the other Hodel happenings in our second term in Dodoma, Tanzania – of being a cook for Cherith's class on an overnight trip to Hombolo dairy farm and accompanying Tobin's class camping trip as the evening speaker. Sending twelve-year-old Cherith, the last native English speaker left in her local class, off to Kenya to attend eighth grade at Rift Valley Academy, of going to visit her there only to be told by her dorm mom that she had gone to Hell's Gate but would be back soon. Harrison bungee jumping from a bridge in Zambia just after we, along with some good friends, survived rafting the Zambezi River beneath Victoria Falls, and of many other such things, all good.

Alas, too soon, our years in Tanzania reached their fulfillment. We left Chichi with some other missionaries who were very excited to have her, and left John with his paternal aunt who was not so excited, making this an extremely difficult situation to say the very least. We choked back tears of love and sadness as the small MAF plane carrying us to Nairobi circled over the Dodoma airport and hangar one last time, to see that the Tanzanians and missionaries who had been there to see us off were in some formation. As they waved their arms, we tried our best to make it out until we could distinguish the letters, *B-Y-E*. We knew what they meant. *Goodbye* in Swahili is *kwaheri. Go with blessing.* We were loved.

Though we live in a much easier day and age than David Livingstone and had only been a few short years in Africa so far, I could still resonate with the speech he gave at Cambridge University in 1857:

> *People talk of the sacrifice I have made in spending so much of my life in Africa. . . .Away with the word in such a view and with such a thought! It is emphatically no sacrifice. Say rather it is a privilege. Anxiety, sickness, suffering, or danger now and then with a foregoing of the common conveniences and charities of this life may make us pause and cause the spirit to waver and the soul to sink; but let this only be for a moment. All these are nothing when compared with the glory which shall be revealed in and for us. I never made a sacrifice.*

On our flight back to the States, we stopped in Germany to visit our friends who had worked at the blind school in Buigiri for years before returning to Germany. Then we went on to Holland to visit two sets of dear friends: First, a couple who had been fellow Moody students in Tennessee and who had worshiped with us at Little Doe Freewill Baptist Church, the Dutch husband alternating at the pulpit with Harrison on Wednesday evenings. Secondly, a Dutch couple with whom we had worked in Dodoma and who now had newborn twins, a tiny girl and boy, Inge and Tom.

Lessons Learned:

Let God do what only He can do – that is,
save the lost, unbind the bound, and heal the sick.
Simply do what He gives me to do.

12

Goodfield, Illinois

The Next Step Outlined
Spring/Summer 1997

S now in April doesn't thrill many, but it sure thrilled the few – specifically Cherith, Tobin and Lizzie when they woke up our first morning in our second perfect little furlough home in the tiny town of Goodfield, Illinois, population of 686. They *oohed* and *aahed* out the window at the still falling snow, and after quickly eating the American cereal so kindly provided in our stocked kitchen, hurried outside for this, their rare opportunity to play in the snow. The first snow that Lizzie could ever remember was on our first furlough when we had gone on a trip out West with Dad and Naomi in their new motor home. It was summer and when we had stopped at Pikes Peak in the Rocky Mountains to throw a few snowballs, Lizzie had been disappointed. Forming her snowball, she said, "But it's so. . .so. . .*cold*, and so. . .so. . .*hard*." But there was no disappointment in this April snowfall in Goodfield. Its soft, fluffy flakes falling like powder on the ground were enchanting – to our kids, if not to the townspeople and the local farmers who were more than glad to see it all disappear in a day or so.

Goodfield was only six or seven miles from the city of Eureka, where we found out there was an excellent summer swim team program. The coach welcomed our kids, agreeing to let them join the summer team, though it was usually made up of students with whom he had worked during the school year. So it was really fun to watch his joy when he saw that these three new members of his team could swim like fish. He got almost beside himself with excitement at the first swim meet, watching Tobin compete. Pacing the side of the pool, he came upon Lizzie, also cheering for Tobin and gleefully shouted, "Look at that boy! Just look at him go! That's your brother, Lizzie, look at your brother go – just look how fast he is!!!"

It was also in Eureka that we went to the Pizza Hut to enjoy pizza not made by my hands, a true pleasure for me especially. (Although Tobin didn't know why I kept saying, "Mmmm" so often while eating it; he said he preferred what I made because it didn't have 'so much stuff' on it, like this one did.) An unusual thing happened while we were there. We hadn't been seated long before a stranger walked up to the table and said to me, "Excuse me, but I think you're my sister." Well, I wasn't sure just what to say and he could see that, so he laughed and introduced himself as Bill, oldest son of my father's third wife, one of my new step-brothers.

"Ooh! Bill!" I said, laughing. "But how did you know who I was?"

He explained that he knew through his mom that we were back in the States and living in Goodfield, and when he saw us here in the Pizza Hut he immediately thought it must be us, but he wasn't sure. When he saw us say hello to another couple that he also knew, he went to that couple and asked if we were the Hodels. Given the affirmative, he headed to our table, ready with the unusual statement of, "Hello. I think you're my sister."

As it turned out, 'Uncle' Bill became an avid supporter of our kids at their swim meets, sometimes taking us all out to a Dairy Queen afterwards to celebrate.

Before school was out for the summer the Goodfield Elementary School asked us to come do a presentation on Africa for the students. We did. Then when the school year ended, the neighborhood kids befriended ours. One Saturday afternoon we had plans to go, as we did some weekends, to Indiana to spend time with family and friends at Faith Evangelical Bible Church, our main supporting church. So when our kids had to come home because it was nearing time to leave, one of them announced to their friends, "We have to go home now because we're going to Indiana this weekend."

"Indiaaana??" said one of the friends with a kind of awe in their voice, "What's it like there?"

Unsure how to answer such a question, our MK shrugged and said, "I dunno. Pretty much like here, I guess."

Encouraged that the school had asked us to come and that others in town seemed interested to know about regions beyond, we decided to hold a meeting at the town's community center to share our life and work in Tanzania. We made fliers announcing the date, time, and venue, and the five of us passed them out to every house in Goodfield. There was a church from our home culture in Goodfield; between the townsfolk and the church members, about thirty guests showed up and we had a lovely evening together. At least, we hoped they did, too.

It was so wonderful living a normal life here in Goodfield, an easy place for Grandpa Hodel to stop by often. He had recently been diagnosed with a slow-acting leukemia, which the doctors told him likely wouldn't affect him for at least ten years. His response to this was to say that in ten years it would be time to die anyway, so he didn't see a problem. Anyway, we made good use of the time we had with him now, the many spontaneous trips to Busy Corner restaurant, where Grandpa introduced Tobin to root beer and cottage cheese, two of his own favorites. We also thoroughly enjoyed the fun opportunity to do normal things with good friends, like going together to watch an excellent performance of *Joseph and the Amazing Technicolor Dreamcoat* at Illinois Central College.

Strange that during this time of normalcy, as I continued with my normal pre-reading mantra of, *Beauty, show me myself and my sin, my Savior and His salvation, souls and my service*, He did – by pointing out to me, good obedient girl that I am, that I had a lot in common with the unforgiving brother of the prodigal son! It came as a big surprise to me, making me ever so much more thankful for *my Savior and His salvation!*

Another strange experience during this time of blessed normalcy came about during the afternoon service, as we were visiting the church on the prairie where Harrison had grown up. I had sat down-stairs in the main assembly for the morning service, but because I had so enjoyed the wonderful fellowship over the lunch hour, I had overdone it and both Harrison's sister and I were late getting in for the afternoon service. We headed up to the balcony in hopes of our late entrance being less noticeable. From our perch there in the balcony I looked down at the sea of dark suits filling the right half of the church, the men's side of that big assembly room. Something about that mass of orderly dark suits struck me as not being real, that it was an illusion – some kind of illusion of permanency that was false, though secure. I whispered something of the sort to my sister-in-law, Jan. I don't know if what I whispered made any sense or not. She only looked at me and said nothing, but I felt she understood.

Other more minor, strange things took place, like the kids asking from the back seat, "How many kilometers is it to Grandpa and Grandma's?" Kilometers? Since when do our American kids think in kilometers? We knew the answer to our question, but couldn't yet know the ramifications – *when they're no longer truly American.* The other strange-to-us question they continued to ask was if we were sure the water was okay to drink. This had been happening since the first time we had arrived back in the States – actually, on our way to the States in the Heathrow airport in London, where they encountered their first public drinking fountain.

* *

Not long after Cherith had convinced us to let her go off to boarding school at Rift Valley Academy (RVA) in Kenya, Harrison had gone to an aviation meeting in Nairobi. Since RVA was only fifty-some kilometers northwest of Nairobi, Harrison went to visit Cherith when he had finished his aviation meeting. Though visiting her was his primary reason for going, he also had an ulterior motive. He met with Roy Entwistle, the superintendent, to ask if there was any chance that he and I could become a part of the school staff. Roy assured him that he was confident there was a very good chance of that. Thus began the process of us switching from working with Mission Aviation Fellowship to becoming a part of Africa Inland Mission (AIM). MAF sent us off with their blessing, AIM welcomed us with open arms, and our beloved and devoted supporters at home backed us all the way. The next step was to spend a few weeks at AIM's orientation at their U.S. headquarters in Pearl River, New York, to ensure that we were a good fit for AIM's work at Rift Valley Academy.

There were quite a few of us candidates that year, perhaps fifty, plus the children of the married candidates. It was an intense time, but worthwhile, and something that we realized after the fact would have been very helpful before heading to Africa the first time. A few things that stand out in my mind, as I look back at this window, are the testimonials of how Beauty had led us individually and as couples to this place, the Muslim with whom we had the most intense session of all, and the fun we had with our kids at a Yankees game and going to the Macy's 4th of July fireworks.

All of us had meals together in a big dining room. After the meal, a few previously assigned individuals would share their testimonies until everyone had had a chance to do so. There was a fascinating variety of paths that had brought us together. When it was my turn, I really wanted to emphasize the truths and wisdom of Solomon[1] – how I felt I couldn't begin to understand how I had gotten here, that I couldn't even have begun to plan such a thing, but that it was meant to happen and did happen – apart from anything I understood.

The session on the foundations of Islam was intended to give us a good understanding of what we would potentially encounter when talking with Muslims about their faith. And did it ever! Looking back, I could sum up what I learned by saying that what we would encounter was the problem of ourselves! This gentleman, in his white gown and Muslim cap, was soft-spoken and articulate in his firm beliefs. He continually praised Allah at every mention of his name, affirming that the true God is One, unique, incomparable, with no son nor partner, and none has the right to be worshiped but him alone. He was quietly adamant that no one shares his divinity, nor his attributes, quoting Quran 112:1-4: Say, "He is God, the One. God, to Whom the creatures turn for their needs. He begets not, nor was He begotten, and there is none like Him." Well, in contrast with his calm assurance, we students began to get hot under the collar as some refuted his Holy Quran with our Holy Bible, each immovable in our confidence of owning the truth. Imagine our utter surprise, when this holy man reached up, pulled off his Muslim cap, smiled and introduced himself as an AIM missionary who ministered to Muslims in the Detroit area! It's hard to pinpoint an exact emotion among the several that I experienced simultaneously at his revelation, but one thing I knew for sure. That was an unforgettable session!

What made the biggest impression on me at both the Yankees game and the Macy's fireworks was the massive size of the crowds of humanity! Though the overwhelming number of humans in one place struck me at both places, it was the behavior in particular of the crowd at the Yankees game that I remember. It kept us so shocked and entertained that we had to remind each other to watch what was happening way down there on the field where they were playing baseball! The thought I remember striking on my mind in the midst of the crowd of two million, even as we were trying to *get to* the fireworks, had to do with the immenseness of Beauty, how He could really love each and every one of these people just as much as He loved me. Impossible as it seemed, I had no doubt that He did. And for that, I was extremely thankful, because just then our three kids and a friend they had made at orientation got into a taxi where there was no room for any more people – and the taxi driver drove away, to take them as close to the fireworks as cars could go! I wondered if I would ever see them again on this earth??

Luckily, we managed to get into another taxi before the kids were out of sight and hurriedly told the driver, "Follow that taxi!!" But inevitably, we soon lost that particular taxi amongst the hundreds of others all trying to get to the same spot! When we got to that spot, where traffic was blocked from going further, we got out, walked a few blocks as one with the throngs of humanity and as we neared State Street, there they were! Cherith, Tobin, Lizzie and their friend, Eric. Unbelievable. Life before the days of cell phones.

* *

One day, soon after we were safe and sound back in Goodfield, Harrison and Tobin came home from shopping in Peoria and had a surprise for me – a shiny new green Cannondale mountain bike! I'm ashamed to say that in spite of my lifelong love of biking, my first reaction was one of chastising Harrison for spending the money. I'm more ashamed of that reaction now than I was then, because now I know the awesome places that bike took me. I remember especially the week-long ride through south-central Kenya with a group of junior and senior high school students, though sandy sisal fields, slick hilly highways, and open savannah where we could feel the giraffes' feet vibrating the ground beneath our tires as they ran away, after having watched our approach from the distance in wonder.

This time as we made our preparations to live in Kenya for the next four years, Harrison and his brother, Herbert, built several plywood boxes and we took everything that we thought could be useful in establishing the dormitory home where we would be living with twelve fifth- and sixth-grade boys – including a used Nintendo PlayStation, donated carpet remnants, two couches and a love seat, an American washer and drier, stove, mattresses, and more, including, of course, my new bike. When all was ready, Harrison and Herbert took it all to a local trucking company, who delivered it to a freight forwarding company in Chicago.

What we didn't know was that, after paying the price upfront, our shipment would sit in a warehouse until early November, at which time we found out the freight forwarding company had filed bankruptcy and our freight wasn't going anywhere. With our mission's help, we then contacted a mission-based freight forwarder who collected our freight from Chicago, consolidated it with other missionaries' freight and put it on the high seas – in time to reach us in February 1998. Unfortunately, we had to pay the full price to both companies.

Lesson Learned:

All that God really requires of me is simply what is good,
that is -
to act justly and to love mercy
and to walk humbly with Him.[2]

13

Kijabe, Kenya

Spurring One Another on Towards Love and Good Works
1997 - 2001

As I now see it, a boarding school for missionary kids is the most well-intentioned institution possible. When we had left for Africa with our children, ages three, five, and seven, Harrison and I had told ourselves that we would never send them to boarding school because they were the precious gifts that Beauty had given us to raise, not to be given away for others to raise. This was one of our lessons in *Never say never*. When the time was right, we like countless others before us, sent our firstborn off to boarding school in another country. When we filled out Cherith's application for admission to Rift Valley Academy, the admissions advisor told us that if there was any chance that we would eventually be sending our other two children, we should also apply now for their admission, because the waiting list was very long and people were applying years in advance for when their children would be old enough or ready to come. We did so with dread in our hearts. And then Beauty rewarded us by sending all the rest of our family to RVA as well, including Harrison and me. You've got to love Beauty's surprises!

Rift Valley Academy functions as a well-oiled machine. As stated on its website: *The academy, a branch of Africa Inland Mission International, exists to provide a quality education in a nurturing environment for the children of missionaries serving in Africa. With over 100 years of rich history, RVA has played an instrumental role in the lives of countless MKs (missionary kids). The current student body of nearly 500 includes more than 20 different nationalities. The families these students represent serve with 80 mission organizations in over 20 African countries.*

We arrived to Kijabe at the same time as El Nino. It basically rained, even poured, from when we got there through Christmas. This was quite a contrast with our life in dry, dusty Dodoma, where it almost never rained. The rare times it did, the compound kids had all gone outside and danced in it while it lasted, which generally wasn't long, and the sun would be out strong again. So it was the reverse that I saw happening out my window here – whenever the sun would break through the clouds for a few minutes, I would see the young mother of the dorm neighboring ours go outside and lift her face and arms to the sky. Then I would join her, soaking in the sun's rays while they lasted.

As we were preparing our shipment in Goodfield, we had anticipated its arrival in Kenya by September as the school year was beginning. Its delay made for months of unadorned living in a new stone dormitory-home mansion in the bleak atmosphere of El Nino. Not only was this a little depressing to us, but it also was to the twelve fifth- and sixth-grade boys living with us, as they compared our dorm to those of the other more settled career missionaries. One of the boys in particular asked almost daily if we had heard anything about our shipment. Oddly enough, during these stark, seemingly unending rainy days, a tune kept playing through my mind, the words of its chorus being, *He's all I need, He's all I need, Jesus is all I ne-ee-ed.* This caused me to reflect on the degree to which I could take Jesus' words literally when He told His disciples not to worry about even the basics.[1]

Our roles at RVA were many and varied. The initial and primary role that we shared with our own children was that of being dorm parents, or as it were, a dorm family – Uncle Harrison, Aunt Pam, big sister Cherith, big brother Tobin, and twelve boys of various nationalities the same age as sister Lizzie. It was a good set-up and we were very happy to be there, welcoming other children into our family. At least I was. I assumed everyone else was.

The only thing was that I couldn't get it in my head that we were back in Africa, because nothing about it had an African feeling to me. For one thing, it wasn't hot. At an altitude of 5,700 feet, it was cool. Plus the large stone building we lived in was even colder; sometimes we actually went outside into the cool just to warm up! And though it was cold and empty, our home was spacious and beautiful and new. A friend from Dodoma, stopping by to see our new place as they were leaving their daughter off for the school year, noted that my bedroom closet here was the size of my kitchen in Dodoma!

Along with that, the campus was large enough and American enough that I couldn't see Africa, apart from the African workers. And in the dorm, we had quite a few Korean boys who tended to speak Korean amongst themselves, making me feel more like I was in Korea than in Africa! But at the edge of the campus where it opened up onto the vast Great Rift Valley, the beauty was absolutely stunningly breathtaking, whether it was Africa or anywhere else. As one missionary put it, waving out into the immensity, "You just know God's somewhere right there."

We didn't know, during our El Nino start, that every student arrival day at the beginning of each new school term seemed to be rainy. We wondered if it was God sharing in the tears of the students and their parents as they parted from each other. These partings were no small sacrifice and painful even to watch. Some, both parents and their children, handled it better than others, but even the ones who didn't openly demonstrate their grief shed tears in the night, sometimes in my arms, and sometimes alone in their beds. And the scene of our Hebrew dorm boy calling out after his father, "Abba! Abba!" left an indelible imprint on my mind.

If I thought our home had been an open thoroughfare for children in Dodoma, I was about to find out that was nothing when compared to this life at RVA, where every day was filled from early morning until bedtime with action! Some of it was self-induced, because we wanted to be involved in it all – not only dorm life, but Caring Community, class sponsors, teaching Sunday School, interim trips with the junior and senior high students, Outreach, and more. So it came as a relief to me when one of Lizzie's friends announced to her in the midst of it all, "Lizzie, your family is such a family family!" It gave me hope that, in taking care of others, I was not neglecting my own flesh and blood.[2]

The system of sharing mission vehicles among the missionaries wasn't practiced here, as it was when we were with MAF in Dodoma. Not long after arriving, Harrison and another missionary new to Kenya began looking for vehicles. Because the used vehicles coming into the country were over-priced and, though polished up, were not mechanically sound, Harrison decided to import a new vehicle since, at the time that he ordered it, new vehicles were allowed into the country duty free through the mission.

In the meantime, a generous Canadian missionary who was going on home assignment agreed to let us use their family's blue Mitsubishi Pajero while they were away. Even though we had been thoroughly warned about the increasing frequency of carjackings, Harrison and Tobin were not expecting to encounter one so soon. Not long after they had left the RVA campus midmorning for an appointment in Nairobi, four men with pistols leapt out of the brush from either side of the gravel road and into the path of the Pajero. Spontaneously, Harrison gunned the vehicle, aiming towards the man most in center of the road. All four men fled and Harrison and Tobin continued safely on, shaken and without an immediate means of letting others know of the danger. When they reached a police post at the end of the road, in hopes that it wasn't syndicated, they stopped and reported the incident. And as soon as they reached Nairobi, they found a phone to call back to RVA to warn any others who may have had plans to travel that day.

Soon after we got our own Nissan Patrol in the fall of '98, we joined a northern safari that had been planned by some AIM missionaries who lived in the north of Kenya for many years. We were one of about ten vehicles traveling in convoy which, at least part of the time, was necessary to be safe from bandits. During the days of travel, we experienced water falls, sliding on sand dunes, digging for gemstones, and driving through wide, dry river beds. In one of them, the locals had hand-dug a deep well, and as they lifted the buckets of water from hand to hand up the stair-stepped sides of the well, they sang in beautiful African harmony.

When evening approached we would stop and set up camp. Each family pitched their own tent and cooked their own meals. After crossing the Chalbi desert, we reached the home of missionaries, Dilly and Ruth Andersen, in Kalacha. A concrete reservoir tank served as a great swimming pool, and a cobra guarded the tool shed against thieves. While swimming in the tank-turned-pool, Tobin lost a contact lens and it was found for him by someone else in the pool! Those are three of the things that stand out among many others in my memories of Kalacha.

But all that was life apart from our regular day jobs at RVA! Shortly after arriving and settling into dorm parenting, Harrison began helping to get RVA set up with the very technology that his fellow Moody student had excitedly told him about only ten years earlier – the Internet! Later on, they would talk about fiber optics, but at this time they were only installing dialup Internet.

Eventually, Harrison became the school's Director of Services. This consisted of overseeing all the non-academic departments, including: building maintenance of sixty-some buildings; the cafeteria where grades 7-12 ate all their meals and grades 1-6 ate most of their meals; care of the sixty-plus acres of grounds; the student health services, including a small infirmary with a few beds for students who were sick enough to require overnight stays; hiring and firing for the 110 national employees and overseeing their payroll; laundry for the 400 boarding students but not the 'station kids,' who, like ours, lived with their own parents; purchasing requisitions for the non-academic supplies required to keep the school running; security, which turned into a really big deal after 9/11; and the purchasing and maintaining the school's busses used for sports, music and other school events, plus maintenance on the missionaries' private vehicles.

Just typing the list makes me tired. It's clear to see – if I had thought that everyone turned to Harrison in Dodoma for help, it was certainly magnified many times over here. Fortunately, here in Kenya he learned that, not only did you not have to, but you weren't expected to meet anyone's entire need. The answer to the frequently asked question of, "How can you help me?" could be satisfied with whatever amount was given. Every little bit was helpful and the recipient went away seemingly satisfied. I learned through example that the answer to, "How can you help me?" could even be with a caring prayer. Perhaps most of all.

Nevertheless, I watched Harrison come home every evening or sometimes after dark, increasingly exhausted, not from the actual service he was meant to be providing for the school – that he enjoyed – but spent from the steady stream of needs too big to be handled.

On the brighter side, my own day job was teaching Swahili. It was offered as one of three high school foreign language options – the other two being Spanish and French. In Tanzania, I had become accustomed to teaching English in Swahili. Now to turn it around to teach Swahili in English to high school students in an international setting – well, I just had to pinch myself to see if it were real, or if I were dreaming. Though looking back to my childhood, I would never even have thought to dream such a dream. Often after a class was over, I thought, "Well, that was fun!"

I came across a little sign that said, "If you really want to know something, teach it." Even though I had learned a lot of Swahili in Tanzania, I knew that I didn't really *know* it, so as I hung that sign up by my teacher's desk in the classroom, I knew with certainty that I was about to learn a lot. And I did. Along with the technicals of this Bantu language, I also became aware of a fundamental concept: language is the rubber and culture the road. Where they meet is in a basic understanding of the people who think in it.

Every weekday, the expatriate staff would gather together mid-morning for chai or coffee. Though it was called 'chai time,' the coffee was also really good and something I looked forward to in the midst of my morning classes. The main purpose of our time together, however, was praying together for each other, the nationals, the nation and nations. It was also a time where any relevant announcements could be made known.

Once a week on Tuesday afternoons, a small group of us missionary women met and headed up the hill to Kiambogo Primary School, where we would divide up into the classrooms and teach an after school Bible lesson. It was a rewarding experience, but could also be frustrating, especially during the rainy season, when no matter how loud we yelled, we could not begin to be heard over the rain pounding on the tin roof. The amazing thing was that the students continued to sit there, crowded together at their desk benches, listening, or at least watching our theatrics. We were probably very entertaining compared with their usual rote learning.

Later on, I replaced my time at Bible Club with teaching as a part of an HIV/AIDS Awareness class in various primary schools in the area. Because the incidence of HIV was extremely high (one town a few miles from us was 50 percent positive), I knew this was a vital program. What was disturbing was the prevalence of personal experience of abuse as an expected part of life among these primary students, especially the girls. It was truly heartbreaking.

I felt the immorality I encountered here to be beyond imaginable limits, but one day my prayer partner put another spin on the topic for me. She gave the example of how shocked and horrified I would be if she asked me if I would want to come over and watch her and her husband have sex tonight. Then she followed that up with, "No? Then why not just come over and together we'll all watch others have it on the big screen." Ah, yes, our culture, too, is far from pure.

I remember the initial Sunday series that our RVA chaplain preached on, our first year at the school. He entitled it *Possess the Land*. It was all about how to possess what God had already given us! We were reminded to remember all the ways in which Beauty had already led us. And long ago, Moses reminded the people wandering around the desert with him that the **reason** God led them there was to humble them, test them, to know what was in their hearts.[3] I felt it was a good way to start, knowing the reason I'd been so beautifully brought here. It was a test to see how I'd handle it!

RVA's excellence in academics and extracurricular activities was all sewn together by an emphasis on the spiritual. They specifically celebrated this aspect during a week labeled Spiritual Emphasis Week (SEW) towards the beginning of every school year. Its purpose was to get everyone on the same page, so to speak. Each year they would invite a speaker from outside to come. I think the first speaker I remember was from England. I don't recall his name, but I can remember that, though a young man, he was recently widowed, his wife having died of cancer. What I recall most clearly was that, in the very midst of her suffering, she had looked at her husband

and expressed what an honor it was to suffer *without being given any explanation at all*. It reminded me of my mom and her attitude towards dying of cancer without ever once asking for an explanation from the One who does all things well.

A SEW speaker from a later year impressed me with the simplicity of salvation in Christ. He explained it as simply lifting our eyes to Jesus as He was there on the cross and saying, *"Yes,*[4] this was for me."* For whatever reason or reasons, I was completely enthralled with the simplicity of the single word requirement for salvation, *Yes*. So as the five of us were on our way to Nairobi one day that same week, I began to wax eloquent to our three kids sitting in the back seat of the Patrol – going on and on about everything that's **not** required, not rules, not tradition, not looks or dress, not anything, just look to Jesus and say, *"Yes."* At this point, I saw that the three of them were just looking at me and Lizzie expressed what was on all three faces, "Duh, Mom." Of course. Their windows of life were not mine. Almost nothing like mine.

A following year's SEW speaker balanced that simplicity out nicely with the necessary complement of emphasizing the truth of *what we sow, we reap*. This speaker gave the practical example of any farmer who plants corn expects corn to come up, and would certainly be surprised at beans growing where he had planted corn! But yet in life, we sometimes sow seeds of ugliness and expect beautiful things to sprout up, and it just doesn't work like that. He warned us all to not believe otherwise; the consequences of what we choose to **do** will be sure. And like the old adage says, *Actions speak louder than words*. I was reminded again of that precious old lady in Wapello's movie-theater-church singing, and felt sure that such a God as she was singing of would definitely not allow Himself to be mocked in the end. I see that as an important aspect of Beauty, too. How we live surely matters. I didn't attempt to wax eloquent on this subject to the kids because I felt I already knew what they would say: "Duh, Mom." It often seemed to me that our kids were more mature in their thinking than their mother was. They've taught me so much in life.

~ ~ ~

Some of the family from home who had come to visit us when we were in Tanzania also came to see where we were in Kenya. The first to come were Dad and Ruth, then Kent and Jan and their family, with a family friend, Jason, and Harrison's father – precious memories. Our little brown John gleefully came back and stayed with us for a few weeks after we had made a road trip to revisit Dodoma, Tanzania. And now Rod, the pastor of our main supporting church in Indiana came, but this time instead of bringing his son, Brett, he brought his wife, Harrison's sister along.

While they were visiting us, we went to visit the Pokot tribe in western Kenya. We had visited this tribe several times as guests of the missionaries who lived and worked with the tribe. Now we had the fun of taking our guests from the States with us. As usually happened, a goat was killed soon after we arrived, to be roasted for our evening meal. As we sat around the fire that evening, Rod was the guest of honor. Tradition had it that the guest of honor was the one gifted with the privilege of sucking the marrow out of a particular goat bone before the rest of us were invited to eat. Rod graciously declined, leaving Harrison, next in the line of honor, to be the recipient.

Pensively holding the bone to his lips, he gingerly sucked. To his relief or dismay, nothing happened. Someone said, "Suck harder!" So putting his usual caution to the wind, he closed his eyes and sucked with all his might. To his dismay, the marrow dislodged and slid into his mouth like a hard glob of slick Jell-o. Having only a second to decide what to do, as all eyes were on him, he swallowed it whole. They told him that it was extremely healthy, but he could only think of it as mucous sliding in a bulb down his throat.

I guess visiting the Pokot tribe was how we really knew we were still in Africa while working at RVA. We went on numerous trips there, together with our good missionary friends from RVA, leaving me with many memories: pitying the people as they worked so hard, digging in unforgiving dry land for a cup of dirty water to drink; being too humbled to even feel honored by the gift of a goat from the two destitute wives whose mutual husband had recently been struck by lightening and killed; giving out grain and the Gospel, but left feeling somehow dirty, with a sense of mocking falseness that was hard to shake off.

Back at RVA, school life carried happily on. Coming up the hill from the center of campus, passing through the Titchie Swot (elementary school) playground and on up the hill to Davis Dorm (the name of the fifth- and sixth-grade boys' dorm/our home), Tobin walked in the front door, which we kept wide open on nice days, and announced, "I LOVE open doors! They make me happy!" How that fit with his dislike of teachers always telling him (and us) that they saw him as having great potential, I'm not exactly sure. While Tobin was in junior high, he and his friends were sometimes more than a handful for their teachers. So much so that during that space of time, when I would see one of his teachers approaching me, I would inwardly cringe over what might be coming. Often I was wrong, and the report I thought was coming didn't, but even when it did, whichever teacher was giving it would always, without exception, add that Tobin was never disrespectful. That was a beautiful thing to hear.

It makes me smile even now as I remember Tobin's response to me telling him *No,* in no uncertain terms, about something he wanted to do. His nodding response was, "That was a firm and sensible answer." He had many such responses, another of them being, in a singsong voice at opportune moments, "I'm getting mixed mes-sag-es!" And if I told him too often that I loved him, his response was, "I *know*, Mom, but do you like me?" I never knew if these responses were original with him or if he had absorbed them from all the Calvin & Hobbes cartoons that he read when he was younger. He had, in fact, been so much like Calvin when he was younger that a fellow missionary on the Dodoma compound had dubbed him 'Calvin.'

The al-Qaeda bombings that brought Osama bin Laden to the attention of the American public for the first time, happened on 8/7/98, which happened to be Lizzie's eleventh birthday. So while we did have fun things planned for the party, she and her friends spent a fair portion of the party time glued to the TV, watching the effects of the truck bombs that simultaneously exploded at two

American embassies – one an hour away in Nairobi, and the other in Dar es Salaam, the largest city in, and former capital of, Tanzania.

A minuscule terror in comparison was the baboon who sprang up out of our garbage can just as I was raising our kitchen trash to plop it in! Its effect was reminiscent to me of the snake on the second to bottom basement step in my youth. I never approached that trash can again without using caution.

Though it was a small, pesky monkey instead of a large baboon, it was nevertheless quite a shock to Lizzie as she ran up the stairs and into her bedroom to grab the PE clothes she had forgotten earlier in the day. I wasn't home at the time, but returned later to find a note on the kitchen counter that I still have somewhere today. It read, "There's a monkey in my room and it's making a terrible mess!!" Indeed, it had made a mess of things. And Lizzie had decided she could do without her PE clothes that day. It was probably an excuse that the PE teachers from America hadn't gotten before – but very possibly could get again during their time here.

Another evening when Harrison and I returned home to the dorm, we found our normally happy Cherith in an unusual state. She had just returned from playing, or rather not playing, in an RVA girls' basketball game. Now that she was safely home, she was able to shed the hot tears of shame and public embarrassment that she felt from sitting on the bench. I felt helpless sitting beside her, watching as her tears gracefully slipped into Beauty's vial.[5]

Cherith's basketball coach had told Harrison and me that Cherith was an excellent player when it came to her physical skill. Her problem, he said, was that she was just too nice to be competitive. For her, the coaches' slogan of 'Ya gotta want it!' didn't supersede her gentle graciousness of not lording it over others. Unless, of course, it had nothing to do with others – like at the basketball tournament at Rosslyn Academy in Nairobi where, cool as a cucumber, she slipped in the necessary free throws to win the tied game. So it was not too surprising that as time went on, Cherith laid down the basketball in favor of the paint brush, to her art teacher's delight.

Neither of her siblings' coaches had this complaint towards them. Being a good Christian school, all RVA coaches stressed that when competing against other schools, it wasn't about winning or losing, it was about how you played the game. Though the point was well-taken, Tobin especially appreciated the one coach he had who was good at reminding them that the goal was to win.

The five of us finished the millennium and watched the new one come in around a campfire at the same Hell's Gate that we had been a little shocked to hear Cherith was at, the first time we had come to visit her when we were still living in Tanzania. But now we were well familiarized with it as a national park. Harrison put aside his cares concerning Y2K and the school, and we all truly enjoyed a night under the absolute awesomeness of the stars in the black African night. There's truly nothing quite like it!

After being in Davis Dorm for three years with fifth- and sixth-grade boys, Cherith asked us if we could move to a regular house for her last year in high school and in Kenya. Though the dorm boys were fond of her, some of them even a little in awe of her, as far as she was concerned, one younger brother was all she needed. And she appreciated that that one didn't hang out of the dorm windows whistling and giggling while watching her and her date walk down the hill toward their movie night activity. It did work out for us to move into a single dwelling house – which we then stayed in for five years, the longest time that Harrison and I have lived in any one place in our thirty-five years of married life.

The week before we moved, we had another special visit from dear friends in the States. We had a great time showing Tim, Linda and their three daughters some of the sights and sounds of Kenya. The most memorable to me was a camping trip near a pool of hippos. It was a beautiful spot in every way that we could see. The problem came in what we didn't see – tiny little black ticks. When we woke up in the morning we found them. On our skin they appeared as a tiny freckle or mole, but they were also places we couldn't see – like up in Lizzie's nose and under one of my eyelids! We all continued to find one here and there for days, especially when in the shower. It was a bit of a scary thing and I felt especially bad about inflicting it on good friends from the States!

When we were still living in Davis Dorm, Harrison had built a deluxe rabbit cage for Lizzie's rabbits. Having experience from the rabbit cage he had built in Tanzania, in this new improved one he had put a wire mesh floor in a section of the cage so that the excrement could fall through onto the ground, leaving the inside of the cage clean and dry. Apparently the rabbits didn't understand the plan because they didn't follow it, necessitating a frequent cage cleaning. So Lizzie was greatly entertained by the sign her father wrote and hung in the wire mesh area of the cage, "Don't be stoo - this is where you poo! Don't be a re - this is where you pee!" I suppose it was particularly amusing to her, since we had had a policy from the kids' earliest days that it was strictly forbidden to call anybody *stupid* ever.

Unfortunately, the same type of biting ants that had once gotten into Lizzie's eyes and surrounded John's small canvas bassinet years ago, on a safari out in the bush to show *The Jesus Film*, had invaded our part of campus and ate away the legs of the rabbit cage. We learned from the Kenyans that these army ants are known to leave only the chickens' bones when they march away. They instructed us to put ashes from our fireplace around what was left of our cage's legs to keep the ants from climbing up and getting to the rabbits – and it worked! But though the ants didn't get to them, these rabbits ended up getting an awful disease that slowly paralyzed them.

About the time we moved into our non-dorm home, one of the RVA guard dogs had a litter of pups. The security guard in charge of the dogs allowed our kids to pick out one of the pups for our own. They were delighted. We named the puppy Obadiah, after the security guard who cared for the pups. Furthermore, it worked out famously because our neighbor's dog was named Amos, so we had a good laugh over having minor prophet dogs.

It was with this same neighbor family that our family rafted the Nile River and then had a picnic at its source. Because rafting the Zambezi River had been such an outrageously wild experience, I was a little afraid of another rafting experience. As it turned out, the scariest part of this trip to me was the cobra that raised itself up high above the trunk of the Pajero and spit at our windshield as we traveled down a dusty road headed to Uganda. The tensest moments of the actual rafting experience were when we capsized and Tobin was spun too far away from the raft to climb back on, so our guide yelled at him to, "Swim right!" It seemed dangerous because there were rocks off to the right. As Tobin obediently swam strongly to the right, the guide continued to yell, "Swim RIGHT! Swim Right!" Tobin continued, until the guide suddenly yelled, "LEFT, LEFT!!! I mean LEFT!!!" I guess we all get our rights and lefts mixed up sometimes.

Along with this same family and other neighbors, one of our favorite outings was to go on motorcycle rides down in the Rift Valley, husbands driving, we wives riding behind. We'd enjoy the wind, the beauty of Africa, and sometimes stop at a duka for some lunch or just some chai. Another time we went spelunking, to the apparent dismay of a whole horde of bats. Those were good times. Often they would be followed up by a card game of Hand and Foot in the evening.

Today's technology has simplified the college application process, but in 1999/2000, when Cherith was deciding where to go to college, it was not yet simple. RVA would take the older students to Nairobi so that they could get on online, but mostly the process took place by overseas snail mail. Because Cherith had somehow gotten interested in a college in Switzerland, Harrison decided the best and easiest way to make a decision was to go see the school. So that was what he and Cherith did – took a trip to Switzerland to visit it. For Harrison, the decision was finalized when he asked someone working at the school if they would send their daughter there and the response was a quick *No*. Although it was followed by quickly trying to remedy that spontaneous answer, it was too late for Harrison to be persuaded. For Cherith, it took a bit longer to accept, but she did.

RVA was a really happening place. To tell of everything taking place out my window there would fill volumes. If you're interested in seeing another window-full, our friend and neighboring dorm dad, Steve Peifer, wrote a book called, *A Dream So Big*. His story gives a vivid picture of life at RVA, much of which we resonate with, having experienced the same – except for the dream itself. We somehow never saw ourselves as having any kind of impact that big.

On our flight back to the States, we first landed in Zurich, Switzerland to go revisit the school that Harrison and Cherith had checked out earlier. While there, we had a lovely time staying with some friends of friends that Harrison and Cherith had gotten to know when they were there. We took great pleasure in the unparalleled beauty of Switzerland and then were struck by the differences in concepts of time as we enjoyed the laid back neighboring country of Italy.

Lessons learned:

We all do the best we can with the beliefs we own.
The secret of having is looking up, saying, "Yes" and receiving.

14

Bloomington, Illinois

Lee Street
Becoming (Re-)acquainted with The West
Fall 2001

M y older brother, Adam, and his dear wife and some of their children had been at O'Hare waiting for us for hours when we finally landed in Chicago. We apologized profusely and told them what had happened – after boarding the plane in Zurich, we had sat for over two hours without taking off. The mechanics were working on a problem on one of the plane's generators. During this time the air conditioner wasn't working, so it got really hot and stuffy. We were all so relieved to finally take off and to get cooled off, but about an hour into the flight, an announcement came over the speaker that they were now experiencing a malfunction of the plane's other generator and it would be necessary to land in London!

They told us not to be alarmed at the firetrucks that would be lining the runway as we landed; they were only precautionary as we were overweight because of having too much fuel to be landing. Sure enough, there they were, numerous firetrucks lined up on either side of us as we landed. Not really a very comforting sight from the air. We imagined that we would be able to get out and stretch after we landed, but no. We were out in the middle of nowhere without any terminal nearby. We must all stay in our seats. It was about this time that one passenger, who had already been traveling for many hours before this whole ordeal began, lost it and had to be dealt with.

Other than being there to greet us, all my brother's family had been waiting to do was hand us the keys to the red Ford conversion van that they were giving us. Yes, giving us! Adam told us when we were ready to return to Africa, we could sell it and go out for pizza with the proceeds. Beauty is as beauty does.

Fortunately for us all, exhausted as we were, the airline gave us a voucher for a room in the airport hotel, so we were able to safely drive the two-and-a-half hours to our next window of life - Lee Street in Bloomington, Illinois.

Arriving in Bloomington, we stopped at a gas station to ask directions to Lee Street, to the rental property of some generous farmers from our home church culture. They were graciously allowing us to live there rent-free for the next six months.

When the college in Switzerland hadn't panned out, Cherith had decided on Illinois State University (ISU) more or less by default. It was in the state that her father called home, the one where she had been born and had lived for a couple years, and her cousin, Jackie, who she knew from visiting us both in Tanzania and in Kenya, was going to go to school there. It was a logical choice – as was us staying in ISU's twin city of Bloomington (ISU is in Normal, Illinois). Our hope was that Cherith living with us for her first semester at university would be helpful as she reentered American culture. RVA provides a Reentry Seminar for the seniors before they graduate, which is very helpful as a preview of the issues a third culture kid (TCK) faces as they attempt to reenter a culture that their parents call home.

Third Culture Kids (TCKs) are a definite culture of their own. Take ours, for example. By the time they'd reached this window of life, they were most familiar with Africa, but they knew they weren't African. They knew they were American, and though they looked American, they didn't necessarily feel it or understand American culture. Who they related to most closely and connected with were others like themselves, no matter what country the others were originally from or living in at present. Thus, they were true TCKs – those in between cultures, those who form their own third culture with others who are the same as them, those to whom an airport can feel like the closest thing to home. To me, it seems like they should have an inside track on the concept of this world not being our real home, that we're just a'passing through, but that has not been my experience. Perhaps because the whole world is their home.

At RVA there were more than a few missionary families represented who had been missionaries for generations. There were those whose parents had been missionaries while they had been students at RVA, and now their children were students at their alma mater of RVA. While we were at RVA, we were fellow dorm parents with a young couple with children. Both sets of their parents also lived and worked at RVA – meaning that there were three generations on both sides of their families right there on campus! It makes me wonder: when there are generations of TCKs in one family, do they still suffer the TCK issues of not truly belonging anywhere – or does life become more like a family-owned business? What an interesting world we live in!

Since we planned to settle into life at this window for six months, Harrison decided to look for a job. First he worked as a security guard at the Alamo, ISU's student bookstore. That made for very long, and mostly uneventful, days. Therefore, when he had the opportunity to work at Darnall, a manufacturer of precast concrete products – co-owned by the good friend in Roanoke who had come all the way to Corbin, Kentucky to pick up us and our damaged car, but to no avail – he gratefully took it. Harrison thoroughly enjoyed the challenge. It was certainly a change of atmosphere from working with missionaries and their already churched children! But along with the refreshing new relationships, the change also included taxing physical work instead of simply sitting at a desk, allowing needs to come to him. More than once, upon coming home so very tired, he unlaced and removed his work boots and dropped to the floor inside the front door in exhaustion. Though we felt sorry for him, the kids and I were very grateful for the paycheck he brought home. It costs a lot to get caught up on four years of shopping in America!

Not long after we settled in, Tobin decided to go see a fellow station kid who had been a good friend to him at RVA and whose family had recently resettled in Pennsylvania. The means that he chose to get from Illinois to Pennsylvania was a Greyhound bus. Though our relatives wondered at Harrison and I allowing him to do this by himself, in a country he was unfamiliar with, Tobin himself didn't see it as a problem at all. His response to their concern was, "How hard can it be when everyone speaks English?"

He went, had a great time with Ben and his family, and began the trip home with not much money left in his wallet. He had to change busses in Indianapolis. Having some time between busses, he looked around, ate, and shopped a little, spending the rest of his money except for some spare change. When it was time to depart Indianapolis, he climbed on the bus and soon fell into a deep sleep. The loud speaker on the bus awakened him, announcing their arrival in Bloomington. He gathered his belongings, stumbled off the bus still half asleep and went into the restroom. When he came out, he was more awake, looked around and noticed that all the cars' license plates said *Indiana. That's weird,* he thought, *how does it happen that all the cars in Bloomington have Indiana license plates??*

You may have guessed by now that Tobin had, in his sleepy state, gotten off the bus at Bloomington, *Indiana* instead of Bloomington, *Illinois*. Same city name, two different states. His bus had left. He learned that to carry on to Illinois would require buying another ticket, but he had no money left. Long story short – he found a phone booth to call home using all the change in his pocket, but not being familiar with phone booths he misdialed and didn't get through. He wandered the streets until someone directed him to the police station. The police listened to his dilemma and in questioning him further apparently thought he seemed strange, and finally said, "Kid, do you have any kind of ID?" Tobin gave them his RVA ID. The officer looked at it and said, "Africa?? You're from Africa?" He suggested Tobin spend the night at the halfway house a few blocks down the street. Tobin walked to it, looked at the place and his over-night companions and decided against it.

When he returned to the police station, the officer had another idea. "Well, why don't you just make a collect call to your parents?" Tobin replied, "What's a collect call?" When he received the answer, he did it. I answered, accepted the charges, and about 10:30 pm, I (Harrison had to go to work in the morning) hopped in the van, very thankful for Lizzie accompanying me, and we headed from Bloomington, Illinois to Bloomington, Indiana. Normally a three-and-a-half hour trip, the pouring rain made us decide on the side of safety to pull over and get a little sleep. We arrived in Bloomington in the wee hours of the morning, so happy to see our Tobin, safe and sound – and he us. Such is life with TCKs.

Somehow, perhaps because of her calm, reserved nature, Cherith's adjustment to life at a secular university with 20,000 students appeared to be less of a challenge than Tobin and Lizzie's adjustment to their new high school of 1,500 students, very few of whom they could relate to. Lizzie entered Bloomington High School (BHS) as a freshman and Tobin as a junior. Both of them made huge efforts towards fitting in – Tobin joining the soccer team and Lizzie becoming part of both the band and the swimming team. We had heard rumors that BHS was known to be a rough place and we had also heard that these activities were where they would find the 'good' kids. This worked well, since these were areas where they fit naturally. My heart swelled with pride as I repeatedly watched each of them put forth valiant effort in stepping out of their comfort zones and up to bat in an arena that necessitated courage from within. I was happy, too, that they *wanted* relationships instead of the easier path of hiding out and waiting for this window to be over. I thanked Beauty profusely for the three very special and unique gems He had loaned to Harrison and me.

Relationships with their teachers came easily, mostly I think, because the teachers had apparently never seen such wonderful, respectful, kind, work-producing students – or at least that was what it seemed like when Harrison and I went to parent-teacher conference and received glowing reports of their conduct and performance. And their days at school always made for interesting discussion at our evening dinner table: The girls who laughed in the halls as they discussed what they named the babies they had given birth to over the summer. The Chinese girl, also new to the school, who watched with Tobin as a punk rocker pass by their lockers, looked at Tobin and whispered, "Scary!" She and Tobin became fast friends.

Not to mention the school bus ride to and from school. Listening to Tobin and Lizzie, I felt that if I had been present **watching** the stories that they were now telling with such animation, instead of simply listening to the *retelling* of the story, I would have seen them sitting quietly, their jaws dropped open in disbelief. I was thankful for the eye-opening experience this window was for them. I thought it could be an important one in helping them relate effectively to others later on, in real life. When they walked out of BHS for the last time to return to Africa where they could be on their own comfortable turf, I felt a gladness in me, knowing that via those two, tiny bits of Jesus had been present in that dark Western place.

When I wasn't occupied with helping our kids orient to this strange Western culture, I was busy with, amongst other things, reading and writing papers for the class I was taking in educational psychology at Heartland, the local junior college. I know it's crazy, but the main thing I remember looking back at that window is not the class, but the placement test I had to take when registering for the class. On the English section of the computerized test, I was required to read an essay and answer some elementary questions about it. That essay is what I remember. It was about a baby whose parents had been teaching him to wave *g'bye* to people. As this baby sat in his seat, watching the leaves on the tree branches blowing in the wind, he interpreted it as the leaves waving at him personally! It struck me anew how infantile we all tend to be in our thinking. Our first response to everything that happens is to connect it to how it affects us personally. In essence, everything is about us! On the other hand, though it seems absurd, who am I to say that the baby's interpretation was not a very valid one, and may well indeed be one of the billion purposes in having those leaves blow in Beauty's wind.

Our weekends at this window were a separate story of their own, as we tirelessly presented our work at RVA to small groups, large groups, churches, home groups, any and everyone who would listen to us. One Sunday in particular, I recall that we visited four different fellowships, all of different flavors. On another Sunday, we were visiting at Kent and Jan's church in the unincorporated community of Taylor, Missouri (consisting of a post office and the church), located between Quincy, Illinois and Palmyra, Missouri. It happened that my brother, Adam, was the visiting preacher there that Sunday. As a part of the regular order of service, we had sung out of the *Zion's Harp*. The song someone had chosen was number 249, *Who Are They Before God's Throne?* When we had concluded the congregational a cappella singing of it, Adam was inspired to speak a few words about the song.

As he spoke, a strange thing happened to me – I had the nearest thing to a vision that I had experienced to date. Before my mind's eye, I could see the *countless throngs standing before Beauty's throne in heavenly light; each wearing a golden crown and shining like the stars so bright, waving palms in every hand*. But instead of being *dressed in white* and *in priestly garments* as the original composer saw them, I saw the *robes of honor they possessed* as a whole spectrum of beautiful colors, as though the throng was representative of people from all nations, tribes, and tongues, *waving their palms in every hand*. It was a breathtaking sight. I know that in reality, all of our robes will be made white by the blood of Jesus,[1] strange as it sounds, but for now, I'm just telling you what I saw, as Adam was talking up there in front of us all in that pulpit. Then, as reality pulled me back to where I was, sitting there in the small world of a separatist church, who loved me completely, yet removed me from their fellowship, I'm sure I must have smiled a rueful smile, the irony not lost on me.

As clearly as I remember seeing my second grade teacher enter the classroom in Wapello Elementary School, crying and telling us that President Kennedy had just been shot and killed, I will always remember seeing the Twin Towers fall on September 11th on the screen at this window on Lee Street in Bloomington, Illinois. Ugly is as Ugly does. Insidious and unfathomable.

Not only was our time in Bloomington full of reconnecting with our Stateside friends and family, we also had the delight of having Bob and Deb, dear friends with whom we labored and laughed while living life together at RVA, pull up to our Lee Street address on their Harley Davidson! Another time, a group of RVA graduates rang our doorbell. When we asked how they found us, they told us they had used this new thing called *Mapquest*. We were amazed; we had never heard of such a thing.

As our time in Bloomington drew towards its close, I could hardly bear to think of sacrificing Cherith to this continent as the other four of us went to live on the far side of the world. Suddenly the small world seemed much too large. In leaving her behind, I comforted myself with the fact that I wasn't leaving her like my mother did me, I would still be in the world right there should she need me. I remember telling Harrison's father that we were leaving him the precious possession of our firstborn child. He and Harrison's mother assured us they would take care of her, even providing their basement bedroom in Roanoke for whenever she wanted to get away from university dorm life. Cherith took advantage of the offer, finding in it a source of comfort and escape.

Lessons learned:

Being human is an entire experience; there is no sacred dichotomy
- no division into secular and sacred. And circumstances do not
simply happen randomly. There is a planned design to everything.
Abundant life and self-sacrifice are congruent paradoxes of truth.
Therein lies one of life's biggest mysteries - the tension of which we
must embrace.

15

Return to Kijabe

Pressing On
2002 - 2005

Tobin, Lizzie and I returned to Kenya in time for the start of the first RVA term of 2002. As hard as it was to go, I still felt like I was taking the coward's way out. It was so much easier leaving Cherith behind in the USA when Harrison was still standing there right beside her, with his arm around her. Harrison was staying until Cherith was settled into the dorm she had been assigned to and had started classes. Then he had the awful job of leaving her behind on her own. I'm still not sure I could have done it and am positive I couldn't have done it as well as he did.

Lizzie and I were walking what they called 'the guard's trail,' a foot path that surrounded the edge of the entire beautiful campus of RVA. Its real function was as a means of our security guard's monitoring the campus – thus its name. It was a perfect September day. A gentle breeze was blowing. It and her thoughts prompted Lizzie's comment, "The wind reminds me of Cherith." The wind. Like the wind that blew against me on my bike rides in Iowa City, cleaning my mind, and the wind that blew the leaves waving *bye-bye* to the watching baby, now it reminded my daughter of her sister far away in the United States of America. *How does the wind work*? I wondered. *How did it clean my mind then, and how does it remind Lizzie of her loved one now?* I do not know and I cannot tell.

Not only the wind reminded Lizzie of Cherith; everything seemed to remind her of Cherith's absence. It made me think back to a time when Cherith was still with us here at our Kijabe window, but Harrison was away to AIM management meetings in Scotland. The four of us were sitting around the dining room table, eating dinner one evening, chatting about our day when Tobin suddenly sighed and said, "I sure miss, Dad. I know he doesn't ever say much, but I just really miss him sitting there." It was true. Normally the four of us all chattered at the table, changing subjects before the previous was completed, leaving Harrison, as he once explained to me, 'unable to get a word in edge-wise.' I got to thinking about Tobin's remark and Cherith's gentle nature and wondered if maybe those who don't strive to make their presence known we miss most of all in their absence.

For their part, Tobin and Lizzie were so very happy to be safely back in their comfort zone. Gone were those times of dreading the approach of Tobin's teachers to inform me of his latest antics, making me realize and thank Beauty that the BHS experience had served him well, giving him just the attitude adjustment he was in need of. Instead, I had the pleasure of unexpected compliments from unlikely sources, such as, "The way Tobin plays rugby is the way he's going to play life." I knew how he played sports; he was coachable and then gave it his all. When he landed on the ground during an intense soccer game and hurt his arm, he told the coach it was okay and kept playing. After the game, he came to Harrison and me and said it hurt real bad, maybe we should get an x-ray. It was broken. And when he had a broken ankle, he hobbled up and down the side of the field on his crutches, cheering his mates onward towards the goal. But he still had his one-liners. To someone showing an attitude of absolute certitude, he quietly commented, "Only fools are certain." He was sounding less like Calvin and more like someone thinking things out for himself.

For her part, Lizzie got straight A's, enjoyed horseback riding, came alive on the trumpet, was a delegate representing Trinidad and Tobago at the Model United Nations, wielded her hockey stick like she meant it, and gave me some of the best advice of my life: "Mom, you might be right, but you need to try to be ridiculously gentle about it." Undoubtedly, my life could have played out much easier if I had taken her advice more often than I did.

I had been assigned a different classroom on the back side of RVA's Kiambogo administration building. The outdoor balcony leading along that block of classrooms overlooked the Rift Valley. If I had picked it myself, I absolutely could not have chosen a more beautiful spot to do a job that I totally loved. I think it was somewhere in that total enjoyment of teaching these delightful students that my fear of being in front of a group began to dissipate. After all, I found them listening to me, to what I had to say, with interest!

Some local Kenyans had made and were selling varnished wooden plaques with verses of scripture on them. I thought it would be a good idea to buy one to use in decorating my classroom. Amongst all the lovely familiar Bible verses, I noticed one I was not so familiar with: *The LORD will fight for you; you need only to be still.* (Exodus 14:14 NIV) I remember thinking, *What an odd verse for a wall plaque.* I was more of the mindset that I must learn to fight against and overcome the things that come against me and in that way produce the balance of holiness.[1] I chose to buy the odd verse. It reminded me of Lizzie's wise advice.

Along with the classroom curtains that I had sewn using African material and the other African artifacts, a huge poster of the Lord's Prayer in Swahili was central to our classroom decor. The poster wasn't just for looks; it was part and parcel of our opening classroom routine. As soon as the students understood the simple phonetics of the language, we began recitation of the Lord's Prayer in every conceivable manner – and this all before they knew the meanings of the words, other than knowing the prayer in English. Those who know how languages work, know that a literal word-for-word translation loses much that is of significance. This process enabled the students to rattle off the prayer like native speakers before they could dissect it into actual words and meanings. In Swahili II, we did the same with Psalm 23. Because I did it with them, year after year for eight years, I can only hope that it embedded in them a fraction of the effect it had on me. Even now, many windows on down the road, if I can't sleep at night, I never count sheep; I rehearse the Lord's

Prayer and Psalm 23 in Swahili – an exercise that never ceases to bring peace to my weary soul.

It may have been at our staff chai time one day that I first heard of a missionary wife who, years earlier, had simply disappeared on a Sunday morning. As I remember hearing it, she hadn't gone to church with her husband because there was some work that needed tending to in the office, so she went there. And was never seen again. Even more than the mystery of it, the effect on me was *Wow. She really disappeared.* It took me quickly back to my long-time desire to not be seen, only heard. The oddest of all possible emotions came over me: I was jealous of her! Absolutely ridiculous, I know. Surely Adam's diagnosis of me was true.

It was also about this time that I again had my childhood reoccurring and exhilarating dream of flying higher and higher and higher still. But this time there was a strange twist to it: while flying, I was speaking in tongues! I've never again had the dream since that night. Apparently, that was the final one. I opened my eyes, as every morning at this window, to the poster hanging beside the bed: *It is for freedom that Christ has set us free. Stand firm, then, and do not let yourselves be burdened again by a yoke of slavery.* (Galatians 5:1 NIV) I was free indeed.[2]

A fellow missionary had introduced me to M. Scott Peck's book, *The Road Less Traveled.* Influenced by that book, I did a ton of thinking and came to the conclusion that each of us is no more important than a single speck of dust in the generations of the universe. Kind of a depressing thought in a way, but that's the conclusion I came to. Since it is far from my intention to leave you, dear reader, depressed, I want to tell you right away – at my next window, a very secular window according to missionary standards, the beautiful truth of it came to me: if we belong to Beauty, instead of being only the value of a grain of dust, we are more like the tiny glittering, shiny diamond of dew, splendorous in the sun's rays, as it sits atop a single green blade of Beauty's grass. I continue to see that as much closer to the truth of the way things are.

A less complicated missionary, Bob, who with his wife came to visit us at our last window on their Harleys, gave me some advice that, fortunately, I think of more often than anything that Scott Peck had to say. Bob's frequent advice was, he said, to himself first of all: *Keep It Simple, Stupid* (KISS). And I so agree with Oswald Chamber's thoughts on the subject:

> Our Lord must be repeatedly astounded at us - astounded at how "un-simple" we are. It is our own opinions that make us dense and slow to understand, but when we are simple we are never dense; we have discernment all the time. . . The mystery of God is not in what is going to be – it is now, though we look for it to be revealed in the future in some overwhelming, momentous event.[3]

Or as put in the fictitious wisdom of the Winnie-the-Pooh:

> An Empty sort of mind. . .can see what's in front of it. An Overstuffed mind is unable to. While the Clear mind listens to a bird singing, the Stuffed-Full-of-Knowledge-and-Cleverness mind wonders what *kind* of bird is singing. The more Stuffed Up it is, the less it can hear through its own ears and see through its own eyes.[4]

Even though I'm convinced that RVA students are some of the sharpest students in the world, I still tried my best to use Bob's advice in my teaching, because I believe that's what makes a good teacher a good teacher. Simplify the complicated.

The real joy of staying at RVA for years was watching the students mature. While I enjoyed all the students, it was natural that I had a special affinity for those boys who had lived with us in Davis Dorm while they were in fifth and sixth grade. Back then, after they had enjoyed their before bedtime snack, Uncle Harrison had always insisted that they say, "Thank you, Aunt Pam," before they trudged up the stairs to bed. He was so firm about it that the rule was, if they forgot, they had to forego their snack the next night. That never happened, mostly I think, because at least one always remembered, followed by a trail of often half-hearted, "Thank you, Aunt Pam"s. So, when after hosting a Caring Community group at our non-dorm house years later, as one of those same boys, a Kenyan, was leaving, he said with all sincerity, "Thank you, Aunt Pam!" He suddenly broke out laughing and exclaimed, "Those words have new meaning now when I say them! I really mean them!" We all laughed.

Maturity and real gratitude are beautiful things. We can only hope that as they matured, they gained understanding of other things that we tried so hard to teach them – for example, the dorm dinner I cooked for them, or some gift that someone brought them from the States, or some rock star's funny comment, were NOT awesome, but that Beauty and His creation are what you truly call awesome! And that God will help you with your homework, but He will not do it for you. That's your responsibility.

While classes shared together were wonderful and made memories, RVA interims were even more so, perhaps because they had a way of making the ordinary everyday relationships come alive. Harrison and I were privileged to be the adult chaperones of several of the trips that the juniors and seniors at RVA chose once a year. Some of these Harrison and I did separately, some together. He was climbing Mt. Kilimanjaro with students while I was biking Kenya with others. Zanzibar, Lamu, and Tanzania were the trips that both of us shared with the students.

The Zanzibar trip happened simultaneously with our twenty-fifth wedding anniversary. I would recommend the idyllic beachside place we stayed while on the exotic island of Zanzibar for anyone's twenty-fifth anniversary – well, maybe without taking a dozen teenagers with you. But as we all swam with the dolphins in that blue, blue water, we really felt like, "The more the merrier!"

The Lamu trip got off to a bit of a unlucky beginning – more for the third chaperone than for Harrison and me. Our flight from Nairobi to the island of Lamu was overbooked. It was decided for us that two of our large group traveling together had to stay behind and go on the next day's flight. What were we to do? Leaving two students behind was out of the question. Two chaperones would have to stay. Rather than splitting up Harrison and me, Karen, who with her many years of being a high school dorm mom, had more tenure than us, graciously agreed to go and leave Harrison and me to enjoy a free night at the Intercontinental Hotel in Nairobi. We rested well, knowing that a long, hot, busy week was before us. What we didn't know about the week was that Harrison would have a knife pulled on him in a dark alley and that I would experience my first sea sickness, a malady I hope to never experience again. Lying in the bottom of that boat, I had the definite impression that this must be what hell was like.

One of the main things that I remember about the Tanzania interim trip is when we all slept in Maasai huts, made of, and smelling of, cow dung and mud. We slept two or three to a hut, sleeping on stick beds or animal hide mats on the dirt floor. Maasai warriors stood guard over us and their cattle during the long hours of dark, in which none of us visitors got much sleep. A favorite memory is one of the students offering a prayer of thanks before our collective breakfast the next morning, "Thank You, God, for the good experience of last night and thank You that it's over."

We felt like we had watched technology happen before our eyes during our years in East Africa. From arriving with a used laptop that we didn't know how to operate, to Harrison helping with the installation of dial-up Internet. From taking students to Nairobi to Internet cafes to apply to Stateside colleges, to being introduced to cell phones first by a few students and then as a school safety measure for those traveling the dangerous roads between us and Nairobi. Finally becoming accustomed to seeing a Maasai warrior, standing under an acacia or baobab tree, garbed in his colorful red blanket, staff in one hand, cell phone to his ear in the other.

Then came the evening that our RVA neighbor called one of the national staff to ask a question about something done in the vehicle shop that day, only to have his call answered in a whisper. Our neighbor asked him, "Willie, why are you whispering?" Willie's answer, "Shh. . .don't talk so loud. I'm here, hiding behind a bush. They're trying to steal our cattle, but we're going to stop them. We've got our bow and arrows with us."

The time was drawing nigh for Tobin to make a decision about what college he planned to attend when he graduated. It appeared that he would have been content to stay forever here, on his own turf, where he belonged and everything was going his way. There was scarcely an upper school girl who had not had a crush on him at some point, sometimes even their little sisters did. I smiled, looking back to him sitting beside Sally Cates, the very gracious, genteel elderly lady he loved to sit with back at the window of church in Tennessee. One day he asked me if he could marry Sally when he grew up. But now it was time for him to grow up, and if it entailed moving away from this comfortable Kijabe window, he really had no desire for it. He wouldn't have minded going to the University of Nairobi; it was the return to the States that he seemed to dread.

One morning when Tobin came to the breakfast table, Harrison told him that time was passing and he needed to make a decision about where he wanted to go to college. Tobin's glum response was, "Surprise me, Dad." The decision left primarily to him, Harrison chose what he believed would be a good school for Tobin, that offered the best financial package and where other RVA students were already attending.

In May of 2002, Harrison received news that his father's health was failing quickly and that he should return home. He did, arriving at Eureka Hospital in Illinois and finding his father in good spirits, lucid and able to enjoy Harrison's company. After enjoying days of quality time together, Harrison took the opportunity of being present in the States to accompany Cherith in her red Pontiac GrandAm to Quebec, Canada, where she was taking summer classes in French. After helping her settle there, Harrison returned to Illinois by train in time to spend some more days with his father before he departed this earth and stepped into eternity, finding it home.

That return trip to the States was the first of several that one or more of us would make before our final departure from East Africa.

Cherith came from the States for Christmas of 2002. As we neared the airport, we saw huge crowds gathered, some groups dressed in traditional African get-up and singing national songs. We joked that everybody in Kenya was as excited about Cherith's homecoming as we were, but the truth was that Kenya's new president, Mwai Kibaki, was also landing at Jomo Kenyatta airport.

It was so wonderful to have Cherith with us once again, especially as we celebrated Christmas together, doing our traditional activities such as going with the large group singing Christmas carols in the Kijabe Hospital on Christmas Eve. When the holidays were over, instead of returning to the States, Cherith flew to Angers, France

197

where she did the spring semester in French, with, she later told me, "No teacher speaking English ever." That sounded scary difficult to me, but what she found more difficult was being American in France. From what I've heard from others, but not experienced myself, being an American in France can be difficult at any time. At this particular time when the United States was making plans to invade Iraq, more than once Cherith received clear messages of disapproval simply for being American. That made her especially grateful for the comment of one French student, "Cherith, we know it's not your fault what America is doing."

In July of 2003, Tobin graduated from RVA. There's a world of emotions, activities and preparations for change packed into that simple sentence. Cherith came from France, for Tobin's graduation and also to be with her graduating class for alumni weekend. Although all alumni are welcome, the students from the class of two years prior traditionally make every effort to be back for this special weekend.

The evening of Tobin's graduation day, our family departed for the States. This time when we landed in London, left our big luggage to be picked up on our return, and flew with just our hand luggage on to Sweden. We had a very special time reminiscing in Sweden with some missionary families we had worked with in Tanzania, had a very cold swim in the Baltic Sea, went on to Norway, and ended up in Denmark, where we attempted to fly back to London – but alas, British Airways had gone on strike and all flights back to London had been cancelled. We waited in a very long line for a very long time only to find out that we could get a flight to Chicago. The problem was that we had left our luggage in storage in London. It could not be taken out of storage without us collecting it. We were then granted tickets on another airline to London, where we arrived to find wall-to-wall people everywhere. There were an estimated 10,500 of us stranded. Eventually, we managed to get our luggage out of storage, and spent the night sleeping on the airport floor, thankful for the cushy Emirates mat that we found unoccupied. We woke up early to be the first in line requesting a ticket for a different airline. Receiving our tickets, we then got in another line for those being accepted by other airlines to help out the situation, and were the last ones accepted to get onto the flight for Chicago! Whew.

This trip back, we stayed in Roanoke, in what had been our home, which Harrison's parents had moved into when we left for Word of Life in upstate New York. With the passing of Harrison's father, his mother had moved into the Roanoke Apostolic Christian Nursing Home, leaving our home open at this time. Though it was good to be home to reconnect with family and friends, our main purpose in coming to the States was to help get Tobin settled in at John Brown University in Siloam Springs, Arkansas. Before leaving Roanoke, Harrison and Tobin spent a couple days looking for a used car for Tobin. They found a good deal on a white Pontiac Grand Prix, and we were ready to head to Tobin's new window of life.

We made the journey from Illinois to Arkansas in our two vehicles. The further south we got, the hotter and more humid it got. Winding along a two-lane back country highway that seemed to get narrower with each tiny town we passed through, Tobin pulled into a gas station. We followed him. Getting out of our vehicles, the 104 degree heat blasting us, the local talk sounding almost foreign to us, not only Tobin, but Harrison, Lizzie, and I, all wondered where we were going, what we were doing, and why. The uncertainty mounted as we continued on. That is why it is hard to say how relieved and comforted I was as we finally entered Siloam Springs to see a signboard that read in large letters:

Welcome to Siloam Springs
Where Jesus is Lord
Welcome to God's country

I could hardly believe my eyes. I had never seen such a sign and never had I ever been so glad to see one! Though leaving Tobin behind there at John Brown University may have been the hardest thing I have ever had to do, that sign, true or not, brought me no small amount of comfort. Later on, when questioning Tobin about everything there, I asked, "So Tobin, is everyone at your college a Christian?" I can still hear his quick reply, "Yep, Mom, they are. There's not a Muslim among 'em." At the time, I didn't know how

Christian higher education worked. Today I have a much better understanding.

* *

Leaving both Cherith and Tobin behind in the States, Harrison, Lizzie and I returned to our home in Kijabe, Kenya. Our many activities, especially continuing to be class sponsors for Lizzie's class – which felt a lot like having seventy kids of our own – kept us occupied and a healthy distance from the grief of Cherith and Tobin's absence. But waiting at Jomo Kenyatta airport for Cherith and Tobin to get off the plane to spend their Christmas vacation from school with us, my mind returned to sitting there on the porch swing in Tennessee, little Lizzie asleep in my arms, Cherith and Tobin's laughter coming to me on the breeze as they played by the babbling stream. Again, it didn't seem like life could get much better than this. We'd be together again, and though the plane tickets cost more than we could afford, I now knew for sure that there's no price you can put on 'being with' – which is, of course, all that Christmas is about, *God with us*. (Matt. 1:23) This truth reminds me of a full page ad that I saw in the local newspaper this past Christmas: *Man reaching for God is called religion. God reaching for man is called Christmas*.

Too soon, the new year was upon us, Cherith and Tobin had returned to their privileged jobs of being educated in the States and we to our jobs, a big one of which was to help our seventy kids raise enough money to go on their final *hurrah*, a trip to the coast at Mombasa, called *senior safari*, or affectionately, *senior safo*. In the midst of all our busyness, we received word that Tobin had broken his jaw in a JBU rugby game. Surgery was required to put in a titanium plate. Cherith missed her classes and drove through a snow storm in Illinois to be with Tobin after his surgery in Arkansas. To say that this was a terribly rough time for all of us is an understatement indeed. I experienced anew the upholding of missionary sisters who understood the pain of being an absent mother and knew how to share the burden of my heart. Missionaries are wonderful people.

It was also during this term of service that RVA hosted an Association of Christian Schools International (ACSI) conference. Though I was aware that the conference would provide high-quality professional development, I was not aware of the effect it would have in shaping the direction of my future. In deciding between the various sessions, my friend Ruth suggested that we try the Teaching English to Speakers of Other Languages (TESOL) session. Torn between the excellent choices, I agreed. It was in that session that Dr. Seaman, a world-traveling TESOL professor from Wheaton College in Illinois, captured me with God's compassionate heart for the stranger and the alien.[5] That combined with my love of language and my vision of it as a vehicle to join people groups together, and presto! I was in.

Baptism Sundays were always a special time at RVA. The baptistry consisted of a permanent concrete structure outside of and behind the gymnasium and there, overlooking the Rift Valley, was where baptismal Sundays took place. It was wonderful to hear the testimonies and favorite Bible verses of the kids, many of whom we knew so well. Harrison had the privilege of baptizing both of his daughters in that beautiful spot. When preparing for her baptism, knowing her father's soft heart, Cherith had asked him not to get too emotional. So when his voice broke with emotion as he was speaking a few words before dunking her, Cherith warned him in a low voice, "Da-ad." He quickly recovered and baptized her. This term it was Lizzie being baptized. Harrison maintained his composure and Lizzie rose up out of those waters glowing like she had just come down off Mt. Sinai.

This term, too, we had some special guests from the States. One was Brent, the medical student son of good friends of ours from the church on the prairie in Illinois. His mother had been especially concerned about her son coming to visit the medical work in Africa. After happening to chat with Cherith and Tobin, whom she found to be 'so normal and relaxed about life in Africa,' she was calmed in her spirit. As Harrison and I were at the airport in Nairobi, waiting for Brent to arrive, we laughed when we realized that we very likely wouldn't recognize Brent since we hadn't seen him since he was a baby! But sure enough, we knew it was him when we saw him

– looking like a perfect cross of his father and mother. It was a real pleasure getting to know him as an adult.

Harrison had a real surprise one day when Joe, a farmer and family friend from the days of Harrison's youth in Roanoke, showed up at RVA! It turned out that Joe was part of a group of central Illinois farmers who belonged to Fellowship of Christian Farmers International, and had just completed a work trip in Tanzania. The group had flown on an AIM flight from Mwanza, Tanzania to Nairobi and had driven to RVA to see the school and give us a good surprise!

In the summer of 2004, Harrison's oldest brother, Steve, his wife, and their three daughters came to visit us. I recently asked his wife, Joyce, what she remembers about the trip. She said she remembered and still tells people today about the awesomeness of the stars in the black African sky – that there's nothing like it. She also remembers: traveling to be with the Pokot tribe; the camels, donkeys, goats, and cows wandering near the road; stopping at a small school where the children sang a few songs to us; passing by a makeshift tavern where the men were drinking at noon; not being able to watch as other Pokot men slaughtered the goat that we would eat that evening; Steve sucking the marrow out of the goat's bone before we ate the ribs, soup, and ugali; me being sick behind our rondoval in the night; and the beauty of the Mombasa coast. Her window brought to mind things that I had completely forgotten.

What I recalled was our Kenyan friend, Willie, lovingly inviting us all to their humble home for a meal. As Willie's wife was preparing the meal, Willie, Steve and Harrison talked farming – a subject they all had in common. Willie told of his deep thankfulness to the Lord for the blessing of his three acres and asked Steve how many acres he farmed. We watched as this conversation changed the short remainder of Steve's life. He had always had a big soft heart, but now, from this new window he had gained into another's life, it was a joy to see his newfound appreciation for the life he had been blessed with and his desire to share it.

At the same time that Steve, Joyce and their daughters got on their flight to return to the States, Lizzie and I got on a different flight to the States. Lizzie wanted to have a look at some colleges in the States to help her make a decision in choosing one – plus we were both longing to spend some time with Cherith and Tobin. As we all had our final breakfast together, we joked with Steve's family that after breakfast in Nairobi, we would have lunch in London and then dinner in Chicago. When we met back together in O'Hare airport, Steve drove Lizzie and me to Bloomington and left us off at my Uncle Ray and Aunt Jeanie's before driving on to their home in Roanoke.

Lizzie and I were so thankful for Uncle Ray and Aunt Jeanie's caring hospitality, not only toward us, but also Cherith and Tobin whenever they could be present with us. It was a wonderful time of being together with friends and family. Brent, who we had recently gotten to know back in Kijabe, even took Lizzie for a ride in a Dodge Viper from his father's dealership in Roanoke. Boy, did she ever feel proud – like she was somebody completely other than her missionary kid self!

Too soon, it was time to once again leave behind life in America and rejoin Harrison and our normal lives in Kenya. Immersed once again in the all-consuming busyness of life at RVA, time passed quickly and soon it was, what we thought would be, our last Christmas in Africa. To make it a really special one, not only Cherith, along with a friend, and Tobin, but also Tartisio and John came to spend the holiday season with us! It was a truly wonderful time of togetherness, one of life's biggest joys.

After the holidays were over and life was back to normal, things got much busier – if that was even possible. Our kids used to laugh about the saying, *'Beware of the wrath of a patient man.'* What they liked about it was how true it was of their favorite man in the whole world, their father. He was known for being a very patient man, but Cherith, Tobin, and Lizzie knew there was a point when his patience ran out – and one needed to be aware of that.

If traffic tests the patience, and we all know it does, Harrison failed the test one day in Nairobi. He had taken our Nissan Patrol into a shop to have the small dents and scratches repaired, and for it to be cleaned up and detailed, inside and out, because he was selling it to his best missionary friend at RVA. The incident happened on the busy afternoon that he picked our vehicle up and was returning to Kijabe. The roundabouts in Nairobi, like many other world cities, can be absolutely crazy. Such was the case in the one Harrison had just entered. The rule of roundabout driving in Kenya is, *when you're in, you're in; when you're out, you're out.* As Harrison entered and was starting around the roundabout, a car from an inner lane of the roundabout pulled over into the outer lane that Harrison had just entered and struck him on the back side of the vehicle. Stopping immediately, and jumping out of the vehicle to assess the damage done to his newly shined beauty, Harrison was relieved to see that the other vehicle had only hit his tire and no damage was done to his vehicle.

The problem was that, though relieved, he was also full of pent-up wrath – so much so that it was through a blind of rage that he saw the other man get out of his car and assess his own damage of a broken headlight and a bent bumper. When the man arrogantly accused Harrison of being at fault (though another driver rolled down his window to shout out the opposite), Harrison, without controlling himself, angrily approached the man, thumped him on the chest with his knuckles, shouting, "This is your lucky day!!" The poor man had no way of knowing that our vehicle had just moments earlier come out of the car shop and the reason he was lucky was because he had done it no damage. With those words, Harrison jumped back in the vehicle and drove on. Glancing back in his rear view mirror, Harrison saw the man, who apparently didn't believe in luck, scribbling on a scrap of paper, though we would never hear from him again.

I was busy doing something when Harrison came home that evening and sheepishly told me the story. Because I was busy, I was only half listening, until I realized what he was telling me! I could not believe he had done something so out of character for him! I stopped what I was doing and looked at him – realizing I hadn't really done so for a very long time. Standing in front of me, I saw that he looked tired, really really tired, like exhausted all the way to his bones. I was thankful that Lizzie's graduation was quickly approaching and silently prayed that we would manage to get safely away from this window.

Finally, it was time for Lizzie and our other sixty-nine kids to graduate and move on to their futures. The main graduation speaker was a good missionary friend of ours from Tanzania. He gave a very inspiring message, one entirely appropriate for an RVA graduation of the world's future missionaries and leaders. The message was on doing great things for God. Though thoroughly and completely in agreement with instilling in young people the fervent desire for doing extraordinary things for God, there remained a still small voice in me, insisting that there was another very important viewpoint to consider. I'll let William Martin's reinterpretation of the Tao Te Ching express this view that I couldn't ignore, try as I might:

Make the Ordinary Come Alive

Do not ask your children
to strive for extraordinary lives.
Such striving may seem admirable,
but it is a way of foolishness.
Help them instead to find the wonder
and the marvel of an ordinary life.
Show them the joy of tasting
tomatoes, apples and pears.
Show them how to cry
when pets and people die.
Show them the infinite pleasure
in the touch of a hand.
And make the ordinary come alive for them.
The extraordinary will take care of itself.[6]

I wanted to be wrong about those small red flags I saw. And perhaps I was. Or perhaps we were both right – just two different windows of looking at the same view.

And so we had come to the end of our time of the many joys and struggles of daily life in living and working at Rift Valley Academy in Kijabe, Kenya. Along with the daily grind, there had also been many getaways in awesomely beautiful spots, places I loved to see Beauty and read His Word – like the time in Nanyuki, sitting outside our room at Mt. Kenya Safari Club, when I read how to guarantee one's self against uselessness.[7] I also learned so

205

much from the animals. I was so impressed by the family nature of wild animals: the dead baby giraffe with its grieving mother sitting beside it; the familial relationships among the elephants – watching the teenagers romp together while the mother helped the baby to walk and patiently taught it to use its little trunk to eat; and watching the lioness – being the usual 'getter of meals' – so carefully stalk her prey. I can never forget the herds of elephant running until we could only see massive clouds of dust, nothing else. And the beauty of the huge red ball of African sun setting on the edge of the savannah, outlining a lone acacia tree, as another day drew to its close. Beauty simply surrounded us and covered us over as we did our daily work, just doing what we found in front of us to do, and doing it with all of our might.

This time it was Tobin who had a double reason for returning to RVA – for his sister's graduation and the return of his class for alumni weekend. Because we would all be returning to the States to stay, Cherith was thinking she would forego the expense of a ticket this time. But as Beauty would have it, Brent's parents decided that we had come to Africa as a family unit and they saw it as only right that we should leave as the same family unit. To make it happen, they sent Cherith to us. Beauty is as beauty does. Fifteen years from leaving the States for Africa, we returned to America. But we were not the same people at all – we had all been changed in the process. Hopefully, for glory and for beauty.

On our way back to the States, we stopped in Morocco, for what was, in my mind, the most memorable family vacation of all. Immediately upon entering the airport in Casablanca, we knew we were somewhere unlike anywhere we had been to date. We had become accustomed to security officers standing about with AK-47s, but we were not used to those same people along with many others shouting! Everyone seemed to be yelling. At first we thought something had really gone down, but finally decided this was normal conduct. We spent the first two nights at the home of a family who were fellow dorm parents with us at RVA, but were now tent-makers here. They were away and had graciously offered us their lovely place.

We began our adventure via train, trusting ourselves to Cherith's ability to speak French, but before long we found a taxi driver named Abdullah who drove us most of our ten days there. Abdullah proved to be both an exceptional and sensitive tour guide. When explaining the importance of the holy men's graves, he asked Tobin (whose turn it was to sit in front with him – we rotated; there had to be four of us in the back seat of his small taxi!) if he believed in these holy men. Tobin answered carefully, "Uh, no, not really." Then Abdullah asked Tobin what holy men he did believe in. Tobin answered, "I believe in Jesus Christ." Abdullah responded with a logical question, "Where was he buried?" It was so logical, in fact, that Tobin began to turn to us in the back seat to ask where Jesus was buried, when he realized and spoke the true answer, "He's not buried; He's alive!" Further conversation led to a discussion of Jesus' ancestors and our belief in the God of Abraham, Ishmael,[8] Isaac, and Jacob. Abdullah, in concluding that we believed in a common Supreme Being, came to a happy conclusion that I've never forgotten: "Oh then – we're cousins!!" *Yes, cousins.* We were sad when it came time for us to part with Abdullah at a hotel in Marrakesh. Along with our payment for his services, we left him a New Testament, in hopes that he'd discover for himself that God has no grandchildren. Indeed, each descendent of Abraham can reach the Father Heart of the One True God in only one way - through His Son, Jesus Christ, the Messiah. No other way. There you have it – the Father's final authoritative Word.[9] Believe and receive it, for your own best interests. For glory and for beauty. And to join in the pleasures forevermore. Because if I've learned one main lesson in writing down this life story of mine it is this: make sure to give credit where credit is due – as in all glory goes to God, the Only Real Author, and not to us, His precious little copies.

Though we had amazing cultural experiences in Casablanca, Fez, and Marrakesh, the picture engraved indelibly on my memory is from our experience riding camels in the Sahara desert – the five of us, each on our own camel, led by a local Bedouin boy. The full moon cast shadows of our five camels on the sand as we rode along in utter silence, nothing but drifts of sand for as far as we could see under the huge dome of dark African sky. After riding an hour or two, our leader decided it was a good place to stop and sleep for the night. He laid out five mats, and there under the stars, we lay down and slept soundly.

A thousand words could not describe the experience of waking to the sun's rays lighting up huge hilly waves of sand, drifted motionless, in every direction as far as our eyes could see. Simply and amazingly unforgettable.

Lessons learned:

There is no price that you can put on 'being with.'
Simple active work and spiritual activity are not the same thing.
Active work can actually be the counterfeit of spiritual activity.[10]
Self-realization only leads to the glorification of good works,. . .
Whatever we may be doing – even eating, drinking, or washing
disciples' feet – we have to take the initiative of realizing and
recognizing Jesus Christ in it. . .
In Christian work, our initiative and motivation are too often
simply the results of realizing that there is
work to be done and that we must do it.[11]
Above all self-care, nourish your soul.

PART III

The Effects

The Lord's Prayer / *Sala ya Bwana*

Our Father who art in heaven,
Baba yetu Uliye mbinguni,

Hallowed be Thy name,
Jina Lako litukuzwe,

Thy kingdom come,
Ufalme Wako uje,

Thy will be done,
Mapenzi Yako yatimizwe,

Here on earth as it is in heaven.
Hapa duniani kama mbinguni.

Give us this day our daily bread.
Utupe leo riziki yetu.

Forgive us our trespasses as we forgive those who trespass against us.
Utusamehe deni zetu kama sisi nasi tutasemehevyo wadeni wetu.

Lead us not into temptation but deliver us from evil,
Na Usitutie majaribuni lakini Utuokoe na yule mwovu,

For Thine is the kingdom and the power and the glory forever.
Kwa kuwa ufalme ni Wako na uguvu na utukufu hata milele.

Amen.
Amina.

16

Normal, Illinois

Out of Africa, Into Normal
2005 - 2009

W hen we arrived at our next window of Normal, we had nowhere to live. It happened exactly as I overheard Cherith laughingly telling someone, "You know how when you don't know what else to do, you move in with your parents? Not my parents, they move in with me!"

It was true. We didn't know what else to do and we did move in with her and her roommate, who fortunately was an MK from Kenya, whose parents we knew and loved. In spite of her joking, neither Cherith nor her roommate could have been more welcoming to Harrison, Lizzie, and me as we invaded the space in their apartment on Orr Street in Normal.

We had celebrated my forty-ninth birthday while eating the most delicious olives, sucking tasty snails out of their boiled shells, and trying to swallow sheep brain when we were in Marrakesh, Morocco. There was so much exotic excitement going on then that I didn't think so much about the age I was turning. But now, thinking about it here in America, I realized why so many people coming through my mom's visitation line commented on the tragedy of her dying so young. At the time, I was eighteen and my younger brother was fourteen. That's what I called young then. Now that I was the same age as my mom when she died, I, too, considered forty-nine to be

211

young. Especially to die. Because she stayed so much on my mind, one day I asked my older brother if he had thought about Mom a lot when he was forty-nine. His answer, "Every day."

Probably for a culmination of reasons, I got sick not long after we moved in on Orr Street. Because of that, one of my main memories of Orr Street is lying in the basement bedroom, sick, reading *The Constant Gardener* by John le Carre. Both the story line and its setting were familiar enough that I related too closely, not making me feel any better.

All of us were really glad when, a few weeks later, we were able to move into our friends' condominium on Ballyford Drive in Bloomington. These friends were former supporters of our work, who then became missionaries themselves. As they made the change from the corporate world to becoming missionaries in Ethiopia, they had sold their home and bought a new condo to have a place to come home to each summer. Now as they were returning to Ethiopia for the year, they graciously allowed us to rent their condo until we could find a place of our own.

We moved into their condo and Lizzie moved into the freshman dorm at Illinois Wesleyan University (IWU) in Bloomington. I started as a full-time undergraduate student majoring in English at Illinois State University (ISU) in Normal, and Harrison searched the papers looking for a job. He soon found one as a truck driver – working for the same farmers who owned the house we had lived in while here in 2001.

That was what we each found ourselves doing, but along with those changes we were each dealing with a whole host of underlying emotions as we made the shift from the missionary world to this present world. Being faced with the daunting challenge of entering the world of eighteen- to twenty-year-old college kids as a forty-nine-year-old woman, I found it helpful to repeatedly tell myself, walking between classes amongst the 20,000 youth, that I was nothing special, nothing great, nor was I dumb old scum; I was just me. Lizzie, on the other hand, had a huge desire to, as she put it, *Be BIG!* In questioning the nature of that desire, she further explained it as *being substantial.* That description helped me to see that she wasn't seeking glory for herself, but rather wanted to be able to show evidence of her essential value, to live a life of significance. And Harrison, for his part, was really struggling with both Lizzie's and my issues, along with another of his own. For lack of another way to put it, I saw him as feeling used and a little tricked. He had just assumed that Beauty rewarded faithful service in more splendorous ways than the mundane that we were experiencing as we struggled through the days and weeks at this window.

Though I was a full-time student, I felt I should get a job to help out with the expense of relocating to the States. Every time I drove by a certain nice-looking building with a playground outside, I would read the sign, *The Baby Fold*, and be intrigued. So one day I decided to go in and apply for a job there. They hired me as a part-time nurse for their Residential Treatment Center (RTC). The RTC was a mental health treatment program for children ages three through thirteen with a variety of severe and complex mental health problems, who need intensive supervision and treatment twenty-four hours a day. The Residential Treatment Center combined a positive living environment and residential school services for children with severe trauma, and psychiatric, emotional and behavioral disorders. Mental health had been one of my favorite rotations when I was in nursing school, but having chosen the path of intensive care nurse, I had never gained experience as a mental health nurse. Now I had the opportunity, and with children – whom I've always especially loved and been fascinated by. It turned out to be a very positive and eye-opening window in all aspects – the children, the staff, physicians, teachers, and the relationships between them all. The other nurses and I bonded in eternal ways, reaching far beyond the job. Later on, Harrison and I took the classes offered to become foster parents and, for a short time, fostered one of the residents who reminded us of our John, who had remained behind in Tanzania.

As a student, I spent a lot of time studying at the kitchen table on Ballyford Drive. One sunny afternoon in the fall, I sat there trying to study, but was mostly reminiscing about my childhood. Through the sliding glass patio door, I watched the farmers harvesting their golden corn in a field behind the condo. The ringing of the phone interrupted my thoughts. I answered it. It was Tobin's rugby coach at JBU. I knew that there had been a game that day and had wondered why Tobin hadn't called to tell about it, as he usually did. The coach told me not to be alarmed, everything seemed to be okay, but he just wanted to let me know that he was in the hospital emergency room with Tobin, who had received a pretty severe concussion. It had been quite concerning because he was out cold for several minutes. They had stopped the game and the team gathered around him to pray. When he came to, he was completely disoriented to time and space, unable to appropriately answer even the most basic of questions. After Tobin was unable to answer who the president of the United States was, another MK on the team from RVA had an idea. "Tobin," he asked, "who's the president of Kenya?" Without missing a beat, Tobin answered, "Kibaki." They all smiled and sighed a huge sigh of relief, thanking Beauty.

The coach asked me if I would like to talk with Tobin. Of course, I wanted to. I asked Tobin what he was doing. "Hangin' out in the ER," he responded. The next time I talked to him, he didn't remember any of the above, or even anything leading up to it.

Irrespective of their nationality, most students from RVA went to college in the States. And when they got there, no matter which state they were in, they tended to keep in touch with one another. So I guess it was natural and shouldn't have taken me by surprise when the students from the class of 2005 began to call either Lizzie or me to say they were coming home for Thanksgiving – and by 'home,' they meant to our place! Though the condo wasn't large, we made do and had a really wonderful reunion of all those who could make it 'home,' plus a few international students who we had met along the way, such as the Korean student with whom I was doing conversational English and the French student who was living on Lizzie's floor at IWU. A few of the students stayed over and helped us get started on decorating for Christmas, even though the five of us ended up going to Florida to spend the Christmas holidays with my parents.

On February 3, 2006, my father turned eighty-five years old. I was so happy to finally be in the States to help celebrate his birthday with him. The effort that it took to organize getting off work and making arrangements for missing classes was well worth it. I drove from Illinois, my older brother, Adam, drove from his home in

Indiana, we met on Interstate 80, and went on to Burlington, Iowa in his car. Plans were already made for Dad and Ruth, Jacob and his wife, Adam and me, to eat at a new place called Martini's Grille, recognized as the most posh restaurant in Burlington.

The uncanny thing about it was that it used to be the old Burlington Hospital, where my brothers and I had all been born and where both Teddy and Mom had left this earth. The building itself was now an office building; Martini's was situated on the fourth floor and offered a spectacular view of the Mississippi River. We fared sumptuously, thoroughly enjoying ourselves and each other's company.

But as almost had to happen, all things considered, there came a point when Dad grew nostalgic over the births and deaths he had experienced in this very building. We listened and then, just before Dad had a chance to turn melancholy in his reminiscing, Jacob retrieved the festive gaiety of our celebration by saying, "These are better days, Dad!" I was glad for Jacob's words, even as it struck me how drastically a view can change out of a single window, depending on the season of life. Beauty can take so many forms. It's hard to immediately recognize them all.

~ ~ ~

In the spring of the year 2006, on Cherith's graduation day from ISU, we moved to our recently purchased home at 1711 Tompkins Drive in Normal, Illinois. Cherith, not wanting to be a bother when we were moving, said graduation was no big deal, she didn't need to walk that aisle; she wouldn't go, she would just help us move. The four of us told her not to be ridiculous; her graduation with a double major and a minor taking up five years of her life was a big deal, and we would be there whether or not she was. She went and we all cheered loudly for her.

It was our move into 1711 that wasn't a big deal – or rather, wouldn't have been a big deal if it hadn't been for those wonderfully nosey Christians at Christ Church. I'd better explain that statement.

When we were still in Kenya, we had come to expect Cherith's report on the excellent good news that she had received on Sunday. Her roommate had happened onto this church first and then persuaded

Cherith to join her at this little white church that looked exactly like a church, with its simple steeple lifting up the empty cross. So it was natural enough for us to join Cherith at this church she had been so inspired at. We were going to go to church somewhere, why not there?

Why not, indeed! Those Christ Church people received us with open arms and made us a part of their family from the moment we walked in. So of course, when the brother in charge of helping folks move found out that we were moving, he repeatedly asked Harrison to let him know ahead of time when moving day would be so he could get the help lined up. Probably it was because we had just lived the previous fifteen years of our life in Africa that the people at this window seemed to be more on the well-to-do side, making Harrison a bit embarrassed to let the moving team know that we had nothing to move, except for the suitcases we had brought with us from Africa – and they fit easily enough into our car. But this well-intentioned man kept pressing until Harrison had to tell the truth of the matter. Guess what? It wasn't long before we had a house of beautiful furniture! Beauty is as beauty does.

And having a home *is* a beautiful provision. Not only as a place to go when you're not somewhere else, but a place to keep things in an orderly, uncluttered manner. For example, Naomi had made full-size bedspread quilts for each of her grandchildren, love and prayers sewn in every stitch. Well, that was her intention. Between her own and Dad's, there were thirty some grandkids. She had started with the oldest grandchild and had made it all the way to Lizzie. She was working on Lizzie's when the car accident happened in Florida. My aunts ensured that Lizzie's got completed. And now I had a place to put such keepsakes until the kids had a place to display and use them. A Little Home to Keep, There's No Joy So Deep.

At 1711, various couples of good missionary friends from past windows – Bob and Deb, Tim and Karen, and Dave and Bonnie – each found us as they came to visit. It was so good to hear of their lives' happenings since our paths had diverged from one another. It's always wonderful to have loved faces from other places reappear in present windows!

It is likewise good to go back to visit those far away windows. Harrison had the chance to do just that when the same group of central Illinois farmers who had visited us at RVA asked him to go with them on their next trip to Tanzania with the Fellowship of Christian Farmer's International. Of course, Harrison was happy to go and they were super happy to have him along.

A sweet comfort comes from our little worlds meeting, such as happened with the passing of Harrison's mother in November of 2006. Her funeral was held in the Roanoke church on the prairie. Along with all those precious loved ones from our past, members of the farming community and Christ Church were also represented. For us, it was another turn on the front benches.

After graduating, Cherith moved to Morton, Illinois to be close to her internship in the treasury department at Caterpillar's Headquarters in East Peoria. Lizzie, after her freshman year, became a resident assistant (RA) in Ferguson Dorm at IWU. I sometimes went to visit Lizzie at IWU, every time being amazed at the difference in atmosphere between her IWU and my ISU worlds. As we would walk across campus, everyone seemed to know Lizzie, greeting her by name. At ISU, I was a complete unknown. IWU appeared to me to be made of green and ISU of concrete. I can still feel that greenness of the grass and the faint warmth of the autumn sun, as I lay there exhausted, on the IWU quad, letting Lizzie's voice flow over me like a healing ointment as she read aloud from Walt Whitman's poetry collection, *Leaves of Grass*. This portion of it was an assignment for my poetry class later that afternoon. As Lizzie read, I was amazed at the coincidence of words and experience:

> *Loafe with me on the grass—loose the stop from your throat;*
> *Not words, not music or rhyme I want—*
> *not custom or lecture, not even the best;*
> *Only the lull I like, the hum of your valved voice.*
> ~~
> *All beauty comes from beautiful blood and a beautiful brain.*
> *If the greatnesses are in conjunction in*
> *a man or woman it is enough. . .*
> *the fact will prevail through the universe. . .*

but the gaggery and gilt of a million years will not prevail.
Who troubles himself about his ornaments
or fluency is lost. This is what you shall so:
Love the earth and sun and the animals,
despise riches, give alms to every one that asks,
stand up for the stupid and crazy,
devote your income and labor to others, hate tyrants,
argue not concerning God, have patience
and indulgence toward the people,
take off your hat to nothing known or
unknown or to any man or number of men,
go freely with powerful uneducated persons
and with the young and with the mothers of families,
read these leaves in the open air every season
of every year of your life,
re-examine all you have been told at
school or church or in any book,
dismiss whatever insults your own soul,
and your very flesh shall be a great poem
and have the richest fluency not only in its words
but in the silent lines of its lips and face and
between the lashes of your eyes
and in every motion and joint of your body. . .[1]

During Lizzie's time at IWU, she was very involved in the campus' Intervarsity Christian Fellowship (IV). When IV held their student missions conference for the first time in St. Louis (normally held at the University of Illinois at Urbana-Champaign), Lizzie, Cherith, and some of their friends decided to go. It was there that Lizzie fell in love with the mission and ministry of International Justice Mission (IJM), but as she understood it, she would never be qualified to be a part of the rather elite staff they were looking for. By this time, Cherith had tentative plans to become a United States Peace Corp volunteer. Unfortunately, whenever she had cause to express this to the representatives of the missions presenting their organization, she felt she was received as a second class citizen. I felt sad for her when she told me this. And I felt sad for the mission representatives who couldn't see the beauty of the heart standing before them.

A wonderful quality of TCKs is that they either don't see skin color or if they do, they value it. Cherith and Tobin tended toward the latter, Lizzie the former. During Cherith's years at ISU, she played a little game with herself. Whenever she encountered a black person, she instinctively knew if they were African-American or if they were African. More than that, she imagined herself to know which African country they were from. If she judged them to be truly African, she would raise the stakes of her game by striking up a conversation with them, asking them if they were from whichever country she believed them to be. She was able to pride herself by most often being correct!

We noticed by listening to Lizzie's frequent mention of the name, that she was becoming very fond of a certain 'Teddy' at IWU. As they continued to spend more time together, she invited him over for our long-time tradition of Friday night pizza. They were already there when Harrison and I arrived home. We instantly liked Teddy and could see why Lizzie did too. We all had a great time together and after Teddy left, Harrison casually commented to Lizzie that she had failed to mention to us that Teddy was African-American. Lizzie asked in complete surprise, "I didn't??" We smiled, thinking back to the time many years earlier when four-year-old Lizzie was naming everything that was different between her and her brother John. She went through many physical traits that differed between them (straight hair/curly hair, black hair/blonde hair, chubby/skinny, tall/short, etc.) before she ever got to the difference of their skin color. I was glad things hadn't changed.

It was an odd experience, being a college student the same time as our kids. I remembered a parent of an RVA student once telling me that they just loved to come visit RVA for a few days because it gave them such a valuable window into their daughter's life. I felt the same when we would visit Tobin at JBU for a weekend. And often, while walking from class to class or sitting in a large lecture hall with a couple hundred other students, I would think of leaving Cherith here on her own, with us in Africa. It made me shudder and sigh. Though she didn't say much, it couldn't have been easy.

For me, at my stage of life, each ISU class was a revolutionary experience in my life thinking. I couldn't understand how the kids around me could sit through classes bored, if not sleeping, when I was finding them to be absolutely fascinating. I had to wonder if the difference wasn't that they didn't have enough real life experience to hang the classroom theory on. The funny thing was that some of them found me too old and conservative to know anything! For example, the next class after presenting my senior thesis on *The Effects of Light and Darkness Throughout Literature*, one young man in the class slipped me a little piece of paper suggesting I read *The God Delusion* by Richard Dawkins. I was not at all opposed to reading from Dawkins' window, but while driving, I heard him in a debate on the radio and knew that life is too short to spend time reading from the foolish,[2] so I didn't. I have no problem with leaving vengeance up to Beauty Himself, confident that He does all things well and won't be mocked in the end- - and leaving me forever thankful that His wrath was satisfied at the cross of His Son, Jesus Christ.

The professor of that class, too, in working with me on that thesis, insisted that there are those who can see and understand more in the dark than in the light. Through it all, I learned to listen to others' views and receive what is of value while still remaining true to who I am. Thus, even in my preference for light over darkness, I can still value the darkness without losing myself, as David Whyte expresses in a line of his poem *Sweet Darkness*:

Sometimes it takes darkness and the sweet
confinement of your aloneness
to learn

anything or anyone
that does not bring you alive
is too small for you.[3]

I had great respect for my professors at ISU, even though not many of them claimed to be a part of the Kingdom of that light I valued so highly. I really felt for one of the few who stood with me on that side. When we were given an assignment in this particular class to persuasively present a topic in front of the class that we felt passionate about, I chose one sentence from a letter written by Saul of Tarsus – turned Paul by the Light, who was, at the time of writing, an obscure Roman citizen without connections. In the oral presentation, I presented myself similar to a courageous gay (though my voice was shaking) who had come out of their closet and into the light, revealing who they really were. I presented the real me, one courageous enough to proclaim that I was not ashamed of the gospel of Jesus Christ, because in it lies the power of God for salvation to anyone in the whole world who will lift their eyes to the cross of Christ, believe by a simple *Yes!* and receive life full and abundant, and pleasures forevermore. I ended by again connecting to the metaphor of stepping out of the dark closet and being amazed at the wondrous freedom of being clearly seen in the light.

When I finished, instead of the usual hands going up to respond in favor or disfavor of the persuasion, there was dead silence. I felt dizzy, like the room was closing in on me, but I heard the professor's voice asking for a response, any response. Finally, one student raised her hand. When the professor nodded to her to speak, she simply said, "The speaker made her point very clearly." Unsteady, I returned to my seat. As I passed by him, I heard the professor mutter under his breath, "If that were me, I'd be crucified."

Speaking of salvation, there was another professor, one in a huge lecture hall, who produced evidence of knowing the Bible inside out, but not believing a word of it. One day when he was railing against evangelicals, not without valid reasons, he especially scorned the idea of salvation. "They want to know if I'm saved!" he mocked. "I ask them, saved **from what??**" The answer was immediately clear to me, though I sat quiet in the sleepy crowd, *From yourself, Doctor, from your arrogant self.*

I sympathized with his railing against Christians who "preach a subtle hatred, the Bible as their alibi",[4] but he lost me when he said his main thing against us is that we are trained that the imagination is evil. To me, that was as ludicrous an idea as salvation was to him. I see imagination as coming about as close to real beauty as we can get in this life!

I consider my window at ISU to have been one of the most effective views in my life. I deduced so many valuable concepts. From rhetoric class: always ask yourself *What is the effect?* From medieval times: what lordship and disciplined discipleship really mean. From poetry: manner of presentation serves a purpose, even the spaces, punctuation and capital letters, or lack thereof. From all classes: to use the truth intelligently, that dogmatism is unable to hear, that *Never* and *Always* are rare occasions, and that context is always king.

Most of the many papers that I was assigned to write at ISU, I wrote while riding my bike. That was easy. Then came the hard work of typing them when I got back to 1711 Tompkins Drive in Normal. That's just how it works for me. In fact, most of this book that you're reading was recalled while riding my bike, first around Lake Freeman in Monticello, Indiana and then in New Jersey parks and on trails. I don't know why things appear so clearly to me on my bike, ideas that good sermons in church only confirm. Maybe it's the wind that does it.

One day while riding in Normal, I happened to be in a turn lane intended for cars, because there was no bike lane to be in. A carful of laughing youth yelled at me out their car windows, "Get off the road!!!" For whatever reason, it made me furious, and I yelled back at them, "I'm a person, too!!" Later, when I told Cherith about the incident, she couldn't believe it, asking me, "You really did that?!" When I affirmed it, she laughed and laughed, repeating it again, *I'm a person, too.* I had no idea what was so funny about it, but her reaction made me think about it a little more and caused me to wonder how this episode fit with my wish to be invisible. Maybe the contrast was what made it so funny to Cherith. Even for me, it seemed like I could see myself in two opposite directions at the same time – invisible and a real person – making me wonder which was the reality.

Through the organization known as International Students, Inc. (ISI), Harrison and I had the privilege of hosting students arriving from other countries to go to school at Illinois State University. Because we would usually pick them up straight off the bus as they arrived from O'Hare Airport, we had the opportunity to catch their first impressions of everything. One such student was a doctoral student from China, whom I'll call Maggie. After she stayed with us for a short time, we helped her settle into ISU's student apartments at Cardinal Court. Our friendship continued and grew quite deep as we each shared our minds and hearts – something we were each willing to do, even though we were very different from one another. For example, I believe each of us lives eternally in some form and Maggie was emphatic that 'when you're dead, you're dead.' It intrigued me that anything that I ever said on spiritual matters, Maggie, though she personally disagreed, would always say, "Yes, that's exactly what my English teacher, May, said in China." Because it happened so often, I asked questions about this English teacher. As Maggie told me about her, I thought I'd like her and wished that I could meet her someday.

At it turned out, Tobin and I both graduated the same weekend in December 2007. I was more than happy to miss my ceremony to attend his. During the night after Tobin's graduation, it began to snow heavily, very unusual weather for Arkansas. Though we left in good time the next morning, it was late by the time we reached Illinois because it snowed the entire trip home, making what was usually an eight-and-a-half-hour trip take hours more. We had no choice but to keep at it, because the following day Tobin and Lizzie had airline tickets to go spend their Christmas holidays with Cherith at her newly assigned Peace Corp site in Kemise, Ethiopia. We arrived to 1711 dead tired, dropped into bed and slept.

I opened my eyes the following morning with one clear question on my mind. *Had Tobin brought his passport with him?* Because he had already begun work with a construction management company in Arkansas, he had only brought the clothes that he needed for his visit to Ethiopia. I quickly got up and went to where he was sleeping, and tapping on his shoulder to wake him, whispered, "Tobin. . .Tobin, do you have your passport?" Tobin opened groggy eyes, looked at me as through a haze, shook his head *no*, and closing his eyes he turned the other way. Anxiously, I shook his shoulders. No longer whispering, I said, "Tobin! Wake up! Did you hear me? DO you have your passport?!" He groaned, rolled over, sat up, looked straight at me as though comprehending but also still sleeping, and said, "No. I don't."

Forcing himself awake, he got up. Before long he had made and implemented a plan. He had called his girlfriend, woke her up, asked her to go to his apartment, told her where to find his passport, and booked her an airline ticket from Siloam Springs to O'Hare airport, telling her where to meet us at O'Hare. He gave her a little time, and then called her back to make sure she was really awake and up. Otherwise, he could imagine that she would easily go back to sleep and when she awoke later, think that she had dreamt a funny dream.

The plan worked like a charm – there she was, the pass-off complete, Tobin and Lizzie safely on their way to Cherith in Ethiopia, and the three of us were off to Ikea Chicagoland to see what there was to see.

On the other end of their journey, things didn't go so smoothly for Tobin and Lizzie. Thankfully, the owners of our condo on Ballyford met them at the airport in Addis Ababa and directed them safely to the bus stop to find the bus going to Kemise. It was then that their difficulties began. It was nothing like Tobin's Greyhound bus experience in the States, where everyone spoke English. Here, no one spoke English or Swahili, and Amharic isn't easy to pick up; even the word *Kemise* is indistinguishable when written in Amharic characters instead of Roman letters. They told the bus driver that they wanted off in Kemise, about a four-hour bus ride away. The driver remembered them when the time came and they got off. But things got more complicated because Cherith, not knowing when the bus would arrive, wasn't there to meet them, and they didn't know how to get to her. Tobin and Lizzie were quickly surrounded by curious Ethiopians, most of whom seemed to want to help. Tobin and Lizzie tried any phrase that they thought might be helpful in describing Cherith, such as *white girl, Peace Corp, clinic. Clinic* was the one that worked – but only partially.

Cherith's role as a Peace Corp Volunteer (PCV) was to provide support to the Ethiopian government's HIV/AIDS program. It was actually an office that Cherith worked in, not a clinic. Therefore when the helpful Ethiopian lad delivered them proudly to the local clinic, Cherith was not there. But fortunately, there was someone with a cell phone there, Lizzie and Tobin had Cherith's number with them, and they successfully connected. Their ordinary adventures were disrupted a couple of days later by the sudden inexplicable death of a government official from the Addis Ababa office, who had come to Kemise to visit Cherith and her immediate Ethiopian supervisor. This and much more was all animatedly reported to Harrison and me when we picked Tobin and Lizzie up at the airport in Chicago a few weeks later.

About a year later, Harrison and I were delighted to also get a chance to visit Cherith in Ethiopia. Everything went much smoother for us as Cherith took us on a circuit of historic northern Ethiopia, visiting Lalibela, Axum, and Bahir Dar, seeing the sights and getting to meet other PCVs along the way. Other than the pleasure of getting a window into Cherith's and the other PCVs' daily lives, the two things I remember most were dramatic in their juxtaposition: the sense of awe I felt as our tour guide through the rock-cut archi-tecture of the ancient Lalibela churches spoke reverently of "The God of Abraham, Isaac, and Jacob," and the experience of using the absolutely unbelievably worst outhouse ever at Haik Lake.

I got to see and hear about Cherith's daily life as the only foreigner in her 99 percent Muslim community, with more camels standing around than I have ever seen in my whole life. The children who threw stones at her as she walked to work every day. The loneliness of living alone without electricity for comfort and connection to the world, and the other inherent dangers. As a mother, my favorite part of it all was when she came home to Normal! I recently heard a perfectly godly mother of missionary children express the way she viewed their work, "It was just too far away. I prayed them home." It made me think of Cherith in Ethiopia. Whether or not it was my prayers that brought Cherith home, I can't say, but either way, when she did come home, she didn't stay for long – just a short stint between Peace Corp placements, the next one being in Guiyang, China.

Our visit to Ethiopia had come at an opportune time for Harrison – between jobs. After working as a truck driver for about eighteen months, he had taken a new position as a facility manager overseeing fifteen branches of National City Bank. A year-and-a-half later, as

225

the banking crisis was beginning, PNC bought out National City and Harrison's department was outsourced to another company, costing Harrison his job. That was when we took advantage of the time off to go spend time with Cherith in Ethiopia. Not long after returning from Ethiopia, Harrison helped a local farmer and friend to harvest his crops. When the harvesting was completed, Harrison looked for other work and found a job at the Peoria BMW dealership as manager of the detail shop.

While Harrison was undergoing that work history, I was simultaneously experiencing my own. As an English major/TESOL minor student at ISU, I had been very keen to work in ISU's English Language Institute (ELI), an intensive English program focusing on enabling international students to successfully enter and complete degrees at Stateside colleges. More than once, I had stopped in to see if there were any opportunities for me to be involved in their program. It didn't happen, but my desire to teach there didn't go away either.

After I had supposedly completed my degree and graduated, I received an email that my hours had been miscalculated and I was short one class from the graduation requirements. When I checked into this disappointing matter, my advisor said that I could come up with my own plan to fulfill the missing hours, but it must be approved by a professor. I quickly got in touch with the director of the English Language Institute and she was agreeable to me teaching there as a practicum. After that semester, the director allowed me to stay on and I loved (almost) every minute of my time teaching and learning from students from around the world, right there in Normal, Illinois!

Along with continuing in a nursing capacity at The Baby Fold, and beginning to teach at ELI, I also took on a role, first volunteering and then teaching, with a county adult literacy program called STAR (Sharing The Ability to Read). These three part-time jobs, along with the private tutoring that I was doing several times a week for some Korean missionary children, kept me more than busy, but I loved each of the jobs too much to give up any one of them.

In the meantime, Tobin, too, had changed jobs, moving from the construction management company that he had worked with when in college to another larger one called Kiewit. This company had hired him to be a part of their federal division, which entailed having a very involved background security check. While the security check was in progress, the company placed Tobin in an underground project in West Virginia. It was a stretching time for him. Every morning, for some months, he was lowered down through a shaft some 400 feet under the earth's surface. Every evening when he came up the shaft, saw the dying light of day and heard the birds singing, he promised himself he'd never go down there again. And then the next morning he got up and did the same thing again. I recall getting a text from him one day, asking me to get him an application to work at the new Carl's Ice Cream shop opening up two blocks from 1711. So he was plenty happy when it was time to move from that project to one building an addition onto a hospital in Hastings, Nebraska. The text he sent from there said something to the tune of, "Hurray for hospitals! They're outside!"

We were glad that, apart from a study abroad that she did in Ecuador one semester, Lizzie was nearby while we were at our Normal window. For me as a mother, one of the most beautiful parts of living in Normal was to have any one of our kids, from near or far, step into the house and call out, "I'm home!"

Another beautiful part of being in Normal was, as I mentioned before, our Christ Church family. Pastor Bob loved, loved, loved the Gospel of Jesus Christ, and he never tired of preaching about the grace of God in sending His Son to die for our sins, and then raising Him from the dead to give us a free and abundant new life. This message of grace was a balm of healing to our work worn hearts and Harrison especially, rarely, maybe never, listened to these messages of grace without his eyes filling with tears of thankfulness.

The missions committee was a natural place for us to fit, and so we did. One of my favorite memories of our mission committee meetings is the dear sister who, though we weren't necessarily using the Bible, just liked to have hers open beside her so that she could touch it if she needed or wanted to. I saw that as a beautiful thing.

While we were in Normal, Pastor Bob held one of his classes on Our Identity in Christ. I thought I already knew who I was, but the structure and nature of this class caused each of us present to become aware in new ways of what a difference it makes being in

Christ, rather than just being ourselves outside of Christ. I already knew that as a part of the universal church of Christ, I am meta-phorically a cell in the body of the bride of Christ, and when He returns to earth to claim us as such, our Heavenly Father has a great wedding supper planned for us – and then pleasures forevermore! But that's all futuristic. In this class I discovered how these truths affect my everyday life here and now. Because it's all true, I have nothing to prove and nothing to hide, and thus, nothing to fear! I felt amazingly free.

It's hard to say which or what combination of all the forces above led to the effect of Harrison and me looking to Asia, but that is what we did. Initially, Harrison's interest was in Tibet, but during our application process, the group disbanded because of political reasons. Had it not done so, my role would have been teaching English. Thus, it was a natural transition for us to turn to an organi-zation that Pastor Rod, from our supporting church in Indiana, had suggested to us almost as soon as we had returned to the States from Kenya. At that time, we were too tired to think of missions at all, and definitely didn't want to think of raising financial support again. Grace and time had healed our weary unwillingness, and we were ready to move on to Teach for Asia (TFA) and Christ Church was eager to send us.

There was a lot going on in our family at this same time, so, as it turned out, the Sunday that Christ Church called us to the front to pray a departing blessing over us, it wasn't only Harrison and me, but also Cherith and Lizzie. Lizzie had graduated from IWU and was going to South Korea to teach English to children in an after school hagwon program. Cherith had been accepted to teach English with Peace Core China. And it had been decided by TFA that we would be a good fit for Laos, though Harrison was still hoping for a place-ment in Tibet in time. So while the four of us were being blessed by prayer up front, Tobin, who had come home from Nebraska for the weekend, sat in the back of the church, looking very sad indeed. Not only had he not been eager to come to this continent, he was even less excited about being left here alone while we all went to different places in Asia, a continent altogether unknown to him.

A few weeks before leaving for Southeast Asia, an unbelievably bizarre accident happened involving Harrison's brother, Steve, his wife, Joyce, and Joyce's sisters. It occurred immediately after Roanoke's fireworks, which were held on July third. As everyone was standing up and collecting their chairs, blankets and belongings, a car accelerated into the crowd, ricocheting Joyce and her sisters out of harm's way, and ran directly over Steve. He was airlifted to St. Francis hospital in Peoria, but went straight on to Glory. It still boggles all of our minds.

We left Normal, feeling anything but.

Lessons learned:

Truth divides. Grace saves.
Take Jesus' words seriously when He warned to be
careful that the light in us isn't actually darkness.

17

Vientiane, Laos

A People of the Heart in the World's Most Bombed Country
2009 - 2010

Not long after we had begun the process of re-becoming missionaries, Marianne, our recruiter, checked in with us as she often did – but this time she was really super excited. She said our financial support was pouring in so fast that she called the director over to see it. "Have you seen the Hodel's support coming in? Look! Look at it!"

As our financial support rolled in, we were humbly put to shame, remembering our unwillingness 'to ever raise support again.' For one thing, the missionary couple in Ecuador who had so touched Harrison's life when he and his brother were traveling through South America, gave us a tithe of the inheritance they had received from a parent's death! Another incident involved a sister from Christ Church who popped over to our house in Normal, giving us a check that was ridiculously more than I knew she could afford. When I initially could not receive it, telling her that I knew she needed that amount more than we did, she said there was nothing for it – that she had received clear instructions from the Spirit, telling her that this money was to be put to His Kingdom's Work, so she had no choice in the matter. Oh my. I sometimes think that there's nothing harder than learning how to receive.

We knew beyond the shadow of a doubt that Beauty was opening the windows of heaven to bless us. What we did not know was Why. He knew. Of course.

Another happening was the day Marianne called to tell me that she had checked back, and the day that we had officially been accepted with the mission was the last day that the mission had been offering their tuition-free master's degree program, so I was in! Unbelievably, inexplicably lucky, I am. The last day. It reminded me of the day that I had reconnected with TFA, to say that we had changed our minds and were not unwilling to raise support so we wanted to apply with the mission. I had called the same recruiter that I had connected with years before when Pastor Rod had sent us the mission's info. In this latter phone call she told me, "Wow, Pam! God's timing is impeccable! This is my last day with TFA. I will get you in touch with another recruiter, Marianne. You will really like her." Unbelievable, inexplicable timing.

Now here we were in Colorado, receiving orientation to be missionaries once again. Only this time, we were training to be professionals of excellence, going places missionaries were not allowed to go – and going with *the cadillac of missions*. That was how I had heard it described by a member of our missions committee. I liked the image of professional excellence better than the missionary image, especially because I had so disliked experiencing the missionary pedestal every time we came back to the States. To me, it was the worst part of being a missionary. Being an incognito missionary appealed to my desire to be invisible and reminded me of the little poem Cherith had recited in such a precious manner so many years ago, at the home school recital back at the Tennessee window:

> *I'm nobody! Who are you?*
> *Are you nobody, too?*
> *Then there's a pair of us – don't tell!*
> *They'd banish us, you know.*
>
> *How dreary to be somebody!*
> *How public, like a frog*
> *To tell your name the livelong day*
> *To an admiring bog!*[1]

All of our sessions at this Colorado window – the large group led by the mission president, the field-specific breakout sessions, and the general logistics – were, like the mission itself, excellent. By excellent, I don't necessarily mean comforting. Sometimes quite the opposite, like the session we had just left, and we were heading to lunch, when Harrison asked me in an uncharacteristically pointed manner, "Do you realize that's how you've lived your life? Based on fear?" No, I had not realized it, but as he asked, the truth of what he was saying shone itself into my heart and mind. I clearly saw what he meant. He was referring to how I had raised our three precious gifts of kids – in fear of anything hurting them, in fear of losing any one of them, in fear of any harm concerning them, as though I were in control of their world. A self-deluded responsibility, like I thought I was God or something. And I had no idea I was doing it. On the contrary, I believed that I had no fear because I so trusted Beauty's care of all. I had successfully deceived myself – not unlike Eve in that primordial garden, knowing exactly what God hath said and hath not said.

It was also not comforting to hear from my brother, Jacob, that Dad had been having some health issues and had been admitted to the hospital in Burlington, Iowa. I had asked if I should return to be with him before leaving for Laos. My brother advised me against it, saying I probably needed to be there, where I was, if I was going to go with the team to Laos.

Everything is so connected. During one session a speaker whose name was *May* and who was a long termer with the mission, told us of some of her teaching experiences in China. Because her name was *May*, it crossed my mind to wonder if she could possibly be our Chinese friend's English teacher, the one who said all the same things as I did when discussing spiritual matters. When the session was over, I asked Harrison if he thought that was possible. No, he didn't, and he laughed when I said I was going to ask anyway. So I waited until May wasn't engaged with others in the group and then asked her if she ever had a student named Maggie when she was teaching in China. Looking at me questioningly, she said, "Yes, I got an email from her this morning. Why?" It was the one and same Maggie as our good friend! May was excited, too, telling us that she had prayed, as Maggie was leaving China to go to school in Illinois, that she would meet some Christians when she got there. We picked Maggie up off the bus when she arrived to ISU in Normal, Illinois. Cool, huh?

When our weeks of orientation in Colorado were over, it was time for us to get on the bus with all the luggage that we had brought for our year in Laos and head to the airport with our new team members. But the next window was not Laos – first we would spend some weeks in Hanoi, Vietnam. . . .

Never have I ever seen the like. I could hardly believe my eyes. There were no stop lights, much less any pedestrian crossings. How was I supposed to cross the street to get to the shop on the other side, even if Harrison did have a firm grip on my hand?? I'll tell you how – I shut my eyes, thankful for Harrison's unflappable calm in such situations, and let him lead me across what should have been a four-lane road, if there had been lanes, which there weren't. Instead, there was a solid stream of motorcycles flowing like a river in each direction. Stepping out into the street, it was the job of the motorcyclists to not hit us. We had been instructed to walk at a slow, steady pace straight across to the other side. True to our instructions, as we stepped out onto the street, the motorcycles began to flow around us just as a school of fish avoids an object in the water. They continued to flow seamlessly behind, around, and in front of us, without slowing or even appearing to notice we were there! I was eventually able to open my eyes, as long as I stared straight to a fixed point across the street, without ever looking around me. I'm sure there was a life lesson in that, but I was too focused on keeping calm and staying alive to receive any other lesson.

Besides practicing crossing the streets, during our time in Vietnam we also had classes on Southeast Asian culture, did an ethnography study in the park, practiced making lesson plans and then did real teaching in a Vietnamese university, rode busses, enjoyed ice cream in the most crowded ice cream shop we had ever been in, and relished eating the local Vietnamese food cooked and served on the street.

One day as we were looking to buy our new cell phones, we took a taxi downtown. After checking around, we decided to go to a coffee shop that we had heard served a good cup of coffee. It was on the other side of town, so we hailed another taxi, went, savored the coffee and explored the surrounding area. For our return trip, we decided to try the motorcycle taxis instead of a car taxi, thinking it would be a fun experience and cheaper than a car. Doing the best they could in English and using gestures, the motorcycle driver and Harrison agreed on a price for him and me to ride on two separate motorcycles to our destination – each believing the other understood. But they did not, and the language barrier won again.

After the scary pleasure of being a part of the motorcycle school of fish, with ease flowing with the other gazillion cycles, osmosing any pedestrian or other external object, we arrived at our destination. Harrison pulled the agreed upon amount out of his wallet, and then it began. The driver refused to take the money, saying they had agreed on a much larger price – an amount more than the air conditioned car taxi we had taken earlier. Harrison insisted that he take the agreed on amount. A crowd began to gather, one man trying to be a go-between. When the driver continued to refuse the amount Harrison was trying to hand him, Harrison laid the money on the motorcycle seat and turned to leave when BAM! A fist struck him forcefully on the back. Rather than turning to fight or be hit again, Harrison hurried into the nearest shop, which was the one we had been looking for cell phones in earlier. The driver made an attempt to follow him into the shop, but the security man at the door prevented this, holding the door shut. The driver was beating on the glass door and shouting. The shop attendant, recognizing us as the American customers who had been in earlier, and having seen the commotion outside the shop's display windows, ushered us into the safety of the recesses of the shop.

Not knowing what else to do, Harrison called the country director of TFA to tell him our predicament. The director gave surprising, helpful and confusing advice. It was surprising to learn that the Vietnamese consider a motorcycle taxi to be as far superior to a car taxi as a fish is superior to huge ship, in terms of the speed of getting somewhere. It was helpful to know that, because of this, they charge more for a motorcycle taxi than for a luxurious air conditioned taxi. And it was also helpful to know that perhaps the agreed upon price had been for one motorcycle, not for both the one Harrison rode on and the one that I rode on. My driver had simply stood by during all the negotiating and the following arguing, seeming almost amused by it all. Harrison's angry driver, on the other hand, appeared to be high.

The director confused us with his further explanation of why motorcycles cost more to use than cars – because motorcycles used gasoline. Acknowledging that we had only just arrived, knew almost nothing, and had almost everything to learn, we accepted everything the director said. Harrison went back outside to pay what the driver wanted. He received it sulkily, because, as we were learning in our classes, we had already caused him to 'lose face' – the worst possible happening in the culture. They shook hands, though again, the driver remained displeased and shame-faced. For us there was nothing to do but seek forgiveness for our well-intentioned ignorance, and continue to live and learn.

Real cultural learning involves a paradigm shift. And that's what happened to me here at this window when the Vietnam War came into conversation. Only it wasn't known as the Vietnam War. Here in Hanoi, that war was known as the American War. We were the enemy. One of the men in our class had been in the Vietnam War and was now here to help Vietnamese university students by teaching them the world's international language. The foe becoming friend. A message of joining together into the harmony of oneness. I loved it.

A favorite experience of this Vietnam window was being present when a choice couple, Jeff and Heather, met each other for the first time. This joy of ours would prove to be made more complete as we moved forward to living life together with them both in Laos, getting to know Heather's parents when they stayed with us there, and meeting more of the family on down the road, back in the good ole USA. But in the meantime, it was at this Asian window that Jeff introduced me to reading the Bible chronologically, in sequence of the time it was penned, causing me to love and eat the words with a new appreciation,[2] one of context, which I had already learned, is king!

* *

Arriving at the airport in Vientiane, Laos for the first time, felt somewhat like a deja vu of our first arrival at the mission field in Dodoma, Tanzania in 1990. I'm not exactly sure why. Perhaps it was their shared similarity of being sleepy, small town country capitals, setting them apart from most of the world's busy capital cities. This airport was more modern than Dodoma's had been in 1990, but upon leaving the airport, the tranquil placidity of flat, open spaces lent the same underlying quaintness of a city that was not in a hurry. I smiled as I recalled sharing with a mission leader in Hanoi, that I was glad that I didn't have to stay there because I wasn't at all sure I could get used to crossing those streets and listening to the constant honking and beeping day and night. This leader had told me that I would love it in Vientiane because I could lie down on the street and take a nap if I wanted to. Yes, I liked it here. Our recruiter had been right in sensing this was the place for us to start out in Asia. So similar to where we started out in Africa.

I can never forget the ride from the airport to the place where we were going to stay for our first weeks in Laos. Gleaming golden temples of religion were everywhere, reaching into the sky, shining gloriously under the hot Lao sun. My spirit lifted. These people were seeking Beauty! They knew there was a spirit world and that it was more important than the physical one. I was enthralled.

Even the roundabouts here showed a totally different way of thinking than those crazy ones in Nairobi, Kenya where you had to fight your way in and around. Here, drivers already in the round-about gave way to let in those drivers wishing to enter! Truly, these people were, as we had been told, a gentle 'people of the heart.' This only increased the ironic pity of learning that the Ho Chi Minh trail running through this peace-loving country had given Laos the distinction of becoming the world's most bombed country – through no fault of her own, simply because she existed between warring factions.

For the first six weeks, those of us new to the Lao TFA team bonded as we did life together, living in a guest house, traveling together by tuk tuk to language school each day, and often eating sticky rice and grilled chicken together under the bare bulbs at the night market.

They say that the more languages you learn, the easier it becomes. Perhaps if my age and the alphabet remained constants, I would have found that true, but as it was, I didn't. Absent was all the joy I had felt in learning Spanish and especially Swahili. Whether it was our age, the strange script of Lao, or the fact that it is a tonal language, the overall effect was that we were hopeless.

To illustrate, one morning as we were sitting in our usual coffee shop, practicing our lesson, we decided to lay out our new laminated Lao alphabet flashcards across the cafe table. We were proud of how good we were doing until the Lao girl mopping the floor reached over, turned one of the flashcards end for end, and continued mopping. We had the 'letter' upside down and didn't even know the difference.

With the help of our team leader, Harrison and I found a house, newly constructed, at the end of a dirt road, on the edge of town, with a lovely Lao-looking swamp with tall green grass outside my kitchen window. We loved the shiny white tiled floors, the many windows, the verandah in front, and especially the neighbors. They were really special people. This house of light was three miles from the language school, and about five miles from our team leaders' home, where our weekly meetings were held. We bought two used bikes and rode everywhere we went, either dripping with sweat or drenched with rain. I smile as I remember riding to our team meeting in pouring rain, both of us singing B.J.Thomas' *Rain drops keep falling on my head* at the top of our lungs. Those were good days.

But there were sad times there, too. For some reason, sitting on our lovely verandah watching the Lao sun set made me cry. I didn't know why. It just felt like every time the blazing sun went down, 'another promise disappeared'.[3] And the darkness of Laos was a thicker darkness than any I had ever known. I recall the evening that I sat, watching the sad rosy dying of the day, when Tobin called. He had gotten baptized that Sunday, in the church he attended in Nebraska. He had done it because he wanted to take a public stand, as an adult decision, for Jesus and His Kingdom of Light. He had wanted it to be a clear, simple statement, but felt that the pastor had confused that clearness by praising him to the congregation for being a missionary kid. He felt sad and alone, so far from loved ones, and went home and wept. Listening to him, I felt helpless, sitting so far away in the dying light of day, but took some comfort in knowing that his tears had gracefully slipped into Beauty's vial, and Beauty counted them precious.[4]

As the weeks and months went by, I continued to watch these beautiful, gentle people of Laos out my window, daily leaving food in the spirit houses outside of each of their homes, to care for their ancestors' spirits. I realized anew how instinctively we humans sense a need to worship something Truly Beautiful. Not having been taught about a Creator Father God, these people worshiped the beauty that they did know – those family members who had gone on to the spirit world. And as they worshiped the spirits of their ancestors, they lived in the hope that those they left behind would do the same for them when they, in turn, left this present world for the spirit world. I sensed a real oneness with these beautiful people and was under no illusion that I was the first to have such thoughts. In the first century St. Augustine of Hippo was recorded as saying:

> Do not think you must speak the truth to a Christian but can lie to a "pagan." You are speaking to your brother or sister, born like you from Adam and Eve: realize all the people you meet are your neighbors even before they are Christians; you have no idea how God sees them. The ones you mock for worshiping stones . . . may worship God more fervently than you who laughed at them. . . . You cannot see into the future, so let every one be your neighbor.

Coming to know our neighbors and other Lao individuals changed me in some way that Africa had not. I began to more clearly see all of humanity as one earthly family. Ever since Cain and Abel, all the families of the earth have had factions. Clearly, our family of humanity is no different. Nevertheless, as in any natural family with all its foibles, humanity remains a family. We all share the same longings, hopes and fears, and the same basic question: *Why are we alive?* The effect of this unified perspective began to revolutionize my separatist missionary thinking.

I realized in a clearer way than ever before that we are all simply products of our experiences and environments. In this communist nation whose primary religion was Buddhism, with no concept of a Creator God in whose image we are made, Beauty was still present, of course. But on taking a closer look than my initial one on our bus ride from the airport, when I had been so thrilled at the obvious spirituality of the land, it became evident that an Ugly presence surrounded and protected this spirituality. On the balustrades of the temples, shrines, and seemingly everywhere was the deity Naga – the Cobra Serpent Protector. From my perspective, the Naga menacingly encircling the shining gold of this peaceful Lao religion was sinister and creepy. I couldn't imagine a religion whose primary deity was the same species as the creature that terrified me so many years ago – there on the second to bottom step of the basement stairs in Wapello. No way. But I now understood that my experience had shaped me and their experience of snakes was apparently far different than mine – if that was their deity! To me, such a deity spelled death and not abundant life.

Simultaneously with sensing this oneness of the human family, along with the realization of each of us being a product of our experiences, I was struck with wonder at my dumb luck of having been born to Christian parents. And as if that weren't dumb luck enough, I also happened to be born American. Funny thing was, that rather than feeling lucky, as I gazed out this Lao window, I felt burdened with responsibility, one that I had asked for no more than I had asked to be born Christian and American. But there it was. What to do with it was my choice. As I seriously considered my choice and made it, things began to change radically. Or maybe things were the same; it was me changing.

Even at team meetings, I seemed to see things differently than most. For example, the verse in Corinthians that says, *Therefore if any man be in Christ, he is a new creature: old things are passed away; behold, all things are become new,* (2 Cor. 5:17) led to a discussion on the meaning of the word *new.* I thought it meant what it said, and was an easy enough word that we as Christian English

239

teachers needn't struggle with it. But then, as my luck would have it, we chose Dallas Willard's book, *Renovation of the Heart,* to read and study together, which easily disproved my simple thinking. Yet, it didn't stop me from feeling a cause to wonder if there wasn't a difference between *new* and *renovated.* From my perspective as a Christian, the difference between **new** and all the **re-*doing*, *-vamping, -modeling** words is similar to the difference between *being* and *doing,* between Beauty's work and our own efforts. I'm so thankful that, in spite of my contrariness, there were still those at this window who became the type of irreplaceable friends that continue to be more precious than gold to me.

Speaking of my contrariness brings to mind a scene that Harrison and I witnessed as we sat savoring our Magnum ice cream bars outside the local grocer one evening. We had noticed a wiry old lady bent over her wares, but had missed the specific event that aggravated her. What we did suddenly see was this same tough, wrinkled woman running pell-mell down the middle of the street, waving a meat cleaver in her raised hand! She was chasing a fit Lao youth who had apparently tried to steal something from her, and she would not have it!! After our initial shock, we were greatly entertained by the scene, as were others. But perhaps I was the only one for whom the scene stayed in my mind for days. Even as I look back to it now, I can clearly see that woman again and know, "There but by the grace of God go I."

Our neighbors were so good about sharing Lao culture with us. We were quickly learning that the Lao love any excuse for a party. While they celebrate with gusto, their many festivals are rich with underlying religious meaning. Not long after we moved into the neighborhood, we saw that people were making small boats out of banana tree trunks and decorating them with flowers. Our next door neighbors explained to us that on the evening of the boat festival, each family would light a little candle and place it in their boat. Then everyone would put their boat on the river and it would symbolically carry their sins of the past year away, taking away bad luck and bringing good. Something about the story reminded me of Aaron in the Old Testament, sending the people's sins away into the wilderness – the main difference being that Aaron sent them on a *goat* and the Lao sent them on a *boat*.[5] The boat festival is also the day that the Naga is supposed to send fireballs into the sky from the Mekong River.

Heading into town on the night of the boat racing festival, we couldn't anticipate the number of people that would be present as the trade fair, food stalls, games, and other activities covered the streets and riverfront. Once in the crowd, I was about to fear never seeing Harrison again should we become separated in the body to body crowd, when I realized that the sea of heads around me all had shiny straight black hair and were about my height. Harrison, with his height and fairness, would not be hard to see above the crowd. Other than the sheer number of heads, the other thing that struck me was the texture of those heads – all shiny and straight, instead of the tightly curled that I realized I had become accustomed to during my years in Africa.

Vientiane's main temple, That Luang, was not far from us and its grounds also provided a great space for exercising, so Harrison and I rode our bikes there most mornings to go running, as did many Lao. When it came time for the big week-long That Luang festival, we didn't want to miss out. It's hard to find words to describe the experience of being among thousands of people during the colorful procession of everyone displaying their large handmade wax temples, the long lines of people placing money in silver bowls, offerings to the monks who were lined up behind the bowls, monks of all ages, young to very old, all wrapped in their bright orange cloth. It was so extraordinarily out of our range of life experiences thus far that even looking back on it, I feel a sense of unreality. The strangest thing of all about it was intangible, the spirit in the air. It was like Naga was everywhere – not frightening, but simply protecting the goings on, there under the hot, hot Lao sun. Thinking about it now, I mostly remember the deep sense of grief I felt, especially when watching the very young and the very old – the beautiful eager-eyed young taking it in as their own, the old having never escaped it.

Though we had been warned against doing so, Harrison and I chose to attend a Sunday morning worship time. There a small group of expatriate believers (non-missionaries) met in a second story room. I don't think there was ever a Sunday morning there that

I didn't feel a kinship to Jesus' disciples, gathered in the upper room in Jerusalem. And every Sunday, I always sensed within me a quiet anticipation that at any moment we were about to experience the second chapter of Acts. In the evenings, a large group of happy missionaries crowded themselves into that same space. We sometimes attended this service, too, enjoying the missionary camaraderie. When Pastor Bob came from Normal to visit us, we went to this evening service. I remember the song that we sang when he was there. It had already been a favorite of mine, but singing blessings to name of the Lord at this window, *both when the sun's shining down on me and when the darkness closes in* seemed especially appropriate, considering the hot Lao sun and the thick Lao darkness.

We had come to Laos to teach English at their National University in Dongdok. But no sooner had we arrived than the semester was cancelled due to Vientiane hosting the South East Asian games (SEA) in December. This had given us the opportunity to spend extra time studying the language and getting to know our neighbors. It also opened up time that we could visit our daughters and see a window into their lives.

First we flew to Guizhou province of southwest China to see where Cherith was teaching university level Business English in the capital city of Guiyang. The sudden switch from hot, laid back Laos to the millions of people crowding the dark, damp streets of Guiyang was a shock to me. When I mentioned to Cherith that the people were so cold and unfriendly compared to the people of Laos, she gave me a fitting answer that changed my perspective, "Mom, there are too many people here to all smile at you." After seeing Cherith's life of teaching, enjoying hot pot with her Chinese students and Peace Corp friends, assembling with her private fellowship, swimming at the natural hot springs where little fish nibbled away the old skin on my legs, and doing endless toasting with Chinese staff, family, and friends, we flew on to South Korea to visit Lizzie.

Lizzie taught English to children in an after school hagwon program; thus her schedule was from mid-afternoon until late evening. The Chung Dahm Private School she taught with had an unrelenting drive for excellence, to such a point that she often felt sorry for her students – going to school all day and all evening. Because she would be teaching when we arrived, she gave us detailed directions on how to find and secure entrance into her apartment. Fortunately, we managed to do just that. Entering Lizzie's apartment, we experienced a sharp contrast compared with the China we had just left behind. Here it felt so clean, spiritually safe, and warm. With the glow of colored lights on her little tree and Boney M. music playing softly in the background, we felt the Spirit of Christmas envelop us. This aura seemed to continue with us as we caught a glimpse of Lizzie's life in Korea, her students, her fellow teachers and friends, the subways, restaurants, and shops, and the world's largest church.

When we returned to Vientiane and walked into our shiny house of light, we were happily surprised to see that Christmas had arrived even here in our absence! The dear team member watching over our place had brought in and decorated a palm tree in fabulous Lao style! Beauty is as beauty does. We were especially thrilled because Tobin was on his way from Nebraska to visit us here in Laos and would arrive Christmas Eve.

It was a wonderful Christmas Eve gift to see Tobin come out of the gate at the Vientiane airport. Looking around as we drove out of the airport, Tobin remarked, as we had, and as each of his sisters would when they arrived, "This reminds me of Dodoma. It feels like I'm home." After a wonderful few days with Tobin at our window came the hard part – saying good bye and watching him go. I wondered why it always got harder instead of easier to do.

When Pastor Bob came to visit us in January, he mentioned in passing that it seemed to him that our family should be working somewhere together. Though it was a dream of all of us, the thought seemed especially ironic to me the following week. That was when I began taking classes for my master's degree. The classes were held in Thailand. Harrison stayed behind in Laos. Tobin was behind in the States, Cherith in China, and Lizzie in Korea. We were in five different countries and I just didn't know how much farther we could get from Pastor Bob's beautiful vision for us. Maybe that was at least partly why I felt so sad, alone, and stressed during my graduate classes. But Beauty did send me comforts. One of them came from His Word, in the technological form of the computer screen of the classmate seated beside me. I forget what the picture

was; I only remember the Words: ***Be still and know that I AM God.***
(Psalm 46:10)

Though the professor and fellow students, most of whom were
confident youths sold out to changing the world, were all very kind
to me, my second comfort came in the form of a new friend, Candy.
Even as we were going around the class, saying our names and
telling a bit about ourselves, the connection happened.

One morning during these two weeks of classes in Chiang Mai,
Thailand, I awoke, having had a dream so vivid in details and color
that I lay paralyzed for long minutes, unable not only to move, but
hardly able to breath. No one had to tell me that this dream, beautiful
in color and texture, but terrifying in nature, was also some kind of
holy ground. I also knew it was the kind of dream to keep to one's
self and wait and see.

When the two weeks of classes were finished, it was time for the
mission's annual conference, also held in Thailand. Harrison now
came to Thailand with the rest of the mission's teams.

I saw Thailand as a strange mix of a country – free and bound,
beautiful and deeply disturbing, Buddhist with Christians everywhere, crowded and spacious, modern and traditional. Because
it is a destination for sex tourism, it is difficult to walk a block
outside of your hotel room to get a smoothie without encountering
numerous prostitutes advertising themselves. In spite of what was
going on around us, the mission's conference was excellent, with the
speakers delivering messages that I can still remember today. One
was from my new friend, Candy, telling about life in Tibet where
she taught English. She mesmerized us with her stories. The capital
city of Lhasa was reportedly built on a demoness who had been
magically staked down by a celestial Buddha, with the foundation
of the Jokhang Temple being directly over her heart. Harrison was
deeply moved by the fear and bondage that the Tibetans lived under.
Afterwards, we talked with Candy again about our desire to live and
work in Tibet. She, too, was keen about the idea and quickly took it
to the powers that be. That's how Harrison's dream of living in Tibet
began to take shape.

In spite of all the good of the conference, when it was over, I was more than glad to leave Thailand and return home to comfortable Laos.

In February of 2010, I was finally teaching English to the University of Laos students at their Dongdok campus. In doing so, I was completely surprised by the joy of why I was born. When Cherith came to visit later that month, she was able to join me in the classroom. She wished that she could enjoy it the way I did, but she said it simply wasn't who she was. For her it was a constant struggle. She loved China, the people, the serious way they thought, their way of life; she just didn't enjoy teaching. I, too, would have been intimidated by the demands placed on her and the sheer number of students in her huge classes. After she left, we devised a plan where I sent her my lesson plans. I loved making them, she loved receiving them. We were both happy.

Something that Cherith said during her visit to Laos that February really struck me, similar to a slap across the face. I can still feel the sting when I think about it. She said that every time we complain about anything, we are insulting God; it's stating that He isn't doing things well enough.

It was as delightful teaching these communist Lao students as it had been telling our little John the Christmas story for the first time. I guess there's just something really fun about giving someone news they've obviously never heard before, especially if it's good news. It was amazing to me the things that these students living in 2009 had never heard of – both old and new things. For example, I once mentioned the Bible and a student raised a hand and asked me, "What's the Bible?" I looked around and they all had blank faces. I asked; no one knew what a Bible was. I took a deep breath, "Well, it's an old book. A very old book. An ancient text." They nodded.

Another 'book' that they had never heard of was Facebook. When I mentioned it and saw no one knew what I was talking about, I asked if anyone could tell us what it was. One girl raised her hand. "Is it like a face (she patted hers) on a book (she patted her book)?"

Nor had they heard of McDonald's. But things have changed quickly, especially in neighboring Thailand, so I feel sure by now they know of these things. In fact, I'm Facebook friends with a few of them now, so I know they no longer think it's a picture of a face on a book.

And out of curiosity one day, considering all the Naga snakes represented all over the place, I asked the girls if they liked snakes or if they were afraid of them. They hated them and were terrified by them. Rightly or wrongly, I concluded that we were not made differently; we really are one human family. Which may be one reason I had a hard time appreciating the monks in my classes refusing to receive the handout or anything else that I held out to them. I would forget that they couldn't take anything from a woman's hand and when they just sat there (not looking at me because that's not allowed either), I'd remember, "Oh, yeah. I have to lay this on the desk and then he'll pick it up." Honestly. As if I was dirty or poisonous or worse. Whatever.

Easter was approaching and I was really searching for a way to present this event in history to these dear students. In fact, I remember lying awake one night pondering on it. I should have just slept because the answer was about to be given me, but I didn't know it.

The following day, my older brother called to tell me that Dad had gone to heaven. He died on March 28th – the same day that he had married my mother so many years earlier. Harrison immediately began searched for airline tickets for us to return to the States for his funeral. But I asked him to give me one day more teaching before we departed. I had an idea.

I knew that Pi Mai Lao (Lao New Year) was coming up and that it was the biggest festival of the year. Because my philosophy of teaching is one of reciprocity in receiving, I would have the students tell me, an interested outsider, all about the festivities involved in Pi Mai Lao. They would enjoy that, I knew. Then I would tell them about the holiday coming up in America – similar to Pi Mai Lao in that it lasted three days and was also partially a religious festival. Good Friday through Easter Sunday.

This was the lesson plan and it went off without a hitch. They were very quiet as I explained the life, death, and resurrection of Jesus Christ – and also about Easter eggs and Easter bunnies.

Then I changed the flow of the lesson by explaining the English way of saying, "I have good news and bad news. Which do you want to hear first?" They had not heard of presenting news in this way, so it led to a little debate of which is better to hear first and why. When one of the students gave his reasoning of hearing the bad news first to get it over with and then being able to enjoy the good news, I affirmed that this was the way I, too, liked to do it. I told them that truly I did have good news and bad news to share with them today, and I would start with the bad news.

When I told them my father had died the previous day, they responded in a way totally in keeping with being gentle people of the heart. They were truly sympathetic and caring. After receiving their precious concern for me, I told them that I wanted to tell them the good news. Explaining that I did not really have to be sad about my father's death. Because he had believed in this Jesus Christ, only his body was dead. His spirit was alive and I would see him again in heaven when I died! They had no doubt of his spirit being alive. Spirits they knew. But the rest they had many questions about. So I left them with the homework assignment of writing down all the questions they could think of to ask about the lesson today – any and all of it. I told them I was going to America to be with my family, and when I came back they should turn in all their questions and I would do my best to answer them.

I loved these students. They were wonderful. But I had no idea what I had just started. Nor was I concerned, which was probably where the trouble started. As I stood there in front of those Lao students telling them the Good News of Jesus Christ, I instinctively knew that it was for this that I was born.

Harrison and I flew from Vientiane to Bangkok, and then from Bangkok to Seattle, Washington. Landing in Seattle, something happened that I was not expecting. As I looked out my window, down at Seattle, a city I was not familiar with, a humongous gush of love washed over me – not only for Seattle, but all of America, a beautiful country who acknowledges God. A country I was unbelievably lucky to be born in and a country I'd be willing to die for – no matter what the haters say.

I don't remember the sequence, but it seems to me that we all five ended up at O'Hare airport, one after another – us from Laos, Tobin from Washington, D.C., where he had recently been transferred,

Cherith from China, and Lizzie from South Korea. Together we all went to Iowa to celebrate the life of my father. I surprised myself by being glad, rather than reticent, to speak at Dad's funeral. Jacob also spoke, as well as a son of each of our step-mothers, and then Adam had the prayer at the cemetery, where we laid Dad to rest, alongside Mom and Teddy.

Back in Laos, the students had their questions ready and waiting. There were so many, and so many excellent ones that I was thrilled to answer! *When Jesus came back to life, did He get revenge on the ones who had crucified Him?* There were so many, I decided to do a couple of them at the beginning of each class. I was aware that this was a communist country, not open to this teaching. I began to consider this as I entered the campus each day and wondered what was the worst that could happen. Would an authority or someone else enter the class one day and shoot me? I just didn't see that happening, but if it did, it did. Actually, as I more clearly explained The Way – and funeral customs, hope, and Easter bunnies, for a few minutes before we began class each day, I had the feeling that this was what I had been born for. Nevertheless, though the girls' toilet was an unpleasant place, I spent a few minutes before class praying there.

Then came the fateful day that it was time for my teaching to be observed in accordance with the mission's protocol. The observation was to be carried out by a fellow mission teacher. Before class, as I went over my lesson plan with my observer, I also told him about the students' questions that I was answering prior to each class, and asked him if he would like to interpret my answers for clarity, since he was a much better Lao speaker than I. His answer astounded me, "In order to honor our leader, I won't do that."

I asked incredulously, "You're going to honor our leader over Jesus??" Now I can see the possible self-deception in my response, but at the time I didn't see it at all.

Long story short – I became more than a little unpopular with the mission leaders. We had no way of knowing what was going on behind the scenes regarding us, but time would show us.

As the school year drew to a close, the students held a party for me. Harrison, with the help of a very special neighbor, threw a big farewell party at our house for the neighborhood. Lizzie was visiting us from Korea and was there for the party. We were so glad and thankful that each of our kids had been able to come to Laos during this year, because the plans were all in place for us to go to Tibet after our summer break back in the States.

Our flights out of Vientiane were scheduled on a Sunday. Time did not allow us to go to church, but we made sure that we did have time to leave off a Lao Bible with some interested neighbors in need. We knew it was the cowardly way to do it – leave the Bible and run off to the airport before we got in trouble. We were counting on the promise in Isaiah being true, that God's Word doesn't return to Him empty, but will accomplish what He desires and achieve the purpose for which He sent it. (55:11)

When we reached the airport, a wonderful surprise met us – the whole church of that upper room - as I liked to think of it, along with some team mates and Lao friends, were there to see us off!

Lessons learned:

My calling (who I was born to be)
must take precedent over my mission (what I do).
Our Lord is dethroned more emphatically by
Christian workers than by the world.
We treat God as if He were a machine designed only to bless us,
and we think of Jesus as just another one of the workers.
The goal of faithfulness is not that we will do work for God,
but that He will be free to do His work through us.
God calls us to His service and places
tremendous responsibilities on us.
He expects no complaining on our part and
offers no explanation on His part.
God wants to use us as He used His own dear Son.[6]
Self-deception is the worst deception of all.

18

Barnes' Basement / Elliot Dorm

Forever Transitioning, Continual Liminality
Summer 2010

S ome dear friends from Christ Church in Normal offered us their
basement as our base from which to travel for the summer. The
space should not be thought of as a basement but as a full home:
kitchen, living room, bedroom, bathroom with all the amenities one
can think of – including a pool and waterfalls! It would have been
a wonderful relief to settle in at this window for the entire summer,
but my graduate classes at Wheaton College were a first priority.

Harrison and I moved into one of the Elliot Apartments on the
corner of President and University Streets on the Wheaton campus.
I started intensive classes, and after his morning runs, Harrison
worked on a myriad of projects: getting Lizzie a visa for China so
she could go visit Cherith when she was finished teaching in Korea;
researching which Mac he wanted to invest in; finishing up our
paperwork for going to Tibet, and a million other small things.

Though the intensity of the classes made them stressful, I thoroughly enjoyed the material, the professors, and the other students,
who were, as usual, many years younger than me. I especially
enjoyed the opportunity of getting to know our friend, Candy, better,
since we would be living and working together in Tibet within a few
weeks. I loved her attitude towards situations as I remember her
expressing it: "Why not use it redemptively?" And I appreciated the

sentiment in her voice as her tidy slender hands lovingly touched my Bible as she softly said, "Wow, this is one well-used Bible."

She, too, was super excited about us being with her in Tibet. She told us that her past year had been extremely difficult. She said she almost felt that she couldn't return for another year if it weren't that we'd be with her this time. Though we were sorry for her rough year and flattered by being able to encourage her in this way, we were also vaguely aware of a red flag waving. We didn't see ourselves as the savior of anyone's situation, and were pretty sure we couldn't live up to that kind of expectations.

It wasn't only we who wondered about the situation. We were thrilled when Candy agreed to spend a weekend with us at the Barnes', and do a presentation on Tibet at Christ Church. She did an excellent job, and the folks at Christ Church loved her. But more than one of our wise friends questioned the logistics when we introduced this beautiful, sweet young girl as our team leader. I assured them it would be no problem and hoped I was right.

Tobin had flown home to be with us that same weekend. So as Harrison, Candy and I left Wheaton for the weekend, we went to Midway Airport to pick Tobin up from his flight. Harrison, who was normally very good with directions and almost never got lost, became confused, missed his exit, but then thought he had it straightened out. When one of us asked him if he was sure he was on the right road, he reminded us that he hated being asked, "Are you sure?" because he was. Candy, seeing he was lost, simply and sweetly suggested that perhaps it was our question that needed to be changed, from "Are you sure?" to "Are you right?" We all laughed. True that.

The Mac that Harrison had decided on and ordered came one happy day while I was in classes at Wheaton. Who knew then that that Mac, along with my Bible and my bike, would become the most constant companions of my life for the next five years?

When the Wheaton on-campus classes finished, we were freed up to settle more completely into Barnes' basement, and to do our traveling from there. Some time the first of August, we made a road trip back to our Tennessee window and had a truly wonderful reunion with those beloved folk there in that little mountain church.

The relationships we had formed years ago were still there, strong and warm. As the Wednesday evening church service commenced, a Little Doe Free Will Baptist tradition that I had forgotten took place. Everyone 'able-bodied' was called to meet at the altar. Kneeling there, I realized how varied my experiences had been, all the while these loved ones had been kneeling here at this same altar. Some of the people who were elderly then were missing now. Those who had been parents were now becoming the older generation. The youth were now the parents and the babies were youth. And here they all were – still kneeling here, praying aloud for all they were worth. In spite of it being familiar, I felt apart from it – as though I were looking on at something very sacred, a community celebrating events that saved, established, and renewed it, linking itself to its past and the successive generations who have gone on before – a community teaching their children as they had been taught, giving expression to their deepest beliefs and allegiances.[1] I sensed that right here before my open eyes was something precious, stable, and enduring. Something I had and had then lost, something established and stable that Harrison and I had never given our children. I wondered if it were a responsibility we had failed at or truly a calling that we had sacrificed for. I supposed time would tell.

If our nomadic lifestyle were a hindrance to our kids establishing themselves as autonomous adults, surely the company Tobin worked for was adding insult to the injury we had already inflicted. His last transfer, from Hastings, Nebraska to Washington, D.C., had only lasted a few months, most of which Tobin had spent living in a hotel overlooking the Pentagon and the Air Force Memorial. Then he had been transferred to Salt Lake City, Utah – where Harrison and I were now flying to see him.

It was early evening when Tobin picked us up at the airport. Wherever he lived, he always made a big effort to show us the real culture of the place when we came to visit him, and this time was no exception. He said that the Mormon Tabernacle Choir allowed the public to come to their practices. Would we like to go? *Of course we would*. It was an excellent introduction to Salt Lake City. And a very strange experience for Harrison and me, because it had a real similarity to the church culture of our youth. Yet at the same time, there was something fundamentally different that was hard to pinpoint.

When the choir practice was over, we walked out of the majestic splendor of their Tabernacle and stepped into the darkness of the summer evening. As Tobin wended his way through the traffic of Salt Lake City, I was mesmerized. The Latter Day Saints temples stood out gleaming against the night sky, and rising above the rest of the city lights. I had an uncanny feeling that though I was in my home country, it had weirdly combined with the country of Laos, where the temples also stood glowing and preeminent over all. As we continued to experience the ambience of Salt Lake City, eclipsed by the religion of the Latter Day Saints of Jesus Christ, my mind dizzied. I continued to make an effort to pinpoint the definitive difference between this religion and my own. They were so similar in their goodness, making the difference so subtle as to be easily misinterpreted, muting its vital importance.

One evening as we were dining out, we got into an intense conversation, in which Tobin asked me, "Mom, are you tough or tender?" I thought again of questions coming closer to the heart of the matter than answers ever did. But this time it wasn't me asking questions of my daddy, the questions that little girls are made to ask. This time it was my grown son asking me a serious question. And one that, though I answered it immediately – thinking he must not know me very well if he had to ask – I continued to think about it for a very long time. It would be a good six months before I came to the right answer.

During this summer, Cherith and Tobin both visited Lizzie in South Korea, their visits overlapping. The three of them went together to a window Harrison and I had never seen – the demilitarized zone between North and South Korea.

Tobin's sadness at having just left both sisters behind in Asia made it harder than ever for me to leave him this time. Especially because he had recently explained to Harrison and me the pain of filling out forms that asked for the nearest relative to contact in case of emergency, and having no one from his immediate family present on the continent. In leaving him, it felt a lot like we were turning away from our own flesh and blood.

But, alas, unrelenting, off we went again, further into the beauty of Enemy territory than ever before.

Lessons learned:

It's not at all about being religious. Or about location. On the contrary. It's all about relationships - no matter where you are. In the words of Franciscan scholar Richard Rohr, *God isn't looking for slaves, workers, contestants to play the game or jump the hoops correctly. God is simply looking for images! God wants images of God to walk around the earth. . . God wants useable instruments who will carry the mystery, who can bear the darkness and the light, who can hold the paradox of incarnation—flesh and spirit, human and divine, joy and suffering, at the same time, just as Jesus did. Watch what Jesus does, and do the same thing!*[2]

19

Lhasa, Tibet

The Enemy's Trophy Showcase
Fall Semester 2010

The missionaries who would be teaching in China all met together in Beijing before going on to their separate areas of assignment. It was a new paradigm for Harrison and me to experience – the caution of taking the batteries out of our cell phones prior to the meetings, to ensure no one was listening in on us. It was especially important to Harrison and me to get used to this precaution, since we would be two of only about a dozen expatriates total in Tibet. We learned that the twelve foreigners in Tibet were being watched at all times – day and night. In light of our mission and calling, this situation we were getting into reminded me of an old Welsh proverb: *Bad news goes about in clogs, good news in stockinged feet.* I really sensed our stockinged feet. They made me feel like a serpent, so I prayed that I would be as wise as one, yet as harmless as a dove. And the paramount importance of stockinged feet at this window also made me see myself as a lamb among wolves.

So it was comforting to have Candy slip a tiny note into my hands as we boarded the bus in the wee hours of the morning while it was still dark, and headed to the airport in Beijing to fly to Lhasa. The note was written in pencil and simply said, *"Fear not, for I am with you; be not dismayed, for I am your God; I will strengthen you, I will help you, I will uphold you with my righteous right hand."*(Isaiah 41:10)

Surprised, I realized that I wasn't afraid, not at all. In fact, knowing that I was going to a high mountain, on the rooftop of the world even, I felt more like another verse written so long ago by that same prophet, *"Get yourself up on a high mountain, O Zion, bearer of good news, Lift up your voice mightily, O Jerusalem, bearer of good news; Lift it up, do not fear. Say to the cities of Judah, "Here is your God!"* (Isaiah 40:9) I was aware that I was not Zion or Jerusalem, and wasn't going to Judah, but I wanted to proclaim good news. I reminded myself again of the slippers hiding my beautiful feet,[1] and once again felt a need to be like a serpent.

Lizzie had finished her contract in South Korea and had flown to Beijing to spend a couple days with us and meet our team. She went with us on the bus to the airport. After seeing us and our team off to Tibet, she got on a later flight that same day and flew to Guiyang to spend six weeks with Cherith, before returning to life in the USA.

~ ~ ~

Arriving on the rooftop of the world, we descended the airplane steps into thin air. That was the main thing that both Harrison and I noticed. At 12,000 feet altitude, the air was really, really thin, so thin we immediately noticed its absence, and had to breathe deeper to get enough. The other thing that we noticed was the sky! It was so, so blue – blue like we'd never seen before. Then I remembered that I had seen it once before – in a dream I had while by myself in Thailand.

As it happened, I had an assignment to keep a journal as part of my work for a Folk Religions class at Wheaton. I will let that assignment show you what it looked like out my window there in Tibet:

August 29th - Well, here I am in our hotel room in the foreign expert building in Lhasa, Tibet. I was stunned to find that, after hearing for years of the awesome beauty of Tibet, the mountains on the hour trip from the airport to the campus struck me as overbearing awful monstrosities polluted with monasteries. It seemed I could sense hordes of the enemy troops hiding everywhere in their ugly crags. This I definitely had not expected! Bizarrely, I wondered if the difference between the whole earth being filled with His Glory and what I was experiencing as I lifted my eyes to these mountains had anything to do with the contrast between the Creator of these mountains and those legions that my spiritual eyes saw inhabiting them now. It will be so interesting to observe these people living here! I have almost no idea what to expect!

August 30th - First full day in Lhasa. One of the first things that we did was to purchase our mobile phones. It was an experience for me – but not one having anything to do with China Mobile or tele-communication. It was the outlandish parade of costumes! Grown men with beautiful coal black hair in long braids laid up over the tops of their heads with a large bright red tassel tied in; one was carrying an adorable toddler bundled up in a snowsuit type outfit with a slit manufactured the length of the crotch out of which she urinated on the linoleum floor at the father's prompting. What these costumes have to do with religion, I don't know – but I guess it must be connected with some form of Tibetan Buddhism. Everything here seems to be. Or is it just culture? Or are culture and religion the same? I've got a lot to learn.

As we were having noodles in a local shop, a beggar came in and walked unashamedly up to our table. It had already been explained to us that giving to beggars in this land is considered an honorable thing to do because it gains one merit with the spirit world. I would have been happy enough to give this beggar money, but I didn't. Why not? 1) I didn't want to be perceived as wanting to gain merit for the spirit world. 2) I absolutely would not give money to him because of the huge colorful demon representation painted brightly on the apron covering the front of his filthy clothes. I really wanted to tell him that, especially #2, was the reason that I would not give to him. What good will I be here, not being able to speak a word of eternal significance?

August 31 - Took our first trip downtown today. Oh my. I climbed on the bus, found a seat, and took a look around me. All around my immediate vicinity were beautiful Tibetan women, thumbing their beads and chanting monotonously and continuously under their breath. I became fixated on the girl across the aisle from me. Without any warning, my eyes filled with tears and I began to weep. Embarrassed, I turned and looked out the dirty window. How can I explain, journal, what happened in me?

When we got off the bus, we headed to the coffee shop of a well-known American. We joined the flow of people. Everyone was walking the same direction. Many of these pedestrians were carrying and fingering their beads, their lips moving soundlessly, unceasingly. Many others were twirling prayer wheels. As we sat and sipped our coffee, I enquired as to the prayers that so many were mumbling. I was told that they are not prayers at all, but a meaningless chant (that doesn't really translate as anything) of six syllables (Om Mani Pedme Hom) over and over again. And the inside of the prayer wheels are filled with sets of the same types of these syllables printed by machine. Do I believe that these syllables are meaningless? No, I don't. Perhaps they are 'meaningless' to the ones uttering them, but I feel pretty sure that they are understandable to the demons. Paul talked about speaking in the tongues of angels. Surely demons have their own tongues. "Why do they do this chanting?" I asked. "To appease spirits and gain merit for themselves," came the answer.

After coffee, we continued on our walk about town. As we neared the famous Jokhan temple, I saw it. There they were – people prostrating themselves facedown onto the ground over and over again, making progress in travel by the length of their bodies with each prostration. Even after having heard about it, I was appalled with the reality of the sight. *"This place,"* I thought, *"is the enemy's trophy showcase. Here he has the people completely under his control – throwing themselves continually on their faces at his feet. All because they fear. There is no pleasure in this sin – only fear. Other sins have pleasure – sexual immorality, drunkenness for love of drink, craving the escape of drugs, but this! No pleasure – he's got 'em altogether."* What a day it's been. What in the world am I doing here? What use am I? Please come, Lord Jesus, and put an end to this gloating of the enemy.

September 1 - Couldn't sleep last night. Read *The Lotus and The Cross* by Ravi Zacharias. It made me realize that the religion of

Buddhism in its high form doesn't have much, if anything, to do with the Tibetan Folk Buddhism that I observed yesterday. Apparently the religion of Buddhism is one of denying self until there is no self to deny – no pleasure or pain. Enquiring, it has been explained to me that 'high' Buddhism is only one corner of the triangle of Tibetan Buddhism. Buddhism simply teaches striving for an awareness, an enlightenment that ends in the non-being state of nirvana and thus escaping the wheel of life and suffering. While that concept may be good for death, the Tibetans apparently can see or have been taught that there are active spirits in the world here where they live – and to deal with that came up with a system that comprises the other two corners of the Tibetan Buddhism triangle: appeasing the demons and attempting to gain merit.

It's so overwhelming. The comfort of this book to me is these words: Prayer in its most basic form is the surging of the human spirit in its weakness, grasping at the Spirit of God in His Strength. My heart surges, "God, help!"

September 7 - Today was our first visit to a monastery. This monastery is the closest one to the Lhasa Teachers' Training College campus that we live on. After stopping for noodles at a Tibetan teahouse, we continued our way on up the mountain towards the monastery Sera. Back in the prime of Tibetan Buddhism, the monks in this monastery were known for their strength and so were considered to be a military power! The contrast this picture created in my mind made me laugh. The peace that Buddhism professes combined with the practical life necessity of preservation via military protection – what a striking contrast of theoretical and folk religion! As if that weren't enough ambiguity for one monastery experience, our coworker told us that she had become friends with a monk who lives in this monastery and she used to visit him often – only to find out that he sits in his 'cell' (room) and watches videos all day and every evening! Reminds me of when it struck me last year in Laos that though the Lao people say they worship different gods than we do as Christians, I wondered as we drove along and could see every household sitting in their houses (with open doors) focusing on the TV god. Do we really serve such different gods on a daily basis?

September 8 - Running beside our apartment, on the other side of the campus wall is a small river. It is filthy and once since we've been here it overflowed it banks with the unseasonal rains, leaving several inches of mud covering several blocks of our part of the city. Today as I look out of our third floor apartment window and watch the dirty water carry its garbage rapidly along, I am reminded of the water that was called 'holy' at the monastery yesterday evening. As I had stood there in the center of that monastery, I was surprised. I guess I had expected a feeling of some sort of peace or something at a monastery, but instead I was mainly left with an impression of pathetic, repulsive filth – maybe created in part by the crumbling buildings surrounding me. I had wondered why the water was considered to be holy. It occurred to me, watching the dirty water flow by – of course! That water was coming down out of the mountains. It was pure and clean. No wonder it was considered 'holy'! Something clean in the midst of that squalor would obviously be 'holy.'

As we were leaving the monastery, Harrison had pointed out a monk, dressed in his red robes, sitting on a crag of mountain up in the distance against the blue blue sky. He was sitting there looking out over the city below. There! That was more what I expected in Tibet! What a picture of peace. Deception – things are rarely what they seem.

September 9 - The famous Jokhan temple. Every time we go downtown, it strikes me again. I've been told numerous times and have also read that the decision of where this temple should be built was determined through divination, but the work done each day was mysteriously undone that night. By further divinations, the king at the time, Songsten Gampo, found out that Tibet was situated on the back of a sleeping demoness. This demoness was apparently jealous of Buddhism coming to replace Bon Po (the very dark religion preceding the entrance of Buddhism) and would only be pacified by building a temple on top of her. This temple acted as a stake in her heart, holding her down. So this temple or 'House of Mysteries,' as it is also called, was built on the heart of the demoness underlying Lhasa and was considered to be a gateway to the underworld. There are two very tall totem poles decorated with prayer flags outside the temple that, because of that story, I think of as gigantic stakes holding down the demoness that Tibet is built on. I asked and tried to find an answer on the Internet about what these poles actually represent, but so far have been unsuccessful. What a place to be sent – a place with a demoness as the foundation. This is what you call enemy territory.

September 10 - This evening our college hosted a banquet at a hotel in town to honor all the teachers for Teachers' Day. It was quite an event – a multitude of delicious looking dishes going to waste as the interminable toasting continued for hours with everyone drinking everyone else under the table because it is the custom. As the most important people of the college gave speeches (in Chinese), I asked the young volunteer Chinese teacher sitting near me what the message was about in English. He replied, "Nothing. It is just blah, blah, blah. . . ." The music was for the most part, quite painful. But when the Tibetan folk dancers paraded onto stage, my attention was captured by their costumes – like something right out of the spirit world. As they began to perform their dance and song, my mind immediately went to what a friend of our daughter told us before we left the States to come here. She said that she knew a missionary to Tibet who told her that she could not sleep at night because of all the demons shrieking. Up to this point, I really had no idea what she was talking about – but I think this *was* that sound – not that of human sounding voices. I'm thankful that I only heard them on stage tonight and not nightly in my dreams!

September 12 - Tibetan children are so very beautiful. My heart is really moved by them and unbeknownst to them of course, when I pass by them my spirit, seemingly of its own volition, cries out to Abba Father that He will draw them to Himself and that they may come to know and serve Him. Today I saw a black smear on a precious little boy's nose. Their faces are often dirty and their noses snotty, but this spot looked different, more intentional or something. I didn't know. Then further down the street I met a little girl with the same black smear. Now I assumed that it must be, as I had thought, intentional. It took asking more than one person before I learned that when parents visit the nearby monastery, there is a monk sitting in front of a huge Buddha statue that places the black mark on the children's noses at the parents' request. The black mark is a mark of blessing – an assurance that the child will be healthy.

September 15 - Here I am sitting and reading the book of Jonah. Looking out of my third floor apartment window, I see, walking along the dirty river below, three Tibetans, one man and two women – walking along, spinning their prayer wheels. It strikes me that, like the people of Nineveh, these people do not know their right hand from their left hand. In my mind, these three Tibetans walking along a river spinning prayer wheels change into three Tibetans, still grown adults, sitting in a playpen of Satan's. Now they are shaking rattles, baby rattles, demon baby rattles. Truly they have no idea what they are doing or why. They are just children of darkness, playing as children do – shaking their rattles.

September 19 - Everyday wherever I go, there they are, spinning their prayer wheels – then today it hit me – *spinning their wheels!* Of course, it's getting them nowhere. And how about me – am I spinning my wheels? How easy it is! Today our city team got together for fellowship and one member brought a message that we listened to on her computer. It was by Francis Chan and was on the parable of the sower. As he spoke about the seed falling on good ground but then the cares of life choking it out, I could see it – me being here in Tibet and getting caught up in the busyness of life here, learning language, sitting in tea houses attempting to 'form relationships' with my students when I can't even speak the same language, joining Bible studies with other expatriate believers, searching endless small shops looking for a can of condensed sweetened milk that I need for a recipe for our next team get-together (there *must* be sweetened condensed milk somewhere, right?). . . . . Me, I am so easily guilty of spinning my own wheels, accomplishing nothing of eternal significance, not even being an obedient child in what He asked me to do.

I sat down and wrote out a personal purpose statement and steps of obedience in accomplishing that vision.

September 20 - Walking home from the noodle shop, we saw another voodoo-looking doll in a box in the middle of the road. Harrison was especially happy to see this because he had been wanting to get a picture of one of these and this time he had his camera along with him. We had been told that we would be seeing these in increasing numbers as it becomes colder, because they represent a sick person or people in some home. When a car or bus inevitably hits the box, the spirits causing the sickness will run away, the sickness will leave, and the person will recover and be healthy again. After Harrison got the picture, a dog walking by went up to the box, sniffed it, and sure enough, lifted his leg and urinated directly on it! Harrison, having anticipated the event as soon as he saw the dog, kicked himself for not getting it on film! Meanwhile, I was pondering the effect of the urine. When we lived in Tanzania, the Maasai considered the urine of their cattle to be medicinal for their own random illnesses. Would the person that this voodoo-looking doll represented, have twice the chance of getting well? Does dog urine scare the spirits away as effectively as a car running over them?

P.S. – note added November 1st – Today we saw a cow in the middle of the street eating the contents of one of these boxes!

September 23 - As we were informed was necessary, Harrison and I went to buy tickets a day ahead of time to visit the hugely famous summer home of the Dalai Lama (before he had been exiled to India). Near the ticket purchasing booth stood a long line of large stationary prayer wheels which the devout would walk along, reaching out to give each one a spin as they walked along. It struck me that, rather than being completely ridiculous, in keeping with the principles of Tibetan Buddhism, this was actually a very efficient practice! The necessity of trying to accomplish the impossible task of appeasing evil spirits and gaining merit from them demanded trying ever harder. An efficient way of trying ever harder is obviously to put more prayers in the wheel one is spinning. Thus, spinning one huge wheel, filled with prayers stamped on paper, followed by spinning another of the same size, is obviously gaining more merit than a small handheld prayer wheel filled with a few stamped out prayers.

September 24 - Today Harrison and I, along with a twenty-one-year-old volunteer Chinese teacher from our college, went to visit the Potala Palace, the former residence of the Dalai Lama. Originally built sometime between 618B.C. - 907 B.C., it is the highest ancient palace in the world and is named 'Buddha of Mercy' after a holy hill in Southern India.

I do not cease to be amazed between the difference in what I expect and the reality of the experience here in Tibet. I guess I expected some kind of experiential encounter with the spirit of Tibetan Buddhism today in this famous site of the Dalai Lama. Instead, the impression made upon me by so much orange and darkness, was one of being in a haunted Halloween house – but one from which the spirits had departed, leaving only a shell of emptiness.

October 2 - Today we visited the holy Lake Namtso, which turned out to be another bizarre experience. Altogether the place was an awesome beauty, combining separate scenes of my life all at one spot – the snow-capped mountains of Switzerland, the beach and waves of Mombasa, Kenya, the wildness of Morocco and northern Kenya, and the wind of the central Illinois prairie and downtown Chicago! Sadly, this intensely beautiful scene was horribly polluted by the trash of faded, ripped prayer flags and khatas (very long white silk scarves that show honor and welcome), like used toilet paper everywhere. But interestingly, it was the wind that really effected my impression. Something about the wind is so cleansing to me, blowing away the chaff. Since childhood, wind has held a fascination for me. Adding to it today was the intrigue of our teammate, who on hearing the mighty wind filling the air with the sound of flapping prayer flags, literally hurried back to our vehicle while fearfully whispering, "I hate that sound." I have no explanation for this experience but am reminded of John 3:8 and of Bob Dylan's *Blowin' in the Wind*.

October 10 - Curious experience today. It really seems that things are never what they seem. The peacefulness that Buddhism sets forth as its basic premise is in direct contrast with the reality of life here as experienced by our teammate, who came to our apartment, very shaken by it all. She was present late this afternoon, as she often is, at a tea house with some of her students when a vicious bloody fight ensued between two girls, one of them being a student of hers. The difference between high and folk religion not only in Buddhism, but also in Christianity struck me, as our teammate told us of her overwhelming fear. Apparently her fear was so profound that her student, with bloodied face, had the presence of mind to see this fear written on her foreign teacher's face and took time out to tell her, "**Don't be afraid.**" This struck me particularly because it has occurred to me in recent days that these words could be among the most frequent expressions found in the Holy Spirit's inspired Word of God. I thought a long time after my teammate left our apartment about the roles each played in that teahouse this afternoon.

October 16 - Today one of my students and her sister took me to visit Drepung, Tibet's largest monastery, which back in the day housed 2,000 monks, but that number is now down to 200-300. Like the earlier monastery we visited, large parts of this one, too, were in shambles. The difference here was that the Chinese were busily rebuilding it for tourism! Nevertheless, there were also plenty of genuine pilgrims, spinning the huge prayer wheels, bowing to the endless paintings and writings of various Buddhas, adding liquid butter to the various vats of butter candles. I really appreciated my student being my teacher today by explaining Tibetan Buddhism to me. Something that I noticed was that she took pains to tell me 'nice' things and tended to avoid the darker side. When I enquired about the truly horrible paintings, she did explain them – they were what happened to those who did bad things in this life. For example, if you killed an animal in this life, that animal would torment you horribly in the afterlife. (Afterwards we stopped for lunch and had the usual Tibetan meal, which includes meat.?)

We stopped with others to listen to a monk teaching. When the small crowd around him all chuckled at the same time, I asked my student what he had said to make them laugh. She said, "He says that Tibetan Buddhism seeks light and good but many hearts of Tibetans are dark."

October 18 - On my daily bike ride, I was really struck by something that my student told me when we visited Drepung monastery the other day. She had pointed out that the Buddhas that are painted on the sides of so many of the rocky mountains, are already shaped there in the stone. The paint is just applied to bring out the shapes that are already present, not carved by humans. This was a different explanation than I had received from fellow foreigners about these endless paintings. They had told us that the Tibetans say that 'these paintings have just appeared all over the mountain sides,' but that the idea is obviously a ridiculous lie because they've *seen* people painting them there. Anyway, this discussion caused me to pause on my bike ride to closely examine the paintings as I rode by – sure enough, the shape of the various Buddhas are **in** the stone and look to be naturally there. Hhmmm. . . . were all those shapes naturally there?! Or were they carved in by Tibetans? Or what?

October 19 - Okay, I have to put up with incense burning everywhere I go because it is out of my control, but I draw the line when it comes to being in my classroom. A student lit incense on my desk during break-time, unnoticed by me as I was doing something with another student. When I looked up and saw it, I frowned, began to cough, and waved my hand in front of my face as though to clear the air so I could breathe. The student, thankfully, took the cue to put it out and then remove it. Thinking about it now, I realize how unfair it was, really, to the student, who, no doubt had every good intention. I remember my visit to Drepung monastery a few days ago when incense was burning at the entrance to many of the rooms. As the pilgrims entered, they would use their hand to waft the smoke into their nostrils. I asked my student why they did this. She answered that it was good for health! Perhaps it is true, and my idea of tar and nicotine has nothing to do with jasmine and other such smoke.

October 20 - Everywhere I go, there are amulets to buy. My students wear them and I wonder about them. Some of them have an evil look, but others are quite attractive in a pretty and Tibetan way. If I buy and wear them as such, with no spiritual significance, does that mean they have none? I am told they are important because they keep bad spirits away (are there any other kind in this religion?) and help to ensure health and safety. It also reminds me of being at the monastery the other day. As I bent down to enter a dark, low doorway, a monk on the inside of the entrance tapped my back with a staff as I entered. Being unsure of significance and relevance, I later asked my student why he did that. She answered that it was for my safety – to keep me safe from evil spirits. What ignorance and blind bondage. How I long for these dear hostages to experience light and freedom.

October 22 - Our team came to Gyantse for the weekend. The trip here took about five hours, partly because of our stops to take in the beauty of glaciers, etc., along the way. Four of us visited Baiju Temple and Pelkor Chode Monastery this afternoon. It is different from other temples and monasteries in that several sects of Buddhism joined together in the venture of building and living in it. Maybe due to the effect of Bon, an indigenous religion of Tibet, this place seemed particularly dark to me. The tantric paintings appeared to be especially ominous and terrifying, but it somehow didn't take on me. I think it might have to do with the explanations we received along the way, "Careful when stepping over the door step into each temple room. . . Those barriers (maybe 8-10 inches high) were built to trip up the spirits so they aren't able to enter and cause problems." Honestly, how can one live in fear of spirits that are that stupid?

October 23 - As our team visited a fort (Tibetan administrative offices in the 1400s) high on the mountain at Gyantse where the British invaded years ago in 1904, an explanation of the stakes that are by every temple (See Sept. 9th) that we had been given by a team member yesterday became even clearer to me today. Yesterday she had told us that the poles could be equated with the Asherim poles in the Old Testament. Huh, I had never considered that possibility and found it interesting. Then today, at the fort, there was a pole that was actually accessible to our examination. I had never known what the poles were even made of but figured it was wood. As we lifted the layers of prayer flags covering the pole, I was surprised to feel cool metal underneath and even more surprised to feel breast-shaped mounds covering the towering pole under those endless stamped prayer flags! At least all the prayer flags covering them make them modest Asherim poles! Indeed, Tibetans seem to be an excessively modest people, but perhaps the cold weather has something to do with this as well.

The physical elements (rocky earth/mountains inhibiting burial, lack of rivers to discard bodies, and lack of trees for burning them) are said to play a part in the reason for sky burials (Tibetan funerals) – where the tradition is to cut the flesh off of the dead, grind the bones and feed them to the birds, bones first, followed by the flesh. This order is used because if the flesh is given first, the birds leave the bones. When we were in the mountains near a sky burial place, sure enough, numerous vultures were circling.

October 24 - Everywhere we travel here, especially along holy lakes, there are little piles of stones. I have grown accustomed to seeing them, but today they struck me again because there were so ridiculously many of them along one lake. Today they struck me funny – as child's play, instead of tiny sand castles there are a gazillion little heaps of stones. When I enquired again as to their purpose in the eyes of the local people, I was told that they were built as small houses for the spirits, so that the spirits will hopefully rest there and not disturb the local people. My immediate response was, "Well, if these spirits know anything about the gleaming gold spirit houses that every Lao home and business provides for their local spirits, these Tibetan spirits must be very jealous and angry at these little stone heaps!"

October 28 - Dear Journal, I believe writing in you has had a cathartic effect and has been very beneficial to my emotional and spiritual health as I've adjusted to life here in Tibet. So thanks, dear journal, for being a safe place to express while I observe, change, and grow.

~ ~ ~

Like my Lao students, these Tibetan students were exceedingly precious to me. Though there were many differences between the two groups, the one primary similarity was their obsession with the spirit world. I went with this similarity, and as I used the material that I had received at an annual Christian Storytelling Conference back in Normal, Illinois, I adapted it to these who lived as though they were more aware of the spirit world than of their physical realities. The beauty of this for me was in presenting The One and Only Completely Good Spirit – something they found almost unimaginable, because all the spirits they knew were terrifyingly out to get them. As I opened class with a few minutes story time, you could hear a pin drop. Never did I ever feel I had such undivided attention, as when those students listened. With all of my heart, I longed for these students to know just One Totally and Completely Good Spirit.

~ ~ ~

It must certainly have been through this same Infinite Spirit that I experienced the things that I did in Tibet. I have no other explanation, apart from the one my brother Adam suggests – that I am simply not right in the head.

The first, and most outlandish, of such experiences happened one day not long after we had arrived in Tibet, when perhaps I still wasn't getting enough oxygen to my brain. I was sitting in a park in Lhasa, praying. Thinking as hard as I can, I cannot think of a way to explain this to you, except to say It presented as an inaudible Voice speaking to me. Inexplicably, and out of context, I 'heard,' "*I have given you a winning hand. Lay it down and go out.*" Huh? *Go out? Go where?* I was willing to be obedient, but I had no idea how to go about it in this case.

The following experiences had more of a basis than that one. Their basis was the Word of God, aka the Bible. But they also came to me strangely, usually in the middle of the night, and appeared, best as I can describe it, as bold-faced lettered text across my mind's eye. The first of these messages that I recall was odd, *Sin is crouching at the door, and its desire is for you, but you must master it.* (Gen. 4:7) Though there were many nights in between, other messages that I remember coming to me in the darkness were, ***Though He*** *slay me, yet will I trust Him,* (Job 13:15 KJV) followed by *Stand by and see the salvation of the Lord.* (2 Chron. 20:17) And yet another, *Let your love be without hypocrisy.* (Rom. 12:9) Though I recognized them as scriptures, I sometimes wasn't aware of their context or sure what they had to do with me. So when I awoke in the morning, I would look them up in my Bible and read them in context, and try to figure out they applied to me and my life here at this Tibetan window.

However, the meanings of other messages were painfully clear to me – such as *Do away with the pointing of the finger,* (Isa. 58:9) *Who made you judge and ruler?* (Ex. 2:14) *Saul was zealous for God, even as he persecuted and imprisoned Christians.* (Acts 22:3,4) *If anyone causes one of these little ones to stumble, it would be better for that person to have a millstone hung around their neck and to be drowned in the depths of the sea.* (Mt. 18:6) There came a day when, after having received all these clear instructions, I was ready, and knelt there surreptitiously by the river in Lhasa and prayed, "I'm ready, Lord. Strike with healing." (Isa. 19:22) Looking back, this was all so very surreal to me.

Over the years of my life, daily Bible reading had increasingly become a lifeline to me. I felt I received strength for the day by reading it in the morning. But often, as the wearisome day wore on, I felt sapped of strength and by evening I was weak. I was explaining this phenomenon to the kids one day when Tobin, in characteristic style, gave me an easy solution: "Why not just read it again during the day?" Good advice, but I just never seemed to find time to do it.

While we were in Laos, I felt such a need to have certain verses with me that I wrote them down on index cards and carried them with me, in my pocket, where I could reach in any time, feel them, and be reminded. One of these that I still carried with me here in Tibet (not the same card, of course – they frayed and faded in time) was, *We use God's mighty weapons, not worldly weapons, to knock down the strongholds of human reasoning and to destroy false arguments.* (2 Cor. 10:4)

Through the years, bike riding had also become a life form of prayer for me. Even so, riding around Lhasa was a different experience than my bike rides at other windows. Here I sometimes found tears running down my face. Then one day in class, an anonymous note appeared on my desk amidst the other papers, "Teacher, why do you cry?" *Oh no. I'd been seen. Why couldn't I just be invisible?*

Part of the problem, I knew, was the extreme sadness and longing I felt as I listened to Over The Rhine's new album, entitled, *The Long Surrender*. I remember crying when listening to it on my iPod while riding my bike around Lhasa. The song that made me ache the most was called *Sharpest Blade*, and in some way, put a new light on my beloved Psalm 23. The emboldened verse became my own heartfelt prayer.

There was a time
I could sleep anywhere—
My feet on a chair,
My heart in the woods;

But love was aloof,
Just a beggar for tips
A mime on whose lips
No promises stood

But you cut me quick
In the light of the shade,
On the edge of the green
Of the yard's sharpest blade;
When nothing I knew
Was all that it seemed

I still dreamed
Of a love to outlive us
I still prayed
That this night would outlast us
And redeem some small thing
Far beyond me

Blossoms begin
Like the tip of a spear,
Or the curve of a tear
From a soldier who weeps;
Seducing the guard
Of lost years falling by
As flowers to lie
On the dead feigning sleep

But you cut me quick
In the light of the shade,
On the edge of the green
Of the yard's dark parade;
When nothing we knew
Was all that it seemed

I still dreamed
Of a love to outlive us
I still prayed
That this night would forgive us
And redeem some small thing
Far beyond me[2]

Things happened on these bike rides. For one thing, it became evident that I was, as we had been told at the beginning, obviously being watched. I liked to have fun with it and would look for a chance to come near and strike up conversations with those monitoring me. They honestly didn't know what to do with me, how to act. Though not to them, my identity was clear to me – I had nothing to hide and nothing to prove. It was fun.

Another thing that happened became my favorite memory of Tibet. Sometimes I liked to ride my bike out into the countryside, on the dirt roads on the backside of the Potala Palace, former residence of the Dalai Lama. It was there that I met who Harrison and I came to think of as 'the manure lady,' our key to real Tibetan life. I first came across her as she was out in the field, placing dried yak dung patties into piles. 'Piles' is too messy a term to describe how the

Tibetans organized the yak dung in storage until they were ready to use it as fuel in their cooking and heating stoves. Their method of storing the dried yak dung is to layer the patties in a very mannerly fashion into shapes similar to Kansas wheat field haystacks. When they finish, the dried manure looks like a giant braided hair-do the height of a haystack. This was where she was the first time I saw her – out in a Tibetan field of yak manure stacks. I thought she was looking my direction as I rode my bike down the dirt path alongside the field, so I waved. She waved back.

Another time when Harrison was riding with me, she was out again, but this time close enough to the dirt path that we were riding on, that we were able to stop and begin conversing. Thus began our friendship. One day she invited us in for their homemade yogurt – the real stuff, from yak milk. I thoroughly enjoyed it, much more than the butter tea I drank with my students in tea shops. Harrison, on the other hand, did valiantly in eating his, as he does not do yogurt of any kind, even in the USA.

But my favorite time of all was when she had me help her one day, in collecting and stacking the dried yak dung into the stacks. Working there, under the blue blue Tibetan sky, with this Tibetan peasant, I could hardly believe my life. This was true beauty. I felt I had arrived. The day before leaving Tibet, we rode our bikes out to say good-bye and to leave her and her household with a flash drive containing good news in Tibetan.

Our departure from Tibet had come unexpectedly, to say the least. And much too soon on our timetable. But it was in keeping with the wildness of the Spirit we had followed in bringing us to this exotic rooftop of the world. I'll try to explain as simply as possible.

As had been forewarned, and as we probably should have known, our relationship with Candy turned rocky. We were willing to be wrong about it, but to Harrison and me, it seemed that when we reached Tibet, Candy instantly turned into a different person than the one we had connected with first in Thailand, and then in Illinois. It was as though she had stepped off the plane and into a new role – from sister and friend into one of literally instructing us in what to do, think, and say. I took very seriously the clear message that I had received, *Let your love be without hypocrisy,* and went in fear and trembling to finally speak to Candy about the situation as we saw it. She assured me it was not her intention to present the way she had. She had good intentions. I believed it then and I believe it now. But as is commonly known, *The road to hell is paved with good intentions*.

Either my attempt at practicing *love without hypocrisy* was unsuccessful, or else Candy had friends in high places that we did not, or both. Either way, the effect of my attempt at communication resulted in a Skype call from Beijing, telling us we were finished in Tibet. The messenger at the other end of the Skype call was no other than May – the mutual friend of our Chinese friend, Maggie. May was kind in telling us that though she knew we would go on with Kingdom Work, it would no longer be with this mission because, this communication with Candy, along with my former contrariness with mission leaders in Laos, proved me guilty of *spiritual abuse*. Ouch.

At the time of the Skype call, I was having the time of my life teaching those priceless Tibetan students of mine. Therefore, Harrison took the call alone. As soon as I stepped into our sunny apartment, I instantly saw by the look on his face that something was terribly and drastically wrong. He blurted out, "We just got kicked out of Tibet!"

I can offer no rational reasoning for my initial, unpremeditated response. I was ecstatic. "Yes!" I said. "Now we are on the front lines!" Nor do I know what I meant. Only later did it occur to me that I was *laying down my winning hand and going out*.

Inevitably, this response of mine was most unhelpful to Harrison's and my relationship. Being in Tibet had long been his dream, and now I had ruined it. This response of mine gave him good reason to question my sanity – which he did.

May had told Harrison that she would Skype back when I was there with him. She did. At this point, Harrison thought to ask if we were kicked out just like that, or if they could offer us some kind of help. She assured us that they were not going to just turn us out into the night; she would check with Link Care, where they had sent others, to see if they had any room for us. We had never heard of Link Care, but were desperate for any care at this point. May also said she preferred the term 'released' over that of 'kicked out.'

Me, too. We were released. Hopefully, for the freedom for which we had been set free. That same freedom that our poster in Kijabe, Kenya had reminded us of each morning as we opened our eyes to a new day.

Though my initial reaction had been one of joy, it was short-lived as the reality set in. In fact, I was so swamped by guilt I couldn't see my way clear. Fortunately, as Beauty would have it, we were not left comfortless. We were extremely touched and encouraged by where He sent the comforts from! One message came from Max in Denmark, a friend who we had worked with in the early 90s at the Tanzanian window. We had not kept in touch through the years, so it was real surprising to wake up to a message saying, *Hi Pam. I hope you are all right. Greetings to Harrison. I sometimes wake up at night and pray for you.*

And another was from a single missionary we had worked with in Kenya, who since the time we had been in Kenya together, had married a widowed missionary whom we also knew. We hadn't heard the news of them marrying each other, and seeing evidence of it on Facebook, I sent a note of surprised congratulations! She replied, asking where we were and what we were doing. When I told her our happening, she replied with the following message: *Hey, Wow. Perhaps it had more to do with China/Tibet than with the organization that you are working with but glad that you are bouncing back. Satan is always trying to remove key people from his kingdom when they get in the way and become too effective. Keep it up.* A third comforting message came from a cousin of mine from Iowa who I very rarely heard from throughout the years. The message simply read: *May you be blessed with vision to see the army that loves and prays for you.*

We were thankful that the mission allowed us to finish up the semester. The students were beyond wonderful in expressing their appreciation for me. They hosted a magnificent party for Harrison and me, complete with recitation, dancing, singing, food, and traditional fun that we had never encountered before. I was happy that staff members also came to the party. The local faculty at this window had been extremely helpful to us and I had connected with some of them as real friends, which hadn't happened in Laos.

In spite of the caring support we received, there were still some real dark times during these days and nights, but Beauty never left or forsook us. On the contrary, there was a day when I rode my bike to a certain pagoda to read and pray, that Beauty gave me a minuscule fleeting glimpse of His Kingdom. I opened my eyes from my fervent prayer for help, just in time to see a towering angelic warrior of Light disappear. Before I could even blink my eyes to clear my imagination, he was gone. Except for a few straggling Tibetans wandering at a distance, I was alone under the bluer- than-ever Tibetan sky. Alone, but without a doubt about His presence and help.

Just a few nights before our departure day, Harrison and I lay in bed, wide-eyed, listening. Because we were older and married, we had been given an apartment in the new building that was for ranking staff. We had heard our next door neighbor was a prominent party member and wondered about the happenings there – veiled visits to his door, men in suits late at night, hushed conversations, or at other times, when we knew he was home, men would pound on his door to no avail. To us, he was always friendly and concerned about our comfort.

But now, he was totally trashing his own place. We heard him yelling and screaming crazily as furniture crashed against walls and boards broke. This carried on for long minutes before Harrison said softly, "Chairman is going to be outa here before us." I laughed softly at Harrison's sense of humor. Then we heard him out in the hall, cursing as he headed down the stairwell, on the other side of our bedroom wall. It sounded as though he were yelling at someone, but we didn't hear the other person. Hearing his cell phone crash against the concrete wall and pieces bounce down the stairs, we knew why we hadn't heard the other party. The steel door downstairs slammed as he left the building. Getting up, we tentatively opened our apartment door. His door stood wide open. We crept over to it and peeked in. It was a shambles – the TV lay broken in the middle of the floor, furniture helter-skelter, bits and pieces everywhere. Cupboards were emptied onto the floor. The faucets were open, water pouring out full force. We could hardly imagine what the repercussions would be.

But we were wrong. From all appearances, there were no repercussions. The next day we saw him in the staff cafeteria as usual.

Later when we met him outside the apartment, he greeted us as usual, chatting a moment or two in his limited English. Apparently life would carry on normally for him, but not for us.

May had checked with Link Care and found out that they were able to accept us. She made our flights accordingly, from Lhasa to Beijing, and then on to Fresno, California. She kindly scheduled us a few days in Beijing so that we could spend some time visiting the Great Wall of China, Tiananmen Square, and the Forbidden City. Since we would be arriving to Beijing on the evening of a special team gathering, May invited us to come to that, saying she would take us out to eat before it started. We accepted and had a lovely time together over delicious authentic Chinese cuisine. We told her the story of our neighbor, and Harrison saying that he would be outa there before us. She thought that was really funny, so we all had a good laugh over it together and knew our time together was not in vain.

When our time had come, we went on our way rejoicing. Well, I was rejoicing. Harrison was still very much in doubt, especially about me.

Lessons learned:

Obedience comes with its own price tag.
Many missionaries are fortunate to be able to please both
God and their mission authorities. But as for me,
I was destined to be one of the few.

20

Fresno, California

A Safe Place to Breathe Easy
Christmas 2010 - Spring 2011

When we landed in Fresno, California, we collected our luggage, got a taxi and gave the driver the address of 1734 West Shaw Avenue, telling him we had no idea where it was, other than we'd been told how to know if we'd gone too far. He, too, was unfamiliar with the address. Together we found it and he helped us with our bags. It was dark and drizzling. We had received word from Link Care that if we arrived after hours, we could find the keys to our assigned house in an envelope pinned to the bulletin board outside the business office. Not that we knew where the business office was, or our house. But we found them and it. Fumbling with the keys in the darkness, trying to find the right one for the front door, we finally managed to get us and our luggage inside and have a look around before unpacking enough to go to bed.

In spite of that start, I still had a strong sense of having arrived at a safe place, especially when I stepped into the house and flipped on the lights. It was a beautiful, three-bedroom home. I couldn't believe our good fortune. Thanking Beauty and our many faithful supporters for this good, perfect, and expensive gift, I fell asleep and slept well.

We got up the next morning to a fully stocked kitchen and refrigerator and made ourselves some breakfast. Sometime later that day, as we were unpacking, there was a knock on the door. The man there introduced himself and was very friendly, but his words still echo in my Link Care memories, "I know you guys are really messed up! Everybody leaves this place before Christmas, but you arrive! Well, anyway, there's only a few of us left here. This is the evening that we usually get together for a potluck dinner, but since we're so few, we're just gonna go out for pizza this evening and wondered if you'd like to come, too." *Of course, we did.*

As we continued unpacking, it became very apparent that Harrison was not sharing my sense of well-being. In fact, though he was as quiet as usual, he seemed really angry. Knowing I had ruined everything for him, I apologized a gazillion more times. He said he wasn't angry at me and he loved me. I knew he did love me, and I also guessed that he just had to be angry, too. I wasn't as concerned by his anger though, as I was by his earlier suggestion of my inherited weak mental background. After seriously considering that possibility, I had rejected it. It seemed to me that my whole problem in life was that I was too much like my father. But here, now, in this place, I was forced to wonder again, *What if I am crazy? What if this place is a sort of mental institute?*

That day and the next ones, though I continued to feel I had reached a safe place, one where there was finally oxygen and I could breathe easy, it was continually tainted by the thought that I might be nuts in my beliefs. We were given a tour of the grounds and facilities, and introduced to a few staff. They all seemed normal and in touch.

Then it happened. I had K-Love radio playing in the background. As I continued to work about the house, doing the dishes, and cleaning up, I listened – to the announcer, to callers, to the songs and I knew. Maybe I *was* crazy, but I was in good company. There were a lot of us! It was a big comfort to me. It felt like we were one big community, those people on K-Love and all of us here in this institution called Link Care. In the coming days I was about to find out more and more the beauty of this healing community, described so well in the words of Henri J.M. Nouwen:

A Christian community is a healing community not because wounds are healed and pains are alleviated, but because wounds and pain become openings or occasions for a new vision. Mutual confession becomes a mutual deepening of hope, and sharing weakness becomes a reminder to one and all of the coming strength.[1]

Our many loved ones and supporters, those who had been with us through thick and thin since we left for the mission field in 1990, were a part of this healing community, too. Pastor Bob sent a message from Christ Church in Normal, saying that he saw great hope in this situation. This showing of support overwhelmed and even befuddled me. What seemed a shameful and condemning situation could also be one of great hope? Then I remembered Bob's love of the good news of grace. I remembered him adamantly preaching that we all need the Gospel every day, saved, unsaved, all of us are the same – in need of the gospel of grace being preached to us every day.

Before we had even gotten into the swing of the intensive 24/7 counseling sessions, my brother Jacob called. When I answered, he first asked, "How's Tibet?"

"Demonic." I answered in one word.

Then he asked, "And what's up with you guys? I mean, what's *really* going on?" (I knew what he meant. He had seen right through our initial communication with our supporters – that we needed a break, that a lump that I had found on my breast while visiting Lizzie in Korea was now oozing dark liquid and needed to be cared for in the States - all true, but irrelevant in light of the real reason!)

I talked for maybe an hour answering his question. When I stopped talking, Jacob summed up with what seemingly took our counselors the next three months to come up with: "Well, it sounds to me like you are just too honest to play games and Harrison has a beyond-human capacity to stuff things." True that. Both of them.

Across the driveway from the Link Care campus was a Denny's. Its warm colors invited us. Inside, it glowed with the warmth of Christmas decorations. It, too, felt safe, and welcoming, and comforting. We went often, using the Denny's discount card available to us as clients of Link Care. Yeah, Christmastime, in Denny's, in California. What were the chances that this was really happening – that this was our life? Why couldn't I shake the feeling that those who had been successful in sending us here were now rejoicing? And how odd the seeming discrepancy between our very real situation and the message of Christmas. Or was it so dissimilar? Either way, later, as I was sitting in the lovely library of Link Care, trying to think how to tell our faithful supporters the truth of the situation in an appropriate way, I found that all I really wanted to do was tell the old, old story of Jesus and His love. It was really the only story I wanted to tell. The one I never get tired of telling, or of listening to, either. Much later, after Harrison had bought a bike for me to peddle around Fresno, I was riding around the university and found a huge statue of Ghandi inscribed with the words, "My life is my message." I liked it. I liked it a lot. But as for me, it seemed more appropriate to say, "His life is my message."

During this quiet spell of the holidays, we did all our psychological testing. When the results came back, our counselors could begin in earnest to help us. As a couple, we were initially assigned a case manager, individual personal counselors, and a pastoral counselor with whom we met together. Along with this, there was a men's group for all the guys and ladies' group for all of us women, as well as a large group where we all met together at the same time. Plus, as our initial Link Care acquaintance, who had quickly become a very dear friend, had told us at the beginning, there was a weekly potluck evening of food and fellowship. I cannot adequately describe the overall effect of this place on me. Groping for words, I can only say that, up to this point in life, I could only imagine such a community. The women's group, especially, was to me church at its finest in this broken world. A place where there was no longer any use to, or even possibility of, pretending. A place where we wept often, laughed freely, and cared deeply for one another, no holds barred. A place where I saw ashes begin to turn into beauty time and time again. For glory and for beauty.

We were only a few weeks into counseling before it became clear to the counseling team that we also needed a marriage counselor. We knew from her name when we met her that she was from the type of people we had grown up with (well, her husband was, since it was her married name), and our pastoral counselor often reminded us of a typical minister from our home church culture. We felt we already had a basic understanding of who these counselors were and hoped they, too, could understand where we were coming from. They did.

On the other hand, I had no idea where my personal counselor was coming from. Nor did I feel like she did me. Nor did I get to know her, though she must have gotten to know me inside out, because I told her everything, all the time. I rarely stopped talking, and she almost never said anything. I felt it unfair that she wouldn't connect with me in relationship, that that surely wasn't what I needed. But, looking back, I think I hardly gave her space to get a word in edgewise and I think that her being someone who chose not to connect with me was exactly what I needed. Thank Beauty! He always knows and is right!

Initially though, I was very frustrated with Dr. Stone. It seemed to me that any time I made any reference to God, which was all the time, since He is my reference point for everything, she said, "God Who?" I know that's not exactly how it was, but that's exactly how it seemed to me at the time.

Both of my brothers called me often during these months at Burn-Out Ranch, as one of them nicknamed the place. Two of those calls stand out in my mind. The first (in addition to that initial one) was from Jacob. When I was venting my frustration with Dr. Stone to him, especially the fact that I heard, "God Who?" every time I mentioned the Bible or anything it said, he surprised me by saying, "But Pam, I think that's really good that she does that."

"What?! Why??"

"Because," Jacob answered, "so many Christians used the Bible so stupidly. I think it's a really good thing if, in your counseling, she just lays that aside. That way there's no chance of it being used unintelligently. This really makes me feel a lot better about the counseling there."

Well, yes, I could see what he meant. After that, I wasn't so frustrated and made, I think, good progress. At one point Dr. Stone asked me, "Why *do* you read the Bible so much, Pam?"

I immediately knew my answer, "For all the *so that*'s."

She seemed taken aback. "That is the first time I have ever received that answer. What do you mean that you read it for the *so that*'s?"

"I mean that I just want to know why. I want to know reasons for what is. When I read *so that,* I know that a purposeful reason is going to follow. I like reasons. If I know the reason, I can understand the rest."

One session early on, I said something to the effect that, although I was soaking in the safe environment of Link Care, I didn't really think I needed to be here. Dr. Stone said, "You're here, aren't you?" Oh, snap. She had me there. So we went right ahead and directly addressed what had gotten me there. After she listened to me tell my story, she told me that it reminded her of a time that she was camping with her son. It was unusual for her to talk this much, especially a personal story. I listened eagerly. When they were camping, her young son shone a five-mile flashlight directly in her eyes in the dark tent. She likened me to the five-mile flashlight. She told me that such direct light is too harsh and thus not able to be received by others. They are simply going to squeeze their eyes tight shut in self-defense against the damaging harshness of light. I considered her words and responded with, "But light doesn't reject light. Darkness rejects light. The flashlight wouldn't hurt in the noonday light." She didn't respond to that, but went on to explain that I needed tools other than a five-mile flashlight in my toolbox. That's what she hoped to help equip me with. I hoped so, too.

There came a point about midway through our months of counseling when I realized that I had become unsure of everything that I had formerly been certain of. I woke up very early one February morning and asked myself what I knew for sure. I wasn't sure. I went to another bedroom so as not to disturb Harrison, with my Bible and a pencil and paper, determined to figure out what I knew. I remembered Tobin saying in high school that only fools are certain. I was willing to be a fool;[2] I just needed to be certain of something. And thankfully, I was.[3]

This gave me a good dose of courage, this being sure of some things. I had lost a great deal of certainty since being at this window. Because I had previously been so confident and clear in my identity,

I had actually been looking forward to getting the results of my psychological testing. This confidence of thinking had set me up for a real low blow.

I had come into Dr. Stone's office that day, happy. I didn't know why she always kept the room so half-lit, shades drawn, soft lights, overstuffed furniture in shades of lush green. It could make a person sleepy. If I had it my way, I'd throw open those curtains and let the sunshine in to energize us. Anyway, it was what it was, I was here, and this was the day I was going to receive the results of who I really was!

Again, as in Tibet, I can offer no rational explanation for what took place next at this window. It was similar to what I had imagined I saw in Tibet, only opposite. Here it was Ugly. Standing there behind Dr. Stone's soft comfortable chair. As Dr. Stone reported on my psychological testing results, I saw her lips moving, but I only heard from Ugly's condemning mouth. He told me that the results of my psychological testing showed that I was a narcissistic, self-deceived fool. Put in other words, I was a self-righteous bitch.

I began to cry. The tears that Dr. Stone had been wanting, waiting, and willing to come, finally came. The ones that I felt she expected when I had told her about my life, from the beginning to the present. Her singular comment had been, "That's a whole lot of sorrow." It had surprised me. I wasn't looking for sympathy. Nor did I think of it as a sorrowful life. On the contrary, I felt I had had so much joy in life. But I felt I had to respond to her summation of sorrow with something, so I naturally defaulted to the Bible, saying that it seemed but a little sorrow compared to the joy.[4] Then I felt silly, shallow, and ashamed, as I saw the bored, half-irritated, 'not God again' look cross her beautiful young face.

But now, as I sat crying, Dr. Stone became very kind. She tried to console me, suggesting that perhaps it wasn't as bad as all that. Tests aren't really fool-proof. They don't know individuals. They just know characteristics common to types of individuals. Maybe the next time I went to women's group, I could ask them their view of me, if they envisioned me as a self-righteous bitch. That's what she told me. I dried my eyes, sniffed some more, and agreed to do that.

Women's group, as I've already described, was as real as it gets. There, we didn't pretend and we didn't care about those experts who collectively determine interpretations of who individuals are. At women's group, we cared about each other, as individuals, badly broken, though created with awesome beauty at our cores, in the image of our Maker. I left women's group that day reaffirmed in who I really was. Nevertheless, there was a lingering question of the basis that had to be present for those personality experts and Ugly himself to come to the conclusion of SRB. It pained me to say the label – that's why I initialed it *SRB*. It was so similar to the mission's diagnosis of *spiritual abuser.* Those terms were impossible to ignore, nor was any amount of knowing myself able to make them easy to bear. Fortunately, the effect was that I was ready to work really hard with Dr. Stone and every other counselor present to supply my toolbox with something other than that five-mile flashlight that had brought me here.

And work we did. One day as Dr. Stone and I were discussing my relationship with Harrison and his family, she obviously wanted to change the focus and pointedly asked, "And so what's your family pathology?"

Once again the answer was simple. Not because I knew it myself, but because my older brother, Adam, had called the evening before and given it to me. (This being the second most memorable phone call of the many my brothers made to me at this window.) In telling me about a situation of his own, and having no idea that he was giving me the answer to what would be my counselor's question the following morning, Adam had emphatically stated, "Pam, we're extremists." So when asked, I had a ready answer for Dr. Stone: "My family pathology is one of extremism." With her, I had not tried to defend the charge of extremism as I had done with Adam.

"But Adam," I had replied to him, "God is extreme – He's extreme in all His ways! His extreme wrath is because of His extreme love for us. His extreme jealousy is because of His extreme glory."

Adam had been irritated and had told me, not for the first time, "Pam, you are so radical. Don't even try saying we're like God."

This had confused me a little and I had tried to explain my reasoning. "But we *are* like Him. I think that's what it means to be

285

made *in His image.*[5] And Jesus even said, "Be perfect, therefore, as your heavenly Father is perfect." (Matthew 5:48)

It may have been the *perfect* bit that made it dawn on me what Adam meant. "Adam," I said quietly, "I don't mean that we *are* God. God is perfect in all His ways – perfect not only in His love, but also in His wrath and His jealousy, which could maybe even be interpreted as selfishness – in wanting glory for Himself, and in *all* His characteristics – unlike us, who are mixed bags and so tainted with sinfulness that sometimes His image in us is all but obliterated. Adam, I don't, for a skinny second, mistake our extremism with God's. He is perfect in all His ways. We are mixed bags in all of ours."

That conversation had helped me to see how I blunder my explanations, sometimes so much so that the beautiful message I intend becomes un-receivable, apparently to the point of being spiritually abusive. That's why, whenever possible, I always prefer to leave it in the words of others – this time the words that Martin Luther King Jr., penned on some scraps of paper from the jail cell he sat in because of being vilified as an extremist:

But. . .as I continued to think about the matter I gradually gained a measure of satisfaction from the label. Was not Jesus an extremist for love: "Love your enemies, bless them that curse you, do good to them that hate you, and pray for them that despitefully use you, and persecute you." Was not Amos an extremist for justice: "Let justice roll down like waters and righteousness like an ever-flowing stream." Was not Paul an extremist for the Christian gospel: "I bear in my body the marks of the Lord Jesus." Was not Martin Luther an extremist: "Here I stand; I cannot do otherwise, so help me God." And John Bunyan: "I will stay in in jail to the end of my days before I make a butchery of my conscience." And Abraham Lincoln: "This nation cannot survive half slave and half free." And Thomas Jefferson: "We hold these truths to be self-evident, that all men are created equal. . ." So the question is not whether we will be extremists, but what kind of extremists will we be. Will we be extremists for hate or for love? Will we be extremists for the preservation of injustice or for the extension of justice? In that dramatic scene on Calvary's hill three men were crucified. We must never forget that all three were crucified for the same crime – the crime of extremism. Two were extremists for immorality, and thus fell below their environment. The other, Jesus Christ, was an extremist for love, truth, and goodness, and thereby rose above his environment. Perhaps the South, the nation and the world are in dire need of creative extremists.[6]

In Adam's almost offhand statement of, "*We are extremists, Pam*," he had given me a world of explanation for the way things were – even to me resonating with the diagnosis I had been supplied with by the counselors – that of *anxiety*. Yes, it was plainly evident that my extremism had led me to this anxiety. And there at the safe window of Link Care, my heartbeat had been, and remains so even now, one with the prayer of the sinful psalmist David, "*Search me, O God, and know my heart; try me and know my **anxious** thoughts; and see if there be any hurtful way in me, and lead me in the everlasting way.*" (Psalm 139:23,24)

As my time at this window went on, I continued to feel that Dr. Stone viewed me as a typical shallow, happy-clappy Christian, like I was covering over the truth of my hurts with a goofy smile. She insisted on me taking a good look at my wounds. I tried to explain that I wasn't denying having wounds, it was just that to me I took the words of Isaiah the prophet literally,[7] as I also did the work of Jesus on the cross. I considered it all to have taken place in the past, and as such, felt my wounds to have already been healed, leaving only scars as reminders. When she questioned my thinking, I had told her plainly, "I believe in redemption." She said nothing. I could see that, although no Christian can argue against Redemption, she didn't really seem to think that it played into the kind of issues we were talking about. I could see what she meant, and knew I probably looked like a dumbo, believing in it so relentlessly. Had my friend, Oswald, been there, he would have done a better job explaining:

287

The great need is not to *do* things, but to *believe* things. The Redemption of Christ is not an experience, it is the great act of God which He performed through Christ, and I have to build my faith upon it.[8]

God cannot give until a man asks. It is not that He wants to withhold something from us, but that is the plan that He has established for the way of redemption. Through our asking, God puts His process in motion, creating something in us that was nonexistent until we asked. The inner reality of redemption is that it creates all the time. And as redemption creates the life of God in us, it also creates the things which belong to that life. The only thing that can possibly satisfy the need is what created the need. This is the meaning of redemption - it creates and it satisfies.[9]

Reality is not human goodness, or holiness, or heaven, or hell - it is redemption. As Christian workers, we have to get used to the revelation that redemption is the only reality. Personal holiness is an effect of redemption, not the cause of it. If we place our faith in human goodness we will go under when the testing comes. And as long as our eyes are focused on our own personal holiness, we will never even get close to the full reality of redemption. Christian workers fail because they place their desire for their own holiness above their desire to know God. "Don't ask me to be confronted with the strong reality of redemption on behalf of the filth of human life surrounding me today; what I want is anything God can do for me to make me more desirable in my own eyes." To talk that way is a sign that the reality of the gospel of God has not begun to touch me. God cannot deliver me while my interest is merely in my own character.[10]

As Dr. Stone had pointed out earlier, having been sent, I *was here* at this window, and I *did* want more efficient tools to do life with. So, at her prodding, I went ahead and dug open each and every wound I could remember giving or receiving in life. It wasn't pretty. Not at all.

Even the 'having been sent' to this window became clearer as our counselors put together the big picture. There was some comfort in the words of our case manager, which he pronounced as a matter of course, "You guys were set up." And apparently, as it typically happens, we weren't alone in that situation. At one of our large group meetings, we were working on yet another type of personality test, one to determine how we are most comfortable relating to and working with others. I don't remember the exact type it was, but it was one that was pretty common amongst our group of about twenty, causing the leader of this session to comment, "And of course, that stands to reason, because you're here and the ones that sent you are still there, in charge." We all had a good laugh over it. Here, at Link Care, a Beauty-ordained setting to restore those wounded in the battle, it was apparently not an uncommon occurrence for clients to have been sent by those who were clever enough to be the ones remaining on the field. Whatever ironic comfort there was in that, we took it, for better or for worse. But, in all seriousness, I felt compelled to repeatedly tell those soul sisters of mine in women's group, "Someone may have meant this for harm, but for sure, God meant it for our good!"(Gen. 50:20) Of this, I had absolutely no doubt.

Of course, those of us at Link Care had not all come by the same route. But as I listened carefully to the stories of each new client, I had to think that, in reality, though they were different situations, there were only a handful of routes by which we had all gotten into our present broken states. It made me realize that Ugly is not very creative. He only takes what was created to be beautiful and twists it into ugly. But, at that, he is very effective.

As the weeks turned into months and our sessions carried on, Harrison and I came to learn the vital importance of early life experiences in shaping the grid on the windows we look out of for the rest of our lives. For me, losing loved ones to death at an early age had an apparently negative impact on my view of living. I had to laugh at myself as I finally caught what they were teaching me – I didn't think it was a negative impact on living, I thought it was reality. Of course, **my** reality – apparently not true for others.

I felt I also got a glimpse out of Harrison's window during one of our pastoral counseling sessions. Our pastoral counselor had told us that the very first time we walked into his office, he immediately thought, "Here are two *very* different people." He was more right than even we knew. For all my trouble with feeling silly for expressing joy, Harrison apparently had an opposite view. At this particular session, our pastoral counselor turned to Harrison and asked, "What does it look like out your window, Harrison?" It was very quiet for a few minutes, and then Harrison began to cry – for what seemed an interminably long time, as the pastor and I sat quietly waiting. I felt so very helpless but took some comfort in believing that those tears were falling gracefully into Beauty's vial, and Beauty counted them precious.

Though I could only imagine what Harrison saw out his private window, something had happened not long before that session that I felt may have given me an insight. Because I was still working on a Wheaton course, I had visited the English Language Institute of Fresno University. The staff there had graciously assisted me and when I was finished, Harrison was waiting for me outside the building in a used car we had recently purchased. When I crossed the street and opened the car door, I saw that he had been listening to music while waiting. I saw his tears before he quickly brushed them away and I heard Susan Werner singing:

Well I come from the rural Midwest
It's the land I love more than all the rest
It's the place I know and understand
Like a false-front building
Like the back of my hand
And the men I knew when I was coming up
Were sober as coffee in a Styrofoam cup
There were Earls and Rays, Harlans and Roys
They were full-grown men
They were barbed wire boys
They raised grain and cattle on the treeless fields
Sat at the head of the table and prayed before meals
Prayed an Our Father and that was enough
Pray more than that and you couldn't stay tough
Tough as the busted thumbnails on the weathered hands

They worked the gold plate off their wedding bands
And they never complained, no they never made noise
And they never left home
These barbed wire boys
'Cos their wildest dreams were all fenced in
By the weight of family, by the feeling of sin
That'll prick your skin at the slightest touch
If you reach too far, if you feel too much
So their deepest hopes never were expressed
Just beat like bird's wings in the cage of their chest
All the restless longings, all the secret joys
That never were set free
In the barbed wire boys
And now one by one they're departing this earth
And it's clear to me now 'xactly what they're worth
Oh they were just like Atlas holding up the sky
You never heard him speak, you never saw him cry
But where do the tears go, that you never shed
Where do the words go, that you never said
Well there's a blink of the eye, there's a catch in the voice
That is the unsung song
Of the barbed wire boys[11]

~ ~ ~

It became increasingly clear to me that my healed wounds were exceedingly inconsequential in comparison to those I had, even with the best of intentions, inflicted on others, especially as there was no way for me to make restitution. The making of restitution had been a vital component in the process of repentance and salvation that I had learned as a youth. So the fact that I could do nothing to remedy the damage I had caused in the lives of those most precious to me, brought me more sorrow than any I had experienced in life so far. Weeping, I asked Dr. Stone if those I had damaged most could recover. She looked at me so tenderly and with sincere empathy answered truthfully and sadly, "I don't know." It wasn't comforting, but I knew it was truth.

Fortunately for me, in a phone conversation later that day, Tobin had assured me, "People are resilient, Mom." In those words of his, I was able to find a measure of comfort and hope. All three of our children were amazingly supportive of our time at Link Care. Tobin reminded us periodically that this was a rare and unusual gift that most people never have the opportunity to receive – a chance to just step back from life and reflect on it. Really, who does get to do that, at least to this extent? When Cherith had finished her time with the Peace Corp, she made her ticket straight to Fresno, California. She stayed with us a week or so before going on to try to establish herself in the States, starting in Washington, D.C., since that was where both Tobin and Lizzie were. After her six week stay in China with Cherith, Lizzie had returned to Illinois. In spite of the love of those who cared for her there, she had found it impossible to stay. Thus it was that she had set her face like flint, packed her meager belongings into her little orange Chevy Aveo, and headed to D.C., where she and Tobin struggled together to make life work for them. It wasn't easy.

Along with the encouragement of our own flesh and blood, we also received the same from many of our friends – both from among those we had left behind on the mission field as well as those long-time friends and supporters Stateside. In sharing with them, we were surprised with the number of times different ones would express their own need, saying, "I think I need Link Care!" Of course, Pastor Bob was amongst our encouragers. In the midst of the worst of our times, he sent a message saying that he saw Psalm 112 as being who Harrison and I were in Christ. I continue to cherish that to this present day.

During the time that Cherith was visiting us, Harrison and I had had a particularly intense session with our wonderful marriage counselor. When it was over and we were ready to go back to the house, I realized our tear-stained faces would give us away, so I asked our marriage counselor, "Whatever will we tell Cherith?" Our marriage counselor's answer showed a lot of wisdom, "You don't have to tell her, or your other kids, anything. They already know."

This marriage counselor was an exceedingly helpful person to our journey. When working with couples, Link Care had one basic question to start with, "Do you *want* this marriage to work?" It was a no-brainer to us. *Of course, we did.* We did so much that we assumed all couples did, otherwise they wouldn't have gotten married. To our dismay, we saw right in front of us, right there in our precious soul-group, that was not always the case. Nor did Link Care force it to be, or needlessly waste resources, if the couple did not want the marriage to work.

But as for Harrison and me, we wanted it to work more than anything, and were willing to go to any length to make it happen. Thus it was that we were ready, even eager, to receive the awful truths of ourselves and what made us tick individually, and why it didn't work when we combined our issues. I continue to sincerely and fervently pray that Beauty has special pleasures in store for these non-judgmental servants of His, who give their lives to helping missionaries, pastors, Christian workers and their families, and other people in the community reach a level of health where they can be more effective in life and ministry. What a calling – helping Beauty's helpers. I honestly can't think of any more beautiful calling.

Though we had only imagined staying at Link Care for six weeks, it turned out our initial friend at Link Care, the one who said he knew that we were really messed up, arriving at Christmas, was right! The mission had initially agreed to use our abundant financial support for up to three months of counseling. At the end of that period of time, Link Care did not feel we were ready to go. In fact, Link Care felt so strongly about the need to help us finish our time at this window well, that when the mission remained unwilling to use more of our financial support for continued counseling, Link Care wrapped up the remaining weeks of our care free of charge. Beauty is as beauty does.

When it came time to leave, we discovered we didn't want to go! Even with its excruciatingly painful times, we had loved this window. Not only Link Care, but also the atmosphere of the city of Fresno. It was just the right size, large enough to enjoy the diversity of its people as well as all the amenities, but small enough to be out in the countryside within a few minutes. And outside of the city, there was California to love! What a state – so much beauty to behold! We made a point of taking it all in, on the weekends, the redwood forests, snow-covered mountains, pristine beaches, and lush vineyards. We also visited friends we had worked with in Kenya. One family lived in Fresno itself, and the other on a lovely farm with kiwi vines and pecan groves!

Apparently it was our enjoyment of experiencing these wonders of California that prompted our case manager's final words to us. In saying goodbye, he encouraged us by telling us that the main thing we had going for us was that we loved having fun together. Yes, that does go a long way towards happiness, especially for a pleasure-seeker like myself.

Telling all of our counselors goodbye was bittersweet. My farewell with Dr. Stone was especially meaningful to me. I had given her a gift of Over The Rhine's album *The Long Surrender*, the one that I had often listened to on my bike rides in Lhasa, Tibet. I drew her attention to the song, *Undamned,* and thanked her profusely for her help in getting my own life undamned. To my exuberant thanks, she just shrugged and said, "You did the hard work. You were willing to consider everything." Yes, she had taught me well the truth that there are so many ways to look at things. But now she got more or less specific about it all and told me that I had come to Link Care for many reasons, none of them being what the mission had said. That was comforting – to know that, at least in her opinion, which I had come to highly value, I was not condemned to what I considered to be the very worst sin in the whole world, that of *spiritual abuse*.

We had no idea what life could hold for us in leaving Link Care. When it came time to leave, we didn't even know whether to turn right or left at the end of the Link Care driveway. I really wanted to think what Beth Moore and Priscilla Shirer had recently promised to us ladies at NorthPointe Community Church was true: that Beauty was able to do waaaaaaaay more than all I asked or could even imagine.[12] But as for Harrison and me, we didn't even know what to ask or imagine. So we left Link Care clueless as to what the day or the night would hold, but having come to a much better understanding of who we were.

Finished with our packing and goodbyes, we hopped into our little red Toyota Corolla, drove to the end of the Link Care driveway, turned right, and wended our way across this beautiful land of the free. Now our only window was that of our Corolla. We took in this land that was made for you and me, from California to the New York island, from the Redwood forest to the Gulf Stream waters – sleeping at nights in our tent, feeling as if we were God's chosen wandering toward our own unknown future. It was an indescribably beautiful adventure. As we stood overlooking the Grand Canyon, the words of a recent sermon came to my mind, "*Hallelujah* is the highest expression of praise." *Hallelujah indeed.* What a land of glory and beauty was ours, from sea to shining sea.

Lessons learned:

Truth hurts and sometimes destroys. Grace saves and heals.
Grace is sorrow dancing. Who knew?[13]
God is not Other. He is our Father and is amongst us, dwelling in and through us who are stamped with the imprint of His image.
Lucifer is Other. He is the ultimate fake, having twisted the beauty he was created in out of proportion and beyond redemption.

21

Washington, D.C.

Justitia Omnibus
Spring 2011 - August 2012

Having wended our way from the West Coast across the awesomely beautiful U.S.A., thoroughly enjoying the journey – yes, even the morning in Idaho when we crawled out of our tent to see the snow gently falling. Along the way we reconnected with those who graciously allowed us in, and eventually we reached Washington, D.C. There we found Cherith, Tobin, and Lizzie, struggling, separately and together, to make a go of it in this foreign country of our homeland. Just as we had done before, when we arrived back in the States from East Africa in 2005, we did again. We moved in with Cherith. But this time it was more difficult. When Cherith had arrived in D.C. three months earlier, she had moved in with Lizzie, who was subletting a one-bedroom apartment. So there we were, the four of us, crowded around the window of a fifth-floor, one-bedroom apartment right off of 16th Street NW, just a few blocks down the street from the White House. Much as I'd like to give you a better view, as I look back on it, it was pretty awful. For whatever reason, it looks a lot worse to me from here where I'm writing than it did at the time, when I was there. I can only tell you what I see.

Not long after arriving, Tobin took me out for lunch one day and explained, in the very kindest and gentlest tones possible, that we had not been there when he needed us, he did not need us now, and we couldn't make up for lost time. I understood and received it in the spirit he delivered it in.

I shouldn't have been surprised when our first Sunday there, at The District Church where we attended with Tobin, they were beginning a new series of sermons entitled, *The Family Mess*. But I *was* surprised and very pleasantly so; it felt to me like God had been expecting us, and had things arranged specially for us. That was a big comfort to me. Beauty saw and hadn't forgotten us.

I loved The District Church, I loved Advent Church, I loved Foundry Methodist Church – all for very different reasons. For one thing, all three churches were within walking distance of our apartment building. More importantly, their services were held at three different times, so I could attend all of them, and be a part of none, which suited me perfectly. At this point, I had nothing left to give. I was just thirsty. All I could do was receive – and what each of these three churches had to give, I soaked up like a sponge.

I loved District Church because it was a fresh sprout and the pastor was a young MK from Africa, like our own kids – though he had grown up in Liberia, West Africa while our kids grew up in East Africa. So this young pastor knew. I loved Advent because it gave a sense of permanency, not totally unlike what I had grown up with, and I loved Foundry Methodist because they lovingly welcomed everybody – not just in words, but in deed.

The message I remember receiving most clearly happened one Sunday morning as I sat in the Methodist Church. The pastor asked a simple question, "Are you a part of holding captive or of setting free?" The answer to that question was as clear as a bell to me. I embraced it without condemnation, perhaps because I was so happy to see the Beauty of the answer. *I was taking a part in holding captive.* What relief to know! To me, seeing the problem clearly is perhaps the most important part of finding a solution.

What I didn't have to give to a church, I had in abundance to give in teaching international students English. It was like the job I had so loved – teaching at Illinois State University's English Language Institute – all over again, only perhaps more so! At the window of this current International Language Institute at Dupont Circle in

D.C., the world again came to me, in classroom after classroom. I reveled in the joy of the job.

I also loved living life in D.C. I could see what Tobin's remark had meant, when after struggling to live, work and fit in, in West Virginia, Kentucky, and Nebraska, he finally transferred here to the Washington, D.C. window. At that time, he had exclaimed with apparent relief, "This I can do! Nobody is from here!" Truly, the diversity was a beautiful thing.

A funny thing happened at Four Eyes, where I was getting my eye prescription updated. I noticed the employee studying me as she helped me to choose new glasses frames, but didn't think too much of it until she asked me out of the blue where I was from. For simplicity's sake, I told her I lived in Columbia Heights. She let it go for a few minutes as I continued trying on the various frames. Then she tried again, asking, "Where did you live before living in Columbia Heights?" Seeing that I had to give a longer answer, I explained briefly. When I said I'd mostly lived in East Africa, she exclaimed, "I knew it! I said to myself, 'There's something African about this woman.'" Startled, I quickly looked down to see what I was wearing. No, it was American as could be. The woman was African – Nigerian, if I remember correctly, but had lived in the States for many years. Every now and then I think about that encounter and wonder what it was she saw in me. I still don't know.

Maybe what she saw in me was something similar to what I saw in the homeless of D.C., especially the homeless women. This, too, is difficult for me to explain, but in each of them, I saw myself. I felt a kinship, knowing of a surety that there, but for the grace of God, went I. Maybe even with the grace of God. Sometimes I thought that by chatting with them, I would see that they were different than me, but it didn't work that way. On the contrary. I can't explain that either – some kind of sixth sense perhaps.

Along with homeless women, I also felt an immediate connection with anyone old. By old, I mean fifty or above. The streets, restaurants, and shops in D.C. seemed to me to be filled with all young people. The majority of them appeared to be fighting gung-ho for justice, to save the world, or at least make a dent in setting things right. Though this seemed to emit an undercurrent of angst, I still found it admirable – something that gets lost with maturity, perhaps. I wondered if that was why there were so few 'old' people in D.C. I wondered where they had all gone, and why. And whenever I saw one, like myself, on the street or in the park, I had to restrain myself from walking up to them and saying, "Will you be my friend?"

At that time, there was one other token 'old' couple at District Church – not as old as Harrison and me, but in relative terms. Naturally enough, we connected and went out for pizza after church. As it happened, Tobin walked with us to the pizza place and sat chatting with the four of us before he had to go meet someone else for lunch. Lizzie knew we were there and stopped by for a few minutes after having coffee with someone. When both Tobin and Lizzie had gone, this couple remarked on how we seemed to have a good relationship with our kids. This was a reassuring thing to hear at this time, especially in light of their next comment. "Yeah," one of them said, "sadly, most of the missionary kids we know hate their parents." Harrison and I were alarmed. We knew lots and lots of MKs, and didn't know any that hated their parents, at least for very long. When I retold the conversation to our kids later, they didn't find it surprising in the least. Shaken, I remember feeling first sheltered from Ugly's effects and then deeply grateful for Beauty's way of escape.

Fortunately for us all, a two-bedroom apartment opened up down the hall. Cherith, with her MA in economic community development, had gotten a job as a barrister at the U Street Starbucks. Lizzie, after working as a temp at International Justice Mission, had gotten a job with Hovde Foundation. Harrison and I and our two daughters all moved from apartment 502 to 503. Along with the additional bedroom, apartment 503 had at least three times the space of 502. More importantly, it was a corner apartment with windows on three sides. Many times, after riding the dingy old elevator, lined in a dark, furry brown carpet, up to fifth floor, and then making two lefts in the long, dimly lit, mosaic-tiled hallways, I unlocked the dark, heavy door of apartment 503 and stepped into what can only be described as heavenly sunlight. It streamed across the light parquet wooden floor and filled every inch of our beautiful apartment. Somehow the contrast always reminded me of the type of despair and joy of which Rollo May speaks:

Happiness is the absence of discord; joy is the welcoming of discord as the basis of higher harmonies. Happiness is finding a system of rules which solves our problems; joy is taking the risk that is necessary to break new frontiers. . . .The good life, obviously, includes both joy and happiness at different times. What I am emphasizing is the joy that follows rightly confronted despair. Joy is the experience of possibility, the consciousness of one's freedom as one confronts one's destiny. In this sense despair, when it is directly faced, can lead to joy.[1]

As Tobin liked to put it when he came to visit, "You guys have the best apartment in all of D.C.!" Thank Beauty.

As it turned out, though, I spent precious little time in that apartment. As mentioned, I taught English at the International Language Institute (ILI). That was by day. By evening, I taught English at the old Carlos Rosario International Public Charter School, not far from our apartment in Columbia Heights. Even though I was teaching English to international adults at both jobs, to compare them would be like comparing apples to oranges. I spent my days with the privileged of the world. By privileged, I mean things like having a student ask me if she could be excused from afternoon classes; the Obamas had invited her and her husband, along with the other ambassadors and spouses over for lunch. I supposed she could.

And there were other students with diplomatic immunity who gloried in being above U.S. law, making what they considered to be good use of it. During his reign, King Abdullah created a scholarship program making it possible for thousands of Saudi students to study in the U.S. One effect of this was that the English language programs across the States filled up with students from Saudi Arabia, including the program I taught in at ILI. This had both a positive and a negative effect on me as a teacher.

It was positive in that I felt I could relate well to these Arabians. There was something about us that was the same. I recalled the taxi driver our family had spent ten days with in Morocco, and I remembered his gleeful explanation to Tobin, "So we're cousins!" That was what I felt like with these students from Saudi Arabia. I knew them as cousins. So I shouldn't have been surprised when numerous of the males, separately, remarked to me, "You remind me of my mother!" Whether or not they meant it as such, I chose to take their warm expressions as compliments. Anyway, it was more flattering than the young man who looked at me wistfully and said, "You make me think of my grandmother."

One day as I was telling a group of students about my father's life, the Saudi guys in the class appeared to be highly entertained. I wasn't sure why until one of them slapped his knee and shouted, "Your father is one of us! A strong man who marries many times!" The others boisterously agreed. I smiled, wondering what on earth my dad would say to that if he were alive. With this kind of affectionate camaraderie between us, I had to remind myself periodically of the reality: the grave difference between the extremism their religion called them to, as compared to the loving extremism of Beauty.

It was much easier for me to relate to the Saudi male students than the females, especially the draped ones. I found this curious, considering my affinity for the homeless women of D.C. As I considered the difference, I realized that I saw myself as homeless, or nearly so, but I could not even come close to letting myself imagine that I had to reach my fingers under the veil covering my face to put a piece of apple, or any other food for that matter, into my mouth. No way. Just no. Watching that, I felt opposing emotions – pity for the human eyes peering out from behind her veils and wrath for the males who made it so. It was easy for me to feel created equal to homeless women on the streets, but I couldn't imagine being equal to this degradation of bondage. As I saw it, it simply couldn't be what we, the pinnacle of creation, were created for.

The negative aspect of all these Saudis, for me as a teacher, came as part and parcel of classroom management. Because my philosophy of teaching has to do with relationship building the receptivity necessary to learn, I found the dynamics of a mostly Saudi classroom difficult. I believed that I would have found a completely Saudi classroom easier than a predominantly Saudi one, because then I would have been better able to implement a successful blanket classroom management. As one of the non-draped Saudi females said one day, "Teacher, you are different. You smile, but you are **very straight.**" This was a completely different base strategy than I had used in a classroom of Lao or Tibetan students, and not one that I would choose for most of the other nationalities represented at ILI. The difficulty of these particular dynamics for me came in finding it necessary to implement one strategy for a taxing group of students. At the same time, I felt I was delivering a disservice to the minority of the class, who were there with the singular goal of mastering the international language of the world – a vehicle that had the potential of taking them more easily wherever it was they wanted to go.

That was the basic situation of my D.C. day window. My evening one, though still teaching the vehicle of English, was much different. My evening students were not the privileged of the world. They were immigrants from various countries. They were here to stay, they hoped. As such, they were in the classrooms of Carlos Rosario as a survival technique towards that end. Most of them had gotten up early and gone to work at low-paying jobs, not only to provide for their own here, but also to send money back to their loved ones in their home countries, who were depending on them for their survival. After their busy days, they were, like me, tired, but also like me, here in class, doing what had to be done.

As we got to know one another, and they shared their joys and sorrows, these students became exceedingly precious to me. In the spring of the year, the school put out a collection of student art and writing entitled, *In Our Own Words*. In an effort to show you a glimpse of the hearts of these students, I want to share with you a couple of my students' writings as they were published in the Spring 2012, Volume 6 edition:

My Most Embarrassing Moment
by Fredy Reyes Toledo

When I came to the United States from Cuba it was difficult at first to feel comfortable in my new country. I didn't speak English. I had many embarrassing moments, but one was especially painful for me. I won't forget it for the rest of my life. It was in the morning in the Metro Station.

I was waiting for the Metro to go to school, when I saw an elderly woman. She was sitting in a chair carrying a lot of bags. Ten minutes later the Metro came. She stood up to take the Metro but forgot one bag. I picked up the bag from the chair. My intention was to give her the bag, but in one moment she looked at me with her bag in my hand and started to shout. "Police, police! This man wants to steal my bag!"

Imagine in a short time I had two policemen behind me. I felt terrible. I almost died. I tried to explain to them what was happening, but I couldn't speak English. Fortunately for me, another policeman came. He was from Puerto Rico and spoke Spanish. I explained to him what was happening and he called the Metro Station supervisor.

Finally, after 30 minutes the supervisor came and they went together to the supervisor's office. They were there checking the camera. I was waiting for 45 minutes. Those were the longest 45 minutes in my life. When they came back they apologized to me, because they saw in the camera what had really happened. It was one of the worst moments in my life, because I tried to explain the truth of the situation and I couldn't. At that moment I understood how important it was for me to learn English. In addition, when the woman started to shout, everybody in the Metro Station was looking at me like I was a robber.

How I Met President Obama
by Terezinha Vitor

It was on Sunday afternoon. I was working at Blair House, the President's Guest House. Blair House was holding a big meeting of different people from around the world for a nuclear summit meeting.

I was in the pantry, because my job is to help the waitresses with the dishes (cups, glasses, plates, drinks, food and so on). I didn't know that President Obama was coming through the pantry. Because of security no one was supposed to be there but when he came, I didn't have enough time to get out, so I tried to hide myself between the cabinets in the pantry. I didn't want the President to see me.

President Obama passed with the security man. I felt relieved when he passed by and didn't see me, but it wasn't true. He came back and saluted me!

"How are you doing? Is everything okay?" he asked. I just answered his questions.

Afterwards I realized that besides being the President, he is a good politician and a wonderful human being.

And, with the writer's permission, there is one more I would like to share with you even though it was not published:

Each Day Is Friday
by Rina Maldonado

Why do people wait excitedly for Friday? Many of them are happy only on Friday because Friday is the last day of the week. Many people work Monday through Friday, but to me, we can be happy each day of the week. When I ask someone which day is the best for her or him, they say, "Friday!" Most of them don't like Monday and the rest of the days because they are unhappy with their jobs; they do the job only for money. I know that money is important but happiness is more important.

We need to be happy every single day – not only on Friday. But it depends on how well off the mind is. Happiness is something decided in advance. In the U.S.A., the common illness is stress. That's why we need to try to be happy each day no matter what – if it is Friday or Monday. It does not depend on circumstances. It depends on choices. Abraham Lincoln said, "Most people are as happy as they have decided to be." It's true. The Bible says, "This is the day that God has made. Let us rejoice and be glad in it." Why not make the decision to be happy every day?

Have you heard the phrase, "Thank God it's Friday"? You and I should also thank God it's Monday, thank God it's Wednesday, etc. A study said that there are more heart attacks on Monday. Yes, I know some days are more difficult than others but we have to have a positive mind. Faith is always in the present. No more waiting on Friday to be happy. Our attitude should be, I'm excited to be alive at this time, today. I'm excited for my family, my health and my opportunities. I have many reasons to be happy at this time. Happiness is your right.

~ ~ ~

Undoubtedly, the stories of these students mean more to me than you, because I know the authors – their struggles, their fight to survive – and I had the privilege to see their beautiful smiles in spite of their hard times. The last writer was going through a really tough breakup at the time I was teaching her, and she would sometimes come into class early to share with me. I valued learning from her, and from the rest of the students.

Another student who gave me pause to consider the privilege that was mine as his teacher was a distinguished, white-haired gentleman. He came from Damascus, Syria, arguably the oldest city in the world, that city where the biblical Paul was converted and received his commission from His Lord. This student was a prominent citizen of Damascus and his grown children had recently decided for him that he needed to be in the States for his safety. At the time of being my student, he was sorely missing his life in Damascus, where everyone greeted him by name. Though the loneliness of being in D.C., where he knew no one and no one knew him, was taking a toll on him, the political situation in Syria prevented him from safely returning. The honor of having this precious elderly man in my class humbled me. I felt privileged to be considered his teacher, when he was my teacher in more significant ways than I was his.

I took great pleasure in my morning walk to the language institute. On my iPod I often listened to Wendell Kimbrough, a new artist I had become acquainted with at the Advent church services. I especially related to the songs on his album entitled, *Things That Can't Be Taught*. The words of these songs fit situations in my current life to a tee. As I tried to explain this to Wendell, I could see that he didn't understand exactly *how* meaningful the words were to me, but thought I was a sweet old lady and received my thanks very graciously.

The walk to work was a little less than a mile-and-a-half and took me about twenty-five or thirty minutes. Between our apartment and my destination, I walked past more than twenty embassies and/or consulates of other nations. I was reminded of the Multicultural Day celebration that Rift Valley Academy hosted at our Kenyan window. To me, the most impressive part of that day-long celebration was the Parade of Nations, a ceremony in which large flags representing the twenty-plus nationalities making up the student body were marched into the auditorium to the music of their national anthems. There's just something thrilling about the nations of the world. To be here in our own nation's capital, walking amongst the nations, and riding my bike around the Washington Monument and the many memorials, never ceased to inspire me. I so look forward to singing Beauty's praises among the nations for real!

After enjoying my private 'parade of nations' walk to work, and soon before reaching the language institute, I always took notice of the huge sign covering the burned out front of the St. Thomas Episcopal Church. It read, "**Make It Happen**." That's all its large letters said, so in my spirit I added on to it: *Mapenzi Yako yatimizwe, hapa duniani kama mbinguni. Yes, Father, make It happen.* My resonating spirit always sensed that *It* was something bigger than helping to rebuild the damaged St. Thomas parish. But I never knew exactly what that *It* was.

I walked on, and when I reached the building with the golden PLO plaque, I walked up the front steps, took the elevator to the second floor, got off and prepared for my day teaching English to the privileged international students there.

Meridian Hill Park, an urban park like no other, lay on the walking route between my day job and my evening one. It became my regular routine to stop and spend meditative time somewhere in this special twelve-acre site, with its lovely cascading fountain, statues, and quietude. I would often go on Saturdays, too, since I found in this spot a place of comfort, solace, and strength. Summer Sunday evenings found me there again, sitting on the outskirts of the drum circle, listening to the native rhythms and watching the crowd of dancers do their thing.

While I was intentionally busy, keeping myself happily con-sumed in my own world of church-filled Sundays and work-filled weekdays, the rest of my family were living out their own stories. On our arrival in D.C., Lizzie and Cherith had put their heads together and decided to combine their respective dreams of running a bakery and having a coffee shop. They convinced Harrison to be the backbone of making their dream come true. Being at a loss as to what else to do, Harrison agreed and went off to The French Pastry School, an exclusive eight-week baking course in Chicago. The girls quit their jobs and chose to go to the International Culinary Center in New York City. Looking online for a place to live while they attended classes there, Cherith found a fellow RVA student from Kenya advertising for a roommate. This friend excitedly welcomed the two of them into her apartment in the Bronx. Because Harrison was already in school in Chicago, Tobin and I drove the girls to the Bronx, helped them unload their scant possessions, and went back to our work-a-day worlds in D.C. The three of them, Harrison alone, and the girls together, had the time of their lives in bread school – the girls being entertained as much by the experience of living in the Bronx as they were by the fascination of bread making and interacting with the characters there. Those two need to write their own books.

When they had all completed their schooling, they began to search D.C. for the perfect spot for their own bakery. Because working at Great Harvest Bread Company had been one of the highlights of Lizzie's college years, they seriously considered a franchise of the same. They spent weeks searching D.C. over and came up with six possible sites. The C.E.O. of Great Harvest came and negated all six locations, suggesting that they look outside of D.C. proper. Harrison would likely have agreed to that, but the girls were insistent on their bakery being in D.C. itself. At this point, Lizzie encouraged the other two that the three of them could strike out on their own and a new search began in earnest, but after a near-go, ended unsuccessfully.

Harrison put on his white baker's hat and began work with the first Paul Bakery to open in Washington, D.C., at 801 Pennsylvania Avenue NW, near the Navy Memorial and across the street from the National Archives. Cherith became first night-baker and then daytime caterer for Panera Bread. Lizzie moved to Arlington and began teaching English to the privileged students where I already was, at the International Language Institute.

Waking at 2:00 a.m. and biking the three miles to work (the metro didn't open until 5 a.m.) to start work at 3:00 a.m., and then finishing sometime between 1-2 p.m. if he were lucky, took its toll on Harrison. Not only were the hours harsh, the work was heavy and demanding. Between his hours, his schedule of having Monday and Thursdays off, and my extensive teaching hours, we rarely even saw each other. Every Saturday, it was my habit to ride my bike to Paul Bakery, and after waving to him in his glass cage, I would get an outside table and wait for him to get off work. Then we had a lovely time together, enjoying the surroundings, including occasional brass bands playing at the Navy Memorial, and talking about everything and nothing. In spite of this sweet time, life as such was unsustainable.

That was when I received a Facebook message from a Finnish pilot we had worked with at the Dodoma, Tanzania window in the early 1990s. We had not been in touch with this couple since our paths had parted in those early missionary days. The message read as follows:

> *Hi Pam and Harrison, Sirpa and I decided to go back to flying after doing other stuff for a number of years (leadership, management, advocacy, child sponsorship). I am now flying C208 in Liberia as a corporate pilot/head of aviation department for an international agricultural company. Sirpa is working as our Flight Ops Administrator. We are looking for a FAA A&P Mechanic, who could run the maintenance and the hangar. Do you happen to know anybody who would be interested in the permanent job, based in Monrovia? Of course, Harrison, you would be perfect guy for the job. Greetings, Roy and family*

Harrison said *YES!* and two weeks later left D.C. for Liberia, stopping in France to take in a seminar on aviation software. Before this opportunity came up, I had already scheduled a vacation for myself to return to the Midwest to visit family and friends. I hated to leave if Harrison was going to be living in Liberia when I got back, but he said, "What difference does a few days make when we have only seen glimpses of each other in the past six months?" So I went.

I left after teaching at my day job. As I was traveling the interstate highway on that perfectly beautiful July evening, Adam called. He told me that it had been quite a day. He had gone to work early as usual. Before leaving for work, he had kissed his sleepy wife and asked her what she was going to do that day. She had replied, "Odds and ends." He left.

He hadn't been at work long when someone he didn't know came into his Goodyear Tire shop. This was unusual, for he knew everyone in this small Indiana town. They greeted each other and chatted cordially a minute or two about the weather. Then this stranger handed Adam a manila envelope, commented, "You're going to want to read that," and he left.

Adam opened the envelope, took out its contents, and read the words on the top of the first page. ***Dissolution of Marriage.*** He read the words again, but they still wouldn't register. There'd been a mistake. This must be for someone else. It simply wasn't possible. He sat down, sensing both blood and breath draining out of his body.

Eventually, he forced himself to read the rest of the envelope's contents. Apparently it was for him. *He had 24 hours to get anything that he wanted out of his home. After that time he would never be allowed back in. By the time he was reading these words, a significant amount of money would already be removed from his bank account.*

Sitting stunned, he saw his first-born son, his right-hand man in the business, outside the big shop window. He was talking on the phone. After he finished on the phone, Adam went to him, showed him the papers, and asked if he had known anything about this. His son, Keith, was pale and shaken. He replied, "That was Mom on the phone. She just told me."

Adam couldn't stay at work. He had to leave, but had nowhere to go, so he opted to go to the post office to see what other news the day held.

Anyway, I think that's what I remember him telling me on the phone as I drove. But I also felt that my ears couldn't be trusted. This was impossible news. It just couldn't be true.

Unbeknownst to Adam, I had known that things weren't good – but the D word had never even come close to crossing my mind. I knew because his wife had emailed me almost daily while we were at the Fresno window, giving me her view of Adam's faults and failures. I had told no one and remember going outside to cry about it, so that Harrison wouldn't see me and ask. I had told her what a wonderful place Link Care was and how it was for pastors and their wives, as well as missionaries – so they would fit right in. I told her Harrison and I had no idea what to do when we left Link Care, so we could come and stay with their four adopted children (of their forty-some foster kids) while she and Adam came to Link Care. I thought how lucky it was that they were wealthy and could pay for Link Care on their own. But she had told me that Adam would never consent to such a thing. Of course, neither of us asked him.

Because, when I was on the phone with him, I simply couldn't think of anything else to say, I had asked Adam if he had told our younger brother, Jacob, this news. Adam replied, "I'm going to call him as soon as I hang up with you." We hung up.

My plans had been to travel until I was tired that evening and then stop at a hotel to sleep. Even though I knew there was no sleep in me, I stopped at a hotel anyway. After I got checked in, Jacob called and we talked until the wee hours. About the years of life and how they work and what would happen from here on out. We simply didn't know and couldn't even imagine.

The next day, I traveled on to where my stepmother was living in Columbia, Missouri. I couldn't bring myself to share the news with her that evening. In the morning at the breakfast table, she asked me to say the blessing. I began with, "Father, this is the day that You have made. Let us rejoice and be glad in it." I stopped and dissolved into tears. My stepmother was kind and tender, believing that I had suddenly gotten lonesome for Dad. I hated to tell her the real reason for my tears, but I did, thanking Beauty that Dad was not here on this earth.

When I left my stepmom's, I travelled on to my original window of Wapello, then on to our Normal window, but I didn't stay there visiting family and friends for as long as I had intended. I went to Indiana and spent the time with Adam at his lake home in Monticello. He was almost out of his mind.

~ ~ ~

Returning to D.C. and teaching, I had an idea! That Wheaton MA program that I had never finished – with everything in such an upheaval anyway, might not now be a good time to finish it up, going to Wheaton campus in Chicago and doing it full-time? I checked with Harrison when he called and it didn't take him long to agree that it would be a good idea. My two main hindrances were the finances of it and where I would live. Harrison immediately assuaged the first by telling me that he had spent $13,000 for an eight-week course and had only gotten a fancy rolling pin out of the deal, and that rolling pin was only because he had graduated with honors! Surely my venture would be more worthwhile than that, he said.

Okay, that decided, I needed only to find a place to live. I had no more than begun to look online when I received a call from Suz, my cousin, one of my Iowa City roommates, and the maid of honor at our wedding. She was excited, "Pammer! (her pet name for me) I know where you can live when you go to Wheaton!" She proceeded to tell me that though she hadn't checked with her, she was positive that I could live with her sister's husband's sister. *My cousin's sister's husband's sister??* It sounded pretty far-fetched to me, but this person did live in Glen Ellyn, a two-minute drive from Wheaton campus. So I sent her a very long email, explaining who I was and what I was about. In the meantime, Suz had told Gretchen about me, and by the time I had clicked 'send' on my explanatory email, there was already an email in my inbox from my new host with four words on it, *Mi casa su casa.* I was good to go. Thank Beauty.

On my final day of walking home from the International Language Institute, I passed through Meridian Hill Park, feeling very nostalgic. I stopped to shake hands with a homeless man whom I often met there. I told him this would be the last time that I would be passing through because I was moving to Chicago. *Chicago, yes,* he knew Chicago. Little did I know, though, this would not be the last time I would pass through this park. How could I know that Tobin and his bride would marry here, in the renaissance-re-vival-style mansion just across the street, overlooking this park? I would be sitting there in the front row. Tobin and his bride, trusting in the grace of Christ to bind them together for life, as best man Harrison, and Cherith and Lizzie as bridesmaids stood by, looking for all the world like a third and fourth generation with the promise of Beauty's love to a thousand generations. I didn't know, saying goodbye to that homeless man, that I would be at this D.C. window again – sitting in profound amazement, on the front row with my father's third wife. I would ask my Father in heaven, "Which prayer of mine in Meridian Hill Park did you hear?" and He would answer, "All of them, My darling daughter. All of them."

As it happened, Harrison returned to the States from Liberia to take part in flight safety training in Wichita, Kansas. He flew first into D.C. and spent a couple days helping Tobin look for a new pickup truck. Having finished my time at this window, I packed up my belongings, turned over my bedroom in our apartment to a person of Cherith's choosing, waved g'bye to the kids, and Harrison and I drove off into the sunset, towards Wheaton, Illinois.

Lessons learned:

Sadness is so small and suffocating
compared to the glorious spaciousness of joy.
Being a disciple of Christ is different than just 'being saved'.
Discipleship requires severe discipline, it's not joyful at the time,
but sorrowful. The glory comes later, with the proof that we really
are more than conquerors through Jesus Christ our Lord.

22

Glen Ellyn, Illinois

A Divine Spanking
August 2012 - May 2013

I will always be able to see Harrison and me pulling into the driveway of that big old home on North Main Street. It seemed so unreal. Though I had never been there before, it was to be my new window – while Harrison would be looking out of his own in Liberia, West Africa. I had been so glad that he was at least present with me as we unloaded what Gretchen termed our 'clown trunk.' And I was refreshed by the eager childlikeness with which this wonderful woman, a few years my senior, had met us at the door and welcomed me into her home and life. It wasn't until much later that I realized that the reason she couldn't get over the amount of *stuff* that kept coming out of our car trunk into her upstairs was that she had no idea 1) how long I was staying and 2) that, like any homeless person, I had brought all my earthly possessions. Apparently, when she had hosted another missionary cousin of mine and her husband, they had come to Wheaton for a conference and stayed a week or two and that was what Gretchen had in mind when she had responded so quickly to me with *Mi casa su casa!* When I asked her, a few years later, *when* exactly it clicked in that I was there for the year, even then she wouldn't tell me. She only said, "I realized it was meant to be and I knew it wasn't polite to ask."

And meant to be, it was. We quickly recognized that though our lives had been very different from one another's, we were fast sisters at heart. Though our schedules rarely allowed us to see one another, when someone commented that our lifestyle made us pass like two ships passing in the night, she quickly responded that it was much more like two Christians passing in the Light. True that. I recognized her as another of Beauty's good and perfect gifts to me.

As Harrison and I were carrying my things up the attic stairs that afternoon, I suddenly remembered a dream I had had prior to making plans to go to Wheaton. In the dream, Harrison was moving boxes up a stairway and I had asked him, "Why are you moving me to an *attic*?!" Now Gretchen and I preferred to call it *the loft*. And what a lovely spacious loft it was – with a window on either end, and even a white steeple of some church or another rising in the distance out the north window, nearest my bed. I learned many lessons from this dear woman, not the least of them being that the Lord is able to give eyes to our feet when we don't know where we're going and that His arm is not too short to do anything.[1]

Though my possessions were in Glen Ellyn, and I considered it to be my address for the time being, in truth, I ended up living much of my time at my brother Adam's, at Lake Freeman in Monticello, Indiana, a two-and-a-half hour drive away. In this painful time of life for him, we connected in more meaningful ways than we had all the years of our growing up. I came to see that one beauty of siblings is to help each other to the finish line of life. There are times when we need all the help we can get. Adam and I sat on his deck over-looking the lake and talked for many hours, sometimes with a full moon shining on the lake and other times with bald eagles soaring in the sunshine. I loved watching the eagles fly, especially because, as Adam watched them, he said he still knew there was a God.

Early on, I saw that no matter how I looked at it, or which place I was at, this was not going to be an easy window of my life. In fact, I discovered that it was anything but easy. I also saw the necessity of making the steadfast decision not to waste the pain. There came a time when, in transitioning back to my attic space from Lake Freeman, I found myself weeping and crying aloud, "Please, God, please," over and over. *Please what?* I didn't know.

314

I loved Wheaton campus. I still love its forthrightness in publicly proclaiming its motto of "For Christ and His Kingdom." *Yes*. Life is about knowing Christ Jesus and making Him known. This truth reminded me of Cherith as a little girl, when she had said to me at our Cicero window, "Mommy, I know what people are made for. Telling other people about Jesus." Perhaps her simplistic circular thinking wasn't so childishly far off after all.

In spite of the confidence I had in Wheaton's mission, I entered her halls in fear and trembling. I had not made it safely beyond our original church without getting excommunicated and I had not made it safely through organized missions without being 'released.' Seeing the obvious pattern and knowing that history repeats itself, a poignant awareness hung continually over me that my track record was not good and my chances of getting safely through Wheaton College without getting kicked out might also be slim.

Whatever doubts I had, however, dissipated completely, at least temporarily, the first time I walked into the fourth floor library of the Billy Graham Center (BGC), and was met, directly inside the door, by my friend Oswald Chambers (not live, of course, but in life-size sturdy poster board)! After all the help he had already lent me on my journey, I knew I was in the right place for sure. I recalled the first time I had met him, in a book in a guest home in Nairobi, Kenya. There he had told me something important about God: *When we choose deliberately to obey Him, then He will tax the remotest star and the last grain of sand to assist us with all His almighty power.* That had bred a huge amount of spiritual confidence within me, for which I had thanked Beauty.

That cardboard statue of Oswald Chambers was *inside* the Billy Graham Center. *Outside* was another story. Every time I climbed those concrete steps to the landing under those impressive white pillars, in my imagination I saw Candy standing there, just as she had been back in the summer of 2010 – laughing merrily, her fine, straight blond hair blowing gently back in the breeze. Of course, every time I actually reached the stairs, she had vanished. Because it happened without fail that she was there, rain or shine – and though the seasons changed, she did not – I sometimes thought of John Nash and wondered if I, too, had *A Beautiful Mind.*

315

Wednesday was my favorite weekday to wake up in the loft. That was because every week on Wednesday mornings at 10:30 a.m., Graduate School Chapel convened in the Chatlos Studio in the west end of the basement of the Billy Graham Center. In that cozy setting, we were gifted with a time of spiritual refreshment and encouragement right in the middle of the busy, stress-filled week. It was a time of some sacramental firsts for me: my first official *lectio divina* and my first participation in Ash Wednesday. Though there were many significant and relevant messages delivered by faculty, grad students, and outside speakers, there is one that continues to ring in my life yet today. The speaker was telling us how she and her husband were working ever so hard to make a go of their ministry, when Jesus' words were brought to their attention: "I am the vine; you are the branches. If you remain in me and I in you, you will bear much fruit; *apart from Me you can do nothing.*" (John 15:5) As they pressed on, trying even harder and harder, the speaker said she heard the Spirit of God ask her, "*What part of **nothing** do you not understand?*" I continue to occasionally remember to think of Jesus as the life-giving Vine, and me as a stem, and ask myself that question.

The one time that I went to an undergraduate chapel is also memorable to me. Dr. Gallagher gave a testimony of the Lord's working in his own life, which I only partially remember. What I do remember is walking out amongst the undergraduate student body, under the distinct impression that I was walking amongst future martyrs, having no idea, of course, who or which ones they would be.

It was Dr. Gallagher's second wife who led the one graduate student forum that I remember more than all the others. She had arranged for many different pictures of different kinds to be placed on the desks and tables in the next classroom. She instructed us to file into that classroom and walk amongst the pictures until we saw the one that we knew was specifically for us. She said we would know when we saw it. I had never heard of such a thing as this assignment, and wasn't at all sure about it. She further instructed us that when we saw the one for us, to pick it up, bring back to our desks in this classroom we were in, and write about it – a prayer, a poem, whatever came to us – and then write the date on the picture.

Carrying my doubts with me, I filed into the next room with the rest of the students. I had only taken a few steps into that classroom, when ***there it was.*** I think it was only the third or fourth picture after entering. I knew, beyond a doubt, that it was for me. Weird, I know. It was simply a piece of 8 1/2 x 11 inch thin brown construction paper. On the bottom center there was a small three-inch-square picture, cut from a magazine. The picture was of a white swan with some light brown coloring on its long neck and forehead. This swan was sitting on some rippling blue-gray water. There were a few thin green reeds surrounding her. None of that was what drew me to the picture. What captured me then and even now, as I look at this picture, is the tiny furry white head poking out from the center of that swan's back – peeking out from under its right wing. But for its little head, it is easy to miss seeing the tiny swan because it is almost totally immersed in the solid fluffy white of its mother.

On the brown construction paper to the left of the picture, I drew an arrow in blue ink to that tiny little head poking out of the white and wrote, *Ha, me thinking I'm so useful in everyone's lives, when actually there I am, that's me!*

On the brown construction paper above the picture, I wrote, *It's me, it's me, it's me, O Lord, standing in the need of prayer. It's me, it's me, it's me, oh Lord, standing in the need of prayer.* Again, with an arrow to that little head.

On the brown construction paper, to the right of mother swan, I wrote, *Safe & secure from all alarm, in the white, fluffy clouds of liminality – safely between here & there. TY, Lord God of All.* Beside the lower left of the picture I dated it, as directed. *~ Jan. 30, 2013*

This picture was meaningful to me on many levels. One of them was that it reminded me of the morning I woke up early in the clean white fluff of a bed in a brand spanking new Hampton Inn in Siloam Springs, Arkansas, with the following words running across my mind:

*no here **or** there*
cocooned in the darkness
surrounded by clean white fluff
safely between here and there

317

Secondly, it reminded me of many Bible verses that had become exceedingly precious to me.[2]

And last but not least, the date reminds me now, as I'm writing, that I had, at the time of writing on this swan picture, safely made it through my rough introduction to Liberia, West Africa, having gone to visit Harrison over my Christmas break from Wheaton.

~ ~ ~

I had thought that I was well-prepared for Liberia. Harrison had told me to think of Dar Es Salaam, Tanzania in 1990, and I would have a good idea of what to expect when coming to Monrovia, Liberia. He was right, that was an excellent help. He also told me that Liberia was almost completely Christian – blatantly Christian all over the place actually, except for a few struggling mosques here and there. Also, good preparation – well, sort of.

Then too, I had learned through a fellow student in Qualitative Research Class that there was a Liberian church group that met together on Sunday evenings at Wheaton church. I quickly joined that and they welcomed me with amens and clapping when I introduced myself as having a husband working in Monrovia! They initiated me into the special Liberian handshake so I could begin practicing early. This was also where I met Bill and Betty Thompson, who had been missionaries to Liberia in the early 1950s. They were instrumental in starting Africa's first Christian radio station on the mission compound known as ELWA, Eternal Love Winning Africa. I also joined the Liberian Bible study that Betty still hosted in her home in Wheaton. When it was time for me to go visit Harrison at Christmastime, I took gifts from the Liberians to their families and from Bill and Betty to those they knew and loved, still working at the radio station at ELWA.

In spite of all that helpful preparation, nothing could have prepared me for what I was about to encounter when I landed in Monrovia and in the experiences that followed there. First of all, there was the ridiculousness of arriving at the airport – never had I ever seen the like. It altogether exceeded the experiences of all my other airport arrival windows, being a part of a body-to-body crowd that was gesticulating wildly while yelling, screaming, pushing, and shoving. Some people even jumped over the conveyor belt in the baggage claim area! I was so thankful that Harrison had the foresight to have a local Liberian with airport clearance come inside to meet me. In the jostling, I feared receiving a broken leg or worse as I tried to remain standing upright while watching for my luggage and gawking in fascination at the goings-on.

Though it was dark as we drove the hour from Roberts International Airport to Sinkor, where Harrison was living, I could still see that he had been right in telling me to recall Dar Es Salaam and vicinity in the early 90s. Then, it was only because I had already seen it on Skype that I wasn't shocked by the contrast of stepping into the shining luxuriousness of his apartment where I, too, looked forward to living when I finished at my Glen Ellyn window.

In the light of the next day, I was more fully able to appreciate Harrison's third floor apartment filled with light from the windows of its balconies on two sides, and its placement a five-minute walk from the Atlantic Ocean. In going out and about, I was thankful and felt smart, already having been taught the Liberian handshake. It didn't take long to discover the standard answer to the greeting of "How are you?" The pat response was, "Thank God." While I appreciated the answer, at the same time it left me a little confused. I, too, thanked God, but at the moment I was actually asking about the person themselves, how they were doing. Later, when I inquired into the explanation for this seemingly rote greeting, I learned that they were thankful to God to still be alive – which I could relate to after my airport arrival experience. It would, in all seriousness, continue to make even more sense as I learned more about their past, and watched the effects in their present lives.

When Harrison and I delivered the gifts that I had been given by Liberians in Wheaton for their loved ones at the radio station on the ELWA compound, we also happened to visit with a Samaritan's Purse helicopter pilot who was in the process of moving his family back to the States. In chatting, they mentioned that they had more pieces of luggage than the six of them were allowed to take on the airline. Because this couple was initially going to be staying with her parents in the Chicagoland area, Harrison thought to offer, and I readily agreed, to take a couple of their pieces since I wasn't using my allotment for this short visit of mine. The beauty of this arrangement was that when Cheryl came to Glen Ellyn to pick up the action packers, she asked if I had time to go out for coffee. *Oh yes, I did.*

Thus began my routine of Thursday mornings with Cheryl at Caribou Coffee in Glen Ellyn. It was in this comfortable, safe setting that Beauty prepared me for the realities of living in Liberia. As Cheryl talked, I came to know Liberians as individuals, along with the wonderful missionaries and Christian workers, but also the dark powers of the spirit at work there. Though I found much of what she had to say shocking, it was in keeping with the realities I would find for myself when I went to live at my next window. Her stories also helped to explain the disharmony between what I had seen and what I had felt on that Christmas 2012 visit. What I had seen with my eyes and what I had sensed in my spirit were in direct opposition. In writing a mini-research paper as an advance assignment for an upcoming intercultural class at Wheaton, I had begun by trying to capture the confusion of this discord that I sensed:

Who Sabotaged the Church in Liberia?

Because I had lived in East Africa for fifteen years, I expected the transition to Liberia in West Africa to be a fairly smooth one. Having been informed before my arrival that the infrastructure of the capital city of Monrovia is currently much like the infrastructure of Dar Es Salaam, the capital city of Tanzania, was in the early 90s, I felt I was prepared in a way that only experience can prepare a person. I was wrong. Indeed, the apt description that I had been armed with was more than adequate as far as it went. Considering that Liberia is still recovering from the horrors of her ruthless civil war (1989–1996; 1999–2003), the resulting lack of infrastructure was not what took me unawares. The problem, as I encountered it, seemed to lay deeper than the infrastructure. What I struggled to wrap my mind around concerning this nation of Liberia, named as such to convey its identity as the land founded by liberated slaves, was the glaring discrepancy between the prolific signage (*below bibliography) proclaiming victorious Christian living and the spirit of the power of the air that I sensed and that was confirmed through the word of testimony of both Liberians and expatriates as I informally conversed and formally interviewed them. As I daily rejoiced in the beauty of the land and, at the same time, grieved in its slavery to the corruption of the glorious freedom its signage proclaimed, a startling, unfamiliar and unbidden question burned in my mind, "What the hell is wrong here?" For once in my life, I had no answer at all. Left without intuitive knowledge, I turned my focus to the academia and research ideology of my current context.

Decision(s) Faced

Faced with the reality of being expelled from missions per se and released into the freedom for which I have been set free, how do I stand firm, and what approach should I take while waiting for the hope of righteousness in Christ Jesus and the accompanying redemption that is possible for the groaning, war torn, church-filled nation of Liberia?

Thus began my research paper. Below are a few examples of the prolific signage that I mentioned in the first paragraph as being below my bibliography:

*Actual Signs in Monrovia

Alpha and Omega Evangelical Bible Church, Inc. a.k.a. Power and Glory Assembly
Be Greatful to God (as spelled)
Be with God Fashion Shop
Blessed Honesty Business Center
Blessed Overcomers Auto Parts
God's Favor Garage
God is One Business Center
God's Favor Computer Parts
King of Glory Enterprise
Look Up to God Food Center
Ministry of Truth Judah Assembly
Miraculous Healing Hand of Jesus Christ Pentecostal Church, Inc.

Mountain of Fire and Miracles Center
My God is Alife (as spelled)
New Creation Bar and Restaurant
No Problem because God Comes First
Religion of the Sound and Sight of God

Coming from the context of Christian Wheaton to Christian Liberia, I had not known enough to expect this collision between my preconceived ideas of a clean, tidy, separate and safe Christianity and what I now sensed as some twisted form of mockery, albeit in a blatantly Christian context. I simply hadn't been able to get my mind around the new context of interpretation that was staring me in the face. The overall effect of it led me to whisper to Harrison in the middle of a dark night that December, "*Beloved, how do we __know__ God IS?*" His answer was soft and gentle, a voice I trusted, "Because, my love, His Spirit witnesses with our spirits that we are His children." (Romans 8:16) *Yes. Yes, of course.* We're His. He has to exist if we do. It's the very mystery of incarnation – being indwelt by the Spirit of Beauty, for reasons beyond the understanding of any of us, and as expressed in the tactfully true bathroom blessing prayer that Barbara Brown Taylor shares in her book *An Altar in the World*:

> *O holy God, in the incarnation of your Son our Lord you made our flesh the instrument of your self-revelation: Give us a proper respect and reverence for our mortal bodies, keeping them clean and fair, whole and sound; that, glorifying You in them, we may confidently await our being clothed upon with spiritual bodies, when that which is mortal is transformed by life; through Jesus Christ our Lord. Amen.*[3]

~ ~ ~

Back at Wheaton, I reentered my classes with a determined zest to finish strong, for better or for worse. So when Dr. Pierson asked me before class if I would stay after class to talk with her, that she had something to talk to me about, I was worried sick. It was difficult for me to concentrate during that class. The whole time I kept wondering if this was it – if and what I had done wrong to warrant being dismissed from Wheaton College. Even though I knew it was probably ridiculous for me to think this way, my past experience of not having known what I had done wrong wouldn't leave me with any peace of mind at this current window.

Therefore, you can imagine my huge relief when Dr. Pierson had these two things to talk to me about after that class: 1) She wanted to thank me for being so welcoming to the international students in the program. She had noticed how I reached out to them. What she obviously wasn't aware of was that I wasn't being intentionally thoughtful. I gravitated towards them naturally, because they were my comfort zone. It wasn't an effort on my part. If anything, it was selfishly motivated. 2) She wanted to let me know of an opportunity she had heard about, to teach English to international students. Would I be interested? *Yes, of course, I would.* How to spell relief!

It seems to me that the name of the class that I took under Dr. Gallagher's professorship is the only thing that I forget about it. That man was so full of the Holy Spirit that time in his classes flew by. Two of the many things that I osmosed there were: 1) Our Christianity has fed us a very narrow slice of God. 2) A reaffirmation that questions tell us more than answers ever can. Because questions reach the heart of most matters more quickly than answers do, Dr. Gallagher had a habit of assigning us to come up with questions instead of answers. One of my questions on the book of Jonah was: *Why did God provide Jonah a comforting leafy plant to give him shade and make him happy* **when Jonah had already made himself a shelter and was sitting in its shade?** (Jonah 4:5,6) That question continued to haunt me in my other missions classes.

For example, it came back to me in Dr. Moreau's class when he assigned us to read Duane Elmer's book, *Cross-Cultural Servanthood: Serving the World in Christlike Humility.* Chapter three of that book is entitled, *Humility, Posture of the Servant.* The chapter opens with the following two quotes and story:[4]

"If you ask me what is the first precept of the Christian religion, I will answer first, second, and third, Humility." ~ *Augustine*

"Humility is the garden of all the virtues." ~ *Chrysostom*

The Monkey "Serves" the Fish

A typhoon had temporarily stranded a monkey on an island. In a secure, protected place on the shore, while waiting for the raging waters to recede, he spotted a fish swimming against the current. It seemed obvious to the monkey that the fish was struggling and in need of assistance. Being of kind heart, the monkey resolved to help the fish.

A tree precariously dangled over the very spot where the fish seemed to be struggling. At considerable risk to himself, the monkey moved far out on a limb, reached down and snatched the fish from the threatening waters. Immediately scurrying back to the safety of his shelter, he carefully laid the fish on dry ground. For a few moments the fish showed excitement, but soon settled into a peaceful rest. Joy and satisfactions swelled inside the monkey. He had successfully helped another creature.

Elmer follows the story with this paragraph:

*The story does not tell us the degree of humility or arrogance the monkey possessed. But, then, that was not the real issue as far as the fish was concerned. The fish likely saw the arrogance of the monkey's assumption that what was good for monkeys would also be good for fish. This arrogance, hidden from the monkey's consciousness, far overshadowed his kindness in trying to help the fish. **Thus good intentions are not enough.** (emphasis mine)*

What I immediately recognized in this monkey was not so much his well-intentioned misinterpretation of the fish's culture – which

324

was presumably the real point of the story and one that is obviously of great value to those heading to the mission field! But because of my experience, what struck me with a much greater impact was the missionary monkey's smugness in a job well done. To me, this story resonated and reverberated with the distaste I had for the missionary pedestal, where I felt even the most well-intentioned were praising us for what I often sensed was us, coming up with our own fig leaf coverings,[5] and making ourselves shelters like Jonah had done. This is all in direct opposition to the way that Jesus told His disciples it should happen: "Let your light shine before men, *so that* they may see your good deeds and *praise your Father in heaven.*"(Mt. 5:16 ESV) For me, though I far preferred that folks praise my Father in heaven for my good works, I didn't even mind much if they praised my father on earth, who had, after all, provided me a life with good choices to choose from. I simply disliked them praising me, or even noticing me at all, for that matter.

In his book, *The Hole in our Gospel,* Richard Stearns quotes Ralph Winter as saying that obedience to the Great Commission has more consistently been poisoned by affluence than by anything else. There are many ways to look at things, and as I mentioned at my Dodoma, Tanzania window, Stearns and I have differing views on poverty, and thus affluence. From my viewpoint, the poisoning in missions comes from misplaced praise – that is, praising the doer of the good deeds rather than our Father in heaven. Either as goers who do, or senders who provide resources, we are all our Father's handiwork, simply doing what we were created to do. All of the glory and praising goes to our Creator, for creating us so marvelously, in His image and likeness, and providing for us so abundantly.

Though Jesus' recorded spoken words, giving the '*so that*' reason for doing good works, are of primacy, others have also expressed both the sentiment of misplaced praise and misinterpreting the need, two of the follies of the missionary monkey.

Anthony de Mellow on misplaced praise:

As the master grew old and infirm, the disciples begged him not to die. Said the master, "If I did not go, how would you ever see?"

"What is it we fail to see when you are with us?" they asked. But the master would not say.

When the moment of his death was near, they said, "What is it we will see when you are gone?"

With a twinkle in his eye, the master said, "All I did was sit on the riverbank handing out river water. After I'm gone, I trust you will notice the river."[6]

And on need:

The trouble with people is that they're busy fixing things they don't even understand. We're always fixing things, aren't we? It never strikes us that things don't need to be fixed. They really don't. This is a great illumination. They need to be understood. If you understood them, they'd change.[7]

And so as not to leave out the words of my friend, Oswald:

It is much easier to do something than to trust in God; we see the activity and mistake panic for inspiration. That is why we see so few fellow workers with God, yet so many people working for God. We would much rather work for God than believe in Him. Do I really believe that God will do in me what I cannot do?[8]

Jesus is saying in Luke 10:20, "Don't rejoice in your successful service for Me, but rejoice because of your right relationship with Me." The trap you may fall into in Christian work is to rejoice in successful service - rejoicing in the fact that God has used you. . . . Our tendency today is to put the emphasis on service. Beware of the people who make their request for help on the basis of someone's usefulness. If you make usefulness the test, then Jesus Christ was the greatest failure who ever lived. For the saint, direction and guidance come from God Himself, not some measure of that saint's usefulness. It is the work that God does through us that counts, *not what we do for Him*. All that our Lord gives

His attention to in a person's life is that person's relationship with God - something of great value to His Father.[9]

To be fair to the missionary monkey, we must express a certain appreciation for his kind, well-intentioned charity towards the struggling fish. But what is charity? Is it as Mitch Albom suggests in his book, *The Time Keeper*, the beautiful taking pity on the ugly? Or is it, as the monkey story suggests, the capable taking pity on those that we view as helpless?

Again, as Dr. Stone taught me back at my Fresno window, there are so many ways to look at things. From my experience, I am in solid agreement with what John penned so very long ago, *God is Love* (1 John 4:8) – that is, real charity is Beauty Himself, pitying our helplessness against Ugly's grip, and sending His Son in the flesh to redeem us and set us free. And I, too, see it as Kayla McClurg expresses it, our beautiful lover is the provider of everything:

What if we were to begin to believe, as Jesus believed, that everything is given to us from God? Nothing is a mistake. Everything has purpose and meaning uniquely suited for our lives. The person who adores me, along with the one who does not like me so much—given. The tasks that weary me, the dreams that never find fulfillment, all my failures and successes—specially designed and given for my continued growth and blessing. What would change? Would I begin to see more clearly? Would I accept the 'what is' more easily? Would I leave the land of complaint and dwell more often in gratitude? What we believe about what is being given to us depends, of course, upon our basic beliefs about God. Do we believe in a loving and divine presence actively weaving in and through our days? Is there an ultimate order and beauty beyond our little perspectives? Does this presence intervene, interact, interrelate, and if so, how so? Is God a nurturing mentor, a loving protector, or a harsh and demanding judge? Does God remain aloof, or rush in to do whatever we ask? Does the Holy One trick us into being and doing what we would not choose, or woo us from our hiding places of fear and regret? What we believe about the nature of God changes everything. When we start to trust the God that Jesus knew, we find the ultimate reality *is* Love. We learn that everything is being given from an endless source of love. The God that Jesus knew was a God big enough for all his need, a God who could be trusted and deepened into, fathomless yet personal. It makes sense to trust such a God as this, to lean back into the grace being provided through all things, to see it all as good. This kind of God is able to capture our imagination in ways that continually unfold, slowly are revealed. In and through all that comes to us, God becomes more and more known, more and more our own.[10]

Not only are there many ways to look at things, it's also true, as written by Bishop Gregory of Nyssa in the first century, that there are endlessly new ways of looking at things:

As you came near the spring you would marvel, seeing that the water was endless, as it constantly grabbed up and poured forth. Yet you could never say that you had seen all the water. How could you see what was still hidden in the bosom of the earth? Hence no matter how long you might stay at the spring, you would always be beginning to see the water. . . . It is the same with one who fixes his gaze on the infinite beauty of God. It is constantly being discovered anew, and it is always seen as something new and strange in comparison with what the mind has already understood.[11]

Returning to the more obvious, and perhaps more positively useful, lesson of the missionary monkey story, the focus is clearly the intercultural aspect of the differences between monkey and fish cultures. So much has been and will be said on the subject of ministering in cultures outside of the one in which we ourselves have swum since birth. My many windows of experience have caused me to ponder deeply on this issue, leading me to the conclusion that we make way too big a deal of distinguishing between local and international scenes of service – seeing that we are one big human family (as opposed to monkeys and fish!), with more similarities than differences. My windows have taught me that obedience to Beauty is the key to everything. Hannah Dagenhart, a friend and fellow graduate student from our time together at Wheaton, wrote about this subject in her blog post: (***bold italics*** mine)

Missions, Ministry, and the Importance of Serving Jesus Where You Are Right Now.

Recently, a friend asked me to write a bit and share about how serving the Lord in international mission work had led me to seek to serve locally. How has following God overseas encouraged me to follow him in my hometown? Since my focus and plans have been shifting over the past few months from overseas mission work to ministry here in the United States, it was a welcome chance to reflect and see the journey that the Lord has been walking with me. Here is what I shared with her:

It was January of '06 when I knew that God had placed a call to ministry on my life. I may have only been a high school student at the time with no knowledge of what a career in missions would look like, but I resolved to be obedient to the Lord. Almost a decade later I am still discerning the call and walking in the Spirit daily to the best of my ability. In the years between high school and present day, I have explored many avenues of missions and ministry, both locally and abroad.

My undergraduate and graduate degrees focused on studying the Word, learning about missions strategies and developing intercultural communication skills. I took weeklong trips to Guatemala and Germany during college, then after graduation I headed out on an 11-month journey touching base in 11 countries. When I came home I spent 6 months serving the youth group at my home church, then took off again for more studies in Illinois and a summer stint in Peru.

International travel and missionary work have been woven into the most recent years of my life in significant ways. As I reflect on the work that my teammates and I did internationally, I realize that those experiences have helped me to better understand and recognize the ***beauty of God*** and His purposes for His people, as well as equipped me to serve my home community and church more effectively. In Kenya we prayed for the sick, preached the Word, visited the lonely, invited neighbors to church, shared the gospel, laughed with children, danced with worshippers, and followed Jesus wherever he led us. Today, as I live in the little town of Statesville, North Carolina, I still gather with fellow believers to pray for the sick. Each Sunday we come together to hear the Word preached. I enjoy visiting and spending time with new friends and inviting my neighbors to church. There are still opportunities to share the gospel and laugh with children each week in Good News Club at the local elementary school. As far as dancing goes. . .well, I attend a Southern Baptist church, but I do occasionally attempt a nice sway/rocking motion with a lifted hand or two (And you better believe I have some good dancing worship in my car when I'm riding solo!)

There were several countries where I had the opportunity to meet with some amazing women, both young and old, and remind them of ***their value and beauty*** in the sight of God (the only One whose opinion truly matters). At home, I have the same opportunities to encourage ladies and show them that their true worth and identity comes from Christ.

Traveling internationally is always an adventure. There are new sights, smells, sounds and surprises around every corner. People may not look like you, speak the same language or have the same customs and cultures. Everything from food preparation to the method of doing laundry could be completely foreign to the mindset you've always known. Church services may vary in length and style; worship and prayer may be expressed in new ways. Still, one thing remains the same – God's glory and his love for his people.

Spending time abroad has enriched my view of God by ***opening my eyes to the beauty*** and diversity among the nations and cultures, along with the unity found in the Christian Church as a whole. I have followed Jesus down the dirt roads of Rwanda and it has given me confidence to follow Him down the paved roads of neighborhoods in my hometown. The Spirit encouraged me to sing and dance in worship with international believers and now I look forward to praying and worshipping with my fellow church members here at home.

Until very recently, I viewed my call as a missionary as a very rigid course that would most likely result in living overseas long-term. As I treasure my past international experiences and plan to continue to learn about culture and communication, I find that I am no longer choosing to define myself as a "missionary," but rather how *the Father sees me as "beloved daughter of God."* If the Lord leads me to the other side of the world or to a small town in the States, I want to be faithful to serve Him. People are people, regardless of where they live, their age, color or social status. And all people have a great need for Jesus. If we know Him it is our mission to introduce Him to everyone we meet, no matter our geographic location.[12]

Well said, in a nutshell. I certainly couldn't have said it better myself.

World Religions Class held a special fascination for me. I'm not sure, but it may have taken on me differently than was intended to do. Rather than proving to me that there is one right religion, its effect on me was both positive and negative. Positive in that it gave me an appreciation of plurality. Negative in that it served to remind me of the falseness inherent in all religion separated from relationship. In other words, religion is as religion does, and it's often not pretty, leaving a bad taste in a lot of mouths.

Clearly, as we watch history unfold, we can't afford to ignore what is taking place outside our present day windows. We simply must not pretend we are all one and ignore the difference between how Ugly kills, steals, and destroys, while Beauty seeks to give life, full of good and perfect gifts, abundant here, with eternal pleasures following forever there! And while we don't have much choice but to let those on the side of Ugly fight and kill amongst themselves, we must do everything within our power not to fight with each other, those of us on the side of Beauty, but to band together and protect one another. I type these words with a sense of passionate urgency.

It may have been this type of thinking that filled me with such joy when I read the final words of a reading by an anonymous author in World Religions Class. I say *final words* because I certainly expected lightening to strike as I read some of the Jewish beliefs, so vastly different from my own! But then the writer concluded by thanking those who read it, and added these glorious words:

May we all work together for the good of the Kingdom of God and forgive each other our disagreements.
I'll close with a saying from the Talmud. When the sages of old disagreed and could find no way to reconcile their differences, they would often allow both rulings to stand as equally acceptable options in Jewish law. When asked how this was possible, it was said that "When Elijah comes, he will explain which of us was right–or why we both were."
In that spirit, I'll also offer this: I have said for many years that, when (if) the Messiah finally comes, the Jews will look up and say, "You're here!" the Christians will look up and say, "You're back!"
– and then we'll all hug each other and laugh about it.
Peace to all.

~ ~ ~

It was in one of my final Wheaton classes, that of Theology, that the feeling of meeting my demise took its final grip on me. Though I tried my level best to behave appropriately, there was just something about us spending an inordinate amount of precious time seriously discussing the thoughts of those who were affectionately termed *dead white men* (DWM). I had not been aware of that term or abbreviation before being introduced to it by fellow students in this class, nor did I ever feel that any of us used it pejoratively. In fact, I honestly wondered if the actual men themselves had said, or even thought, the things that have since been attributed to them. I specifically wondered this about John Calvin, who Tobin had supposedly been so much like as a growing boy. I earnestly wondered if Calvin had, in truth, taken it upon himself to have added the extra words of *total, unconditional, limited, irresistible,* and *perseverance* to the respective biblical truths of *depravity, election, atonement, grace,* and *sainthood* – truths that were already complete without those additional stipulations. I wanted to think that he had not added onto these truths, but that instead, those of us living since had somehow misinterpreted him. Because I have learned by an excruciatingly painful path to understand, remember, and not forget above all, that *no prophecy of Scripture came about by any prophet's own interpretation of things,* (2 Peter 1:20) I can relate to, easily love and forgive misinterpreters, as I hope they can me, too! The only real shame is the harm done to the truth of Beauty.

I sometimes wonder what our motivation is for quenching and harming the Spirit of Beauty – to what end and purpose? What is the reason that we yearn for *totality, unconditionality, irresistibility,* and *unbroken determination?* Is it because, as Parker Palmer suggests, we resist limits placed upon us?

Resisting Limits

One of our problems as Americans—at least, among my race and gender—is that we resist the very idea of limits, regarding limits of all sorts as temporary and regrettable impositions on our lives. Our national myth is about the endless defiance of limits: opening the western frontier, breaking the speed of sound, dropping people on the moon, discovering 'cyberspace' at the very moment when we have filled old-fashioned space with so much junk that we can barely move. We refuse to take no for an answer. Part of me treasures the hopefulness of this American legacy. But when I consistently refuse to take no for an answer, I miss the vital clues to my identity that arise when way closes—and I am more likely both to exceed my limits and to do harm to others in the process.[13]

And if we do, in our humanity, yearn to break through all limitedness, why then, would we choose to think of *whosoever will* as being *limited* to our special 'atoned for' group? Does this show our innate desire to be more special than others, through nothing we have done? Without forgetting my identity, so clearly formulated during my Normal window at Christ Church, along with the mandate to be separate and peculiar, (2 Corinthians 6:17), I, at the same time, resonate and have experienced what Thomas Merton emphasizes as a need to awake from our dreaming:

Awaking From Separateness

In Louisville, at the corner of Fourth and Walnut, in the center of the shopping district, I was suddenly overwhelmed with the realization that I loved all those people, that they were mine and I theirs, that we could not be alien to one another even though we were total strangers. It was like waking from a dream of separateness, of spurious self-isolation in a special world, the world of renunciation and supposed holiness. The whole illusion of a separate holy existence is a dream.[14]

No matter the reasons, because I was unable to remain silent in theology class and thus voiced truths that were clear to me from Scripture and about which I was passionate, I feared the wrath and power of dear Dr. Stetina. I did and do really like her as a person and admired her as a professor, but my experience had taught me that, as with other respected religious leaders at my past windows, she had sway over the success of my current intended path – for better or for worse. Therefore, you can imagine the tremendous relief I experienced when I received a line from her that read, "Thanks, Pam, for always bringing us back to Jesus." Whew. THAT's how to spell relief!

But in spite of it, and even along with the Jonathon Edwards notecard that she had laid at my usual seat at our u-shaped table, I still remained aware, the entire last semester, that I might at any moment cross the line and be out. Upon seeing the Edwards notecard, I had quickly looked up at her. She was watching me and smiling, offering the explanation of, "It's for you. I thought if you read the back of that card you might like him better." I turned it over and read:

And my mind was greatly engaged, to spend my time in reading
and meditating on Christ; and the beauty and excellency of
his person, and the lovely way of salvation, by free grace in
him. . .And found from time to time, an inward sweetness, that
used, as it were, to carry me away in my contemplations; in what
I know not how to express otherwise, than by a calm, sweet
abstraction of soul from all the concerns of this world; and a kind
of vision, or fixed ideas and imaginations, of being alone in the
mountains, or some solitary wilderness, far from all mankind,
sweetly conversing with Christ, and wrapt and swallowed up in
God. The sense I had of divine things, would often. . .kindle up a
sweet burning in my heart; and ardor of my soul.
Jonathan Edwards, *Personal Narrative*
Young Jonathan Edwards Contemplating Nature
Painting by Ann Holman, 2010
Acrylic on canvas, 24 x 18 in.

And I did like him. Much better. I could relate so well to his sweet love of Christ. Plus, I also realized that Dr. Stetina, and people like her, who held Edwards in what seemed to me, unduly high regard, in actuality simply felt about him the way I experience Oswald Chambers – a friend who continues to daily help us along on our own earthly journeys.

~ ~ ~

One day as I was studying in Wheaton Public Library for an enjoyable change of scenery, I received a text from Cherith, informing me that she had an interview the following day in NYC with Jeffries, a global investment banking firm. The following weekend, when I was sitting on the deck overlooking Lake Freeman in Indiana, I received a follow-up text from her, "On the bus – off to a new life in NYC!" As it came to pass, Cherith ended up moving seven times in 2013 alone. Which then made Lizzie stop to consider and she realized she had lived, studied and/or worked on four continents in five years. Tobin's summation of that was, "That just can't be healthy." Maybe or maybe not – either way, I finished up at my Glen Ellyn window, hugged Gretchen a sad goodbye, promising to stay in touch, joyously greeted Harrison at O'Hare airport, and without waiting for graduation, headed to Adam's in Monticello, then on to D.C. and NYC to see the kids.

While there in NYC, Harrison and I visited the World Trade Center Memorial. We finished and were walking back to the ferry to return to Cherith's apartment in Jersey City. As we were about to cross a street, we noticed the blockade and asked the policeman standing there why we couldn't cross. He informed us that President Obama was coming. It seemed odd to us, as it was a nearly empty street and we were the only ones right there on the sidewalk, but sure enough – here came the presidential limousine! Barack waved at us, we waved back, and carried on to the ferry, wondering if that had really just happened.

We returned to D.C. the next day, since that was where our departure for Liberia was scheduled to take place. Sitting at Northside Social in Arlington, enjoying a parting drink with Harrison and Lizzie, I received an email from Wheaton College, showing me my semester grades (all A's, thank Beauty!) and informing me that *all* requirements had been met for my graduation from Wheaton's TESOL/Intercultural MA program! I rejoiced exceedingly, thanking Beauty again and again for His goodness to me! I didn't actually believe it until I saw it with my own eyes in the plain print before me.

I had been the last on our theology class roster to present a hymn, which was a significant part of our grade. I had worn a veil from our original church culture and presented the hymn that had so moved me years ago, *Who Are They Before God Standing?* I had no confidence that Dr. Stetina had approved and had not yet received feedback from her on it – nor had I received her grade or comments on my final creedal paper. Thus, my occasional tormenting fear of not finishing well had continued to revisit me. But Harrison and Lizzie both found me to be absolutely absurd. They had never had any doubts whatsoever about my success. To my total exuberance at seeing this email, announcing my successful completion, Harrison's half-irritated comment was, "I told you so," and Lizzie's was, "You're a silly goose, Mom." They were right and I was so glad and thankful they were. I love, love, love being wrong! Especially when it means Beauty's love wins!

En route to my next window of Liberia, Harrison and I had twelve hours layover in London. Reminiscing about doing the same when our children were young, we went to watch the changing of the guards at Buckingham Palace. It was a chilly, cloudy day and not many people were around. So imagine our surprise when the Queen's state limousine came driving out the palace gates! Harrison and I happened to be standing very near the gates, so when the Queen waved in her graceful queenly manner, we waved back at her, in our excited American manner! Then we went and had a cup of tea to warm our bones and wondered if that had really happened.

Lesson learned:

Don't waste the pain.
Our Father God is trustworthy. Receive and trust in His goodness.
The Beauty of God never fails and His Love
eventually Wins - for those who repent of themselves and
their agendas and turn to receive His Life.
Use the truth intelligently and in context.

23

Monrovia, Liberia

The Enemy's Playground
May 2013 - August 2014
Red Dust on the Green Leaves
A Kpell Twins' Childhood

Go up-country, so they said,
To see the real Africa.
For whomsoever you may be,
That is where you come from.
Go for bush, inside the bush,
You will find your hidden heart.
Your mute ancestral spirit.
And so I went, dancing on my way.

An overladen lorry speeds madly towards me
Full of produce, passengers, with driver leaning
Out into the swirling dust to pilot his
Swinging obsessed vehicle along.
Beside him on the raised seat his first-class
Passenger, clutching and timid; but he drives on
At so, so many miles per hour, peering out with
Bloodshot eyes, unshaved face and dedicated look;
His motto painted on each side: *Sunshine Transport,*
We get you there quick, quick. The Lord is my Shepherd.

The red dust settles down on the green leaves.

I know you will not make me want, Lord,
Though I have reddened your green pastures
It is only because I have wanted so much
That I have always been found wanting. . . .

From *The Meaning of Africa* by Davidson Nicol[1]

When I arrived in Liberia this time, there was nothing in the airport to shock me. Then, as our driver sped us along, from Roberts International Airport to Sinkor in Monrovia, I watched out the window of the Toyota Hilux and didn't think anything, really. It was just what it was, that's all. As they say, A is A; it is what it is. Not that the observations of my Christmas visit weren't still there, glaring at me. They were there. Nothing had changed. The city was still dark and without any electricity except for generators. I now knew that not only was there no system of electricity in this country apart from generators, but the postal system was near nonexistent as well. I knew this because I had sent Harrison a card every single week from the time I had arrived back in Glen Ellyn in January and it was now May and he had received two cards. Pity, they were such beautiful cards full of love. I hoped they blessed whoever might have them.

I simply felt ready to accept things for what they were, wise enough to know that I could not make a difference. At least I didn't see any way that was possible. Though I was ecstatic to be here, with my beloved husband – here where we were supposed to be, together, as planned before the foundation of the world in accordance with Beauty's pleasure and will – still I knew my being of any affect here was quite out of the question. Apart from my purpose in fulfilling Harrison's joy, I felt small and insignificant in the big scheme of things and ready to sit quietly, watching and waiting to see what would happen.

Along with this view of being small, and waiting in silence to see what would happen next, my desire to disappear had remained strong, causing me to continue to resonate with both the words and the musical pathos of an Over The Rhine song entitled *Drunkard's Prayer,* but to me was the prayer of my heart to Beauty Himself:

You're my water, You're my wine
You're my whiskey from time to time
You're the hunger on my bones
All the nights I sleep alone
Sweet Intoxication
When Your Words wash over me
Whether or not Your lips move
You speak to me
Like an Ocean without waves
You're the Movement that I crave
And in that Motion I long to drown
And be lost *not to be found*[2]

~ ~ ~

Immediately following my arrival to stay in Liberia, I spent my days observing the unpleasant realities of my new window. I went daily to the beach to read, think, and talk to the locals. They taught me a lot quickly, reinforcing concepts that Cheryl had explained to me, on our Thursday mornings together at Caribou Coffee, back at my Glen Ellyn window. Things like: "We Liberians don't trust anyone, not even our mothers." "Many of us Liberians don't get married anymore because women are bad. They will never be true to you, because no man has enough money to keep a woman from selling herself to someone else." "When we get sick we go to the witch doctor." Because most of those I spoke with said they were Christians, I then asked questions, in an attempt to distinguish if their Christianity made any difference in the things they were telling me. Their answers were either negative or supplementary, such as "Well, we Christians call the witch doctors 'traditional medicine.'" I also deduced that no one died in Liberia of natural causes; young or old, the cause was always that a curse had been placed on them by someone.

Even though I'd spent years of my life at other African windows, it was at this Liberian one that the African spiritual worldview was so exaggerated as to come into sharp focus for me. As I watched through this particular African window it looked to me as though the inhabitants outside viewed God and Satan as equals. Depending on where one was determined who won. In church God won. Outside of church it was iffy, the darkness having a really strong hold. The bright spot in this was that the Africans had no doubt as to the reality of Satan and his demons, no doubt at all - unlike my culture of origin where he is often considered more or less a comical figure dressed in red and holding a pitchfork.

It was there on the beach near our apartment that I met Blessing, a friendly, happy, young woman. She was especially happy when I mentioned that I went to church on Sundays and even more delighted to learn that Harrison and I were going to the same church she went to, Monrovia Christian Fellowship (MCF)! And thus began a long-standing, close, and increasingly complicated friendship. I had initially been naively unaware that she was a beggar woman, and this was her preferred way of caring for herself and her children, all from different men. When I asked why, as a Christian, she had children from several men, none of whom she had married, she explained to me that though she knew it was wrong (I had not said that), still that was the way her mother had done things and she expected her daughters would, too. I quickly learned that it was the way of the vast majority. Whether or not they were Christians, and regardless of what church they went to. I know this partly because Blessing and we went to the same Pentecostal church. There Pastor Momolu boldly preached the pure unadulterated truth, soundly condemning the dualistic African worldview I presented above. I admired his audacity to speak so directly into the lives of the large congregation who assembled there in the heat, Sunday after Sunday.

It was also at Monrovia Christian Fellowship that I first became acquainted with MacDella Cooper, an interesting and lovely woman who has been called 'Liberia's Angel'. Even though I didn't know that at the time, I still took her words seriously when she said, *"Liberia is never going to make progress until the people stop working against each other."* Later, as I sat eating spicy potato greens on the porch of a local place with Harrison and a GVL pilot, I heard a commotion across the narrow street. Looking up, I watched in horror as a group of several Liberians dragged one of their own over to a sharp-edged iron post and vigorously beat his head against it – for what, I didn't know. My mind went back to my first African window of Dodoma, where Tanzanians had beaten one of their own nearly to death for stealing a can of margarine out of my basket at the market.

Considering what MacDella had spoken about her own people, her fellow Liberians, it looked to me, from my collective windows, that though her words may have been especially true for her beloved nation of Liberia, the problem didn't seem at all limited to Liberia. From where I sat, it seemed a problem of epidemic proportions, extending not only to many peoples, but to even, or maybe especially, their religions – supposedly loving their own, but definitely not their neighbors. I recalled reading a story by Chaim Potok of a Jewish Rabbi who found it difficult to rebuke his people, always discovering good in them, no matter what they did, and who would not permit his synagogue to use electricity because the same current provided light for the nearby Catholic church.

As the days passed by my window, I became accustomed to seeing things the way they were: an occasional group of developing youth, most noticeably girls, walking along the highway, having come out of their secret society bush school where they were being prepared for the responsibilities of adult Liberian life, naked to the waist but covered (from head to toe) with white chalk – like a ghastly appearance of ancient tribalism clashing with modern day life; hearing of children who had disappeared, being sacrificed, especially near election times, because of the political power to be gained through the shedding of human blood; constant police corruption; parents pushing their young girls on the streets, to be used for as cheaply as a dollar or even for candy; spirits in the ocean pulling swimmers under and drowning them; people turning into animals at night and back into themselves by day; and much more.

My love of reading and learning led me to books to help me understand what was otherwise incomprehensible to me. Helene Cooper's life story in *The House at Sugar Beach* was especially helpful to me. One comment of hers explained so much: "*In Liberia, we put on civilized airs, but the truth was that we always seemed to be teetering one step away from something dark and savage."* Reading Helene's book gave me a view through a Liberian's window, while Nancy Sheppard's book, *Confessions of a Transformed Heart,* gave me a missionary view to which I could easily relate while learning much about the complexities of Liberia. Thus, I found it, too, extremely helpful.

A third book that was influential in shaping my thinking and understanding was the memoirs of Liberia's current president, and Africa's first woman president, Ellen Johnson Sirleaf, entitled *This Child Will Be Great.* In spite of the rumors and growing dissatisfaction of the people, and in spite of the annoying commotion her daily motorcade made careening down Tubman Avenue, directly in front of our apartment, still I respected and admired President Ellen. I was pleased when a crazy man in downtown Monrovia once mistook me for her. So when I heard from local sources that the thoroughly Christian President Ellen never makes any major decision without first checking with Chief Zanzan Karwah, the head shaman of Liberia, I could only hope the connection was not as strong or as influential as it was reported to be.

~ ~ ~

This window was a new experience for me, going to live in a foreign country without having to ask people in my home country to give me money to be who I am. I liked it; I discovered it was a joy to not get paid for who I am – something that does not change for me, no matter what I'm doing. Who I am is not something that requires, or can even be measured in, money. I prefer being paid for what I do. This new situation seemed to open up many additional doors of opportunities and friendships. And the beauty of it was that it didn't close the old, familiar doors!

It was Wendy who had first welcomed me into the missionary circle. That happened my first day there, when I was at Sprigg's Airport with Harrison. She happened to be there, too, with her husband, who was a pilot with Samaritan's Purse. She warmly introduced herself and invited Harrison and me over for dinner. In getting to know us, Wendy noticed from our story that we were only a short time in Tibet. She briefly commented on it, "So you were only in Tibet a short time. Why was that? Did it not work out?"

Grateful to her for her kind way, I responded, "Right. It didn't work out."

Her wonderful response, "Yeah. Sometimes things don't."

And that was the end of that. Forever. I saw in her the image of her Father, choosing not to dwell on, or even remember, shameful pasts that are now forgiven.

Wendy, along with Kathy, wife of the other Samaritan's Purse pilot, took me under their wings and made me a part of not only what they affectionately called the 'aviation wives' group, but also introduced me to the ELWA (Everlasting Love Winning Africa) compound Bible study group that met on Wednesday afternoons. This group was comprised of not only the missionary ladies who lived in the compound, but other missionaries who didn't live in the mission compound. It also included other Christian expatriates who, like the new me, weren't technically missionaries, i.e., didn't raise financial support from churches, friends and family to be there, doing what they were doing. We were one big, happy, connected group where labels didn't matter. When potlucks were held, it was emphasized that both the families of missionaries and Christian workers were welcome. *Yes, Harrison and I were first Christians and secondly, we were doing work.* I loved it.

Initially my work consisted of tutoring individuals who were not first language English speakers, but needed to improve their English skills to function effectively here in Liberia where English was the official language. At this point I need to say that Liberian English varies so much from Standard English that I had struggled to understand anything when I had arrived for my visit the previous December. At that time, Harrison had already been in Liberia for six months and thus had adjusted his ears to Liberian English. He kindly repeated everything anyone said to me so that I could respond! But English it was, and for those of other languages, English still had to be learned, as the language of communication.

I tutored various and sundry ages and nationalities of students at my Liberian window, my first one being a German engineer who worked at the Club Beer factory, which is also where I tutored him. The beer factory sent a driver from their plant on Bushrod Island to pick me up in Sinkor, a distance of about twelve miles. The ride alone was an experience for me. The poem at the beginning of this chapter contains a description not unlike both the driver, named Victor, and me, his first-class passenger:

> An overladen lorry speeds madly towards me
> Full of produce, passengers, with driver leaning
> Out into the swirling dust to pilot his
> Swinging obsessed vehicle along.
> Beside him on the raised seat his first-class
> Passenger, clutching and timid; but he drives on
> At so, so many miles per hour, peering out with
> Bloodshot eyes, unshaved face and dedicated look;
> His motto painted on each side: *Sunshine Transport,*
> *We get you there quick, quick. The Lord is my Shepherd.*

Unable to exert any control over the situation, I focused out the side window of the old jalopy and watched the dark scenes of city poverty, struggling to come to terms with the inert apathy of resignation everywhere.

While continuing to tutor individuals, I also helped the small, mixed-nationality staff at New Africa Technology Company (NATC) develop their professional English, specifically to be more effective at recording the services and products they provided. NATC also provided me a ride to and from our apartment in Sinkor, but the experience stood in contrast to my wild rides with Victor to and from the beer factory. NATC employed their favorite taxi driver to collect and return me. Peter was a kind, elderly, gentle, observant man, who drove in that same description, a rarity among Liberian drivers, and especially among taxi drivers! I smile now as I think of our relationship. He was a sweet encouragement to me during those days.

Meanwhile, the new academic year was arriving in Liberia. The big news, even making international news, was that *all* of the 25,000 high school graduates applying to the University of Liberia failed the English entrance exam! President Ellen went on public record as saying, "Our educational system is a mess."

Armed with my new MA in Teaching English to Speakers of Other Languages (TESOL) – and these 25,000 Liberian high school graduates were apparently speakers of a language other than English as we know it – I found this turn of events completely fascinating. After reading the following article, I took it upon myself to find this James Dorbor-Jallah, who had administered the test, and visit with him:

Admission Standards Toughened at University of Liberia

James Butty
August 27, 2013 1:45 AM

A private consultant said the days are over when students were admitted into the University of Liberia through bribery or based on how many important people they known.

James Dorbor Jallah was hired by the university to manage and administer this year's entrance examination.

Nearly 25,000 high school graduates who took the exam failed.

Minister of Education Etmonia David-Tarpeh reportedly said she would discuss the issue with university officials. However, she expressed doubt that all 25,000 students failed the admission exam.

Dorbor-Jallah said students seeking admission into the university would study harder if they are made to understand that admission is based on personal ability and not through bribery.

He said he was hired because the university has had problems in the past about the credibility and integrity of its admission exam.

"There is a perception in our society largely that once you take the University of Liberia admission exam, if you do not pay money to someone, or if you do not have appropriate connections, you would not be placed on the results list. So, the University has been grappling with how they could manage the process whereby people's abilities would be truly measured on the basis of their performance on the examination," he said.

Dorbor-Jallah made it clear he was not speaking as spokesman of the University of Liberia but rather as a private citizen who was contacted by university president, Dr. Emmet Dennis to help restore public confidence in the university's admission process.

He said the 2013 admission exam was no different from previous exams that had been administered by the university in terms of subject matter content.

Dorbor-Jallah said the exam tested high school graduates based on the curriculum of the Ministry of Education.

But he said unlike previous exams, the faculty senate of the university decided that this time around, results would be reported on the basis of raw scores.

"To gain a pass and admission, one would have to make or earn 60 percent in mathematics and 70 percent in English of their raw scores, not curved or scaled results. So on the basis of that, we administered the exam. We went through the tabulation of the results, and it turned out that 308 of the more than 23,000 candidates actually did meet the threshold score in mathematics of 50 percent or above. But absolutely no one was able to reach the threshold score in English of 70 percent. That is why the university has reported that no one passed its admission exam," he said.

Minister of Education Etmonia David-Tarpeh reportedly said she would discuss the issue with university officials. But she expressed doubts that all 25,000 students failed the admission exam.

Dorbor-Jallah said he made a commitment to the university that he and his team would document the process in such a way that the results can be replicated by anyone.

"If the minister is interested, or if any practitioner in the educational sector is interested, I'm sure the university will be willing to go through the process," Dorbor-Jallah said.

He said he and his team tried to lay the foundation for the University of Liberia to see how an examination can be conducted and how the integrity can be preserved.

"We hope that the university will continue on this path so that there can be a restoration of public confidence in the process and people can begin to know that whoever merits admission into the university is the one who gets admitted and not for any other external factors," he said.

Dorbor-Jallah said there is also a message that Liberia as a nation can draw from the mass failures of this year's university admission exam.

"For the country as a whole, I think this is a clarion call that we need to all see that the king is moving around naked and not pretend as though the emperor has his finest clothes on," he said.

He said Liberia as a nation must begin the process of soul-searching by carefully analyzing the root causes of the mass failures because the future of a nation depends on the education of its youth.

~ ~ ~

Having long known of Samaritan's Purse (SP), I, like many fund-raising missionaries, had envied those working with the organization, in that they had the privilege of being 'paid' missionaries. Now, being in Liberia, with a Samaritan's Purse office close at hand on the ELWA campus, and associating with those working with SP, I had wanted nothing more than to work with them – especially as I heard they had an opening for a new program working with orphans and vulnerable children! I hadn't been able to think of anything more desirable than working to help orphans and vulnerable children – genuine religion at its purest!

But after my visit with Dorbor-Jallah in his office in downtown Monrovia, the fact that I didn't hear anything from Samaritan's Purse about my application, no longer bothered me, at least very much, because it seemed obvious that I had my work cut out for me teaching freshman English! Dorbor-Jallah had carefully explained to me that the heart of the issue was more the corrupt system than the lack of English abilities. The deeply entrenched system of ability and performance having nothing whatsoever to do with success made it a foolish waste of time for students to spend time studying. I myself was wise enough to know that there was nothing I could do to even make a dent in that kind of entrenched evil. However, I knew I could teach English and I hoped and dared to believe that I could teach it in such a way as to make students want to learn for the pure joy of learning. Leaving Dorbor-Jallah's office, I was determined to do that. If the University of Liberia wouldn't have me (and they wouldn't, for their own reasons – another whole story that I came to understand, forgive, and thus, will let go), then I'd find somewhere else to do so.

That somewhere else was directly beside the University of Liberia and was a private Catholic school called Stella Maris Polytechnic (SMP). Indeed, it was close enough to the University that the gunshots fired during a student protest there set the students in my classroom on edge, making it difficult to concentrate. But I'm getting ahead of myself.

Among the first of many memorable windows of SMP was the staff in-service held before the fall semester started. We had already broken for lunch and had reconvened for the afternoon sessions, when the speaker opened it up to any of the faculty if they wished to speak. I had noticed that my new colleagues were predominately male, with less than a handful of us being female. It was a female colleague who rose and went to the front. I still don't know if the audience knew what to expect or not, but I know that I would have been totally blown away had not Cheryl prepared me so well over coffee in Glen Ellyn. This female colleague became completely impassioned as she shouted, "Our educational system is a whore-house! Gentlemen, this has got to stop!!"

I was once again thankful for Beauty's gift of Cheryl to me, letting me know ahead of time how things worked – such as the way to get good grades is via sex with the teacher. And that this was only one manifestation of such realities of life in Liberia.

I was also thankful for Aloycius, the driver assigned to Harrison by Golden Veroleum Liberia (GVL), the company Harrison worked with. He had already become, first Harrison's and then my, fast friend, but now, as he drove me to and from SMP, he became vital to me, a cultural informant who told me what to expect – even when it was far different than I had been told. And it amazed me how he was always right! For example, I had been told by my Liberian boss that I would have no more than fifty students in any class. As Aloycius drove me home after classes, he listened to me tell about my morning, and he told me, "The students like you. You teach different than Liberian teachers. They will keep coming. You will have more." And keep coming they did, up to around 150 in one class – dragging little wooden desks in with them and packing themselves solidly into the room! That didn't count the ones who stopped by and stood at the door or the windows to just listen in for a while. Those 150 names were just taken from the attendance sheet roster I passed around each class, for them to sign in. This was my feeble attempt to figure out how I was going to give grades, as I had informed them upfront that I wasn't interested in their money or sex. I had enough of both as it was. They had laughed. I truly enjoyed teaching and learning from these students.

At the same time, I felt so sorry for them. Sitting in their library doing my last-minute preparations before class, I became disconcerted whenever I looked up from what I was doing. All around me sat students with dark, vacant stares. It was plain to see that they weren't present there in the library, but rather in some other disturbing realm. It made me shudder. This happened sometimes in class, too. At the beginning I would think this one or that one was unfriendly, only to realize that they hadn't seen me at all – and when they did notice my presence, their faces would break into a warm smile. I knew I could never understand the atrocities these precious young people had been through. Their whole generation had known little else than their country's brutal civil war, many of them having been the child soldiers the war was infamous for, learning the necessity of not trusting anyone – even their mothers. All of them had suffered tragically in ways that I didn't even want to comprehend or think about for too long. Reading about it in narrative accounts was almost more than I could stomach.

Apart from the terrifying realization of their past, I had the time of my life teaching these students. The conditions present made it an extremely overwhelming amount of work. I gave it my all, exhausting myself in one semester there. Nevertheless, my memories of the time spent with these students are precious and priceless. I learned so much from my little glances out their windows as they responded to Langston Hughes' essay *Salvation*, and Hans Christian Anderson's *The Emperor's New Clothes*. I learned more than I wanted to know about their culture and beliefs as they presented, and I read, the 'research' papers they attempted to write from interviewing their elders. As I was teaching them the differences and similarities between Liberian and Standard English, they taught me other, possibly more important, things. Such as the absolute necessity of changing *KISS, Keep It Simple, **Stupid*** to *Keep It Simple, **Sweetie,*** because to say **stupid** is the serious equivalent of putting a curse on someone. Or that things happen in Africa they do not expect me to understand, like everyone knowing there was a man out at Harbel, Liberia's famous Firestone plantation, whose head turned into that of a pig at night. And many, many other such things.

Sadly, it was during this time that our driver, Aloycius, was unjustly fired, for reasons unknown, and never explained to him or to us. Perhaps it was because I could so relate to him in this, along with the close friendship Harrison and I had both formed with him, that I reacted so strongly against this injustice. My efforts were to no avail, except for the deep appreciation from Aloycius at the time, as well as his strong continued friendship to this day.

Because my classes at SMP were all held in the morning, I could still make it to the weekly Wednesday afternoon Bible study held on the ELWA compound. My Dutch friend, Aaf, picked me up almost as soon as I arrived home to the apartment from class and off we went, chattering away to fill each other in on what had happened with us since we had last seen each other. Unlike me, Aaf was a courageous driver and adept at avoiding the many attempts by the police to pull us over for some bribe money. Once on our way home from Bible study, the policeman simply stood in front of our approaching car and Aaf was unable to get around him because of other traffic, so we had to stop. The policeman came to the passenger side of the station wagon where I sitting and said to me, "You aren't wearing your seat belt!"

Confused as to what he could mean, I looked down and then back up at him, replying, "Yes. I am."

"But you just now put it on."

"No," I said truthfully, "I put it on when the car started, back at ELWA."

At this point, I heard Aaf mumble under her breath, "*Stupid!*" and she eased her way back into the traffic without glancing at the officer. I had to disagree with my students' understanding of the word. I knew Aaf was not cursing the officer; she was just stating a fact about how she saw the situation.

Because our ELWA Bible study group decided to do Beth Moore's *Mercy Triumphs Over Judgment* study on the book of James, I experienced an amazing epiphany. Beth Moore had, for a long time, felt like a good friend to me, though I had only met her in person once, back at the Nairobi, Kenya window. Our conversation went like this: to my profuse thanks for her help along my rough and joyful path, she had simply replied, "It just keeps me out of the pits, that's all. All glory be to God." *Yes.*

During this study, Beth and one of her daughters opened up our view to the person of James, not just as a writer of Scripture who presented a seemingly different message than the rest of the New Testament writers. They introduced us to him in a way that we felt we were really getting to know him, as a fellow human, one of us, in flesh and blood, who had lived in the same household with Jesus Himself, as they were growing up in the flesh – no doubt, being irritated with this perfect sibling's constant presence! Imagine living with a perfect human sibling who was full of grace and truth (John 1:14, 17) and never ever erred on either side, not in harshness with truth nor in enabling licentiousness with grace.

During this study on James, I was struck with the distinct impression that I was, at long last, getting a view out my beloved husband's window! Imagine my shock at my own blindness – I, who thought I saw so clearly! I now had a completely fresh view of who Harrison was! And this view was brought to life to me via the human person the biblical James may have been, judging from the distinctive flavor of his writing.

This clear glimpse out my beloved's window gave me a new functional understanding of how he had, of necessity, missed what I had seen out my very separate window. Like James compared to the other New Testament writers, Harrison's was just a different way of looking at things, a valid, practical way, revealed through works. But these pure works that James wrote of surely cannot be the same works that one beloved pastor's wife, under the influence of a *living white* evangelical Bible scholar, wrote of:

What Jesus is saying in Luke 13:3 (*I tell you, no! But unless you repent, you too will all perish.*) is if you want to enter into My Kingdom, if you want to follow Me, if you want to be forgiven of sin, if you want eternal life, you have to start by hating everything you are apart from Me, recognizing that all the good about you is filthy rags, despising everything about you. And now, since all that you might have earned, or all that you might have gained, or all your so-called works have been redefined as wretchedness, and you have seen yourself as consummately unworthy, you are just in the perfect place to reach out, to cry out for mercy and grace. So the real message of the gospel is the message that you need to start by hating everything that you are.

Though I rejoiced in seeing out this new window, which opened up wide to me as I memorized the book of James, I had a hard time shaking the sadness I felt about those, like the sister quoted above, whose experiences and views have given them cause to hate themselves and disdain others. I believe with all my being that the writer John penned the truth, no matter what any of us say or how we see things: God is love, and light, and in Him there is no darkness at all.[3] From this window, being made in the image of such a God precludes hating anyone, especially ourselves, since the second greatest commandment tells us to love everyone we come into contact with in the same manner that we love ourselves.[4] Of course, it obviously all flows out of the *first* commandment – to love the Lord our God with all of our heart, soul, mind, and strength.[5] A really important thing is to keep the main thing, *the main thing* – to be real in our love, not mixing up who God is, who we are, and who others are.

~ ~ ~

Because the Wednesday afternoon Bible study in the ELWA compound was for ladies only, Harrison and I were happy that there was also a Sunday evening one, which we could go to together. It was held twice monthly and usually, but not always, held in a missionary's home in the ELWA compound. An astounding thought that stands out to me from that group was when Frieda mentioned, almost in passing, that Jesus, as He walked as a human on this earth, was filled with His Father's Spirit and never sinned. She went on to point out that we who are also His children, likewise have this promised Spirit within us, and thus, have the potential of walking by, in and through, that selfsame Spirit – if we so choose to. It's up to us.

~ ~ ~

As Christmas 2013 approached, Harrison and I bought a small, already decorated tree from a street vendor. As Harrison carried it the short distance home on his head, we met and chatted with several people we knew, both national and expatriate, making me realize that I felt at home here at this window. I felt settled and happy. Odd, I thought, to feel so safe and secure in such a setting as this strange window.

I had decided to be friendly with the plethora of beggars that existed on Tubman Avenue, and especially outside the grocery stores. To make it a game, instead of an irritation for me, I developed various ways of dealing with them. I especially enjoyed the one where, upon them asking me for money, I would smile, and offering my right hand, say, "Excuse me, I don't think I know you yet. Hi, my name's Pam. What's yours?" Thus, I got to know a few of them as people, rather than beggars.

The closer it got to Christmas, the more often we would see the Long Devil, a character dressed up with very long trousers hiding his stilts, dancing to the beat of the drummers following him, and collecting money from all who didn't want curses put on them simply by not giving. Along with this, the beggars, as well as casual acquaintances, would constantly ask everyone for gifts by saying, "Give me Christmas." In accordance with the game I used to entertain myself, I resorted to explaining in friendly terms that in my culture, gift giving is reciprocal. *People give each other gifts; it's not a one-way street.* This apparently seemed acceptable, coming from my friendly white face, and after the amiable conversation, the seeker moved on to another, ever hopeful.

The best thing about this Christmas was that Cherith, Tobin, and Lizzie all came to Liberia to be with us. Unfortunately, just before their arrival, Harrison became extremely ill with a virulent strain of malaria, unlike any we had experienced in East Africa. On top of that, Cherith had found out in an airport on her way to Liberia that the contract she and her teammates had been working under at Jeffries had been suddenly terminated and they had all lost their jobs! At first she had thought the teammate informing her was joking, but not so. It put a definite damper on her time with us. More than once, I caught her wringing her hands, and knew she was wondering what would become of her. Lizzie, too, was going through some distressing times, finishing up an internship and uncertain of what was next in her life. In spite of these obstacles, we managed to have good times together, showing our kids our daily lives, traveling to Chimpanzee Island and the lovely beach at Robertsport, and cheering loudly together when Tobin confided in us that he was thinking of asking his girlfriend to be his wife!

But rather than sugar-coating the truth, I'll let the story Lizzie wrote afterwards tell it as it happened, from her window:

Liberia

We landed in Liberia in complete darkness, the first warning about its nature. It was a thick darkness; the kind you could almost push up against, arms extended in front of you, moving darkness aside the way one does with water to make space for the body to enter. Besides darkness there was heat, a humidity that pulsated in rhythm to the hum of evening insects. This combination of darkness and pulsating heat is one I have never experienced in any place outside of the continent. It is how I know I'm in Africa.

It was almost Christmas and the five of us were going to be together — my older siblings and my parents and me; my sister and I flying in from JFK and my brother from Washington, D.C. Being American and yet having spent years in East Africa with my missionary parents, I found it ironic and yet appropriate to be going "home" for the

355

holidays to a country I had never been to and knew little about. Before the trip I glibly told people that home is wherever your parents are. Afterwards, if someone asked, I'd say I didn't have a home.

When we landed on that dark airstrip I instinctively understood that this trip was a marker: it would divide time into before and after, both shedding light to interpret my past and setting the stage for the future.

The second warning was that my father did not meet us at the airport. He had come down with malaria the day before our arrival and was burning with fever, too weak to manage the stairs leading down from my parents' fourth floor apartment. So only my mother and the driver, a dark, beaming, and courteous man named Samson, came to pick us up and drove us forty-five minutes into the heart of Monrovia, where my parents' tall gated apartment building stood directly across from Monrovia's newest and most expensive hotel, the Royal. Facing each other across Tubman Boulevard, the two buildings looked like funny-mirror interpretations of each other; both with shiny interiors and impossibly high prices, both standing tall above the shorter and shabbier apartments, groceries, and convenience shops surrounding them.

On the drive into the city, I looked out my window at the darkness, broken here and there by dim lights in roadside bars showing people huddled together in the darkness, dancing or arguing or laughing, gesticulating wildly. As we drove past them, their faces and movements were captured like photographs in my mind, as real and as momentary. Between the lights in the thick darkness I thought of Liberia's brutal history and imagined death everywhere.

But when we reached the apartment, it was bright and clean and my dad was there, and I kissed him, and didn't feel death.

We went to sleep that night in an oversize bed with a wonderfully hard mattress and the cool of the air-conditioning coming in from the living room. I woke up with the bright orange light of the sun to the hustle and bustle and ceaseless honking on the street and felt well and alive.

My brother arrived the next afternoon and we celebrated being reunited with a dinner of pork chops, fresh vegetables, orange-mango juice, coffee, and moringa tea. When we were together it was good; we were a unit, we five belonged to each other, and none of us was alone. It happened more rarely, now that we were adults, but when we were all together like this, the identity of family member pushed all other identities into the background and took prominence. And so I forgot myself again, as I always did at these times, and was lost among my siblings and my parents and the burning African sun.

On Christmas day, we decided to go to the beach at the missionary compound called E.L.W.A (Everlasting Love Winning Africa), figuring that its restricted public access would make it less crowded and cleaner than the beach across from the apartment, which we referred to as poo-poo beach for the human excrement that scarred it. Both this beach and its inhabitants were casualties of Liberia's twenty years of brutal conflict. Drugged-up and hollow-eyed boys lived there, spending their days medicating under makeshift cabana style party spots. Displaced after the war, they were now completely detached from society. One evening, my family walked down this beach, and my father's face clouded with fear as the sun began to sink. It was no place to be after dark. The boys showed others exactly the same amount of care that had been given to them, making the place lawless and frightening. There was nothing peaceful about this beach. Even the ocean waves struck me as restless and angry as they foamed up onto the rocky shore.

Ready for a better beach experience, on Christmas day my family loaded up the Patrol with everything necessary for a day at the beach and drove to the missionary compound. It was Christmas and it was sunny; I tried to relax but was troubled. We had gone Christmas caroling with E.L.W.A missionaries at Liberian houses in the compound the evening before, and the memory of it disturbed me. The Liberians *who appeared in their doorways to watch us sing looked at us with blank, scornful eyes. It made me conscious of how White we were, with our neatly packaged family units and carols and the adolescents holding their adopted African brothers and sisters as they sang Joy to the World. The whole thing felt like an incongruent overlay onto the black African night. Standing there in the darkness and humidity, singing Christmas carols, I could not orient myself, and became as rootless as a note sounding into the night, existing neither here nor there, appearing and disappearing without a trace, the memory of it the realest thing about it.*

At E.L.W.A. beach, the day was unremarkable, warm but not hot and bright without being blinding. We set up our umbrellas and a large gold tablecloth we were using as a substitute beach spread, big enough for the five of us. After a time, a crowd of about one hundred began to gather on the beach in front of us, and the word was that a boy had gone missing, a fairly regular circumstance along the beach. It is a Western conception that beaches are places of luxury and entertainment. In Africa, a beach is a resource for fishing and other income. Beaches offer utility but also danger; Liberians have a real fear for the ocean that is absent among tourists. Nevertheless, it was a holiday and many locals had come to the beach to socialize on their day off.

I was lying on the outside of our spread, enjoying the sun's warmth but feeling agitated and wondering about my place in things. When my siblings got up to go in the water, I went with them. My sister and I were in the shallower water near the shore, a little above waist height, and my brother swam further out. I was playing a game, planting myself in a particular place in the sand and trying to see how long I could go before losing contact with it as the waves pushed and pulled. Suddenly I heard my brother yell, "Hey guys, I found the boy." He took a deep breath and dove purposefully down into the water. When he came up he was holding a dark, thin African child. I heard my voice weakly yell, "help." "Hold his head," my brother said as he struggled to swim the boy in. I did. Water was pouring out of the boy's mouth so that it looked like he was foaming. His tiny body felt smooth, almost slimy. More than an hour had passed since the crowd had gathered on the beach, and we knew the child was already dead. We swam him to shore. In the shallow, standing part of the water, people rushed to help us. They grabbed the boy as soon as we reached them and carried him to higher ground. A crowd of bystanders instantly surrounded them, and I never saw another glimpse of the boy's tiny body.

We walked calmly over to our umbrella and sat down on the gold tablecloth turned beach spread. The sun was still shining, not too brightly, there was a slight breeze rustling the trees, and the day was fine. Our American friend remarked on the high incidence of this kind of thing in African society and gave his recommendations to the young African girl with him. We sat there, then, the five of us and this neighbor and his girl, and watched people surround the place where the boy's body lay. We watched police and taxis come and go. We watched people in the crowd taking pictures with their cellphones. We watched the crowd watch as foreigners performed CPR. We watched the water hitting the shore and felt the sun warm on our faces, and other conversation continued and other concerns returned. Soon we stood to go. I'd lost track of the conversation, thinking about the boy's thin body and smooth black skin, and wishing to wash my hands. "Are you okay?" my family wanted to know as we walked away.

With that question, the emotion of the trip, the darkness when we landed, the confusion of caroling, my sense of identitylessness, and now this fact of the dead body in the water and the utter insignificance of that fact welled up in me like a gathering tsunami and finally crashed into an angry and confused statement, which I spat out like a poisoned root. "I hate Africa."

That night the darkness came and in the morning it went, but in me it was still dark. I took the meaninglessness of the boy's life and death as personally as if it had been my own, and felt crushed by insignificance and futility.

The next day, my family was back in the Patrol, driving the dirt road to the beach at Robertsport, which had been recommended by the American neighbor. The vibrant red of the dirt and the jarring jolts of potholes comforted me. They were proofs of reality when I felt as insubstantial and ephemeral as a Christmas carol in Africa, sung and forgotten as soon as it ends, leaving no proof it had even existed at all.

Now and then the dry bush along the road cleared and gave way to small village communities where I saw women carrying colorful buckets and loads on their heads, or sitting on short three-legged stools holding babies and talking or working on small projects. At once I felt envious of them and ashamed of my envy. As restricted and impoverished as their lives may be, I was drawn to their simplicity and cohesion. And if their lives were no more significant and enduring than the smooth-skinned boy's, at least the song of their lives was in harmony with the natural rhythms of their environment; life and death, sickness, suffering, were all contextualized and no one asked for or expected more. A boy could die without shaking up the order of things, because death was everywhere and was as natural as life. But my world demanded meaning and explanation, and the boy's obscure death projected into my world without fitting into it, jutting out like a broken limb that I could not set straight.

We eventually got to Robertsport Beach and it was as flawless as an advertisement in a travel magazine — crystal clear water all the way to the sand, gently rocking waves, no rocks, no weeds. We set up our beach umbrella, laid out the tablecloth turned beach spread, kicked off our shoes, and applied sunscreen. There were only a few tourists on the beach and some African men sweating as they pulled in their fishing nets. I tried to be normal and cheerful and keep things light, but my mood didn't match the scene before me, and I couldn't stop my eyes from continually welling up in the confusion and dissonance of it all. Everyone in my family spoke to me very gently the whole afternoon, and I knew they were being careful with me, the way you are careful with a child who is hurt or frightened. I closed my eyes and lay there and thought about the smooth-skinned boy and the Christmas carols and the red dirt road and I felt hurt, like the boy's death was a wound that had been ripped open. I lay there beside my family and let the sun seep into my skin, felt the salty spray of the ocean, and held the darkness at bay.[6]

~ ~ ~

Gone was the joyful little girl and her triumphant 'tude that had brought so much sunshine to our early windows. Sadly, she had been replaced by someone who didn't even seem to like herself, thus causing her to struggle in all her ways. We hoped and prayed that she would recover with time. As for me, I was willing to give it as long as it took, confident that time would tell.

~ ~ ~

From the beginning of 2014, I had this increasing sense of anticipation. Like something was just about to happen and I had no idea what it was. But anticipation may be too positive of a word; perhaps *impending* better described whatever it was I felt I was holding my breath over. I often felt it most strongly sitting on the balcony meditating – that same balcony where Harrison and I literally watched corruption take place below us, unbeknownst to the practitioners.

As the year began afresh, the director of American International School of Monrovia (AISM) contacted me, asking if I would come in for an interview. He thought he had a position that would be open when the school started up after the Christmas break. *Of course, I would.* I went and I accepted the possibility of filling a position that the director believed was 99.99 percent vacant, having heard through the grapevine that the upper school (grades 7-9) English teacher was not returning after break.

The ink was barely dry on my signature there on the dotted line, committing myself to complete the contract of the missing teacher at

AISM, when Samaritan's Purse contacted me, They wanted to know if I would be interested in the program manager position for the orphan and vulnerable children's program!! I could hardly believe the bad luck of this timing! Or was it?

Kendell, the SP country director, suggested that I come into the office anyway, to discuss my potential involvement with this program or another one. I did. As he, I, and two other SP staff talked together, Kendell said that he just felt we were missing something unseen that we should pray about. We did right then, but we still didn't see what we were missing, so I saw no choice but to fulfill the missing teacher's contract. Not only that, after I had been at the American International School for some weeks, the director invited me to sign a contract to continue teaching there the following school year (2014-15). Not wanting to make the same mistake twice, I first got in touch with Samaritan's Purse to see if there were any potential possibilities for me to work with them. Receiving an answer in the negative, I went ahead and signed the new AISM contract – after doing as Harrison advised, and reading all the fine print.

At AISM, I had the honor of teaching the few privileged children living in Liberia – those of my own nationality, various other nations, a few privileged Liberians, and primarily the children of the Lebanese. Basically, those with the backing of pocketbooks, ensuring that anything that did work in Liberia was theirs. Though I thoroughly enjoyed teaching and learning from these few students, to me, the honor did not compare to teaching English to the traumatized young adults at Stella Maris Polytechnic. But then, though the two student bodies were close geographically, they were worlds apart in experiential choices, making them incomparable. This made me struggle with what surreptitious spirit lay hidden in the sunny innocence of that beautiful American school.

Quite a few of my responsibilities at AISM, I found out about after I was already there and in the routine of teaching. This was fine with me, as the work load was negligible, having just come from teaching in a Liberian college. What wasn't fine with me was being bossed around by what the local Liberians termed 'Congo' – the descendants of those early settlers who had been slaves in the West and, when freed, came on ships to Liberia to rule the natives who had always lived on the land. Even that experience, I appreciated. It gave me an opportunity to relate in a small way to those many natives of this land, who were treated without consideration of their own potential by those who considered themselves far superior, for whatever reasons. Anyway, the additional jobs gave me the opportunity to know more people, which is always a plus – especially when they are as lovely as Phiarum.

Phiarum, a Buddhist from Cambodia, was the library assistant. I came to find out that I was the librarian, which was great, because libraries are among my favorite places to be! One day as I was sitting in that library, preparing for class (I had so few students that some of my classes were held around a table in the library), I heard Phiarum humming as she re-shelved books the students had returned. As the actual tune came into my consciousness, I stopped typing up my lesson plans to listen more intently. Was it possibly *Amazing Grace* that this Buddhist was humming? As I listened carefully, I could no longer doubt it. I cleared my throat and simply asked, "Phiarum, are you humming *Amazing Grace*?" Smiling, she replied, "Yes, I am. I just love that song. It is so beautiful." *Yes. Yes, it is. Beautiful indeed.*

One particular assignment that these students thrilled to do was to write poems inspired by paintings from Cherith's website.[7] I found their poetry to be superb, and sometimes Cherith would post one of the poems with the particular painting on her website, pleasing the students exceedingly. Though they wrote the poems in silence, or with soft background music playing, so as not to influence one another's impressions, oftentimes a theme was clearly evident across their work. One time their individual poems were so much of the same ambience, after reading them aloud, they decided to combine them into a masterpiece!

Because of my many windows, I have the awesome privilege of being Facebook friends with students around the world. Imagine my delight when I received the following message from a Kenyan student I had taught at this AISM window in Liberia before her family moved on to Cairo, Egypt:

Hello Ms. Hodel, In English we are given a prompt or quote each week and have to write something about it in any form.

363

The prompt this week was, "One's destination is never a place, but a new way of seeing things." - by Henry Miller.

And I wrote a poem about it. I was always a fan of poetry, but you made me like it more. Here is a poem which I hope you share with your students or the person you will have coffee with.

I am so gratified to not only share it with someone over coffee, but to share it with you here, with her permission:

When going to a place you have never been before
You don't just see a place
You see so much more
You don't just see trees or rocks or sand
You don't just see hills or snow or grass
No, You see people
That live and breath
You see people doing things that you never did
You see people that you don't know
You see folks that plant seeds that you have never grown
And it 'ought to be scary at first
To see and not really understand
But in a day or two
In a year or a few
You will grow a forest of knowledge and learn
You and these people
Will not just greet
No these people will talk! Yes Speak
Maybe, about the weather
But maybe not
You may speak about things you learned
About things taught
About dreams that sought
About plans you made
About people you forgave
About things you foresee
About horrors that you wished did not exist

And you and this people will be strangers no more
Yes! You and these people once strangers
Will make something grow
You'll make something die
You'll make something go
You'll make something fly
And before too soon
Yes! Before not too much
You'll make something happen
You and these people
All of a sudden
You and these people once strangers
You
will
become
one

by Patricia Kamara

~ ~ ~

The school year ended successfully on all accounts. We packed away our books in an orderly fashion and faithfully did our inventories. Ebola had already become an issue. At first it was just one that we mostly joked about. For example, when our crazy charming American director met me in the breezeway between classes one day, he congratulated me on something, raising his hand to high-five me; then as my hand was almost to slap against his, he pulled away saying, "Haven't you heard there's Ebola around here? We can't be touching each other!!" We both laughed. But not for long.

Soon the cases were increasing with scary rapidity and missionaries fled the country, leaving the nationals and expatriates to carry on. Then some weeks later, we watched as they returned in a valiant effort to take this plague by force and be the solution. I wondered. I sat on the balcony and pondered the big picture – about our role and God's role, and if this was the unknown that I had been anticipating. I hardly thought so, but then again. . .

~ ~ ~

School was out when Wendy called me to ask if I would like to help out at the Ebola clinic that had been set up on the ELWA compound. She herself was helping out, as was Nancy Sheppard and Nancy Writebol, also friends from the ladies' Wednesday afternoon Bible study. She suggested that with my nursing background, I would be especially suited to the task of understanding the importance of caution in helping the doctors and nurses suit up before going into the ward and decontaminating them when they came out in their Tyvek hazmat suits.

Wow, what an opportunity for real adventure! How many people can say they've worked in an Ebola unit?! That had been my immediate line of thinking. Just as quickly, however, that thought was brought captive by a motivation check within my spirit. I told Wendy I would think about it and let her know. Thus began an internal struggle. I listened to it carefully. I heard the Spirit within me whisper, *"Rest,"* to my insatiably adventurous spirit. Though the insatiable adventurer knew she was tired, she believed the need to serve others was great, and surely she should tend to it with her God-given nursing skills!

That's when I happened upon a letter that was written to some Hebrews long ago, and in it, I read these words: *For the one who has entered His rest has himself also rested from his works, as God did from His.* (Heb. 4:10) What really struck me were the last five words! I had to wonder at my audacity – God rested from *His* work, and I did not think I needed to rest from *mine*! Could I take the risk of refusing the rest that even God took?

During another conversation over dinner a few evenings later, Wendy asked me if I had had time to think about volunteering at the ELWA Ebola clinic. I responded that I had, and I had decided not to do so. Wendy accepted my decision graciously and without reservation. I offered no explanation and she requested none. Again, I saw the loving and non-condemning image of our Father in her, and was incredibly thankful to Him. And to Wendy, for her uncommon sense, in spite of all the absolutely amazing experiences she was having, doing as God had called *her* to do – volunteer at the ELWA Ebola clinic.

Of course, it's not possible for God or us to rest all the time. That's clearly not practical and is also not the point. Bill Haley of Coracle explains the real point, "Few ideas are as practical and helpful in our spiritual development as understanding the relationship between our true self and false self, and our growth in the direction towards Christ himself living in us in our *own unique ways*." (emphasis added)

This topic of Haley's matters immensely to those of us who want to grow in Beauty and thrive in life. It is part and parcel of the epiphany I received through gaining the long-awaited glimpse out of my beloved's window! It is manifested in a clear view of who God is, who we are, and who our neighbors are, and not getting the sequence of commands mixed up: 1) loving our Heavenly Father first and foremost, passionately and above all else, and 2) loving everyone we come into contact with *in the same way* that we love our God-loving selves. To love others *more* or *less* than we love ourselves is to love falsely. To love others *more* than we love ourselves is to err on the side of falsely sacrificing to/for others, as though they are our idols, redirecting the love that is meant only for God. To love others *less* than we love ourselves is to err on the side of misinterpreting ourselves as a god or goddess, thus more worthy of love than our neighbors.

~ ~ ~

In her book, *In Harm's Way: A View from the Epicenter of Liberia's Ebola Crisis*, my missionary friend, Nancy Sheppard, wrote about our last ladies' Wednesday afternoon get-together on the ELWA compound before she and her family were returning to the States for a family wedding. As it happened, it was also the last get-together before Harrison and I were returning to the States to spend some time with our family, a vacation that we had scheduled long before the Ebola crisis. Nancy had been one of those volunteering at the Ebola unit in the ELWA compound. Here is her description of her feelings and the happenings of that Wednesday afternoon:

I felt a bit guilty for leaving my spot at the Ebola ward. After the first week of working every night, Mark [Nancy's husband] had jokingly asked it it were possible for someone whose name was *not* Nancy to be trained for the job. [Nancy Writebol was also volunteering.] Thankfully, there were several people *not* named Nancy willing to be recruited. By the time my family was ready to leave, Eric Buller and Wendy Simpson were working regularly in the ward. Additionally, Samaritan's Purse had new volunteers heading toward West Africa.

The day before our departure, I took Jonah and Jared [Nancy's sons] with me to the ELWA campus. Although I was very busy trying to pull everything together for our trip, I wanted to say goodbye to my friends.

I drove over to the duplex my friend Melanie Ness and her family shared with the Brantlys. Melanie had planned a little event, complete with nail polish, chocolate and hot beverages. By the time I arrived, Amber Brantly and several others were already chatting.

We had a sweet time of fellowship and I felt very privileged to have such good friends with whom to share. The Ebola crisis was on everyone's minds, of course, and much of our talk was about it. We were all keenly aware of the need for God's wisdom and protection for everyone, but most obviously for those working in the ward. In addition to concern for their husbands' safety, Beth Fankhauser and Amber Brantly were dealing with the practical realities of caring for their children and homes while having husbands working in the Ebola ward in addition to their normal doctoring duties.

As Beth, Amber and I talked, it crossed my mind I had an insider's view that could encourage them. Watching Dr. Fankhauser, Dr. Brantly and Dr. Debbie in the ward had touched me deeply and I inevitably cried when I tried to talk about it. While Beth and Amber were home at night with their children, I was with their husbands in the Ebola ward. I knew what they were doing during those long hours.

"Your husbands are doing such a great job," I said to Beth and Amber, who listened attentively. "It's just amazing to watch them work with the patients. They are so gentle and kind. They are being the hands and feet of Christ to these people. It's a really beautiful thing."

~ ~ ~

As Nancy had shared from her heart, I could easily see the amazing beauty she spoke of in Amber and Beth's doctor husbands being the hands and feet of Jesus to those suffering with Ebola. And as Nancy shared her own experiences, I remembered listening to Wendy's, and was touched again, seeing the incredible beauty of these friends of mine, also being the hands and feet of Jesus, serving the doctors who were serving the Ebola patients. And yet, along with this vision of communal beauty, and possibly for the first time in my life, I felt no condemnation for declining an offer to serve others. I had been obedient to the Spirit of Beauty in His direction to me. It felt a little like I was being introduced to my true self. Weird, but wonderful – and immensely freeing. I thanked Beauty.

On Saturday, July 26th, Liberia and I shared another birthday. Liberia turned 167 and I turned fifty-eight. The following day, July 27th, I heard Harrison gasp as he was checking his email before we went to church. When I asked what was wrong, he responded with disbelief in his voice, "Kent Brantley has Ebola!"

We had plans to go to Victory Family Church to celebrate their second anniversary. Some friends of ours were missionaries there and we wanted to rejoice with them in their church plant's second birthday, as we had the first, a year earlier. During the celebration after the church service, we received a phone call from David Writebol, the leader of our small Sunday evening Bible study group. The group was scheduled to meet in our apartment that evening and David was calling to say that he and Nancy would not be able to be there because Nancy had tested positive for Ebola the day before. We were absolutely, wordlessly, stunned.

The next few days were a struggling journey for Harrison and me, as we followed Nancy and Kent's conditions, and seriously

369

stressed over my own fever, sore throat, muscle aches, headache and abdominal rash. Because these were also the same as the beginning symptoms of Ebola, we couldn't help but think "what if. . .?" The thought terrified Harrison. It did not terrify me. Though I didn't want to die the awful death of Ebola, I was totally ready and willing to go home. For me there was just one stipulation, I was not willing to die on the opposite side of the world from Cherith, Tobin, and Lizzie.

Because our flight to the States was in a few days, I lay awake at night, asking myself if I was willing to lie at the airport screenings that they had begun conducting. From what we had heard, the temperature-taking devices they were using were far from accurate, but the question remained: if questioned, was I willing to lie that I had not had a fever in the last two weeks, and that I had not been in contact with anyone who now has Ebola? In the dark, I knew the answer. I was. I was willing to lie to just get on that plane and get to the kids – a behavior that we, and everyone else, had railed against Liberians for doing.

When I told Harrison in the morning that I was willing to lie, he was incredulous. "You would really be willing to lie and even take Ebola to America?!?" *I would.* And thus began the most eye-opening lesson for me yet – of what happens when one's children have become their idols, creating a mess that Dr. Seuss accurately diagnosed as *so big and so deep and so tall, we can not pick it up. There is no way at all!* A real hard lesson in the false me. Harrison and I did not share my physical symptoms, or my struggle, with the kids or anyone else. Only with Beauty.

The day for our departure came. My fever had gone. I felt great – the only remaining symptom was the strange abdominal rash. The scanning thermometer at the airport recorded my temperature as incredibly low. No lying was necessary. I boarded the airport jubilantly. I wasn't even bothered that it seemed to be taking us an extra long time to take off. Eventually, the captain came on to explain the reason – the Peace Corp was evacuating Liberia, and some of them were having difficulties getting to the airport. We would wait on them. Happily.

Because we remained in transit to another flight, nothing was made of our arrival in London Heathrow airport. That is, until we went to board for D.C. The gate attendant looked twice at my passport, nudged her counterpart working beside her, and pointed to it, asking me if we had really just come from Liberia. The two gate officials looked at each other, he shrugged and said in a low voice, "There's nobody here now." She motioned me onward. Jubilance again!

Arriving in Dulles Airport in D.C., again not a single thing was made of us having come from Ebola-stricken Liberia. Perhaps the world in general didn't know, or choose to care, what was happening so far away in Liberia. Well, soon enough they would.

Lizzie, after updating her Facebook status to, *Have I said recently how much I love airports? Because I do. Especially when waiting to pick up parents coming from Liberia!* was standing there – a glorious sight – waiting for us as we exited customs and immigration, with a beautiful bunch of flowers in her hands. No sooner had we greeted joyously (me taking care not to kiss Lizzie. . .just in case), than Tobin called her to ask if we had arrived yet. Lizzie responded to him with, "Yes, they're here. Mom's kissing the ground!" We all laughed. I wasn't, but it wasn't because I didn't want to. It was just that I didn't want to make a scene.

Lessons Learned:

We are not God. Not even close.
Thus we cannot save the world from God's decisions.
Grace happens where love and truth meet.
Always remain situationally aware. (from Brian, thanks!)
Even in seeing things for what they are,
remain kind. (from Gilles, thanks!)
Recognize real when you see it.
(from Brian and Gilles, thanks, guys!)

24

From Pillar to Post

Homeless in the U.S.A.
August 1, 2014 - November 15, 2015

Lizzie took Harrison and me to her apartment in Arlington, Virginia, where she had prepared us a favorite meal. It was incredibly delicious. We spent the night in her absent roommate's empty double bed. Early the next morning, Lizzie and I caught the bus to go see Cherith, now living in Brooklyn, working as a temp in various financial offices. The following morning, Harrison flew from Reagan Airport in D.C. to Wichita, Kansas, to take a one-week course on propeller assembly procedures. While he was away, I moved us into a darling little attic apartment in D.C. that we had arranged to rent from Josh and Jen before we had left Liberia. It was perfect.

But in my mind, I will always connect that perfect little space with the news I watched our world receive – of first Dr. Kent Brantly, and then our friend, Nancy Writebol, being flown to Atlanta's Emory University Hospital so that they could be saved from the death grip of Ebola. We listened to the effects of Donald Trump tweeting that doctors who treat Ebola patients "are great," but shouldn't be allowed to seek treatment back home if they get sick, adding that the U.S. cannot allow Ebola-infected people back – people who go to far away places to help out are great, but must suffer the consequences! Not stopping there, he said the U.S. must "stop all flights from Ebola infected countries or the plague will start and spread inside our borders."

And sure enough, we soon received word from British Airways that they were canceling all flights to/from Liberia, including our return tickets.

In the midst of all the controversy, I was encouraged by the poem John Piper composed, "inspired positively by the Samaritan's Purse workers and negatively by Donald Trump"-as introduced when first published in *World* magazine:

> Today a thousand dead. And more
> To die. A common ache, like flu,
> Then nausea, a fever-soar,
> A hopeless clinic interview:
> "There's nothing we can do."
> The bleeding has no bias. These:
> A child, a chief, a friend, a nurse,
> Liberian, and Leonese,
> From Guinea, Texas, taste the curse—
> And kindness, from the Purse.
> Samaritans, six thousand miles
> From home and care, subdue their fears,
> And wonder if a sneeze defiles,
> Or if a healthy fluid clears
> The curse. Perhaps their tears.
> But now two treasured ones, struck down,
> Contagious still with death—and love—
> Fly back to us, our joy, our crown,
> A touch of grace, a gentle dove,
> Yet through a plastic glove.
> While in our land we see today
> Another virus spreading, dumped,
> More deadly, in the soul. They say,
> "Why bring them home?" Though you be stumped,
> This grace will not be *trumped*.
> John Piper[1]
> August 3, 2014

Of course, Donald Trump was not alone in his thinking, and was influential in the ensuing panic that would escalate for months, especially in our beloved U.S.A. Trump was undoubtedly voicing what others, less bold, were thinking. And from a purely self-seeking, self-protecting, intellectual viewpoint, he did make sense. I cannot judge the man because I don't know him – indeed, have never even met him. But letting his fabulous track record speak for itself, he has, from my window, gotten the main things all out of order: ignoring God, loving himself supremely, and letting others fall wherever they can best serve his interests.

As Ebola threatened to be a real plague, wiping out the land in its exponential rapidity of travel from body to body, place to place, President Ellen, of necessity, closed all the schools in Liberia. Harrison and I were at a loss as to what to do next – with no return tickets available, and me on hold for teaching. GVL, the company Harrison worked for, came to his rescue with a plan for him. Their corporate plane had had an issue while at their oil palm plantation in Butaw, near Greenville, Liberia – a place that even Cherith, Tobin and Lizzie could picture well, one of the GVL pilots having flown them there when they were visiting us over Christmas. Now Harrison's immediate boss was calling from Accra, Ghana to inform Harrison that he would get him a ticket on Brussels Airline, an airline still flying into Liberia. His boss told him that they needed him to be there. ASAP. Harrison went.

Our month in the perfect attic was over and another couple was ready to move into our spot. Phil and Mona, a couple associated with our original church culture, lived in Arlington, not far from Lizzie. They kindly invited me to stay with them in their lovely home until I knew what else to do, where else to go. I gratefully accepted.

~ ~ ~

After spending some precious time with Tobin, Lizzie, Phil, and Mona, I packed up my luggage again and travelled on to my brother Adam's lake house on Lake Freeman, near Monticello, Indiana. For how long, I had no idea. By this time, the worldwide news of Ebola had Americans approaching a state of paranoia. Neighbors on both sides of Adam, who were like family and had always hugged me on arrival, were now afraid to even touch me. They inquired about Harrison's health frequently and cautiously. Not only them, but many other friends and family were equally concerned about Harrison's health, and even if he would return home alive. For once I was not worried – at least, about his health. His well-being was another thing. But as for his health, systems were being put in place in Liberia wherein, upon entering any store, facility, anywhere, one must first wash their hands in the chlorine bleach water waiting at the doorway. Some places also required temperature to be taken before entering. Along with that, Harrison had made the firm decision not to come into bodily contact with anyone, not even to shake hands. Under these conditions it is impossible to get infected with the Ebola virus – at least, from another human. For a country of people to whom touch is as natural as breathing, this new situation was challenging, to say the least. Traditions and other aspects of West African culture also made it extremely difficult to curb the spread of the virus.

It appeared to me that Adam was pretty much in agreement with the thinking of Donald Trump – now that I was safely sitting beside him, taking in the beauty of our surroundings at Lake Freeman. He definitely thought that Harrison should get home, now and quick, while he was healthy. When I shared with Adam an article interviewing Nancy Writebol that I had read in *Christianity Today*, where Nancy had said that Ebola is a spiritual battle, Adam scoffed. So I went quiet. I wish I could have told him then what I know now – the beautiful victorious end of that spiritual battle as expressed in the August 2015 newsletter about David and Nancy. But, of course, I couldn't, because I couldn't yet clearly see that conquering outcome.

But now that it has come to pass, I sent a message asking Nancy if I could share it with you and she responded with this message:

Hi Pam always good to hear from you. Trust you are doing well. Would love to read your book and we are honored that you would want to use our prayer letter. Please feel free and thank you for asking. Wish you were here! Blessings dear one!

And here is that letter:

Writebols 2 Liberia

"Come over to Macedonia and help us." **Acts 16:9b**

Responding to need. Proclaiming the Gospel. Equipping the church.

"And after some days, Paul said to Barnabas, 'Let us return and visit the brothers. . .and see how they are.'" Acts 15:36

The Ebola Survivor who Came Back

"Did you ever ask God, 'Why me?,' when you knew you were infected?," a reporter asked Nancy in an on-camera interview. Her answer to this question always meets with looks of surprise. She responded, "I never asked God, 'Why me?,' but my question for him has been, 'Lord, what do you want me to do with this?'"

And then comes the follow-up question: "Will you be going back to Liberia?" In the weeks and months that have followed Nancy's release from Emory Hospital (now a year later), and after much prayer by you on our behalf, Nancy and I have followed God's continuing call upon us to serve him. We returned to Liberia for a short visit in March and then full-time in June. The glorious unfolding of God's story continues to be amazing!

"Are you Nancy? I'm so happy to meet you, and I thank you for coming back to Liberia, you give us so much hope!," is the new normal for us as we go to the market, or to a shop. Many Liberians have expressed to us ways that Nancy's return has encouraged them to continue to trust God for their lives. More than the celebrity status, though, is how God is using Nancy's experience to minister to the Ebola survivors we meet. Two ministries are examples: Trauma Healing and the Ebola Survivor's Clinic.

Nancy was trained to be a facilitator in Trauma Healing. In July, Nancy and the Trauma Healing team from the US trained 82 leaders from churches, organizations and NGO's. Nancy presented parts of the training course to two groups of forty participants. Nancy meets weekly with two groups of women to help them in dealing with various trauma by taking their pain to the cross.

In the once-per-week Ebola Survivor's Clinic at the ELWA Hospital, Nancy serves with SIM's Dr. John Fankhauser and is a welcoming face, able to identify with our patients and their problems, connecting them with resources and loving them in the name of Jesus.

A New Country Director

In March, I (David) took up the responsibilities of the various SIM ministries and missionaries in Liberia as the Country Director and the Executive Director of ELWA Ministries. I don't mind saying that the job still scares my socks off! Carrying forward the strategic vision and direction for SIM, and managing the several ministry units (radio, hospital, school, etc.) with over 200 staff and a budget of tens of thousands of dollars per month is a staggering load. What will God do through all of these things?

Through it all, God brings me back to **Joshua 1:7-9** "Only be strong and very courageous, being careful to do according to all the law that Moses my servant commanded you. Do not turn from it to the right hand or to the left, that you may have good success wherever you go. This Book of the Law shall not depart from your mouth, but you shall meditate on it day and night, so that you may be careful to do according to all that is written in it. For then you will make your way prosperous, and then you will have good success. Have I not commanded you? Be strong and courageous. Do not be frightened, and do not be dismayed, for the LORD your God is with you wherever you go."

Here's a list of the exciting things that God is doing as we return to Liberia:

- Partnership with the Evangelical Church in Liberia (ECOL) to care for Ebola Survivors and their families through care groups in local communities.
- Radio broadcasts of Trauma Healing Institute stories.

- Post-graduate level seminary, Evangelical Seminary of West Africa planning to start classes in January of 2016
- ECOL Theological Seminary and Professional Studies planning to train pastors in rural area.
- ELWA Hospital construction of new facilities scheduled for completion in May of 2016.
- Expansion of ELWA Academy to offer high school education.
- Radio ELWA plans to complete new studio and production facilities in 2016.
- Returning SIM missionaries and adding new missionaries to provide support for expanding mission opportunities.

Nancy and I look forward to sharing with you in the months and years ahead all that God is doing in Liberia. We can't wait to hear what God will do with you as you pray and respond!

By Prayer

- Thank God for all the ways He has been a present help and strength to us and has made us to be useful in His hands for His work, especially in Liberia at this time.
- Pray for us as we strive to make the most of every opportunity to glorify Jesus and make His Gospel known.
- Pray that Nancy and I continue in good health, and remain faithful to His calling work and plans.

We have seen God work in many powerful ways through the prayers of His people. Let's keep on praying!

~ ~ ~

During August, while we had been staying in Josh and Jen's attic, I had started going to yoga classes with Lizzie and loved it. So when I found out that there were yoga classes in Monticello I joined in there. I found these sessions to be greatly beneficial to me – mind, soul, and body. Our instructor always encouraged us towards self-awareness and to gracefully accept what is. J.J.

Heller's music was sometimes playing softly in the background and because she had ministered to us in song one Sunday at our Fresno, California window, this music helped connect my past with this new experience of yoga. And then our instructor always ended with the words, *The light in me salutes the light in you.* When I got back to the lake house, I would enter and greet Adam with those same words. Adam would smile, but shake his head, no doubt thinking that I just couldn't be right in the head.

Sitting there alone at Lake Freeman, in the extreme beauty of those autumn days, in what seemed to me to be my own private paradise, it struck me: *This is how Beauty takes care of His homeless!* I was overwhelmed with thankfulness. Some days the beauty was more than I could take in as I sat contemplating the riches of life as expressed in the over-abundance of beauty out the window of that special autumn of 2014 overlooking Lake Freeman.

~ ~ ~

Before Harrison had left for Liberia, our friend, Eva, had given us a book by Mark Batterson entitled, *Draw the Circle: The 40 Day Prayer Challenge.* Harrison and I were only a few days into taking the challenge together when he was called back to Liberia, leaving me to continue on with the challenge on my own. Batterson's challenge was so instrumental in my life that I voraciously read the rest of his books, in that same spirit. Somewhere in one of them, I think it may have been *The Circle Maker,* Batterson challenged would-be authors to simply *do it; write as an act of obedience, whether or not one person ever reads it.* So sitting there at a window that I wouldn't have planned, but one that would be the envy of any author, I began writing, and if now you are reading it, I thank you from the bottom of my heart for giving me the honor and privilege of sharing my windows with you. And I would *so* love to know your story, too, as you see it, from your window! I really would. If you're willing to share, please email me at simplymywindow@gmail.com.

~ ~ ~

One weekend, I left that beautiful lake window to return to Gretchen and my Glen Ellyn window. Though it was an absolute delight to spend time with Gretchen and her friends, my real purpose in returning to Chicagoland was to join Leslie, Tobin's fiancee, in watching him run in the Chicago Marathon, this being the race that would qualify him for the Boston Marathon. The day of the race dawned stunningly beautiful and stayed that way the entire day. As I stood there, watching the runners, I was struck by the realization of a beauty even greater than that of nature – of a countless throng of individuals, in many different colors, each with a different stride, each pricelessly unique in the sight of their Creator, all alive and running as one race. The reality of this beauty overcame me, leaving me with an immense sense of both insignificance and significance.

~ ~ ~

Back at Lake Freeman, I received troublesome news. The director of the American International School of Monrovia was trying to renege on the fine print of the contract that I had signed for the 2014-15 school year. That fine print said that in an unforeseen event of a calamity closing the school, the teachers would continue to be paid for a stipulated period of time. After Adam heard Harrison and I discussing the situation over Skype, he asked me about it. When I gave him an explanation, his response was, "So you're screwed, right?"

I don't remember how I answered, but I do remember what I thought. *No, no. I'm not.* I was confident that I knew and trusted Someone in high places who protects and provides. Thus, I chose not to allow myself to be placed in a professionally inappropriate position of screwage. At Adam's question, I felt a quiet and patient anger rising within me and knew I was not and would not be a victim. My parents had raised me well, giving me the choice of easily knowing my value.

In the end, I received all that I rightfully had coming, thanked Beauty for it, forgave and prayed blessings, not curses on that delightful, but deluded director.

~ ~ ~

Through a dear ex-missionary friend, Gail, who with her husband, Don, runs a similar place in Pennsylvania, I came to know of Cedar Lane Missionary Homes (CLMH) in Laurel Springs, New Jersey. Cedar Lane Missionary Homes seemed to me to be an ideal spot to be in transition because it was nearly halfway between Cherith in Brooklyn, New York, and Tobin and Lizzie in Washington, D.C. The problem was that the place was for missionaries and I wasn't currently a real one. I decided to risk it and contact them anyway. They wonderfully and graciously accepted me in spite of myself! Little did I know that this new window would leave me feeling less self-centered in thinking that Beauty had awesome ways of caring for me, one of His homeless, because here I wasn't homeless alone – the place was full of 'homeless' missionaries, all being taken care of in an abundant way, beyond anything any of us could think to even imagine!

It was Friday, October 31st, Halloween, when I arrived at my new window. It was dusk and a gray drizzle was falling. I couldn't find my apartment, 103A. The whole thing was somehow reminiscent of arriving to Link Care in Fresno, California. But this time, I was alone, without Harrison. After finally finding my apartment, I went to get a bite to eat at Wendy's. The place was full of precious children in contrasting degrees of grotesque ensembles with their less-than-excited parents. It all added to the gray drizzle and my aloneness.

Then I went to get gas, and was surprised to discover that it is New Jersey law that no one fills their own gas tank – the station attendant must do so! This was going to be another interesting new window, I was sure.

As I slowed to turn onto my new street of Cedar Lane, I noticed a warm glow of candlelight coming from the church windows, immediately on my right. Those glowing stained glass windows drew me

381

in without any resistance on my part. Inside, I found myself at the first night of Laurel Hill Bible Church's mission conference. I was late. As I found a seat in the warm darkness, Doubting Thomas was already spotlighted on the stage. His soliloquy drew me in – his doubt, his clear reasoning. He had seen Jesus on that cross. He knew what happened on a cross. You died. Dead was dead, no matter what anyone said. In the quiet of the dark silence, his soliloquy continued. Thomas told what it was like from his window, to think like that, and then to have Jesus actually appear in front of him – alive, kindly asking him to touch His side, see His hands, to stop doubting and believe. Even though I knew this character was just a pseudo-doubter, I still felt goosebumps on my arms as he fell to the floor of the stage, and in an agonizing cry, called out, "My Lord and my God!'

~ ~ ~

The next morning, when I opened the stocked refrigerator to find *Simply Orange* juice waiting on me, I just had to text Adam the news since we shared our love of the brand! He immediately responded, "You're spoiled." *Yes. Yes, I am. I'm a spoiled lucky girl.*

Also on the first morning at this window, there was a knock on my door, with a lady asking me if I would please move my car from in front of the garage door, because a Trader Joe's delivery was about to arrive. The kind lady told me after I had moved my car, I should come back and she would show me the garage. Confused, I quickly agreed to move my car.

The evening before, when Harrison had called from Liberia, I had told him that our apartment had an attached garage. He had responded with, "No way! That's great!" After seeing what was in our garage, I could hardly wait for his daily call so that I could tell him that it was far *better than* a garage – it was a food bank stocked chock full with free food, fresh flowers, fresh produce, meat, toiletries and more! *Simply beyond anything that we could ever have imagined.* And that was not all that these missionary homes were provided with. There was also a boutique of quality used clothes and a yard sale room with miscellaneous everything – all at no charge for the missionaries. Here we were as cared for as any alien, orphan, or widow, should be – by those with true religion.

Tuesday morning prayer meetings at this window were also reminiscent of my Link Care window in California, the same authenticity present as at our women's sessions, but with two basic differences. The first was that we participants weren't so seriously wounded as those of us at Link Care had been at the time, and the second difference was the presence of both brothers and sisters. Our hearts were one, our aches deep – especially for missionary kids – and our joys so large as to be overflowing all over the place.

The nations were represented in our small prayer circle, either by representation of missionary service or by actual nationality. With all its abundant provision, its picturesque setting, and its representation of the nations and their languages, I felt this window was my closest to heaven yet. I even had the joy of tutoring a German-born, Portuguese-speaking Word of Life missionary to Brazil! Though everyone was totally free to pray in their mother tongue, I loved it when one Korean sister prayed in English, "Lord, you know how many MKs have hurt, and a strange feeling of people – how to treat them." Exactly, expressed in her third language in a way that not only God, but all of us parents understood perfectly. I liked her words in stating it better than the way I would have expressed it in my mother tongue.

Though there were used bicycles provided at CLMH, I retrieved my beloved LeMond from Lizzie's apartment in Arlington and rode it daily, as I had ridden bikes at my other windows. (Except the Liberian one, where Harrison had told me that no way would he get me a bike there; I would get myself killed. *Basi.*) Imagine my surprise when, while riding at Gloucester Township Park in New Jersey, I came upon a small golden sign on a park bench with the same *Make It Happen* message as the huge sign at the burned-out St. Thomas Church in D.C.! Only here the message was slightly different, as its tiny golden inscription proclaimed, *We Make It Happen*. I wondered about that – if it's possible that *we can make it happen*. Somehow I just didn't feel I had that kind of power on my own.

~ ~ ~

At long last, Harrison successfully finished up his work in Liberia and was heading home to us! We, especially I, could not have been happier. Because of the Ebola crisis, he would have to undergo a minor ordeal of reporting his temperature to the county health department every morning and evening for twenty-one days before he would be freed up to be the best man in Tobin and Leslie's wedding party.

Before leaving Cedar Lane to go to Dulles International Airport to pick up Harrison, I quickly posted my status on social media:

Off goes the happiest woman in the world ~ to Dulles International Airport to pick up her Beloved!

Then under the Tibetan-blue sky of the New Jersey day, I left my perfectly provided safe missionary home and traveled the smooth wide roads of the U.S.A. in our comfortable well-functioning car, soaking in the last of Mother Nature's autumn beauty, and singing praises to her Creator Father. I truly could not have been happier.

When I got to the airport and parked in the organized spacious parking lot and entered the sparkling clean airport, I checked the efficient sign that told me Harrison's flight was ahead of schedule. To reassure myself, I easily found the well-marked information desk and immediately went up to the friendly lady behind the desk who was not already busy with someone else. Even though I knew the answer from having repeated this procedure countless times before, I checked to see if all the internationals flights came out of the same gate. "*Yes,*" she assured me, "*they do.*" Seeing there were only fourteen baggage claims, I asked where baggage claim fifteen was. She smiled and told me that they shouldn't really call it fifteen, because the international travelers come out with their luggage, which of course, I knew, too. Suddenly I had flashbacks to my first arrival in many other airports around the world, particularly that Liberian one, and laughed out loud.

Then I realized I really needed to use the restroom. With the memories of all the restrooms of all my windows, I entered this sparkling clean American airport restroom with a renewed sense of the awesomeness of the country Beauty had set for my original bound and habitation. After using the restroom, out of sheer thankfulness to Beauty, I knelt, there in the privacy of my stall – thanking Him for every little and big thing, including my thankfulness for being born American and for the government that He had put in place, making a country that works – for my good, one of her many people.

When Harrison finally walked through those quadruple wide doors, pushing his inevitable load of baggage, I was struck. I looked at him with fresh eyes, deeply grateful, and finally saw that it was not for his own benefit that he was bearing the load of all this burdensome excess baggage. No, it was for my good. With an overwhelming sense of gratitude and in that deep place where we truly see and know, I saw Harrison, and though I didn't have the vaguest clue of where our next window was going to be, I did know that it was going to be an awesomely beautiful one. A very beautiful window for sure. *Yes, the best is yet to come.*

Lesson Learned:

Choose Life Now and don't look back!

ACKNOWLEDGEMENTS

I want to sincerely thank:

~ Aunt Jeanie, for encouraging me, more than once, when I needed it most.

~ Daniel McBurney, who, in his own way, showed me the beauty of simplicity, and Dr. James Pearce, who skillfully and permanently removed any doubt I ever had.

~ Nancy Sheppard and Staci Floyd, for helping to clear my spirit so I could write.

~ Dr. Robert Dawson and his wife, Estelle, for establishing, and those who followed, for maintaining, Cedar Lane Missionary Homes where I've graciously been given space and time to write.

~ My sisters in faith, who prayed this book into being, especially Joanne Callahan, without whom this book would likely still be in the prenatal stage. Thanks, Joanne, for laboring beside me to birth it.

~ Our three children, Cherith, Tobin, and Lizzie, who finally got it through my thick skull, that my windows are not theirs. Not even close.

NOTES

All Scripture quotations, unless otherwise indicated, are taken from the *New American Standard Bible*, copyright The Lockman Foundation 1960, 1962, 1963, 1968, 1971, 1972, 1973, 1975, 1977, 1995.

All Oswald Chambers quotations are used by kind permission of Oswald Chambers Publications.

Chapter 1 Wapello, Iowa
1. Isaiah 5:4ff, Luke 20:9-21
2. Poem by Larry Moser, aka 'Jacob' in this book. Used with permission.

Chapter 2 Iowa City, Iowa
1. Sykes, Mr. & Mrs. Seth. *Thank You, Lord* lyrics. Assigned to Singspiration, Inc./ASCAP, 1940, 1945, renewal 1968, 1973.

Chapter 4 Schroon Lake, New York
1. Singer, L.E. and Don Wyrtzen. *Finally Home* lyrics. New Spring, a division of Brentwood-Benson Music publishing ASCAP, 1971. Used with permission.
2. Jeremiah 15:19 NASB

Chapter 6 Cicero, Illinois
1. my experiential paraphrase of 2 Chronicles 16:9

Chapter 7 Hampton, Tennessee

1. Chambers, Oswald. *My Utmost for His Highest*, June 30th. Grand Rapids, MI: Discovery House Publishers, 1963.

2. Croft, Steve. *Pierce My Ear* lyrics. Dayspring Music, LLC, 1980.
3. Paris, Twila. *Faithful Men* lyrics, from album *Kingdom Seekers*. Star Song Records, 1985.
4. Updike, John. *Self-Consciousness*: *Memoirs*. New York: Random House, Inc, 1989. (p.246)

Chapter 8 Dodoma, Tanzania

1. Hoffman, Showalter and Elisha A., *Leaning on the Everlasting Arms lyrics*. Published 1887.
2. Rilke, Rainer Maria. *Letters to a Young Poet*. USA: Merchant Books, 2012. (p.15)
3. Matthew 26:11, Mark 14:7, John 12:8, also Deuteronomy 15:11

Chapter 9 Rolling Prairie, Indiana

1. Romans 12:19 KJV; Leviticus 19:18; Deuteronomy 32:35,41,43; Psalm 58:10, 94:1; Isaiah 35:4; Jeremiah 11:20, 20:12; Nahum 1:2; Hebrews 10:30; 1 Thessalonians 4:6

Chapter 11 Return to Dodoma

1. Isaiah 42:8; 43:11, 48:11, Exodus 20:3, Psalm 83:18

Chapter 12 Goodfield, Illinois

1. Proverbs 16:1,9; 19:21; 20:24; also Psalm 37:23-24, Jeremiah 10:23
2. Micah 6:8; also Deuteronomy 10:12,13

Chapter 13 Kijabe, Kenya

1. Luke 12:22-34
2. Isaiah 58:6,7
3. Deuteronomy 8:2 NIV, with 1:8, 4:1, 9:23
4. 2 Corinthians 1:19, 20
5. Psalm 56:8 NLT

Chapter 14 Bloomington, Illinois

1. Revelation 7:14

Chapter 15 Return to Kijabe

1. Chambers, Oswald. *My Utmost for His Highest,* December 4th. Grand Rapids, MI: Discovery House Publishers, 1963.
2. John 8:36
3. Chambers, Oswald. *My Utmost for His Highest,* April 21st. Grand Rapids, MI: Discovery House Publishers, 1963.
4. Hoff, Benjamin. *The Tao of Pooh.* New York: E.P. Dutton, 1982.
5. Deuteronomy 10:18,19, 23:7, 27:19; Psalm 146:9; Leviticus 19:34; Ezekiel 47:22; Exodus 22:21-23; Numbers 10:31,32
6. Martin, William. *The Parent's tao Te Ching: A New Interpretation.* Cambridge, MA: Da Capo P, 1999.
7. 2 Peter 1:3-11, specifically verse 8
8. Genesis 17:20
9. Hebrews 1:1-4, 3:6, 4:14, 7:28, 9:26, John 1:1-5, 14:6, Colossians 1:15-20, 3:11 Romans 4:13-25, 8:17, 1 Corinthians 2:7, 8:6, Acts 10:34-43, 20:21, 28:22-31; Galatians 3:7-29
10. Chambers, Oswald. *My Utmost for His Highest,* July 10th. Grand Rapids, MI: Discovery House Publishers, 1963.
11. Chambers, Oswald. *My Utmost for His Highest,* July 11th. Grand Rapids, MI: Discovery House Publishers, 1963.

Chapter 16 Normal, Illinois

1. Whitman, Walt. *Leaves of Grass.* a poetry collection, first published in 1855.
2. Psalm 10:4, Psalm 14:1, Psalm 36:1, Psalm 53:1
3. Whyte, David. Belonging. Langby, WA: Many Rivers Press, 1996.
4. Over The Rhine. *All Over Ohio* lyrics, from album *Meet Me At The Edge Of The World.*

Chapter 17 Vientiane, Laos

1. Dickinson, Emily. *I'm Nobody.* Published 1891.
2. Jeremiah 15:16
3. Ortega, Fernando. *Angel Fire* lyrics, from album *This Bright Hour,* 1997.
4. Psalm 56:8 NLT
5. Leviticus 16:10, 20-22
6. Chambers, Oswald. *My Utmost for His Highest,* December 18th. Grand Rapids, MI: Discovery House Publishers, 1963.

Chapter 18 Barnes' Basement / Elliot Dorm

1. Hiebert, Paul G., R. Daniel Shaw, and Tite Tienou. *Understanding Folk Religion: A ChristianResponse to Popular Beliefs and Practices*. Grand Rapids, MI: Baker Books, 1999. (p.302)
2. Rohr, Richard. *Things Hidden*. St. Anthony Messenger Press, 2008.

Chapter 19 Lhasa, Tibet

1. Isaiah 52:7, Nahum 1:15, Romans 10:15
2. Over The Rhine: Karin Bergquist, Linford Detweiler and Joe Henry. *Sharpest Blade* lyrics, from album *The Long Surrender*. Used with permission.

Chapter 20 Fresno, California

1. Nouwen, Henri J.M. *The Wounded Healer*. New York: Doubleday, 1972.
2. 1 Corinthians 4:10, 1:18-21,23,25-28, 2:14, 3:18
3. Psalm 46:10, 86:8, Job 19:25, John 16:13, Exodus 3:14, 6:2, 8:10, 9:14, Deuteronomy 4:7,35,39,6:4, 7:9,10, 11:1-32, 32:39, 1 Samuel 2:2, 1 Kings 8:60, Psalm 100:3, 86:8, Isaiah 43:10, 44:6,8, 45:5, 46:9, 10:6-8, Jeremiah 10:6,7, John 8:28,58, Hebrews 13:8, 12:29, 10:31,36 Mark 12:32, 1 Corinthians 8:4,6, Revelation 1:8, 4:8
4. 2 Corinthians 4:17, Romans 8:18, 1 Peter 1:6, 5:10, Hebrews 12:2
5. Genesis 1:27, Ephesians 4:24
6. King Jr., Martin Luther. "Letter from Birmingham Jail." April 16, 1963. http://www.mlkonline.net/jail.html
7. Isaiah 53:5
8. Chambers, Oswald. *In The Presence Of His Majesty*. Sisters, OR: Multnomah Books, 1996.
9. Chambers, Oswald. *My Utmost for His Highest,* December 17th. Grand Rapids, MI: Discovery House Publishers, 1963.
10. Chambers, Oswald. *My Utmost for His Highest,* July 31st. Grand Rapids, MI: Discovery House Publishers, 1963.
11. Werner, Susan. *Barbed Wire Boys* lyrics, from album *Club Passim*. Used with permission.
12. Ephesians 3:20

13. Hodel, Rachel. https://profunditties.wordpress.com/?ref=spelling Used with permission.

Chapter 21 Washington, D.C.
1. May, Rollo. *Freedom and Destiny*. New York, London: W.W.Norton & Co, 1999.

Chapter 22 Glen Ellyn, Illlinois
1. Isaiah 59:1, Numbers 11:23
2. Psalm 17:8, 36:7, 46:1ff MSG, 57:1, 59:16b, 61:4, 63:7, 68:13, 91:1,4, 131:2; Ruth 2:12; Isaiah 4:6
3. Taylor, Barbara Brown. *An Altar in the World*. New York: HarperCollins, 2009. (p.200) Taken from *The Book of Occasional Services*, 2nd ed. New York: The Church Hymnal Corporation, 1988. (p.147)
4. Elmer, Duane. *Cross-Cultural Servanthood*. Downers Grove, IL: InterVarsity P., 2006. (p.27-8) Elmer gives credit to Ann Templeton Brownlee for originating the story, although he was unable to locate the source. This version is Elmer's own, and the degree this story overlaps with that of Ms. Brownlee is unknown.
5. Genesis 3:7
6. de Mello, Anthony. *Taking Flight*. New York: Doubleday, 1988.
7. de Mello, Anthony. *Awareness*. New York: Random House, 1990.
8. Chambers, Oswald. *My Utmost for His Highest*, June 1st. Grand Rapids, MI: Discovery House Publishers, 1963.
9. Chambers, Oswald. *My Utmost for His Highest*, August 30th. Grand Rapids, MI: Discovery House Publishers, 1963.
10. McClurg, Kayla. *Everything, Given From God*. Inward Outward seeking the depths. Used with permission.
11. Gregory of Nyssa. Quoted in *Untamed Hospitality* by Elizabeth Newman. Grand Rapids, MI: Brazos P., 2007.
12. http://hannahdagenhart.blogstop.com/2015/02/missions-ministry-and-importance-of.html Posted by Hannah Dagenhart at 11:21 PM. Used with permission.
13. Palmer, Parker. *Let Your Life Speak*. San Franscico, CA: Jossey-Bass, 2000.

14. Merton, Thomas. *Conjectures of A Guilty Bystander*. New York: The Abbey of Gethsemani, 1965,1966.

Chapter 23 Monrovia, Liberia
1. portion of poem from *The Meaning of Africa* by Davidson Nicol. Used as the opening poem in John Gay's book, *Red Dust on the Green Leaves* by permission. Copyright 1973 by InterCulture Associates.
2. Over The Rhine: Karin Bergquist and Linford Detweiler. *Drunkard's Prayer* lyrics, from album of the same name. Used with permission.
3. 1 John 4:7,8,16; 1 John 3:10; 1 John 1:5
4. Mark 12:31; Leviticus 19:18; Matthew 7:12; Luke 6:31; Galatians 5:14; James 2:8
5. Matthew 22:37; Deuteronomy 6:5, 10:12
6. Hodel, Rachel. https://profunditties.wordpress.com/ Used with permission.
7. http://www.rebeccahodel.com/ Used with permission.

Chapter 24 From Pillar to Post
1. http://www.worldmag.com/2014/08/a_virus_more_deadly_than_ebola http://www.desiringgod.org/poems/ebola. Used with permission.

CPSIA information can be obtained
at www.ICGtesting.com
Printed in the USA
FFOW04n0046290316
22758FF